SURVIVING STATE TERROR

Surviving State Terror

*Women's Testimonies of Repression
and Resistance in Argentina*

Barbara Sutton

NEW YORK UNIVERSITY PRESS

New York

NEW YORK UNIVERSITY PRESS
New York
www.nyupress.org

References to Internet websites (URLs) were accurate at the time of writing. Neither the author nor New York University Press is responsible for URLs that may have expired or changed since the manuscript was prepared.

Library of Congress Cataloging-in-Publication Data
Names: Sutton, Barbara, 1970- author.
Title: Surviving state terror : women's testimonies of repression and resistance in Argentina / Barbara Sutton.
Description: New York : New York University Press, [2017] | Includes bibliographical references and index.
Identifiers: LCCN 2017034143| ISBN 9781479861576 (cl : alk. paper) | ISBN 9781479829927 (pb : alk. paper)
Subjects: LCSH: Victims of state-sponsored terrorism—Argentina. | Women—Crimes against—Argentina.
Classification: LCC HV6433.A7 S88 2018 | DDC 323.3/4092282—dc23
LC record available at https://lccn.loc.gov/2017034143

New York University Press books are printed on acid-free paper, and their binding materials are chosen for strength and durability. We strive to use environmentally responsible suppliers and materials to the greatest extent possible in publishing our books.

Manufactured in the United States of America

10 9 8 7 6 5 4 3 2 1

Also available as an ebook

CONTENTS

1

Women, State Terror, and Collective Memory

The past lives in the present, and traumatic pasts still throb and ache. This is often true for individuals and societies, as memories of war, displacement, genocide, and other forms of "social suffering" are not easily stored away.[1] Their painful marks defy oblivion, and past traumatic situations shape and erupt in present circumstances. Many of these memories are culturally mobilized and transmitted through oral and written narratives, ceremonial rituals, and political performances. They can also become embodied memories that inhabit the lives of both individuals directly affected by traumatic events and those who belong to the same mnemonic community.[2] At stake are not only the lifeworlds of people who experienced unbearable loss and unspeakable suffering, but also broader society's ability to learn, rebuild, and change. The recent history of state terrorism in Argentina is a case in point; and the survivors of this political repression have key stories to tell. This book focuses on the voices of women survivors of state-run clandestine detention centers (CDCs)—a group whose perspectives have not always been heard. What might attending to these voices reveal about the nature of state violence and its relation to gender and power? What might we learn from them about survival and resistance, about collective memory and human rights?

Three decades after her captivity in one of the clandestine detentions centers of the last military dictatorship in Argentina (1976–83), survivor Marta García de Candeloro remembered a poignant lesson she learned from another former detainee called Ledda.[3] The story featured unlikely protagonists: the ants that were free to move around in places of utter unfreedom, namely, the secret sites where so many people were tortured and "disappeared" during the period of state terrorism.[4] Marta recounted the story in 2007, in the context of her testimony for the civil society organization Memoria Abierta (Open Memory). In this testimony, she wished to highlight more than horror. Although she did not remember exactly Ledda's words, she offered the gist of the story:

[I]n summary, what I got from it was: That those ants should not be killed; they should be left alone because they were going to freedom and returning; and they were going in and out. That was the contact with the outside. [. . .] I will never forget that thing of Ledda's as long as I live, because it had to do with the things that life clings to, no?—in order to live in a situation where you were . . . tortured . . . where it was as if your body did not belong to you, but where those things were a sign of life.[5]

In her testimony, Marta was apparently referring to survivor Ledda Barreiro, a woman who was detained in the same site as Marta. According to other sources, the story traces back to Ledda's daughter, Silvia Muñoz, who was "disappeared" by the regime while pregnant. As Ledda explained in one of her public appearances, the exhortation to not kill the ants wandering around in a CDC reportedly came from her daughter and was witnessed by fellow detainees who survived to tell the story.[6] Eventually this story was turned into an illustrated children's book, *Marimosa y las hormigas* (Potes 2014), about colorful butterflies held captive by big and evil bugs and about the bonds of solidarity that the imprisoned butterfly Marimosa forged with a group of ants, which symbolized freedom. Various human rights organizations and public institutions then began to use *Marimosa y las hormigas* as part of their work to promote human rights education and collective memory among school-aged children.[7]

The journey of the ants' story, originally told and retold by women survivors of state terror in Argentina, encapsulates many of the themes of this book. The story itself certainly takes us directly to a place of extreme oppression, but it does not end there. Importantly, as Dori Laub (1992, 62) mentioned in relation to Holocaust survivors' testimonies, this story hints to "the very secret of survival and of resistance to extermination." From this story we learn about resilience, compassion, and solidarity in the midst of horror; about the power of collective efforts and the unyielding pull of freedom. That these notions become salient in the memories circulated among survivors, and then shared with the public, also speaks to the desire to draw broader lessons from experiences of unimaginable suffering and terror.

In considering how the story was retooled for a children's audience, another important theme addressed in this study emerges: the transmission of memory, particularly to future generations. The central role of women as transmitters of collective memory and culture also becomes apparent. While oftentimes these processes of transmission stem from women's socially ascribed roles as mothers, grandmothers, or teachers passing on cultural knowledge, I would like to expand and problematize this frame. In Ledda's memories of her disappeared daughter and the quest to find her grandchild, the centrality of gender-mediated family bonds is evident. However, Ledda and other women in this study have shared many other vital experiences and perspectives, including as political activists, beyond those associated with normative gender expectations.

Finally, as memories are repeated, transmitted, and resignified, variants of the ants' story point to the social construction and "labors of memory" (Jelin 2003, 5) dedicated to keep critical insights alive. Consistent with Joan Scott's (2001) elaboration of the notion of "echo," the retelling of the ants' story—as well as many other stories of survival—can create new resonances and meanings. Through echo, utterances are repeated but not exactly: "repetition constitutes alteration" (291). The innovations introduced through repetition prompt us to consider present investments in transmitted stories. That the ants' story comes to us decades after its point of origin speaks not only to the open wounds left by the events that prompted the story but also to the lessons that contemporary societies still need to learn from these experiences.

* * *

During the last dictatorship in Argentina, the state armed and deployed a repressive apparatus that perpetrated massive human rights violations (CONADEP 1984; Duhalde 1999). This regime promoted a "culture of fear" (Corradi, Fagen, and Garretón 1992b, 1) and aimed to "discipline a society with strong political concerns" (D'Antonio 2009, 89), persecuting with special vehemence those whose social or political activities challenged prevailing power relations. In the geopolitical context of the Cold War and leftist and popular movements that sought major societal transformations—including through armed struggle—the dictatorship proclaimed itself in defense of "national security" and "Western and Christian civilization." In the name of this cause the military regime kidnapped, tortured, and "disappeared" a wide spectrum of people.

Among these were members of guerrilla, religious, political, student, labor, and social justice organizations as well as many other people categorized as "subversive." Over five hundred CDCs proliferated all over the country (Ministerio de Educación n.d.). These were places where military, police, and security forces carried out a systematic plan of brutal repression. Women detained under the framework of "subversion" were disciplined using a variety of methods, including sexual violence and other gendered repertoires that intensified oppression (Aucía et al. 2011; Balardini, Oberlin, and Sobredo 2011; Bacci et al. 2012; Lewin and Wornat 2014).

This book is based on oral testimonies of fifty-two women who survived CDCs during the period of state terrorism in Argentina. While repression began before the 1976 coup d'état,[8] I focus on the dictatorship period because this is when the methodology of torture and disappearance became systematized and implemented on a massive scale (Duhalde 1999). It is also the period in which the discourse of human rights gained a foothold and grew in Argentina, with long-term political and cultural implications (Carassai 2010). The testimonies I analyze were collected by Memoria Abierta, a consortium of several human rights organizations, some of which emerged as a direct response to the illegal and devastating violence that the state unleashed.[9] Memoria Abierta's Oral Archive provides public access to stories, experiences, and other information about the period of state terrorism as stated by the people directly affected by the events, literally in their own voices.

For much of the post-dictatorship period, the voices of survivors were scarcely heard outside judicial spheres (Longoni 2007), and this has been especially true for women, as aspects of their experiences became virtually unspeakable and inaudible. For instance, systematic sexual violence in CDCs was a seemingly taboo topic for decades. Even though testimonies of such actions were already present in the 1984 *Nunca Más* report by the National Commission on the Disappearance of Persons (CONADEP),[10] judicial proceedings tended to subsume sexual violence under other crimes (Duffy 2012). Furthermore, Argentine society failed to fully reckon with the gender-based violence that women experienced in CDCs. However, in recent years, projects with feminist sensibilities have provided needed accounts and analyses to help reverse such trends, particularly in relation to the silencing of sexual and gender violence.[11]

In the past few years, advances have also been made in judging sexual violence in trials for crimes against humanity committed during the dictatorship (Balardini, Oberlin, and Sobredo 2011; Duffy 2012). This book adds to feminist works on the topic by developing an analysis that includes women's body narratives and testimonies of survival as well as their assessments of their journeys and the messages they hoped to convey with their testimonies. These women's testimonies contain more than experiences of suffering and horror. Their accounts offer an opportunity to reflect on visions and strategies for social change, for building a present and a future that take the recent past into consideration.

Furthermore, the voices of these women are *political* ones, not only because they speak directly to political issues, but also because many of them have had significant activist trajectories that informed their perspectives. During the democratic transition, survivors' past political identities were often silenced. As Ana, a survivor quoted in Guillermina Seri's work (2008, 12), argued, "it is as if the only respectable witness is the one who 'had nothing to do' with politics, the one who was there 'by mistake.'" While the study of survivors' political histories is not the central focus of this work, social and political activism was an integral aspect of many women's testimonies. This background infused their experiences in the camps, their survival strategies as well as their more current viewpoints. Various survivors reclaimed aspects of these political experiences, but they sometimes offered critical retrospective assessments of them as well.

Women's political voices defy the silent and subordinated place traditionally ascribed to women in the body politic and tell of the specific ways such subordination has been enforced and contested. Citing theorist Giorgio Agamben, survivor and scholar Nora Strejilevich noted in her testimony that the military regime implemented techniques aimed to turn captive people into "bare life," stripped of rights, identity, and all traces of social belonging.[12] In this study the testimonies of the women, who exercised their voices even when speaking from bodies marked by horror, strongly countered such attempts. These women offered their narratives not simply as traumatized, raped, and humiliated bodies, but as persons with other important things to say beyond victimization. Their varied, nuanced, and broader perspectives are critical contributions to collective memory.

Using Argentina as its case study, this book shows how centering women's voices and experiences can offer a more complex and fuller grasp of how state violence operates, how it is countered, and how it is remembered. Based on testimonies of women survivors of state terror, the book accomplishes several goals: (1) it shows how state violence is *gendered* beyond the use of sexual violence; (2) it underscores ways in which state violence, resistance, and memory are *embodied*; (3) it expands our understanding of women's experiences in relation to the dictatorship *beyond motherhood*; (4) it emphasizes *women's agency* instead of simply focusing on victimization; and (5) it takes into account women survivors' political voices as vital to the process of *collective memory transmission*.

To provide a road map to this book, I will briefly sketch its structure. The remainder of this chapter addresses important developments in collective memory and human rights struggles in Argentina, situating this case in the Latin American context. The focus on women survivors and the use of gender as a key analytic are explicated, along with my research approach and personal implication in the study. In chapter 2, I delve into the process through which women survivors come to "tell terror," to give testimony about their experiences of clandestine detention. I offer an account of the tension between silence and talk and body and voice in this process. I also explore these women's reflections about torture and the human condition as they grappled with memories of unimaginable cruelty. Chapter 3 focuses on women's body narratives and examines the place of women's bodies in human rights violations. I analyze not only repressors' use of motherhood and sexuality as oppression resources, but also how gender scripts inflect torture and torments beyond overtly sexualized strategies or those related to the treatment of pregnant women. Chapter 4 presents an analysis of women's embodied ways of coping with, negotiating, and resisting the oppressive conditions of the camps. I emphasize the role of the body in such dynamics and how the body became a carrier of memory and a vehicle for voice. Chapter 5 highlights the value of listening to women survivors' testimonies as political accounts, recognizing these women's political and historical agency and their contributions to the crafting of visions for the present and the future. The book's conclusion, chapter 6, draws the political and theoretical implications of the study in relation to central themes:

human rights, transitional justice, and collective memory; gender and state power; and bodies, vulnerability, and agency.

Collective Memory and Human Rights Struggles in Argentina

December 10, 2013, marked the thirtieth anniversary of the return of electoral democracy to Argentina. The administration of President Cristina Fernández de Kirchner called for a people's celebration (*fiesta popular*) at the emblematic Plaza de Mayo, the public square at the heart of Argentina's political history. The fiesta—occurring in the midst of a polarized political climate and police work stoppages that gave way to lootings, violence, and deaths in several provinces—nevertheless commemorated three decades of constitutional governments uninterrupted by military takeovers. During the twentieth century, the military toppled constitutional presidents and established de facto governments multiple times. The last military dictatorship (1976–83) was notorious for its level of atrocity. December 10, which is also internationally celebrated as Human Rights Day, aptly symbolizes the connection between democracy and human rights aspirations in the Argentine imaginary. However, as much as different democratic governments intended to rein in armed and security forces, and to break from a past of blatant human rights violations, the process of democratization has been far from easy and straightforward.

The last decades of electoral democracy were not devoid of threats to the institutional order or major political crises. In fact, the legacy of state terrorism has continuously affected political developments. After the dictatorship and under the administration of elected president Raúl Alfonsín (1983–89), CONADEP documented the dictatorship's human rights violations in the report *Nunca Más* (Never Again) and a civilian tribunal convicted members of the military juntas in a historic trial (Juicio a las Juntas).[13] However, during the same presidency, and in the context of military rebellions, the laws known as Punto Final (Full Stop, no. 23492) and Obediencia Debida (Due Obedience, no. 23521) were enacted in 1986 and 1987, respectively. These laws limited further prosecutions and ensured the impunity of repressors for years. The next president, Carlos Menem (1989–95, 1995–99), pardoned convicted military officers and members of armed political groups, advocating national reconciliation. While justice was being denied via impunity laws, special judicial proceedings called Juicios por la Verdad (Truth Trials) took place in different parts of the country in lieu of regular criminal trials. The Truth Trials further established the record of the military regime's atrocities, but could not impose penal sanctions.

As a grave economic crisis and concomitant social unrest unfolded in December 2001, the democratically elected president Fernando de la Rúa declared an *estado de sitio*, an exceptional measure that allows for the suspension of certain constitutional guarantees. The population responded with massive street protests rallying under the cry "Que se vayan todos!" ("They must all go!"), aimed at politicians. De la Rúa resigned, and four interim presidents followed until the 2003 presidential election of Néstor Kirchner.[14] Among the groups agitating for social, economic, and political change during this activist surge were the formerly established human rights organizations. Activists in the human rights community made connections between the legacy of the dictatorship's political-economic agenda and the contemporary woes of neoliberalism, including the rising sovereign debt, unemployment, and poverty. The administration of President Néstor Kirchner (2003–7) responded to some social movements' demands through increased efforts to redress human rights violations of the past. Figuring prominently among the changes during his administration were the annulment of impunity laws and the opening of trials against people accused of participation in crimes against humanity. This commitment continued during the presidency of Cristina Fernández de Kirchner (2007–11, 2011–15), including trials and convictions of hundreds of the military and security force members as well as some involved civilians (CELS 2013). In 2015, center-right candidate Mauricio Macri was elected president, generating uncertainty about the fate of state-supported initiatives in relation to the period of state terrorism.

Overall human rights advocacy and protests have shaped public discourse and influenced democratic governments' transitional justice policies. Resorting to different strategies, depending on the political environment and the actors involved, human rights organizations have maintained an active presence (Andreozzi 2011a). During the democratic period beginning in late 1983, the Argentine state adopted various measures with human rights orientations, for example, the trial of the military juntas and ratification of a number of international human rights treaties.[15] During the Kirchners' administrations, human rights organizations' concerns gained momentum after years of impunity. In addition to efforts to bring perpetrators to justice, state and nongovernmental initiatives fostered human rights education through schools and the media, held special commemoration days, created sites of memory, and organized cultural events in line with the theme of "Memory, Truth, and Justice." Susana Kaiser (2015, 195) points out that besides the possibility of judicial accountability, the trials for crimes against humanity have functioned as "public spaces for collective memory making, political arenas for competing memory battles, and forums in which new information and perspectives about what happened under state terrorism continually emerge."

Contemporary contexts influence how individuals, families, groups, and nations remember the past, including state-sponsored atrocities; and memories of the past in turn affect current values and debates (Zerubavel 1996; Jelin 2003). This embeddedness of memory in social and historical milieus, and their beyond-individual character, has led scholars to devise terms such as "collective memory" or "social memory" to refer to such phenomena (Halbwachs 1980; Zerubavel 1996; Olick, Vinitzky-Seroussi, and Levy 2011). Federico G. Lorenz (2004, 17) points out that "[s]ocial memory is essentially dynamic. It grows and changes, constantly recovering or burying facts and meanings." Furthermore, we need to think of memory in the plural: multiple, shifting, and contested memories that are affected by power relations (Jelin 2011). The testimonies of the relatives, comrades, and friends of the disappeared, as well as the sometimes overlapping testimonies of survivors themselves, have all helped to document state terror and its effects as well as contributed to the construction of collective memory.

Rather than being merely the sum of individual recollections, collective memory has also been formed in a relational manner through political dialogue and contestation, shared commemorative spaces and events, public protests and demonstrations, and the discourse that human rights organizations generate in their interactions with the state and civil society. In the politics of collective memory in Argentina, we can see how narratives of distinct social actors at different points in time emphasized, problematized, or silenced particular versions of the past and the participation and responsibilities of different groups and individuals in it (see also Rabotnikof 2007). While the most obvious divide is between people at opposite ends of the political spectrum (e.g., military supporters vs. members of human rights groups or leftist political organizations), the field of memory making is neither homogeneous nor static within either side of the divide. Collective memory making is an ongoing process, even as "emblematic memory" is instituted (Steve Stern cited in Crenzel 2011a, 1071) and categories of atrocity victims have been set literally in stone with monuments (Vecchioli 2001). Political developments in Argentina, such as impunity laws, the opening of judicial proceedings, and new generations of human rights activists, have shaped how and what is remembered. These trends have also had considerable influence on survivors' ability and impetus to speak.

In the human rights movement arena, features of the past that have been highlighted or silenced have shifted over time and in relation to the intervention of different social actors and to political events. For instance, scholars note that some early human rights achievements during the democratic transition, for example, a measure of governmental response through the formation of a truth commission and the trial of the juntas, were partly grounded in humanitarian appeals and language. However, this approach tended to depoliticize and silence the activist histories and identities of many of the disappeared and survivors (Otero 2010; Crenzel 2011a). This framing was later modified by sectors of the human rights movement—particularly, though not exclusively, organizations of children of victims of state terrorism (HIJOS)[16]—who have reclaimed the activist, even revolutionary, histories and ideals of many of the disappeared (Cueto Rúa 2010). Mothers of the disappeared, known as Mothers of the Plaza de Mayo, similarly reclaimed that activist legacy, expressing, "Our children gave birth to us" (Borland 2006, 126; Jelin 2014, 151). Silence and oblivion still permeate aspects of memory making even among members or supporters of such organizations. This is evidenced, for example, by fragmentary or taboo topics in family narratives, which in turn are significant to the construction of social memories (Cepeda 2013). In addition, what can or cannot be communicated about a traumatic political past depends on multiple factors including timing and whether societies are willing and able to listen to testimony of such trauma (Felman and Laub 1992; Caruth 1995; Jelin 2003).

The trauma and open wounds associated with state terrorism in Argentina point to the connection between collective memory and human rights, though this connection has been articulated in different ways depending on social context and field of study. Andreas Huyssen (2011, 608) argues that "contemporary memory studies should be linked more robustly with human rights and justice discursively and practically to prevent memory, especially traumatic memory, from becoming a vacuous exercise feeding parasitically and narrowly on itself. But [...] unless it is nurtured by memory and history, human rights discourse is in danger of losing historical grounding and risks legalistic abstraction and political abuse. After all, the abstract universalism of human rights is both a problem and a promise." In contemporary Argentina, the most prevalent collective memory discourse is integrally related to the language of human rights and the critique of state terrorism that human rights organizations have advanced—much of which was taken up by the state (e.g., Vecchioli 2001; Alonso 2009). Sebastián Carassai (2010) shows how human rights discourse—a political frame that was relatively rare in Argentina before the last military regime—came to be strongly associated with denunciations against the dictatorship.

While the linkages between notions of "memory" and "human rights" persist, different political actors beyond traditional human rights organizations have also adopted these concepts with disparate goals. For example, Valentina Salvi (2010) illuminates this dynamic through her study of the discourse of *memoria completa* (complete memory) that organizations allied with the military have deployed. These groups dispute the terrain of memory making by drawing on the language of human rights organizations, but with opposite goals. Human rights discourse also emerges in contemporary social movements, for instance, those supporting sexual rights, marriage equality, and women's abortion rights (Biglieri 2013; Hiller 2013; Sutton and Borland 2013). It has also been present in discourse denouncing the marginalization and invisibility of ethnoracial communities such as Afro-Argentines or indigenous groups (Sutton 2008). These groups have focused on political issues different from the dictatorship's human rights violations, but they also make discursive and symbolic connections to that history. Political developments of the new millennium, such as the neoliberal economic crisis of 2001 as well as cultural and legislative changes spearheaded by the women's movement, have also affected how the past is interpreted and how lessons of that past are applied to contemporary Argentina.

Although this book is centered on the Argentine case, its contributions can be placed in a broader geographical and political context. After all, Argentina was not the only country that experienced repressive regimes around the period of this study, and many of the themes addressed in this book have hemispheric overlaps and significance. As Brian Loveman (2011, n.p.) summarizes, military rule had spread throughout the region around the time of the last dictatorship in Argentina:

> Long-term military governments, with changing leadership in most cases, controlled eleven Latin American nations for significant periods from 1964 to 1990: Ecuador, 1963–1966 and 1972–1978; Guatemala, 1963–1985 (with an interlude from 1966–1969); Brazil, 1964–1985; Bolivia, 1964–1970 and 1971–1982; Argentina, 1966–1973 and 1976–1983; Peru, 1968–1980; Panama, 1968–1989; Honduras, 1963–1966 and 1972–1982; Chile, 1973–1990; and Uruguay, 1973–1984. In El Salvador the military dominated government from 1948 until 1984, but the last "episode" was from 1979 to 1984. Military governments, though inevitably authoritarian, implemented varying economic, social, and foreign policies.

It is important to note that although human rights violations were committed at the hands of military governments in various parts of Latin America, atrocities have also taken place under the watch of civilian governments that did not hesitate to turn against their own citizenry. For instance, the Tlatelolco massacre in Mexico—when state armed forces fired against students assembled in a large demonstration on October 2, 1968—took place under a civilian government.[17] Furthermore, in some countries and periods civilians technically were at the helm of the government, but real power remained with the military. As an example, Mainwaring, Brinks, and Pérez-Liñán (2001) mention that in El Salvador—between 1982 and the 1994 elections—the "military and the paramilitary were beyond the control of the civilian government and ruthlessly killed tens of thousands of leftists and purported leftist sympathizers" (45). Regarding Honduras, Joanna Mateo (2011) states that the military dictatorship that ended in 1981 gave way to a "*democradura*:

a nominally democratic government that is really under military rule," which continued using "death squads, torture, and other 'dirty war' tactics aimed at rooting out communism" (90).

Whereas the impact of local political affairs, histories, and conflicts cannot be overstated, we should also keep in mind the influence of transnational factors that played a role in repression and resistance in Latin America. In the context of the Cuban Revolution in 1959 and rising leftist insurgencies and movements in the region, Latin America became one important theater of operations of Cold War contests between the U.S. and Soviet Union superpowers (Brands 2010). The United States played a key role both ideologically as well as logistically in supporting various repressive regimes to extricate communism and other leftist-inspired movements threatening to disrupt hegemonic power relations. The National Security Doctrine—with its focus on the "internal enemy" and allowance of "extralegal methods"—was adopted among various military forces across the continent with devastating consequences (McSherry 2005, 20; Menjívar and Rodríguez 2005). Many of these regimes became infamous for persecuting, torturing, and disappearing members of their own populations, and even coordinated repressive activities with other countries in the region to kidnap or kill exiles and other political targets. This is evidenced, for example, by collaboration in the exchange of information, capture of prisoners, and assassination of political targets among the military regimes that integrated Operation Condor during the 1970s. This secret network brought together Argentina, Bolivia, Brazil, Chile, Paraguay, and Uruguay in regional counterinsurgency operations, "later joined by Ecuador and Peru in less central roles" (McSherry 2005, 4; see also Lessa 2015).

The spread of political violence and state terror in various countries in Latin America also led to the emergence of testimonies, human rights organizations, and memorial cultures specific to each country but in dialogue with each other. Referring to countries of Latin America's Southern Cone, Emilio Crenzel (2011b, 3) points out that the "narrative shift represented by the prevalence of the human rights discourse was the result of ties forged by political exiles and relatives of prisoners and disappeared persons with transnational human rights networks, in particular in the United States and Europe, and of the emergence of human rights organizations in Argentina and Chile, and at a later stage and with a lesser impact in Uruguay. In sum, the unprecedented strength gained by the culture of human rights in the region was, ironically, a product of the dictatorships."

From organizations of families of the disappeared to initiatives to fight impunity, human rights solidarity networks, the creation of sites of memory, truth commissions, and trials for crimes against human- ity, there has been a cross-fertilization of ideas, lessons, and strategies among different countries in the region.[18] Argentina has been a trail- blazer in transitional justice initiatives, which served as reference to other Latin American countries and beyond. Kathryn Sikkink (2011, 87) points out that "Argentina helped invent the two main accountability mechanisms that are the focus of much of the debate on transitional jus- tice: truth commissions and high-level human rights prosecutions." She also refers to the strength of the human rights movement in the country and the persistent efforts of activists and public officials who strove to bring accountability where impunity for human rights abuses reigned. Efforts to investigate human rights violations through prosecutions and/ or truth commissions have taken hold not only in Argentina but in other countries in the region such as Bolivia, Chile, Ecuador, El Salvador, Gua- temala, Haiti, Honduras, Mexico, Nicaragua, Panama, Paraguay, Peru, and Uruguay (Sikkink 2011, 269–70).

In crafting collective memories, demanding truth and justice, and making connections between past and present, the testimonies of people affected by human rights violations in Argentina and beyond have been crucial. They have not only provided necessary firsthand accounts of the events in question, but also contributed to a collec- tive memory-making process concerning these events. However, as memory scholars note, testimonial accounts should not be taken as simply transparent reflections of the facts narrated. Testimonies are crisscrossed by the "multiple temporalities" of narration and by what victims can tell and societies hear at specific historical moments (Jelin 2014, 141). Which voices are authorized to speak, in what capacities, under what conditions, and about which experiences? These factors also mold the texture of collective memory at every point in time. This book shows the critical significance of women's testimonies to a more complex understanding of the past.

Centering Women's Testimonies, Visualizing Gender

The testimonies of survivors of clandestine detention are among the most direct accounts of the workings of state terrorism. Despite fear, threats, and intimidation, a number of survivors, along with relatives of the disappeared and members of human rights organizations, had started to denounce what was happening before the dictatorship ended. Their willingness to testify was later encouraged or accompanied by different state and civil society initiatives during the democratization period. These included the formation of a truth commission, subsequent trials, and the production of myriad books, documentaries, and artistic and political performances.

Survivors' accounts have been essential for piecing together how state terror operated, including kidnapping procedures, detention conditions, the location of clandestine sites, and methods of "disappearance." Their accounts have acquired particular importance because individuals who could have provided further details—repressors and their accomplices—have generally denied wrongdoing and refused to provide information, including on the fate of the disappeared.[19] Survivors' testimonies have provided crucial evidence in trials for crimes against humanity—evidence ever more important because as time passes some sorts of proof become harder to retrieve. For example, as has also been the case with places of atrocity in Chile and Uruguay (Gómez-Barris 2010), some buildings have been demolished or modified. Many corporeal injuries are no longer visible either. At the same time that some traces of evidence fade, changes in political and social contexts allow previously silenced dimensions of experience to emerge, enabling new personal, political, and academic analyses about the period (Partnoy 2009; Jelin 2014).

This book focuses on the (embodied) voices of women because their diverse and complex stories are vital to social memory. Even when the experiences of women are recognized, they often tend to be limited to normative gender roles such as those of mother, wife, or caretaker. For example, Mothers of the Plaza de Mayo is one of the groups of women who became well known in relation to the period of state terrorism in Argentina. These women confronted the military regime at a very dangerous time in order to demand the safe return of their disappeared children, and many of them remain politically active today.[20] A related group is the Grandmothers of the Plaza de Mayo. These women search for their grandchildren who were born of women in captivity, or who were kidnapped by state forces along with their parents. These children were appropriated and raised under false identities, often by repressors or families connected to the regime. It is not surprising that these activist groups of women are known in and beyond Argentina given their public visibility and the significance of their continuous work.[21]

My interest, however, is to bring to the fore women whose experiences and perspectives have received less public and academic attention: women survivors of CDCs.[22] Some of these women are also Mothers or Grandmothers of the Plaza de Mayo, but it seems their relationships to the disappeared have overshadowed the visibility of their experiences as persons who were themselves temporarily disappeared. While their sufferings as mothers/grandmothers *and* as survivors of clandestine detention are entwined in the narratives of some of the women who have this double status, it is significant that the discourse most readily expressed and heard in the public sphere is one that resonates with the figure of the nurturer and caretaker rather than the survivor. As is often the case, gender scripts afford women more legitimacy to speak on behalf of others than to speak about their *own* experiences.[23] Furthermore, some of the political trajectories of women who became Mothers and Grandmothers of Plaza de Mayo, preceding the founding of these organizations, contradict the usual narrative about apolitical mothers turned activists (Vecchioli 2005) and tend to be obscured in public discourse.

Women's struggles as mothers and grandmothers have continued to come under the spotlight for good reason. The loss of daughters, sons, and grandchildren is an enduring wound, fueling these women's ongoing activism. At different points, they still had expectations for the disappeared to return alive. As time passed, this hope receded. However, one of the effects of "disappearance" as a state terror tactic is that it hinders the possibility of closure for the relatives and friends of those taken away. As survivor and Grandmother of Plaza de Mayo Ledda Barreiro noted, "We don't even have their bones." The absence of bodies precludes certainty about the death of their loved ones and undermines the possibility of mourning. Activist efforts have generally shifted toward establishing truth, demanding justice, and contributing to collective memory. In the case of the search for persons presumed alive today, such as appropriated grandchildren, relatives cannot process their loss as a past trauma. Rather, it is an ongoing struggle to locate and reunite these now-adult persons with their families of origin.

The magnitude of suffering that so many women experienced over the loss of their loved ones does not fully account for the predominant public and academic focus on mothers or grandmothers. Prevailing gender ideologies and relations have not only shaped opportunities and constraints for collective action under the dictatorship, but also influenced how the dictatorship is remembered. Many scholarly works have analyzed how the mothers of the disappeared were able to draw on normative gender roles, especially mothering, to challenge the military regime in ways that might have been more difficult for men to do (Fisher 1993; Bouvard 1994; Bellucci 2000). This has also occurred in other Latin American countries where women confronted authoritarian regimes or made demands on behalf of the disappeared (Safa 1990; Stephen 1997; Bejarano 2002). Prevailing gender expectations make it more acceptable for women to advocate for their children, and in some cases there is an implicit expectation that "benevolent" sexism might protect women to some extent (for example, the idea that state forces would refrain from attacking women).[24] Gendered struggles illuminate particular paths to women's political participation as well as significant dimensions of women's experiences of state terror. Elizabeth Jelin (2001, 129) notes that "personalized symbols of pain and suffering tend to be embodied by women—Mothers and Grandmothers in the case of Argentina—while the institutional mechanisms seem to 'belong' to men." As significant as such feminine political interventions have been, a wider set of women's narratives still needs to be heard.

Why is it that some sorts of women's experiences have gained greater attention than others? Why, even when the focus is on women disappeared, is it the mother figure that emerges more visibly in public representations—for example, in silhouettes depicting pregnant women in street protests or public art? These representations are effective in drawing attention to the gender-specific plight of women, including the experiences of captive mothers and pregnant mothers-to-be. No doubt the agents of state terrorism found in motherhood a bountiful arsenal to enhance the suffering of their victims. These relevant dimensions of experience are incorporated in this book's pages. Yet this project also sheds light on women's experiences and perspectives beyond maternity. A broader range of women's testimonies is vital to a deeper understanding of state terrorism; and it is also necessary to the construction of a collective memory that recognizes with greater complexity women's experiences. These testimonies also enable us to see some connections to contemporary times, including persistent discourses and practices of gender violence—for example, from blaming women for gender-based violence to sexualized epithets and representations leveled against women in political positions.[25] It seems that one key strategy for silencing women's political voices is to sexualize and reduce them to objectified bodies.

Memories of the past and present-day circumstances are entangled in a number of social issues of feminist concern. On one hand, social memories inform current political projects: for example, the language of human rights infuses much contemporary political discourse, including local understandings of the globally disseminated notion that "women's rights are human rights."[26] On the other hand, current developments also offer new tools and possibilities for digging into and interpreting the past. For instance, feminist and women's movements promoted cultural and institutional transformations that have provided a framework to address gender-based violence in "normal" times. This in turn extends to understanding sexualized violence in CDCs. In the past decades, legislation passed, training was provided to judicial workers, assistance centers opened, demonstrations were staged, and a myriad of other activities and debates were generated by state and civil society organizations to raise awareness of, prevent, and end gender-based violence.[27] These developments have also indirectly influenced the ability of society to grapple with silenced topics such as rape and other forms of sexual violence in the context of state terrorism. Women's organizations, feminist and human rights lawyers, and survivors have new legal and discursive tools with which to revisit these state crimes, traditionally surrounded by impunity.[28] Still persistent difficulties to prosecute such actions as crimes against humanity speak to the continued need to make visible and contextualize these women's experiences, in Argentina and beyond.[29]

Oppressive gender ideologies permeated CDCs. The testimonies of women in this study reveal a spectrum of violence that hurt women in specific but diverse ways. They spoke of state crimes that are well known by now, such as those involving the killing of women after they gave birth and the appropriation of their newborn babies. But these women also narrated less discussed situations, such as the case of Adriana Arce who related: "[G]iven that I was pregnant, they had to perform an abortion without anesthesia." They also spoke about various forms of sexual violence. Marta Bianchi heard a repressor threaten, "how pretty [. . .] this one . . . we rape her." Susana Jorgelina Ramus, who suffered rape and torture, described "the feeling of humiliation that one has" in both situations. Women who tried to resist the repressors' harassment by shouting and swearing were met with sexualized epithets such as "little golden pussy" (*conchita de oro*) (Celeste Seydell) or "little painted lips" (*boquitas pintadas*) (Gloria Enríquez), terms that asserted the subordination of captive women as women.[30]

Among the people disappeared were women who had considerable political experience—those who on the one hand seemed to fascinate the military and on the other were treated as objects of reform (Bacci et al. 2012). In some camps, versions of "recuperation" or "rehabilitation" were implemented to change the ideological and political outlook of the prisoners. In the case of women, there was an additional twist: turning these captives into properly feminine women. Marta Álvarez recalled that in the CDC operating in ESMA (Escuela de Mecánica de la Armada/School of Naval Mechanics), the military discovered in the militant woman someone who "could think and develop her own ideas, and engage in political conversations, and discuss history, discuss politics, and discuss the economy. So, one had to find in that activist the feminine essence, let's say, to. . . . That was the process of recuperation, at least with women: that we start doing ourselves up, that we start discovering motherhood, that we start talking about the kids."

At stake was the dispute over different modes and ideals of femininity. Through the process of *recuperación* ("recuperation") captive women's political femininity had to be left behind and replaced by a model of domestic/ated femininity, imposed as a condition of survival. The ability to survive, however, was never guaranteed. These examples remind us that various guises of state terrorism also drew on existing ideologies and hierarchies in society (see also Gómez-Barris 2009, 55). Dora Barrancos (2008, 147–48) argues: "No doubt, there is a gender difference in the attributes with which the horror of state terrorism was invested: the rapes, the birthing conditions and the abduction of newborns increased the victimization of women. [. . .] I absolutely do not claim that women suffered more than men, but that broader repertoires of torment were inflicted on them, there were more alternatives for suffering." In this book I analyze the narratives of women survivors, exploring the gendered dimensions of their experiences as well as how they made meaning of their overall journey. I listened to these women not only as victims, but as agentic political subjects who, in giving testimony, offer vital insights about the past as well as tools to understand the present and build a future.

These connections between past, present, and future are particularly important when it comes to understanding and responding to various forms of violence. While the specificity and contexts of oppression need to be accounted for—for example, in CDCs, in regular prisons under a "state of exception," or in homes raided by state forces with little to no restraint—it is worthwhile to consider how particular languages and practices of violence "travel" across different sites, periods, and circumstances (Alexander 2005), including in dictatorship and democracy (Sutton 2010). What are the overlaps and continuities between the violence of state terrorism addressed in this book and forms of violence that persist and morph in the post-dictatorship period (e.g., Auyero and Berti 2015)? In the Guatemalan context, for example, the works of Victoria Sanford (2008) and Cecilia Menjívar (2011) show how *impunity* has been one of the threads that tie together the recent history of state terror and the "postconflict" violence that women have experienced, including feminicide. This theme of impunity is also relevant to Argentina as many survivors became actively involved in trying to obtain accountability for massive human rights violations and end the impunity that most perpetrators enjoyed for years. In some cases, these efforts included the demand of justice for sexual crimes that occurred in CDCs but that share some features with sexual violence in other contexts.

Nancy Scheper-Hughes and Philippe Bourgois (2004) argue for the need to think about violence as a *continuum*, including genocide and other types of violence (19), and make "existential leaps in purposefully linking violent acts in normal times to those of abnormal times" (20). The violence continuum includes "all expressions of radical social exclusion, dehumanization, depersonalization, pseudospeciation, and reification which normalize atrocious behavior and violence toward others" (21). This normalization is something that is also a component of the "multisided violence" that Menjívar observed through her research in Guatemala (2011, 19). As we shall see, some of the women in this study reflect on the connections between different expressions of violence and challenge normalization. They draw on their experience of state terrorism to critique the structural violence of neoliberalism, the violence of "security" forces and culture in democracy, the abandonment of the poor and the vulnerable by state and society, and pervasive violence against women.

In examining societal responses to violence, it is also possible to observe overlaps across periods and circumstances, as certain approaches are borrowed and retooled, working synergistically and/or providing similar interpretive frames. For example, consider Chile's dominant state response to the military dictatorship's crimes *and* to normalized forms of gender violence that continued during the post-dictatorship period: Parson (2013) and Hiner and Azócar (2015) show how the prevalent framework of "reconciliation" that had been promoted in relation to the dictatorial past was also applied to violence against women within families, in both cases betraying justice aspirations. Alternatively, consider how human rights discourses can be fruitfully extended to situations that at first sight might not be obviously linked. In this sense, some human rights organizations in Argentina have worked to connect the dots by expanding the human rights frame beyond the dictatorial past—though not without obstacles (Bonner 2014). A case in point is the Centro de Estudios Legales y Sociales/Center of Legal and Social Studies (CELS), which has not only produced reports on issues related to state terrorism, but also published research and legal perspectives on a broader range of contemporary human rights violations, including those pertaining to gender inequality and concerning women in particular (e.g., abortion, the treatment of women in jails, violence against women).[31]

As evidenced by the evolution of truth commissions and other transitional justice measures in different parts of the world, concrete synergies are possible between feminist and human rights work in relation to the legacies of state violence and armed conflict. In fact, feminist analyses of militarization, political violence, and war have found some echo over time in transitional justice mechanisms, which have become more attuned to the role of gender inequality and the specific forms of violence that women are particularly likely to experience. Nesiah et al. (2006, 8) point out that while early truth commissions such as Argentina's CONADEP did not incorporate a gender lens as central to their work, later truth commissions in "Guatemala, South Africa, and Peru paid particular attention to gender, even though their mandates were formally gender neutral. In countries like Haiti, Sierra Leone, and Timor-Leste, gender or sexual violence was explicitly incorporated into the mandate, and these topics were identified as critical avenues of investigation."

In the judicial realm, the international trials for mass atrocities in the former Yugoslavia and Rwanda during the 1990s were critical in paving the road for prosecuting other cases of sexual violence in connection to armed conflict and generalized or systematic attacks against the civilian population (Outreach Programme and the United Nations n.d.). The Rome Statute of the International Criminal Court, which entered into effect in 2002, includes rape and other forms of sexual violence among the actions listed as war crimes and crimes against humanity (ICC 2011). By the time of this writing, 124 countries had joined as state parties to the Rome Statute (ICC n.d.). At the local level, victims also started to seek justice for sexualized violence in the context of armed conflict and repression. Among other advances, in 2016 the judiciary in Guatemala "issued an exemplary ruling in convicting two perpetrators responsible for subjecting Q'eqchi' women to sexual slavery and domestic slavery in the military base located in the Sepur Zarco community in the 1980s" (WOLA 2016, n.p.). What is significant about the case is not only the court's ruling, which considered sexual and domestic slavery and sexual violence as crimes against humanity, but also the agency and resiliency of eleven women survivors who pursued the judicial case despite the odds and social stigma (Burt 2016). In Argentina, too, some inroads have been made in judging sexual violence in connection to state terrorism. The first conviction issued by an Argentine federal oral tribunal for sexual violence committed in CDCs was in 2010 in the city of Mar del Plata, in the case of Molina (no. 2086/10) (Balardini, Oberlin, and Sobredo 2011; Duffy 2012).[32]

Women have been particularly likely to experience sexual violence in the context of armed conflict and repression, and the seriousness of the crime demands redress. At the same time, as Kimberly Theidon (2011) observes with regard to the experiences of women in the recent history of armed conflict in Peru, there is the danger of circumscribing the workings of gender oppression to sexual violence, as if that was the only or main form of suffering that women experienced. Theidon mentions, and I also find in this study, that women survivors have many more things to say. Gender inequality—and the ways in which it permeates militarization and state and political violence—includes but transcends sexual violence.

In this book, I embarked on a project that centers women's experiences and that treats gender as a key analytic. To be clear, I conceptualize gender as more than an identity, and certainly not as one that is interchangeable with, or a shorthand for, "women." Throughout this work, I pay attention to gender norms, gender ideologies, gendered institutions, gender as a system of inequality, gender as a dimension of social location, and gender as a performance.[33] Also, following theorists of "intersectionality," I see gender not as an isolated category but as one that intersects and is mutually constituted with other categories of difference and inequality—such as class, sexuality, age, race/ethnicity, nation, and bodily ability—which have specific salience in particular historical and social contexts.[34] Some of these intersections become evident in my analysis of the archived testimonies of women survivors of state terrorism in Argentina. Yet one limitation of archival work is the inability to probe more deeply into details of narratives already recorded, even though I sometimes suspected that particular intersectional dynamics might have been at play.

Another issue to consider is the critique of gender binaries within the field of women's, gender, and sexuality studies. Scholars advancing this critique have stressed the multiplicity, fluidity, and instability of gender identities, and some have also questioned the very category "women" (e.g., Butler 1990; Scott 2001). Following Butler (1995, 54), the use of quotation marks—in this case around the term "women"—is meant to indicate its contested character. Joan Scott (2001) points out the historicity of the category and the role that activist and academic identifications have played in constructing "women" as a seemingly stable subject, while also minimizing the differences among those deemed to compose the category. In discussing feminist attempts to inscribe women in history or gain rights for women, Scott (2001, 287) posits that the "identity of women [. . .] was not so much a self-evident fact of history as it was evidence—from particular and discrete moments in time—of someone's, some group's effort to identify and thereby mobilize a collectivity."

The problematization of "women" as a category of identity may raise questions about the wisdom and politics of a study focused on *women's experiences*—this time leveled not from an antifeminist perspective, or one that considers feminist analysis unnecessary, but from within a feminist field that has been in dialogue with poststructuralist, queer, and trans studies. Challenges to the notion of gender as fixed and binary mean questioning the most taken-for-granted categories of identity and experience. Who belongs or does not belong to the category "women" cannot be assumed, and the notion of "cis privilege" (see, e.g., Serano 2013) helps reveal previously unnamed advantages accrued by those who feel aligned with the sex/gender designated at birth, including "women" who fit normative definitions.[35] However, even if we recognize the unstable, historically specific, and complexly layered dimensions of the category, I would like to assert the value of foregrounding the experiences of a sector of the population who identify and are socially treated as belonging to a group called "women." This is the case, even if we are cognizant that "women" is not a homogeneous group and that in practice gender cannot be disentangled from other categories of difference and inequality. All in all, a critique of gender binaries and heteronormativity can help enrich understandings of state violence and the differently precarious experiences of those targeted. At the same time, it is important to recognize that the politics and concepts of contemporary movements and academic fields do not always travel smoothly across historical and/ or geopolitical formations.

Identifying and being perceived as "women" has significant quotidian and political implications, as well as embodied dimensions. In the case of this study, it is critical to analyze how gender ideologies permeated the specific forms of violence that members of masculinist institutions— such as the military, police, and security forces—perpetrated against women. Furthermore, various dimensions of suffering in CDCs were related to the materiality and phenomenology of gendered bodies, including the culturally mediated experiences of pregnancy, menstruation, and sexualized body parts. As cases of sexual and domestic slavery in the context of armed conflicts also illustrate, those considered "women" (especially if poor and also subordinated based on race/ethnicity) have been especially likely to be forced into allegedly womanly tasks, from doing the laundry and cooking for combatants and soldiers to providing them with sexual services. The situations of women during the armed conflicts in Colombia (Amnesty International 2004) and Guatemala (Burt 2016; Gago 2016) are cases in point.

Although this study focuses on "women," it does so not from an essentialist perspective, but from one that recognizes the social construction of the category as well as a spectrum of gender identities. Later in the book, the analysis of femininity in the extreme context of state-run torture centers shows the performativity of gender and how it is produced through power relations. Additionally, examples of women who exhibited traits or behavior associated with masculinity show the contestation of gender norms and how supposedly natural gender attributes do not necessarily attach to particular kinds of bodies. Narratives about people who embodied "abject" sexualities and gender identities/expressions—including testimony referring to the solidarity of *travestis* detained by the police—also reveal the importance that the state attributed to the disciplining of gender and sexuality. State power was one of the vehicles through which the contours of gender and sexuality were produced and enforced during the period of state terrorism, though not without negotiation and contestation (D'Antonio 2015).

This study's focus on women's lived experiences of state terror, as well as their activist perspectives, helps account for relatively neglected aspects of the recent history of Argentina and other parts of Latin America. For too long history was written as if women were not worthy of attention, and were thus subsumed under the generic masculine subject. The voices of women were silenced. Here I am highlighting women's voices and embodied experiences, recognizing the challenge of foregrounding "women" without essentializing or homogenizing those deemed to belong to the category.

Memoria Abierta's Oral Archive: Crafting a Method

Human rights organizations are a good place to start when looking to understand the workings of state terror and how particular groups were affected. A number of these organizations have steadily accumulated knowledge and experience in denouncing and pushing for accountability for state-sponsored atrocities, and they provide a wealth of documentation about the abuses that took place as well as the context of the events. This book is indebted to the tireless work of organizations committed to building collective memory in relation to the period of state terrorism in Argentina—in particular, the civil society organization Memoria Abierta. Indeed, Memoria Abierta's Oral Archive, which started in 2001, provides a treasure trove of firsthand accounts of the recent past of state terrorism. Among Memoria Abierta's projects are a database on CDCs, a centralized database of documentation stored in various member organizations, and the Oral Archive. These projects have been part of the broader efforts of civil society and state institutions to promote "Memory, Truth, and Justice" regarding human rights violations.

The testimonies I analyzed were video-recorded and stored as part of Memoria Abierta's Oral Archive, now located in one of the buildings of the former Escuela de Mecánica de la Armada (ESMA), a facility where a notorious CDC functioned during the dictatorship. When I started this project, the Oral Archive contained more than seven hundred testimonies of different groups of people who were affected by state terrorism. These groups include relatives of the disappeared; public officials, artists, professionals, and intellectuals; activists and members of social, religious, labor, and political organizations; people exiled and deported; and political prisoners and survivors. Testimonies of women who survived CDCs fell into the latter group.

Memoria Abierta recognizes its work as contributing to the "construction of social memory" (Memoria Abierta 2005, 2). This is not a politically or ethically neutral activity. The politics that influenced the Oral Archive include a commitment to provide a "selection that accounts for state terrorism, that contributes to the formation of a historical consciousness able to interpret and represent the past in order to configure another future" (6). This requires a political positioning by Memoria

Abierta with respect to the recent past as well as consideration of a number of ethical dilemmas regarding the interviews in the Oral Archive: from what to ask and how much detail of horrific situations to solicit to how to negotiate painful emotions and the memories that the interview process itself prompts. As Memoria Abierta (2005, 4) put it, how to "record terror without (re)producing it"? Memoria Abierta's team had to grapple with this and other challenges. A careful, caring, and reflexive praxis has characterized the work of creating and sustaining the archive. Keeping all this in mind is important given that, as Diana Taylor (2003, 19) observes, the materials in an archive are not unmediated; they cannot be understood "outside the framing of the archival impetus itself." She adds: "What makes an object archival is the process whereby it is selected, classified, and presented for analysis" (19).

In Kirsten Weld's book *Paper Cadavers*—about archives of state repression in Guatemala—it becomes apparent that not only the content of an archive but also the goals and process of creating it are important. Weld shows how an archive can be a technology of power and control, even of warfare, at the hands of a state bent on persecuting those deemed enemies. However, that same amassed information can be transformed by human rights activists/archivists into tools for accountability, historical memory, and democratization (see also da Silva Catela 2002). Weld (2014, 6) argues for the need to pay attention to what she terms *archival logics*, that is, an archive's "organizing principles" and "reasons for being." In the case of Memoria Abierta in Argentina, a central goal is "to make accessible all documentation regarding the last military dictatorship for the purposes of research and the education of future generations."[36] The Oral Archive is part of the organization's efforts "to raise social awareness and knowledge about state terrorism in order to enrich democratic culture" (Memoria Abierta n.d.-b). In this archive, the voices of people directly affected by state violence have a privileged place.

While incorporating the voices of those targeted by state terror is paramount to understand that history, it is also a delicate matter, as we are talking about people who themselves and/or whose relatives, friends, coworkers, or fellow activists suffered unspeakable violence. I was not privy to the work of constructing the Oral Archive, yet informal conversations with members of Memoria Abierta gave me a sense of the conscientious and detailed work that goes into arranging, recording, and making available even a single testimony (let alone hundreds of them, as was the case by the time of my research). The "messiness and complexity" of creating an archive may be lost to those who have the opportunity to consult them (Weld 2014, 23), but the existence of an archive such as Memoria Abierta's surely helps to build collective memory, and has been central to this book and the dissemination of knowledge it may allow.

In addition to relying on Memoria Abierta's interviews, as a feminist sociologist I brought more intangible resources to the project: a "gender lens" (Howard et al. 1997) and a "sociological imagination" (Mills 1959), which I used to analyze women's testimonies of state terror. I began my project with an interest in women's body narratives and survival strategies. These interests partly derived from previous research for my book *Bodies in Crisis: Culture, Violence, and Women's Resistance in Neoliberal Argentina* (2010). There I examined different forms of violence (e.g., interpersonal, structural, and political) by focusing on diverse women's embodied experiences in contemporary contexts. The enduring wounds of state terrorism were also part of the analysis, and one of my interviewees for that book was a survivor of clandestine detention. In addition, I analyzed women's political activism, in ways that revealed not only oppressed but active and resistive bodies. The present work continues and deepens some of the lines of inquiry from my previous research, this time focusing exclusively on women survivors. A previous project on militarization in international perspective for the edited volume *Security Disarmed* (Sutton, Morgen, and Novkov 2008) also influenced my approach for this book.

Taking into account my research interests, the diversity of CDCs, the time period I had delimited (1976–83), and the conditions of use for different interviews,[37] I viewed and analyzed fifty-two testimonies of women survivors who were adults or teenagers at the time of their detention. These testimonies were recorded from 2001 to 2011 and range in length roughly between one and six hours each, in one or more sessions. I first read the written summaries, keywords, and other descriptors of the interviews that Memoria Abierta provided. I used these descriptions as a preliminary way to familiarize myself with the interviews, though the amount of information and level of detail provided varied. While some summaries contained terms more explicitly related to my initial research interests (e.g., "body," "health," "survival"), in most cases I had to use other information as cues of content related to my specific inquiry, including references to bodily themes such as pregnancy or torture.[38] As I began watching the interviews, I became intrigued by emerging information, such as responses to a question concerning transmission of memory to future generations and the message that the survivors wanted to transmit based on their overall experience.

The interviews were conducted by members of Memoria Abierta's team, which includes scholars, archivists, and other researchers trained to work with testimonies. The interviews were tailored to each person giving testimony, but presented a similar pattern and a logical chronology. The general sequence, with some variations, is as follows: First, interviewees were asked to introduce themselves and talk about their family of origin. Next, they were often prompted to address the role of politics in their lives and to reflect on the social, cultural, and political context of the 1960s and 1970s. In many cases, this included interviewees' activist histories and experiences of political violence prior to the coup. Interviewees would then talk about the last military dictatorship, their experiences of abduction and captivity in CDCs, their subsequent passage to the legal prison system and/or release, their post-detention life (including exile in some cases), and the transition to democracy. In this last section interviewees would usually refer to issues connected to the politics of memory, truth, and justice regarding human rights violations. Significant developments included the work of the CONADEP, the trial of the military juntas, the Truth Trials, impunity laws, judicial proceedings outside Argentina, and other transitional justice and memorialization initiatives.[39] The interview session generally concluded with survivors' retrospective reflection on their overall journeys, and the message they wished to transmit to other people who might view their testimonies, including future generations.

Interviewees did the great majority of the talking, narrating their experiences, sharing anecdotes, and emphasizing what they thought was important. Interviewers gently guided the sessions by briefly interjecting key questions, with some variation in the topics addressed depending on both interviewers and interviewees. The only person on camera was the interviewee. This created an illusion of being face-to-face with the person giving testimony. At times, I would almost forget that a screen separated me from the women interviewed, or that there was a temporal discontinuity—in some cases several years—between the time when the testimony was rendered and the moment I viewed it. The timing of the testimony is important because it shapes the content of interviews. For instance, the period of economic and political crisis around 2001 and the annulment of impunity laws and reopening of trials later in the decade seemed to influence some interviewees' narratives.

In accordance with the protocol of Memoria Abierta, I had to view all the testimonies in situ, as full copies of the testimonies cannot be borrowed from the archive and no recording devices are allowed in the room to copy the materials. This poses the challenge of how to collect and analyze data without the possibility of audio-recording the interviews at the archive. After conversations with colleagues and members of Memoria Abierta, I crafted a method that took into account the need for accuracy, the feasibility of the study, the hours of archive operation (which led to concentrated work of four to five hours per consultation), and my own constraints as a researcher (such as pain in my hands preventing me from speed typing for long, uninterrupted periods). In the end, my main instruments for recording information were a pen, a paper notebook, and a laptop. I did a preliminary search of the Oral Archive's database in January 2013, retrieving written summaries of interviews with women survivors. After clearing permission with Memoria Abierta and the Institutional Review Board of my university, I returned to the archive in June 2013. I viewed the interviews in stages during the period between June 2013 and July 2014.

Day after day I immersed myself in the world of testimonies, facing women who survived state terror and came forward to share their stories. I began by watching the entire interview, writing down as many details as possible. While the work consisted of archival research, there were overlaps with the active listening strategies of in-depth interviewing.[40] Yet Memoria Abierta's interviews were not designed to follow my own research goals and questions. Thus I needed to be attentive to narratives—sometimes appearing unexpectedly—that had direct relevance to my study. For ethical reasons and given the richness of the archival materials available in Memoria Abierta, I made the decision to use those sources instead of conducting my own interviews. I did this to avoid potentially burdening women with the task of retelling a difficult story they might already have told multiple times, in order to serve my research agenda.[41]

While the testimonies I listened to were rich in stories and information—and constitute an extremely valuable legacy for future generations—reliance on archived oral interviews presented a set of limitations when compared with conducting my own interviews. These limitations included the impossibility to follow up with questions, obtain clarification on particular aspects of the narrative, get a better sense of the context of enunciation, and more directly address my own research agenda. Additionally, interviewees might have been more willing to talk in confidential interviews about issues that they would rather not discuss in video-recorded testimonies for posterity. At the analysis stage, I also had to rely more heavily on my detailed notes and transcripts of selected passages, as opposed to having repeated and free access to the tapes of the full interviewees. Despite these limitations, I believe it was important to embark on the journey of listening to and working with the accounts of women who offered their testimonies with the expectation that they would be heard. I wanted to be the kind of interlocutor who would not only learn from these women's testimonies, but do something useful with their stories. Hopefully this book is a testament to the value of listening to survivors' archived narratives.

Memoria Abierta's interviews address issues similar to those elicited in judicial testimony, such as details about CDCs and the people there, but they also consist of contextualized life narratives. These accounts include interviewees' childhood memories, subjective assessments of political events, emotional recollections of fellow activists, accounts of life after detention, and other information that would not necessarily find its way into judicial proceedings. These aspects of the testimonies helped situate my particular research interests and questions within a larger set of experiences, worldviews, and biographies. At the same time, interviewees did not talk about some experiences addressed in more detail in judicial venues. For instance, I sometimes found out about aspects of interviewees' experiences (e.g., rape cases) from judicial documentation, not the oral testimonies I worked with. This reminds us of the partial and subjective quality of testimonies and their variations according to the time and place in which they are given, the purpose they serve, and the issues women may want to address in one venue or another.

Implicated Research

To work with CDC survivors' testimonies is not only to connect with someone else's trauma, but also potentially to be traumatized. How can one be immune to the barrage of sinister and painful information that these narratives convey? How can one remain unscathed after looking at horror in the eye, even if vicariously? Fernando Reati, a scholar and former political prisoner who along with CDC survivor Mario Villani wrote *Desaparecido* (Disappeared; 2011), tells of a ritual he devised to deal with the impact of listening to testimony of atrocities, to enter and leave the horrific world the survivor narrated. Washing his hands before and after working with testimony was his way of delimiting the work space and time, separating it a bit from the rest of his life (Veiras 2011). In my case, I had not created any particular strategy to deal with the emotional aspects of this research. Yet soon after I started the process of listening to survivors' testimonies I felt the full weight of the project and realized I had underestimated how personally taxing it would be. As Laub (1992, 72) notes, "There are hazards to the listening to trauma. Trauma—and its impact on the hearer—leaves, indeed, no hiding place intact. As one comes to know the survivor, one really comes to know oneself; and that is not a simple task."

As I became immersed in the stories of these women, furiously taking notes for hours at a time day after day, the images, sounds, smells, and feelings associated with torture centers permeated my consciousness. I would leave the archive with my back and neck hard as rock, and not just from intensive and sustained note taking. I was also in desperate need to share what I heard and learned. For a variety of reasons, however, it was not always easy to find interlocutors in my everyday life, with some exceptions.[42] "Who wants to talk about women in clandestine detention centers after an exhausting day of work?" someone in my social circle explained to me during a dinner party. "If you are going to talk about torture, then NO!" interjected another one after I was asked about my research. Given that memories of this recent history are far from settled, and political differences can create wedges even among people who care about each other, it is not always easy to discuss these topics. I wondered what unpleasant ghosts my work might summon amid my family and community of origin, and what the risks might be of pushing too hard when I needed to talk about the narratives to which I was bearing witness.

While I had written about the dictatorship and its aftermath in previous work (e.g., Sutton 2010; Sutton and Norgaard 2013), this project required digging deeper and even more directly into a history that many still prefer not to hear or think about. Listening to these women's accounts of state terror also meant listening across multiple registers: the content of the story, the manner in which it was narrated, and the way it engaged my own biography. As I listened to these women, I could not help but make connections with events I remembered from childhood, linguistic turns I had heard, places I had visited, or difficult conversations I had had with relatives or friends. I started to see my own life in a different light, including the cities and landmarks I was familiar with and the people I have known. I entertained disturbing questions. How much did everyone really know about what was going on back then? What is the true reason for continued silence about this topic in some social circles today? Is it only political differences that keep talk about state terrorism at bay? Did anybody I know participate in repression? Childhood memories of specific events or interactions came back in flashes. And yet some things remain almost unthinkable, or at least unspeakable.

Although the testimonies I heard are vivid reminders of the horror that took place in Argentina, my *own* memories growing up during the dictatorship do not generally reflect this horror. They are fragmentary and erratic, blending knowledge based on what I "remember" with images and frameworks acquired as an adult. What I came to know about the dictatorship has been shaped not only by my own experience at the time, but also by later testimonial, political, and academic writings; documentary and feature films; human rights groups' political protests; the trials of members of the repressive state apparatus; media information aired during the early transition to democracy; and conversations with relatives, friends, and survivors. Only in hindsight can I start to make sense of what I "knew" happened under the dictatorship, putting together the pieces I witnessed as a child.

I was six years old in 1976 when the military took power and thirteen—and in my first year in secondary school—when the dictatorship ended. I grew up in a sheltered middle-class family, with the luxury of feeling safe at a time when many adults and children experienced sheer terror. My life continued its normal course: Our summer vacations in Mar del Plata, a town by the ocean, were not suspended; Papa Noel continued bringing his gifts each Christmas; during the 1978 soccer World Cup, I cheered passionately when the Argentine team scored goals. I went to the same school all of my childhood and teenage years, never having to hide or run away. Weekend meals at Grandma's were almost a religious ritual. And I only got amused smiles from adults, when I thought as a young girl that to be president of Argentina one had to be a military officer.

Yet I also remembered moments that disrupted the appearance of safety, the privilege of obliviousness. Episodes here and there served as hints that something was not normal after all. I remember these episodes from the perspective of the girl I was, though now interpreted from the critical distance adulthood provides.[43] Normalcy was once interrupted when I was vacationing with my family in Mar del Plata and we heard gunshots on our block. My grandfather was coming from the airport and he and the taxi driver had to rush into the house. I wondered what was going on. Why did the taxi driver come into our home? It was dark and the streets were occupied by the military. They were supposedly confronting *guerrilleros* (guerrillas) who lived in our neighborhood—or so I was told. I was sent back to bed. That night, I rested uneasily, not terrified but somewhat fearful. I never knew what had happened to the alleged guerrillas (or "subversives" in the military lingo), but after that day a variation of the kids' game *ring-raje* (ring-and-run) emerged: "Who dares to touch the door of the *guerrilleros'* house and then run away?" we kids would ask. Touch and run. As children, we managed to normalize state terror, to adopt the framework of those in power as we constructed our neighbors as scary beings. Their raided home became our haunted house.

Not only did the testimonies I listened to merge into my personal history, but they also challenged me to connect with women whom I was beginning to know, but who did not know me. They did not know I was listening to their words, or that I was moved by their stories, or that I was crying, feeling angry, or at times even laughing with them. Although a screen separated me from these women, I developed a sense of connection with them through active listening (see also Einwohner 2011). I was receptive to their words and gestures, hearing their stories and experiencing diverse emotions, but with no possibility of a true bidirectional encounter. As in face-to-face interactions during ethnographic fieldwork or interviews, I felt varying levels of affinity with different women. While each story offered unique insights and engaged me in specific ways, some testimonies struck more of a chord than others. For various reasons, these women's narratives shook me, moved me, or challenged me in different ways. However, in all cases the need to engage in mindful listening was ever present (Bacci et al. 2012), as were the dilemmas and contradictions that hearing stories of atrocity entailed. Memory studies scholar Marianne Hirsch (2014, 339) warns of the traps of "identification and empathy" when listening to the pain of others: "[M]y work with postmemory has introduced a distancing awareness emphasizing that 'although it could have been me, it was decidedly not me.' I thus prefer to think in terms of a form of solidarity that is suspicious of empathy, shuttling instead between proximity and distance, affiliation and disaffiliation, complicity and accountability."

What produces the point of encounter between a person giving and the one listening to testimony, even if they have never met? How can the right balance "between proximity and distance" be struck? (Hirsch 2014, 339). These questions came into stark relief after I heard a testimony I found particularly moving. Something about this testimony shook me with particular force. It might have been the woman's words, her unspoken modes of communication, or my own projections that made me feel especially connected to her. As I witnessed the suffering still present in her face and hand gestures, I wished I had magic powers to heal. I wished I could cross the barrier of screen and offer some comfort. Of course, it would have been audacious to presume that I could have provided any solace or that she would have welcomed it. I realize that I was treading the perilous edge of "appropriative empathy" Hirsch mentions (2014, 339). I was clearly not an "objective," detached observer, but how could I navigate the emotions this type of work triggered? In my notes I reflected on the paradox that my feelings about this testimony presented: although I felt connected to this woman, she would not be able even to spot me on the streets.

A serendipitous encounter sometime later challenged me to revisit the emotions and the dilemmas that working with video-recorded testimonies of traumatic events presents. One chilly night in Buenos Aires, I crossed paths with the woman whose archived testimony had so moved me. A friend and I were standing in a packed theater lobby, waiting for a play to begin. As we were chatting, I scanned the crowd and realized with surprise—almost shock—that this woman was just a few meters away. She was waiting to see the play, too. Although she had given her testimony about a decade earlier, she looked nearly the same. For a split second we made eye contact. I do not know whether I stared at her or made any other involuntary gesture, but she walked toward me and stood silently by my side for what seemed to me like two or three minutes. I was paralyzed, unable to say a word, standing almost shoulder to shoulder with this woman I felt I knew but who I assumed would not recognize me. In a sense my assumption was true: she did not know who I was. And yet this brief encounter somewhat defied the notion that the affinity I experienced was just illusory—even if we both were there by coincidence. For an instant, I considered talking to her, but before the idea even took form I knew it would be inappropriate and invasive to do so. The fact that she gave testimony did not entitle me to bring up her experience of state terror on a Saturday night at the theater, or to unexpectedly approach her as she carried on with her life. While I certainly would have liked to tell her how much her testimony affected me, I abstained. It was not the right place or time. Even so, this unexpected encounter, in a city of millions of people, somewhat vindicated my feeling that perhaps the connection I felt with this woman was not a mere figment of my imagination.

The lack of direct research interactions with the women on whose testimonies this work is based raises questions about the nature of this qualitative study, my research positionality, and my responsibility as someone bearing witness to survivors' traumatic memories. Despite the fact that I did not conduct the interviews that yielded the testimonies, my positionality was not one of a distant observer. My approach can be described as a form of *implicated research*, applied to archival work. While terms such as "implicated" or "engaged" are usually used in relation to research that involves face-to-face interactions with research subjects, such as ethnographic and participatory methods, my own work did not involve such live encounters (e.g., Whitmer et al. 2010; Flores 2011). However, this project implicated me—in the sense of being entwined or entangled with the issues under study—in multiple ways: as a woman, an Argentine citizen, and a supporter of feminist and human rights causes. It ultimately implicated me as a human being, confronted by atrocities committed by other human beings.

As a scholar examining social suffering and trauma, the notion of "implication" is also significant in another way. Michael Rothberg uses the concept of "implicated subjects" to describe a particular connection to experiences of trauma: neither victims nor perpetrators, but "more than bystanders" (2013a, xv). He explains: "I use the deliberately open-ended term 'implication' in order to gather together various modes of historical relation that do not necessarily fall under the more direct forms of participation associated with traumatic events, such as victimization and perpetration. Such 'implicated' modes of relation would encompass bystanders, beneficiaries, latecomers of the postmemory generation and others connected 'prosthetically' to pasts they did not directly experience" (Rothberg 2013b, 40).

The women in this study spoke about a history that implicates me as someone who grew up in Argentina during the dictatorship, maintains important connections to the country, and feels invested in its future. While my personal memories of the dictatorship do not come from direct experiences of fear and terror (e.g., witnessing or suffering torture, having to hide or flee), they have triggered critical questions about how ordinary people process, normalize, and distance themselves from information about state violence. I have tackled some of these issues in previous work (Sutton and Norgaard 2013; Sutton 2015), yet the present project raised the stakes by bringing me closer to the stories of those who suffered the brunt of state terror. This project generated ever more disturbing questions, prompting me to examine my own life and the social contexts in which it has unfolded more deeply.

My involvement in this project is also related to my political commitments. My interest in this type of work grew out of and echoes the widely shared demand by members of the human rights movement that state-sponsored atrocities never again be committed. Rather than tainting the work with subjective or political motives, I believe that understanding and disseminating information about the contexts, lived realities, and effects of state terrorism are important particularly given the power of the state and its expected role as guarantor of rights. This project also flows from feminist political and scholarly awareness that women's experiences and perspectives, particularly with respect to issues construed as men's domains (e.g., politics, the economy, militarization), have not always received due attention (Enloe 2004; 2013). I hope this work encourages the examination of linkages between past instances of state violence and forms of state-sponsored/perpetrated/enabled violence that women and other marginalized groups continue to experience in different parts of the world (e.g., INCITE! 2006; Riley, Mohanty, and Pratt 2008; Sutton, Morgen, and Novkov 2008).

Though I currently reside in the United States, I maintain strong ties to Argentina, spending extended periods in the country, visiting family and friends, conducting research, and interacting with activists and academics. I inhabit a transnational space, straddling cultures, languages, and geographies. This enables connections as well as dislocations. My transnational positioning allows me to put in dialogue what I observe in Argentina with my lived experiences and knowledge as a U.S.-based scholar. Similarly, as I continue to learn about the history of state violence in Argentina and its rationalizations and circumstances, disturbing questions emerge about U.S. political developments as well. I refer specifically to the post–September 11, 2001, U.S.-led "war on terror" and the notions of "national security" that permeate much state violence. Such notions have undergirded not only wars in Iraq and Afghanistan, yielding countless victims catalogued as "collateral damage," but also torture and torment of detainees, extraordinary rendition programs, indefinite detention in prisons of dubious legitimacy, drone attacks that are far from surgically precise, and increased surveillance and profiling in the name of eradicating terrorism (e.g., Welch 2003; Danner 2004; Del Rosso 2011; Constitution Project 2013).

Torture, disappearance, and the gendered dimensions of political and state violence are not simply matters of the past or characteristic of dictatorships. They are part and parcel of how contemporary wars are being conducted, for example, in the context of the global "war on terror" and neoliberal democracies where people continue "disappearing." In news stories about such events we rarely hear from the tortured individuals themselves; and women's experiences seem to be particularly likely to be silenced in the public debates about torture. This book tackles such silences and addresses how gender is imprinted in militarized conceptions and practices of "security," including those that resort to brutal and illegal interrogation and confinement. These matters remain urgent and significant beyond Argentina.

Besides offering insight about Argentine politics and the operations of state terror in general, the testimonies I viewed and listened to also open up a space to reflect on "big questions" concerning the human condition, questions we might not think about on a daily basis. These narratives exposed me to profound dilemmas about the meaning of being human, living and dying, and surviving. I heard witness accounts of the human capacity for extreme cruelty, yet these testimonies also spoke to human resilience and the ability to transform trauma in creative and positive ways. The ants' story that opens this book points to the resilience of life in a place of torture and death, of the resources of human beings in extreme situations, and of the community and support network that is necessary to sustain and bolster those resources.

As I started to share these stories in academic settings and through conversations with friends, family, and acquaintances, I confronted a spectrum of reactions reflecting the still-contested dimensions of memory concerning the recent Argentine past. I strove to be reflexive about my own standpoint and approached the project with a sense of responsibility that marked each stage of the process. Although I rely heavily on the words of women survivors, the analyses presented here are not simply transparent reflections of their perspectives. As a writer I have played a central role mediating these women's narratives. Furthermore, the institutional context of an archive also shapes what is said and not said in individual testimonies in the first place. The accounts in this book are the product of a collaboration of sorts: between the survivors who were willing to record their words for the archive, members of Memoria Abierta who collected and made the testimonies available, and myself as a researcher who listened to and worked with these stories. I hope that my analysis resonates with women survivors' lived experiences, honors their courage in voicing their stories, and helps advance understandings of oppression, resistance, and survival.

2

Telling Terror

[T]he moments of confusion, of terror, of torture are mixed
with moments of relative calm, when they would perhaps
sit me there and let me bathe, and they even prepared *mate*
[a traditional infusion] for me. But it gets all mixed up, that
is, I can't tell you if everything started with a torture session
or everything started sitting at a desk drinking mate at the
naval base. I cannot remember, I cannot piece together the
sequence, but there were several days where . . . I think at
the beginning, that first morning they sat me in one place,
at a desk, and then it was like things started moving quickly,
toward torture and interrogation, and confinement, and
isolation, and the pressure of terror.
—Liliana Gardella

As Liliana's testimony in Memoria Abierta shows, accounting for the
multiple and disturbing layers of experience in clandestine detention is
far from a straightforward undertaking. Lapses in memory or difficulty
in piecing the events together are often entwined with vivid recollections of horrific or unsettling events. Grief, loss, and trauma permeate
the narratives of women survivors, even as they powerfully assert their
voices in defiance of silence and oblivion. How do women survivors
"tell terror"? What is at stake in the process of remembering and giving
testimony about experiences of state terror? What is the significance of
silence and talk, body and voice, in these women's testimonies?

In order to better understand the content of survivors' narratives of
political repression, it is important to have a sense of the social context
from which repressive state actions developed. Thus this chapter begins
by situating interviewees' narratives in relation to the period of social
and political mobilization that preceded the last military dictatorship
and the escalating state violence that ultimately reached the women in

this study. Keeping this period in mind is necessary since, as will be discussed later, a number of these women reclaimed their histories of social and political activism (and/or their disappeared relatives' participation), and talked about the intense political commitments that characterized their lives before the last coup d'état. Needless to say, these political experiences do not make these women any less victims of the brutal state repression they suffered in the clandestine detention centers (CDCs). However, they do offer a window into the radical political projects that the military regime tried to quash chiefly through the annihilation of political activists, their relations, and anybody else categorized as "subversive."

Before diving into the analysis of women's narratives of clandestine detention, it is also essential to remember that giving public testimony about these events—for example, in trials, commissions, or other institutions—has entailed an often onerous and painful commitment for survivors. Even if testifying can also be empowering, it demands a significant investment of time, energy, and emotion. It can also involve a level of physical risk, depending on the context. The fact that Jorge Julio López—a survivor and key witness in one of the trials for crimes against humanity[1]—disappeared once again after testifying in 2006, this time while living in a democracy, is a stark reminder of how high the stakes can be for those who publicly give testimony. Testifying can potentially mean returning to conditions of threat and bodily harm. The dictatorship was intent on silencing civil society, and most particularly those targeted through physical torture and disappearance. Breaking the silence was both an individual and a collective process. Thus, themes related to silence, voice, and embodiment are important here. How and why did these women decide, sooner or later, to offer their testimonies? What value and challenges do they attribute to these efforts? How are body and voice implicated in the testimonial gesture?

After addressing the process by which survivors have claimed their role as witnesses—giving their testimonies in various venues—this chapter begins to delve into their memories of state terror, including how different women conceptualized the torments and torture they endured. Their accounts help to visualize the indelible marks of the traumas they experienced, beyond narrow definitions of torture. As women survivors grappled with memories of unimaginable cruelty, they also posed troubling questions about the human condition, particularly as they tried to make meaning of the perpetrators' actions. While survivors' narratives cannot settle these difficult questions, in dealing with these issues, several survivors reveal a perhaps more subtle form of suffering than that evidenced by the brutal inscription of violence on the body. These devastating stories convey a pain for humanity, a sense of grief for actions that can defy basic assumptions about what it means to be human. These are not merely abstract theorizations but insights grounded in these women's concrete lived experience of terror in the camps.

The Backdrop of State Terror

On March 24, 1976, a military coup d'état launched a seven-year dictatorship in Argentina. The language of the de facto military authorities' first communiqué shows that the regime was not interested in just subduing insurgent armed groups, but had broader power and control aspirations: "It is communicated to the population, that from this date, the country is under the operational control of the Junta of General Commanders of the Armed Forces. It is recommended to all inhabitants that they strictly comply with the provisions and directives emanating from the military, security or police authorities, as well as that they be extremely careful to avoid individual or group actions and attitudes that might require the drastic intervention of personnel in operations."[2] The reliance on ambiguous concepts and the inclusion of the elastic notion of "attitude" as potentially attracting repression were among the tools that enabled state authorities to persecute a broad spectrum of people.

During the last military dictatorship, the state carried out a violent repression against the civilian population, targeting people deemed "subversive." The figure of the subversive was an ideological construction of a dangerous Other that had to be suppressed at all costs (Duhalde 1999). Among other things, this figure masked the diverse universe of people who, from the military perspective, fit this blanket categorization. People who were kidnapped by state forces and taken to CDCs were alleged subversives, no matter whether or not they had ever taken up arms. Individuals from all walks of life were caught in the repression. Even though many of the people abducted by state forces were part of armed political organizations, with different levels of responsibility and participation in armed struggle, such affiliation did not justify the illegal and brutal treatment they suffered at the hands of the state. Ironically, while the dictatorship instituted the death penalty for certain crimes of public order, it did not really apply it in the legal sense (Lorenz et al. 2010; Hood and Hoyle 2014). In other words, the regime did not implement its own overt—though illegitimate—laws, and instead proceeded to kidnap and execute people without trial. "Official denial" (Cohen 2001) was part and parcel of how the de facto government implemented its so-called "war against subversion."

As was the case with the disappeared more broadly, the women featured in this study constitute a socially and politically diverse group. At the time of the dictatorship and in previous years, this group of survivors had varied occupations, including student, teacher, cashier, seamstress, psychologist, catechist, journalist, actress, lawyer, factory worker, homemaker, and university professor, among others. Many of them were social and/or political activists. They participated in community, labor, religious, and political groups, including guerrilla organizations and/or their mass political fronts. A number of them were relatives or acquaintances of persons already catalogued as "subversive" or had helped people targeted by the regime. They experienced illegal detention in different types of secret prisons in terms of size, structure, and geographical location and with regard to whether the military, police, or other security forces were in charge. As a whole, these women offer essential perspectives about the spaces and actions of state terror in Argentina.

In addition to their experiences of state repression, many of these women also shared relevant accounts of the popular mobilization and cultural changes that took place during the sixties and early seventies and the ways these societal developments were interwoven with their lives. That period not only was marked by "a strong radicalization of middle-class and working-class sectors" but also represented "a break with respect to previous practices and subjectivities" in terms of gender relations, sexuality, and women's political and workforce participation (Andújar et al. 2009, 10; see also Felitti 2000; Martínez 2009; Gramático 2011; Oberti 2015). Several women in this study talked about the sense of possibility they experienced during these heady days, and highlighted the sheer joy and intensity that their commitment to activism

entailed, even as they also dealt with conflict in their organizations and/
or faced state or paramilitary repression. They told anecdotes about their
participation in marches, student demonstrations, community meetings, *volanteadas* (pamphlet distribution), labor conflicts, and heated
debates in the university, at the workplace, or among the union ranks.
Such memories also include the escalation of paramilitary violence and
state repression during the lead-up to the coup, from tear gas and other
violent tactics aimed at disbanding political protests, to the disappearance of fellow activists later on.

The social and political transformations that survivors narrated in
Argentina can be placed in the context of larger international trends at
the time, including movements in which young people played central
roles. Examples of these events include the civil rights, antiwar, feminist,
and sexual liberation movements in the United States; the 1968 general
strikes and popular rebellions in France known as the French May; and
the Tlatelolco massacre that followed massive student demonstrations
in Mexico City in the same year. The Cuban Revolution provided in-
spiration to other revolutionary movements in Latin America, and the
decolonization and national liberation struggles in Africa and Asia also
influenced activism elsewhere. Some interviewees related their experiences to social and political events beyond Argentina's borders. This international context also became important, for instance, in situations of
exile during the political repression in Argentina.

Argentina was going through its own period of turmoil during the
1960s and 1970s. A series of civilian and de facto military presidents followed the 1955 overthrow of popular leader Juan D. Perón (president of
Argentina from 1946 to 1955). In 1966, a military regime took over the
government of another elected president, Arturo Illia, under the banner of the so-called Argentine Revolution—this was really a military
dictatorship with the intention to stay in power indefinitely, but which
lasted from 1966 to 1973. In the meantime, Perón continued to have a
significant influence in the course of events in Argentina even though
Peronism had been proscribed and Perón exiled. In the early 1970s, his
followers, including an active movement of young people, were mobilizing to return Perón from his prolonged exile in Spain.

The economic and political measures adopted by the military's Argentine Revolution as well as its general authoritarian approach met

with resistance from various groups. This regime intervened in public universities (and repressed students and faculty), strove to discipline labor (reducing salaries and undermining sectors of the workers movement), favored the industrial capitalist class (including foreign capital), dictated conservative morality norms, and implemented censorship (Calveiro 2005). One example of the popular discontent that was rising across the country was the 1969 Cordobazo, a joint uprising of students and workers in the province of Córdoba, which sent ripple effects among activists all over the country. This mass protest met state repression, and the results of the confrontation included up to thirty deaths, hundreds of wounded, and numerous arrests (Romero 2013). Historian Luis Alberto Romero notes that there were divergent evaluations of the event but "[w]hatever the interpretation, one thing was clear: The enemy of those people who massively went out into the streets to protest was the dictatorship, behind which lurked the manifold presence of capital" (2013, 181).

The insurrections of the sixties and early seventies included diverse social movement organizations that aimed to advance social justice causes, be it under Marxist-spectrum ideologies or under Peronism. Such movements included armed political organizations with revolutionary ideals: "The first guerrilla organizations had emerged—with little significance—in the early 1960s, under the influence of the Cuban experience. They were revived with Che Guevara's Bolivian campaign, but their real genesis was to be found in the country's experience with authoritarianism and the conviction that there was no alternative to defeating the dictatorship except armed struggle" (Romero 2013, 189).

Pilar Calveiro (2005) notes how the recourse to violence had become commonplace in Argentine politics for much of the twentieth century, with military coups often toppling elected governments since 1930. She argues that in the late sixties "[t]he military violence began to be reproduced and to find a response, also violent, from other sectors of society" (37), and that the guerrilla organizations "represented a challenge to the monopoly of violence, exerted by the Armed Forces, by a sector of civil society" (38). As part of their armed struggle, guerrilla organizations launched attacks on military and police facilities, held hostages for ransom and/or prisoner exchange, engaged in armed confrontations with state forces, and perpetrated politically motivated killings (Romero

2013). Most notable among such armed revolutionary groups were the ERP (People's Revolutionary Army/Ejército Revolucionario del Pueblo) connected to the PRT (Workers' Revolutionary Party/Partido Revolucionario de los Trabajadores) and the Montoneros (armed branch of Peronism), which was in turn associated with various mass political fronts, such as the Peronist Youth/Juventud Peronista (JP), the Peronist University Youth/Juventud Unversitaria Peronista (JUP), and the Peronist Working Youth/Juventud Trabajadora Peronista (JTP).

In 1973, the military regime gave way to elections, still banning Perón from running for the presidency. The stand-in Peronist candidate, Héctor Cámpora, won election to the office under the rallying call "Cámpora to the Government, Perón to Power." He resigned after a few months, and was replaced by interim president Raúl Lastiri. That same year new elections took place and Perón won the presidency with a 62 percent majority (Calveiro 2005; Lorenz et al. 2010). However, his term was short-lived, as he died in 1974 and was succeeded by his third wife and vice president María Estela (known as Isabel) Martínez de Perón. While Perón's deceased second wife, Eva Perón (known as Evita), had enjoyed enormous popularity among the poor, the working classes, and their allies, that was not the case for Isabel. Her brief government was marred by economic problems, political divisions within Peronism, and spiraling political violence. This violence included high-impact actions by guerrilla organizations as well as repression by paramilitary groups such as the Argentine Anticommunist Alliance (AAA), which hunted activists and political opponents. In 1975, the state-led Operation Independence (Operativo Independencia)—which aimed to "neutralize and/or annihilate the actions of subversive elements" in the province of Tucumán[3]—was one of the precursors of the state terror unleashed with full force during the dictatorship.

The social and political commitments of many of the women in this study reflect the political context of the time, including a varied range of more or less combative activist organizations embedded in different realms of social and political life in Argentina: schools, universities, workplaces, poor and working-class neighborhoods, and religious communities, among others. A number of women reported their affiliation to more than one group in which they had participated simultaneously or over the years.[4] Given their political activities and sympathies, several of these women experienced closely the heightened political violence and repression that preceded and increased after the military coup of 1976. Some went underground along with their organizations, and many lost fellow activists, family members, or friends to detention, armed confrontation, or disappearance. When the military took power on March 24, 1976, starting the self-designated Process of National Reorganization, some of these women were already exhausted, tired of being on the run, feeling afraid and/or defeated. Despite the terrible conditions of their kidnappings by state forces, a couple of these women suggested that they could finally stop anticipating what they had feared would happen. The horror they encountered, however, was well beyond what many could have ever imagined.

All of the women in this study share in common their passage through CDCs, but the conditions and length of clandestine detention varied. Some of them were held captive for hours or days, while others were disappeared for months and even years. Whereas some survivors were kept in one clandestine center, others passed through several of these places, which could involve suffering the "initiation ceremony" (Calveiro 1998, 60) of torture repeatedly and in different sites. Within CDCs, forced labor was part of the daily life of selected detainees, though not necessarily during the entire period of captivity.[5] The circumstances of their liberation also differed: some were released directly from a CDC while others were first "legalized" and transferred to the nonclandestine prison system (which also involved abuses, but where they at least had recognized existence within the legal system).[6] Before being released, some of these women were subjected to a regime that entailed working during the day for more or less extended periods in places outside the camps designated by the repressors, such as ministries or businesses. The end of the clandestine detention did not necessarily mean freedom, but rather gave rise to varying degrees of "surveilled freedom" and control by the repressors. Upon release, some of the women went into exile and some of those who stayed in Argentina went into forms of "internal exile," temporarily cutting off their ties to their previous history, moving to different towns, and trying to start anew. No matter the path they took, the experience of captivity continued to plague the lives of many survivors. Escuela de Mecánica de la Armada (ESMA) survivor Munú Actis referred to this lasting burden: "[I]t is like a kind of backpack that one has attached. And one gets up with it, goes to sleep with it, then everything takes much more effort."

Counting the Losses

The testimonies of women survivors emerge from a place of profound loss and suffering stemming from state terrorism. In summary, besides torture and disappearances, repression also included the appropriation of babies of captive women, theft of property belonging to detainees and their families, slave labor by kidnapped persons, continued intimidation and threats even after their release, births and abortions in deplorable conditions, and sexual violence, among others. In their accounts, interviewees repeatedly recounted painful personal and social losses. These losses happened in a traumatic manner and were therefore particularly difficult to process (Caruth 1995; Jelin 2003). Sometimes during their testimonies, a cracking voice, a look of disbelief, or tears rolling down the face offered hints of the deep emotions that these losses evoke. Even though many survivors were able to rebuild their lives, rechannel political concerns, find sources of joy and connection, and even flourish personally and professionally, the weight of trauma and loss becomes apparent in their narratives.

Loss appears strongly on a *personal* level: loss of fellow activists, family, friends, loved ones—concrete people who were missing, killed, or forced into exile. That is, there was a universe of persons that in one way or another were gone. After all, as Norma Berti explained, a central strategy of repression, specifically torture, was the destruction of the "relational world" of those in captivity: "[B]ecause torture is not just something that threatens your own self but that threatens your whole world, that is, your relational world, no? I mean they want to go and kill the people who had something to do with you. [. . .] [I]t is a moment of . . . I think of utter desperation, either due to the physical pain, or due to the desperation of trying to save that relational world, that affective world that has surrounded you and that at that moment runs a grave risk, no?" As in the case of Norma Berti, in most testimonies one can quickly glimpse the *group dimensions* of personal suffering. Through these stories it is possible to re-create the political and affective "networks" of people (Águila 2008, 75) who were "falling" (being kidnapped, murdered) or experiencing other forms of political persecution. Although these interviewees survived, many of them are still waiting to know about the ultimate fate of *compañeros/as* (fellow activists), friends, colleagues, children, grandchildren, partners, spouses, or other relatives.

The *life trajectories* of survivors were changed forever. Women in this study referred to unfinished, destroyed, or stunted vital projects: work, study, family plans, and places of residence. Some of these women spent years in clandestine prisons and/or in indefinite detention in the regular prison system.[7] Some could no longer pursue their chosen educational paths. Others had problems reinserting themselves into jobs, even due to the accusation of having "abandoned work" while in clandestine detention. Some had to start their lives anew in different towns or foreign countries. Others missed precious time raising their children, and could communicate with them only through letters or sporadic visits. Some women lost their pregnancies because of torture or forced abortions, or traced to the experience of captivity the health problems of sons or daughters who were very young during the women's detention, or who were born around that time. Still, these costs do not fully reflect the time, energy, and efforts that survivors expended in dealing with the physical and psychological consequences of captivity.

For many of those who were activists, another dimension of loss was the *sinking of political projects* in which they had been deeply involved, projects that were "annihilated," in the words of survivor Norma Berti. In talking about their activism before the coup, several women mentioned the joy that it entailed, the bonds of solidarity with compañeros/as, the sense of possibility that animated their work, and the feeling that the utopias they envisioned were around the corner. Politics emerged as an all-encompassing activity and orientation that had colored all aspects of many of these women's lives. As state repression increased, as many activists had to abandon their studies, jobs, and homes in order to hide, and as people around them started to be killed or disappeared, joy gave way to horror.

At the *broader social level*, various interviewees lamented the loss of a "very valuable generation" (Raquel Odasso), "great people" (Marta Álvarez), "all of our generation [. . .] many who I think would be valuable to have today" (Laura Schachter). Beyond their loved ones and other concrete people absent from their lives, they also outlined the wider implications of state repression against a generation of people who were predominantly young at the moment of their abduction. What is the social cost of a missing "generation" and of a cohort of survivors who have had to spend much of their lives recovering from trauma?

Indeed, as survivors recounted their losses, their reflections also suggest that Argentine society overall has suffered a significant loss: missing many people who could have positively contributed to the present and future of the country. At the same time, while it might be tempting to idealize those who are no longer here, Laura Schachter, who was a student activist in the seventies, noted: "[W]e belonged to a moment in history, where we are products of that moment. And that doesn't make us better or worse. [. . .] Nor do I think that we lost the best ones. We lost those who were like us, and that's what makes it more terrible." With this statement Laura implicitly countered the narratives that have placed the disappeared on a pedestal of heroism, and that in the same move could reduce survivors to irrelevancy, or worst, traitor status.[8]

The traumatic losses that the women in this study narrate are part and parcel of the recent history of Argentina and therefore have clear social dimensions. They involve not only individuals who were directly affected by state violence, but also various social institutions, political and economic sectors, and society as a whole, with varying consequences and levels of responsibility. Still, not everything is losses. Survivor and Grandmother of Plaza de Mayo Ledda Barreiro pointed out that "yes, we lost irreparably," referring to the people who disappeared, including her own daughter. "But we also won," she said. This is associated with the fruits that the struggles of human rights organizations have yielded over the years, including the debilitation of the power of the military, the achievement of a measure of justice through trials for crimes against humanity, and collective memory "demonstrating that history can also be written by the defeated."

Living Testimony

Breaking the Silence

The testimonies of survivors have been crucial to advance human rights organizations' demands for "Memory, Truth, and Justice." Indeed, survivors provided firsthand accounts of the workings of state terror. Many survivors offered their testimony soon after, and even before, the dictatorship ended, including in international forums, in the Argentine truth commission (CONADEP), and in the Trial of the Juntas in 1985. Yet in line with writings on trauma and its effects on people's abilities to share their experiences (e.g., Felman and Laub 1992; Caruth 1995), a number of survivors took a long time to tell what happened to them or to narrate particular aspects of their experiences—to loved ones, to the general public, in judicial proceedings, or in the sphere of human rights organizations. For one, the ability to talk or the motivation to be silent about these issues has been mediated by emotional marks, including fear or guilt for having survived (Bacci et al. 2012). Survivors' possibilities and willingness to give testimony (or not) were also affected by political contexts: the fear experienced during the dictatorship and the first years of democracy, the criminal prosecution of repressors soon after the end of the regime, the impunity laws and pardons under constitutional governments, and finally the political changes and judicial decisions that led to the annulment of impunity laws and the opening of trials for crimes against humanity in the 2000s.

While some women in this study started to denounce the human rights abuses upon their release from captivity, or even while still imprisoned (e.g., to international monitors or to the regular prison authorities), other women were not able to speak openly until much later. Some could not talk about such events even within their intimate circle. During the dictatorship, silence was pervasive, and in the case of survivors the effects of terror could have a powerful silencing effect. According to survivor Laura Schachter, "[O]ne of the objectives [of the dictatorship] was that one would not speak. And I believe that it was the terror, I mean, they left us terrorized. On the one hand, one tried to be with people who knew, or knew something, so as to make it not necessary . . . I mean, one felt close to those people. But not even then could we talk about it, not even with my sister was I able to talk until recently. [. . .] Nobody asked, one would not tell."

The mandate to not speak, not ask, and not know was a key mechanism in the operations of power of the dictatorship (e.g., Hollander 1996; Sutton and Norgaard 2013). The imposed silence, embodied by the idea that "nothing happened here," was one way of sustaining impunity. In the case of former detainees, this mandate was not just a diffuse effect of the context of fear but had been explicitly conveyed to them with threats by repressors. Furthermore, their own terror-filled captivity experience served as a cautionary tale.

The title of Memoria Abierta's book *Y nadie quería saber* (And Nobody Wanted to Know; Bacci et al. 2012)—which quotes the words of survivor Alicia Morales—evokes how the position of the listener also helps to define the contours of the speakable. Certain survivors' experiences became unspeakable partly because of the inability or unwillingness of a society to listen (Laub 1992; Jelin 2011). While on one hand stories of atrocity can be unbearable (Feld 2002), "not knowing" permits people to continue life as if nothing had happened, distancing themselves from the disturbing emotions and dissonance that thinking about these issues may elicit (Hollander 1996; Sutton and Norgaard 2013). In cases of sexual violence, survivors sometimes kept these experiences silent in order to protect loved ones from the suffering that such information involved, as well as due to feelings of guilt or shame (Zurutuza 2011).

The obstacles that survivors encountered in voicing their stories in Argentina can also be placed in a broader perspective, in relation to societal reactions in other cultural and political contexts. Anne Cubilié argues that generally

> survivors of atrocity become deeply uncomfortable signifiers for the post-atrocity societies within which they live, excessive to structures of normality that privilege forgetting, getting over and getting on with things through the denial of the terror of death, especially the possibility of mass death. Survivors have come to be figured by us in the form of "ghosts" who haunt our cultural imaginary. Configured as the uncanny [. . .] and vested with a power and wisdom that have literally been brought back from the realm of the dead, they are valorized, memorialized, and heroized, but we cannot—will not—hear them. (2005, xii)

Based on survivors' accounts in varied political contexts, Cubilié also points out that even when heard, there are often limited and standard sets of survivor accounts to which audiences might be willing to listen. And yet while the point about the inaudibility of certain stories seems to hold in the Argentine case, in her book *Traiciones* (Treasons), Ana

Longoni (2007) argued that rather than being *heroized*, survivors of state terrorism in Argentina had more often been viewed with suspicion, even deemed *traitors* by people with whom they might share some political affinities. It seems like the "'stock' stories" (Cubilié 2005, xii) that survivors were allowed to tell for much of the post-dictatorship period were in the constricted space of judicial or truth commission realms, and demanded the silencing of important dimensions of experience, such as political identities and agency. In the context of binary constructions of agency/victimhood, the recognition of survivors' political involvement and (constrained) agency in the repressive milieu of the camps could go against their recognition as victims deserving justice and reparations (Macón 2014; Park 2014).

Survivors' feelings of guilt for having survived—which can influence their ability to talk—were often compounded by the perceived, expected, or actual reactions of other people. The words of Susana Jorgelina Ramus, who was held two years in the clandestine camp in ESMA, illustrate a survivor's efforts to grapple with feelings of culpability. A potentially accusatory audience is present in her text:

> The glasses need to be perfectly clean; I have to see and see myself in the situation. It cannot be that that shadow of guilt slides in, guilt for living, guilt for thinking that the behavior was not the appropriate one, guilt for my father's death, the same day and almost at the same hour of my kidnapping/guilt for abandoning my daughter, guilt for wanting to live to see her, to feel her close to me, to see her grow up, to accompany her and tell her about her father/guilt for the rapes, for seeing how they kidnapped our compañeros and not saying anything, guilt for feeling scared and more than afraid about torture, about pain, or death. Faults that are not so. Because in that situation it was impossible to choose, or because each one did what [they] could. And who can judge. The one who can, throw the first stone. (Ramus 2000, 52–53)

Several survivors refer to the pain of being treated as suspects for having survived the arbitrary power over life and death that the repressors deployed.[9] Ana Longoni (2007) recounts the suspicion with which even people in leftist and human rights circles regarded survivors. A binary frame depicted those who remain disappeared as heroes/martyrs and those who "reappeared" as (potential) traitors, including the idea that they traded their lives for some sort of collaboration with repressors (Park 2014). Such notions overlook the complex and impossible situations confronted by detainees as well as the multiple examples of the arbitrary nature of events surrounding who died and who survived—which could not be simply traced to any particular action by survivors. As testimonies such as Emilce Moler's suggest, the question of why some people lived and others died should be directed toward repressors, who were the ones who made those decisions. Yet, this question was too often posed, with a suspicious tone, to survivors. Elisa Tokar mentioned "that question, 'and why did you survive?' no?, which is so terrible. [...] When the question should be: 'Why did these sons of a bitch kill so many? And what a joy that you are alive.'"

In the case of women, the specter of the "bitch and traitor" (Longoni 2007, 143)—who supposedly survived thanks to her sexual relations with the oppressor—also weighs as another possible basis for ascribing culpability, regardless of whether the woman had sexual contact with her captors.[10] The stigma of the "whore" is part of a shared social imaginary. Repressors called Elisa a "Montonera bitch" while they tortured her; she could potentially become "traitor bitch" in the eyes of those who would blame her for surviving; and in turn the repressors were "sons of a bitch" for the atrocities they perpetrated (Elisa redirected the accusatory finger, but the figure of the "whore" somehow remained to signify the negative—so naturalized is the "son of a bitch" insult). Survivor Marta Álvarez proposed that if people knew about the feelings of guilt that many survivors had already carried, perhaps the accusers would abstain from continuing to blame them. Though guilt operates in a subjective manner, independently of someone accusing, this inhospitable context did not help survivors to share their experiences in CDCs.

In any case, a number of women were ultimately able to *tomar la palabra* (take the floor and speak) (Bacci et al. 2012, 85), some encouraged by political changes that favored their testimony as well as greater societal openness to listen to their words. With regard to sexual violence, cultural and legal changes influenced by feminism and women's movement organizations nationally and internationally have helped open spaces to address previously silenced gender issues (Zurutuza 2011; Jelin 2014). Sometimes testimony came after survivors' personal and therapeutic work. Many survivors wanted to contribute information to obtain a measure of justice, and several did so when encouraged to process their experience with others who underwent similar situations. Since the 2000s, increased attention to these issues in the public sphere has emerged in conjunction with multiple state and nongovernmental initiatives under the banner of "Memory, Truth, and Justice." The testimonies of Memoria Abierta can be understood as part of that process.

Even though the weight of silence and the difficulty of talking are mentioned in various testimonies, the effort to overcome this challenge was also articulated. Survivor Liliana Gardella explained: "It always concerned me that our difficulty in talking, meant, [or] it would end up meaning in practice, besides a very high personal cost, that society would never find out, that always there would be a piece . . . because we survivors do not talk about the deepest of the repression." While remembering a traumatic past can be difficult and painful (Levi 1989), many survivors still decided to offer their public testimony. Giving testimony involved multiple dimensions, from helping to process the trauma and obtaining justice to being "included in the conversation" about events directly relevant to their lives and the broader political society (Partnoy 2006, 1668). Reminiscent of Holocaust survivor Primo Levi's "'duty to remember,' to testify 'in the name of others'" (Jelin 2003, 62), some survivors of state terrorism in Argentina also referred to the need to give testimony as a "responsibility" or a "debt." Testimony was invested with a moral dimension, construed as a way of being a face and a voice for the disappeared. In this sense, testimony was also conceived of as a "privilege." Adriana Arce explained that already in captivity she began the task of remembering, of telling herself repeatedly what had happened, so as to not forget and be able to denounce it. She recalled that her chances of surviving to testify were slim: "[M]ost likely I would not be able to be, like I am today, telling this, no? Which continues to be a privilege, because there are many who cannot be telling, well, what I am telling you. Thus it increases the responsibility that we have."

Similarly, Susana Jorgelina Ramus, who published her experiences in the book *Sueños sobrevivientes de una montonera* (2000), recounted the effort that revisiting such painful experiences represented, while also emphasizing her perceived duty to give testimony. In her testimonial interview with Memoria Abierta she explained: "[A]t the beginning it was very hard work because, well, perhaps I would read things in my journal and they were so intense that I could not continue, no? And then . . . well, then I had to make an effort, and did it, no? But . . . it also seemed to me that it was a kind of debt to . . . which I believe that we who survived have with respect to those who couldn't, couldn't tell. [. . .] And since they cannot tell what happened, well, someone has to give testimony, no?" Relatedly, Laura Schachter concluded: "And even though what happened to me was very painful, and marked my future life, I am here to tell it, and I already feel it is a privilege."

These words show how the impetus to testify can partly arise from a sense of responsibility toward those who disappeared, whose ability to speak was shut out by state violence. At the same time survivor and scholar Alicia Partnoy, who reflects on the idea of *speaking with* instead of *speaking for* others,[11] also points to the dilemma that the voices of the disappeared represent: "Yet we can only 'speak without' those who have not survived" (2006, 1668). Referring to Primo Levi's writings on Nazi atrocities, Giorgio Agamben (1999, 33) elaborates on the "lacuna" that testimony presents, on the impossibility of having "complete witnesses" of the extermination experience. Survivors were the exception and cannot really speak from the perspective of those who experienced the whole process of annihilation and died as a result. As such, survivors tread through a difficult terrain, narrating their own stories and struggles while also giving an account that has collective dimensions and that includes those who are no longer around to speak in their own words. Survivor Nora Strejilevich's literary work in *Una sola muerte numerosa* (A Single, Numberless Death) (1997) is an example of the weaving of her own and other people's experiences to generate a more collective account of clandestine detention. Survivor Ana Di Salvo remembered the book that she and fellow captive Martha Brea said they would write, based on their experiences in clandestine detention. Though that project never came to fruition—as Martha Brea never returned from captivity— Ana spoke of her own testimonial practice as a figurative way of writing the book that she and Martha had aimed to produce.

Hence, in addition to the significance that survivors' experiences have in their own right, their narratives also bring to the fore memories of those disappeared by state terror: a mother tenderly described the dreams of her son who was illegally detained and brutally assassinated as a teenager, another survivor talked about the poem that a fellow detainee wrote for her while in detention, and yet another one fondly remembered a comrade whose advice helped her resist torture without giving away names of other people. These micro stories powerfully evoke and convoke the disappeared, even if they cannot really bring them to the conversation in order to tell their own stories. These ways of expressing voice, speaking for/with/without, complicate notions of victimization, reclaim the humanity of the "disappeared," and assert forms of agency, solidarity, and resistance.

Survivors' willingness to testify has also been strongly associated with the hope that the transmission of their experience would serve a meaningful purpose. The aspiration that it "be useful" (*que sirva*) appears in different testimonies. A number of women expressed the expectation for their testimony to contribute to social memory and justice, to give information that might lead to the persons disappeared or appropriated by the dictatorship, to recover the many gestures that weave survival and solidarity, and to provide a foundation for building a better society in which state terrorism *never again* is implemented. Marta García de Candeloro connected "leaving things that are useful" with the idea of living, which according to her involves passing on something from other people: "At the end of the day that's life, no? To be able to leave something. [...] [W]hen the other is not [here] and you feel you have things of that other, of parents, or whomsoever, of compañeros. [...] [O]ne is perpetuated in that, in what one was able to leave of the other. And then I think that life is that: being able to leave things that are useful. That already justifies life, no? Even if to say, 'I have another opinion.'"

In their testimonies, these women reported incidents that involved other persons in captivity, many of whom they never saw again. They also expressed how their own lives were transformed through contact with fellow captives. Gestures of solidarity, political speech, or funny personal characteristics were vividly recalled through concrete anecdotes. Somehow, and following the reasoning of Marta García de Candeloro, survivors' testimonies have been partly about leaving or passing on something of those who are no longer around—from descriptions of their ways of being in the world to stories about shared experiences in clandestine detention, all of which help to build collective memory. In her testimony, Marta Álvarez concluded with the hope "that this will be useful. That something will be useful for us for once. Great people died. I miss them [dries her eyes with her hand]."

The initiative to speak more fully about the painful experiences of captivity was sometimes facilitated by collective testimonial projects, outside the judicial process or other state-led initiatives. For instance, this was the case of the book *Ese infierno: Conversaciones de cinco mujeres sobrevivientes de la ESMA* (That Inferno: Conversations among Five Women Survivors of ESMA; Actis et al. 2001). In her testimony in Memoria Abierta, Elisa Tokar recalled her participation in this book: "Personally, it helped me to really give a full voice to . . . to . . . those things that anguished me so much and that I could not put . . . put a name on them, no? The fact that other compañeras have gone through the same as me. [. . .] [I]t was like . . . it helped me to put words to . . . to . . . to that anguish, no?, that pain, to give a name to those things that had happened to me." As Elisa's narrative suggests, finding resonance in the experience of other women was helpful to understand her own experience and to process traumatic memories. Furthermore, although the issues that brought these women together are obviously political, this horizontal dialogue between women and the type of analysis generated—which started to touch on "personal" issues related to the body—are reminiscent of so many groups of women in the feminist tradition who discovered that "the personal is political" and that there is a system of gender inequality that marked their experiences specifically. Part of the power of the book can be traced precisely to its collective character: "With their words, these women dismantle a sinister repressive apparatus conceived by men who possessed the violence of weapons, the *picana* and the phallus as a symbol of domination and abuse" (Daona 2013, 68).[12]

Laura Schachter also spoke of her participation in a collective project of testimonies for the book *Los chicos del exilio* (The Children of Exile; Guelar, Jarach, and Ruiz 2002). She pointed to the kind of contexts that facilitate survivors' ability to express voice: "The book is done by a group that is very close to me, so it was my testimony and that of the others; we had several meetings. This was something done very attentively, very . . . it was done by people who care about me. [. . .] It was the best way. [. . .] I mean, I felt like it gave me the possibility to talk. It truly was good for me [. . .] it was a relief to have been able to give testimony there." These words convey the healing qualities of certain forms of testimony, of certain ways of expressing voice, which help to process trauma. However, as Laura suggested, to make it so—and so that the act of testifying does not result in revictimization—certain trust and conditions for listening and sharing need to be in place.

While the testimonies of survivors in trials for crimes against humanity are critical sources of evidence, the testimonies in Memoria Abierta and those that appear in texts such as the aforementioned books provide further texture and layers of meaning about the recent past. The stories that emerge in nonjudicial venues are constituted, in the words of Elisa Tokar, as "living testimony" not subject to the conventions or formalities of the legal system (Feld 2002; Jelin 2011). In that way survivors can account for aspects of experience that may not have legalistic value but are significant for social memory. For example, Cristina Comandé—who was a political activist in her youth—emphasized the solidarity and mutual support that occurred in situations of extreme degradation in CDCs. Marta García de Candeloro even spoke of the "beauty" that can be found in certain dimensions of the experience:

> Everything else is already in my testimony, everything else is the horror, and everything else also has great beauty. It seems strange, no?, to say that all that . . . but it has the beauty of knowing what a human being is, what our limits are, what it means to want to live and to be able to live. [. . .] When people say, "Oh, how could you endure?" What do I know how we were able to endure it. No one is prepared for that. What happens is that in extreme situations, we humans have things we do not know we have. The *cosas de vida* [things of life] that we have. How in everyday life sometimes little things depress us, and it is all right that they make us feel depressed [laughs], and we feel bad. And you believe that that thing destroys you—a problem at work, a family problem, a problem . . . and you cannot go on anymore. And when you experience an extreme situation, you begin to manage unconscious mechanisms you do not know if you have, and they also belong to human beings, and they make you to see life from another . . . to hold on to life. And understand life.

This passage provides a clue that besides contributing to attaining justice or to the writing of history, there is much more that the testimonies of women survivors convey. These women certainly "tell terror," but as we

shall see, they also interrogate the human condition, expose the gendered contours of repression, and express political knowledge that is
critical to understand the past, create the present, and build a future.

Testimony, Body, and Voice

It is more than words that are offered in the transmission of memory
through testimony. The act of testifying enlists the body in significant
ways: the body stores memories; the body conveys meaning related to
lived experiences; and the body expresses different forms of testimonial authority. Though this study focuses only on women, it is worth
considering how gendered power structures have influenced the content of survivors' memories, including the kinds of gendered events that
feed memory; the significance attached to such events; and whether the
speaker will be believed or perceived with suspicion when testifying.

The body is the repository of the memories that are given voice
through testimony. Margaret Randall's (2003) interviews with Nora
Miselem, a Honduran activist who survived torture and sexual violence
in clandestine detention in Central America, shows how Miselem conceptualized her "body as an archive" of such painful memories (127).
Pilar Riaño-Alcalá and Erin Baines (2011), who engaged in dialogue
with survivors of atrocity from Colombia and Uganda's armed conflicts, refer to the "archive in the witness" (416). This archive includes
survivors' bodily scars, wounds, and pain, which evoke and inscribe
memories of atrocious events. Riaño-Alcalá and Baines also mention
how testimonial embodied practices, such as oral storytelling and artistic performances "create living archives in the moment of bodily
inscription, when memories are re-storied in the body of the teller/
performer and received and accepted by the listener/audience" (431).
Similarly, various women in this study speak of their visible and invisible bodily scars of human rights violations, which are part and parcel
of their testimonies.

As other scholars have noted, through their embodied testimonial
practices survivors not only tell their recollections of *what happened*,
but also convey *meaning* about such events (Hirsch and Spitzer 2009;
Riaño-Alcalá and Baines 2011). Hand gestures, pregnant silences, a
choking voice, flooding tears, and other embodied expressions are inte-

gral aspects of testimony and point to the present salience of past events. Survivor-witnesses' oral accounts include the expression of emotion through the body. Indeed, they convey "affective memories" of a difficult piece of individual and social history (Stockwell 2014, 31). These embodied acts can have a more collective impact, in the sense of deeply affecting the listeners in public settings such as the courtroom (Macón 2014) and contributing to shape "memorial cultures" with long-lasting impacts (Stockwell 2014, 34). While the recorded testimonies of Memoria Abierta sometimes leave out the full display of emotions—recordings were usually paused when interviewees seemed overcome by the intensity of the emotion (e.g., crying)—the transmission of affective memories is still operative in these oral accounts, and emotion still managed to filter through. In any case, in watching these video-recorded testimonies, one is not confronted with a piece of paper, but placed in front of another embodied human being (even if separated by screen). Survivors' embodied/affective presence has an impact on the understanding of events in ways that a written transcript or disembodied voice may not fully accomplish.

Nora Strejilevich referred to the act of testifying as "*poner el cuerpo* [literally, 'to put the body'] in the narration of a truth: 'I say this was this way.'"[13] She implicitly associated the meaning of this act with the authority that masculine corporeality confers—connecting the word "testifying" to testes and testosterone. In some way this relates to how the possibility to speak authoritatively is predominantly ascribed to men. What are the possibilities for women's testimony and speech, particularly in the public sphere? To what extent can women use their embodied experiences as a basis for truth claims? In the case of many women survivors, the bodies that have come forward to narrate their truths are bodies that suffered beatings, threats, harassment, torture, and/or sexual violence. Yet time and again various types of gendered violence—occurring beyond CDCs and in "normal" times—are heard with suspicion or outright disbelief, and many women have been shamed or revictimized when daring to denounce them. Silence, then, can be a (precarious) refuge for women confronted with such an onslaught. In some cases, women's silence can also be a way to wait for the social and political conditions to be ripe for speech, so that their stories can be truly heard (Dossa 2003). In other cases, women may exert their agency

by choosing not to give testimony, not to be constrained by the institu-
tionalized formats of testimony (Macón 2015a).

As survivors' testimonies demonstrate, sooner or later many women
did speak out, including about seemingly taboo topics such as sexual
violence. They positioned their resilient bodies with strength to express
voice, "telling terror" to family, friends, judges, human rights organizations, and the general public. This embodied positioning, this poner
el cuerpo, imposes various costs—in time, physical effort, affective and
mental energy, and even exposure to threats and intimidation. Referring to repressors, Marta García de Candeloro explained: "[T]hey anticipated that we would get out and nobody would say anything because
we would be scared to death. We have experienced fear, and we continue experiencing fear now when we are threatened because of this or
that. We continue feeling afraid, but there is something that is much
stronger which is not wanting that these types of things happen to anyone [. . .], not even the worst enemy—if one has . . . if one can have
someone as an enemy." Many survivors recognize the social value of
testimony and see that it can also be personally beneficial in terms of
processing traumatic experiences and fulfilling justice goals. Munú
Actis explained: "*[P]onemos el cuerpo* [we put the body] each time that
we relive that history, and we declare, it hurts but it is good for us"
(Actis et al. 2001, 284).

In examining the dimensions of testimony we can see that "the
body" is integral to "voice" across multiple registers. The body can be
the grounds that confer authority to voice (though this is inflected by
power relations in specific contexts). Testimony also implies an investment of bodily resources (material, emotional, and energy-related). In
addition, the survivor's body matters to voice in another way: the body
"gives birth to [the] story" that testimony conveys. This is so in the sense
that survivors' stories are "anchored" in embodied experience (Dossa
2003, 68): suffering bodies, bodies of evidence, maternal and sexualized
bodies, resistant and resilient bodies. In other words, bodies are sites
and vehicles for voice.

Sometimes it is the *silent* body that conveys meaning and "testifies"
to a history of violence and social suffering. This can be expressed, for
example, through ill symptoms and other embodied marks of trauma
(Dossa 2003; Darghouth et al. 2006): Survivors of state terror surely

know of the physical/emotional effects of captivity, even long after the event. Although silence should not be necessarily equated with passivity, as it can be an expression of agency (Fiona Ross cited in Dossa 2003; Hyams 2004; Gómez-Barris 2009; Davidovich 2014), it is also important to recognize that the bodies of many survivors did more than silently assert meaning. This is especially significant given that in the context of the military dictatorship, silence was politically and brutally imposed on the body politic and on the concrete bodies of people held in CDCs, with long-term implications. Thus it is not a minor detail that many survivors strove to overcome terror and have been able to poner el cuerpo through their testimonial voices.

In giving testimony, women survivors have claimed the position of witnesses. Parin Dossa points out that "becoming a witness means taking the responsibility of stating what happened" (2003, 67). Consistent with the Latin American tradition of *testimonios* (Beverley 1987), women survivors talked about their own suffering and survival as indicative of a more collective story of what happened in Argentina. These are oral narratives of political repression told in the first person, which, like other testimonios, derive significance from the social truths they attest to and the "plural self" that underpins the narratives (Strejilevich 2016, 434, drawing on Doris Sommer). Yet it is important to note that whereas this book is fundamentally based on such narratives, one difference from typical texts in the testimonio genre (e.g., Menchú 1984) is that I, as the book's author, did not directly elicit the testimonies, nor is this book written by the protagonists/witnesses of the events narrated. Still the accounts incorporated here serve to denounce a history of atrocity and recover the struggles and political agency of those directly affected.

The Latina Feminist Group (2001, 19) asserts that testimonio can be a valuable tool to "theorize oppression, resistance, and subjectivity." Survivor and writer Nora Strejilevich (2016) points out that testimonio has "been an inspiring genre for women who need to delve into the innermost echoes of torture and repression. The feelings anchored in their bodies lie at the heart of women concentration camp survivors' experience, and they seek other voices with whom to enter into a dialogue within this framework. They often focus on the gender-specific repression they suffered—such as sexual abuse and the kidnapping of their children—and present their stories in oral/written patterns or in literary form" (434). Similarly to the accounts of other women who lived through authoritarian regimes and armed conflict in Latin America,[14] a number of the testimonies featured in this study point to the gender-specific dimensions of violence, activism, revolutionary struggle, and repression.

The collective story of "what happened" in the context of state terrorism in Argentina is multifaceted, and it is gendered—and yet many of these aspects of experience had been silenced until recently. Experiences of sexual violence, which have gained increasing attention (in the judicial sphere, publications, and documentaries) in more recent times, are a case in point. The fact that the events on which this book is based were recontextualized decades later through women survivors' testimonies adds another layer of value to the analysis. This is the case because the passage of time allowed for a "longer view" and reflexivity about the personal and political ramifications of state terrorism, women's participation in political activism, the transitional justice process, the contemporary relevance of human rights frames, and other critical aspects of experience that the women who share their stories were able to think about with the benefit of hindsight. In other words, the value of these testimonies rests not simply on their ability to transmit "what happened" but also in their capacity to help us interpret important aspects of a turbulent past. This is a legacy of the testimonial practice.

Testimony has also been a way—though not the only one—for survivors to exert agency in response to brutal state violence meant to totally erase their subjectivities and ability to resist. Cecilia Macón (2014) argues that through their affective testimonies in the context of trials, women survivors in Argentina have defied the dichotomy of agency and victimhood: they have exposed their vulnerability (for example, to sexual violence), but this practice of embodied and emotional denunciation also has an empowering potential. Women's testimonies of state terror in various spheres can operate as a form of "subjective restitution" (Macón 2014, 29), and may also constitute ways of "telling to live" (Latina Feminist Group 2001). Even though these survivors have carried deep wounds, the perpetrators' attempted erasure of their subjectivities and the shattering of their lives did not succeed. These women endured, and in testifying they asserted their voices. A number of survivors testified in the judicial sphere, including to denounce the sexual violations they experienced. As Macón points out, "by choosing to become complainants, [these women] decide to expose their suffering through action" (2014, 32).

The testimonies of Memoria Abierta have a different function than those performed in the judicial sphere, but they also "expose suffering through action." In doing so, they present a variety of narrative and affective textures. There are testimonies that focus on presenting very detailed accounts of places or events of detention; some contain more in-depth reflections on the meanings attached to such experiences; others also elaborate extensively on political histories, for example. As other researchers have noted, silences and omissions are also pregnant with meaning (Hyams 2004). In the case of testimonies, silence delimits the contours of the speakable or what's desired to share at a particular point in time or in relation to a real or imagined audience. For instance, while some women preferred not to elaborate on their experiences of torture in the Memoria Abierta testimonies, others provided vivid details of the procedures and the suffering they went through. Some women denounced sexual violence in the context of judicial trials but did not speak about such themes in the Memoria Abierta interviews.

Furthermore, while testimony can revive the pain of previously lived experiences, certain familiar forms of narration can also offer a space of safety for some survivors. Patricia Erb recounted how testifying provided some relief to her emotional suffering, but only after multiple iterations:

So basically what I did was to tell my story again and again and again. It was painful but [. . .] it was cathartic also because I started to dream less about it. When I came out [of detention], night after night I would wake up with nightmares and screaming. [. . .] But in telling and telling [the experience] it didn't appear in dreams again, because I was living it and talking about it. And I think it is something that I have no interest in closing on a square; it is a part that is better to have alive. Of course, after the years I've realized that my story follows a little path, you know, a little path where sometimes I even use the same words. So it is quite protected, and when someone brings up a memory that is, sometimes is . . . [points to her jaw] like a tooth [ache], the pain is intense. And this little path is quite safe because I have walked it a lot. [. . .] I gave lots of testimonies.

Here a particular path for the expression of voice—a repeated "formula"—helps to keep at bay painful embodied emotions, demarcating the possible ways in which testimony may be given.

In the Memoria Abierta testimonies, the embodied emotions expressed by women survivors varied: While some accounts were interspersed with crying, nose blowing, or a breaking voice, other interviewees offered seemingly more detached or dispassionate descriptions, showing little emotion. The combination of body language and words sometimes conveyed a kind of disbelief about what the speaker herself experienced or witnessed—as if such atrocities were impossible or could swallow a person's sense of reality. For instance, Viviana Nardoni referred to the Calamita CDC as a kind of "limbo": "It is difficult for me to imagine it as a real place where I was." In some testimonies, individual women's sense of humor or mischief emerged in the narratives as they recalled how detainees managed to trick or disobey their captors, or as they fondly remembered fellow activists or detainees. Stories of solidarity also injected emotion into some of the testimonies. For instance, a woman told about the comforting kiss of a detainee she did not know. Another one remembered a prisoner who strategized to help her avoid rape. And yet another one narrated how a young woman detainee, who was eventually "transferred" (killed), taught her how to breathe calmly and how to survive in the midst of horror. Stories about praying, joking, singing, or playing games with other detainees also emerged in the testimonies.

In listening to these accounts, it is difficult to predict what would be emotionally hardest for different interviewees, or at what point emotions would betray the composure of the narration. After all, traumatic events are processed in heterogeneous ways, so it might not be possible to anticipate what the triggers are for specific persons—even if one assumes that the topic of the interview itself promises to be emotionally challenging. Is it the personal memory of torture that which might make someone express sorrow or anger? Is it recalling the disappearance of a son or daughter? Is it remembering a mock execution that which prompts disturbing emotions? Is it the memory of a captive woman who returned without her baby after giving birth? Is it a truncated political project? These are examples of situations that elicited different interviewees' emotions as manifested in body language, tone of voice, and explicit words. I now turn from *how* these women remembered to aspects of *what* they remembered from their time of clandestine detention and the meanings they attached to such experiences.

Remembering Terror

The women in this study agree in their denunciation of CDCs: places where horror, perversion, and the total distortion of human relations were common currency. Picana, waterboarding, hoods, shackles, nudity, beatings, threats, sexual abuse—countless forms of degradation were deployed in the camps. Besides using the materiality of the body as a privileged source of suffering, repressors exercised a varied repertoire of psychological approaches, such as mock executions, threats of harm to loved ones, and techniques designed to generate disorientation, isolation, and the disintegration of the person's identity. The exercise of the macabre was the order of the day, including the enactment of seemingly ordinary gestures and activities, but with the twist of deeply repressive contexts. Thus, the wrapped gift with a ribbon that a repressor gave a pregnant detainee, Susana Reyes, was a little hood for her baby resembling those used to blind prisoners (see also Bacci et al. 2012). This gift replicated in miniature one of the emblematic objects of repression, as if being hooded was the inherent condition of the woman and hence the baby she was expecting. In the ESMA, repressors sometimes took captive women on pseudo-dates to restaurants and hotels, or talked with them about their lives as if they were partaking in traditional romantic relations or friendships. While many cases of sexual abuse occurred in the context of obviously violent interrogations—like actions involving insertion of electric prods or other objects in genital areas—it is important to note that sexual abuse also occurred in situations such as the alleged dates. These were scenarios in which the kidnapped women did not have a genuine option to refuse or consent to sexual "relations" and, therefore constitute sexual violence (Aucía et al. 2011; Bacci et al. 2012; Forcinito 2012).

While the conditions of captivity in secret prisons presented variations, ambivalences, and contradictory situations, human rights violations were the common denominator. Besides the fact that individual freedom was illegally infringed upon, many survivors were hooded and/

or shackled for long periods, including days or months. They were also subjected to interrogations that often involved torture. In many of these places, detainees were assigned numbers or codes to replace their names. The denigration of the person appeared to be a primary objective. Survivor and scholar Nora Strejilevich narrated this experience as such:

> In any case, the initial process is of depersonalization. You are no longer the person who wears those clothes, who has that name. You are a code and someone completely anonymous. You already became an N.N. [someone with no name, anonymous] at the moment that you can no longer see. That is, not only you cannot identify them [the repressors], but directly you can no longer identify the world to which you belong. Nor will others identify you in the same way because you are a code. So you stop being a person and you live in the margins of humanity. No longer are you a human. There is a theorist who talks about—[Giorgio] Agamben—who talks about . . . "bare life," no? Already you become a biological being, which is an abstraction because we are actually social beings who are inscribed from birth with our own name and such. So it is an abstraction generated by power. But at that moment you feel like they take away everything that identifies you . . . they steal that, they tear that to shreds, and on top of that you are with clothes that you realize that belong to someone who no longer needs them. Then, well, it begins the . . . everything that is sinister. [. . .] I was tortured as everyone else at a table with . . . where they tied your hands and feet like . . . like being crucified . . . like a crucified being to whom . . . electricity is applied— which is one of so many tortures, and I was lucky that this was the only one that was applied to me.

Nora's "luck"—being tortured with electricity—is articulated in comparison with the abuses that other women suffered, such as rape. Marta Bianchi—who was kidnapped for several hours, eyes covered, tied up, and verbally threatened with rape—also pointed out that she had "great luck": "I have suffered a lot but, I was not. . . . There are people who suffered far more and were tortured and disappeared." Certainly, the majority of people who went through CDCs ended up being "transferred"—the euphemism used by repressors to (not) name the fact that they were sending persons to be murdered. It is in relation to this magnitude of horror that survivors sometimes minimized certain types of violence that they experienced (Bacci et al. 2012, 90).[15] Having been spared of some forms of torture and suffering could lead survivors to feel shame or guilt. For instance, Susana Muñoz, who was beaten and confined in isolation in a cold cell while in detention, expressed, "I do not like hearing about torture, because I feel like I benefited in some way; so I feel like I ashamed." And yet what constitutes torture cannot be taken for granted, as there can be discrepancies between legal, judicial, international, or medical definitions and interviewees' subjective experiences.

Many of the practices to which survivors were subjected certainly meet international definitions of torture or "other cruel, inhuman or degrading treatment or punishment" (in the words of the United Nations convention banning such acts). While there is variation between different international institutions' definitions, those advanced by organizations such as the United Nations and the World Medical Association include "physical and psychological forms of suffering and require coercive intent by perpetrators" (Green, Rasmussen, and Rosenfeld 2010, 529). The UN Convention against Torture and Other Cruel, Inhuman or Degrading Treatment or Punishment, which brings together 162 states as parties of the treaty,[16] defines torture as

> any act by which severe pain or suffering, whether physical or mental, is intentionally inflicted on a person for such purposes as obtaining from him or a third person information or a confession, punishing him for an act he or a third person has committed or is suspected of having committed, or intimidating or coercing him or a third person, or for any reason based on discrimination of any kind, when such pain or suffering is inflicted by or at the instigation of or with the consent or acquiescence of a public official or other person acting in an official capacity. It does not include pain or suffering arising only from, inherent in or incidental to lawful sanctions.

Setting aside the masculine generic language, which makes women invisible as potential targets of torture (more about this in the following chapter), we can see that this definition covers many of the acts that women in captivity experienced.

Still some survivors challenged what they perceived as narrow interpretations of torture, pointing to a wide range of torments that they
experienced or defined as torture and that may not be always recognized
as such by the state or society.[17] They argued for a more expansive conception about which forms of suffering constitute torture in the repressive context of clandestine detention. In that vein, Eva Orifici, who went
through several secret prisons, recounted that when detainees would try
to talk with each other, they would get hit with sticks or kicked:

> That was . . . that was a form of torture. Then there was another torture
> that they could do, such as drills simulating that they were going to kill
> you; [. . .] leaving you hanging. [. . .] Because of that I have [. . .] till I
> die a concrete problem in the whole area of arms, cervical vertebra, due
> to hours and hours of being . . . left hanging, no? [. . .] I mean we have
> tortures and injuries of all kinds but . . . this is what perhaps sometimes
> you are told in the court, like this is not . . . "Oh, no, torture is, well, if
> they did the submarine to you, or applied picana."[18] And with the rest it
> seems that there are different . . . in this so sickening matter, like there is
> a certain category of violation of rights, no? So that's another thing that
> has . . . to be recognized as a society.

Similarly, Carmen Lapacó—who survived clandestine detention and
then became a Mother of the Plaza de Mayo as she searched for her
disappeared daughter—presented an expansive perspective on torture,
including physical and psychological components well beyond the more
archetypal forms of torture embodied by the use of electric shocks or
waterboarding: "I was beaten; I suffered some physical aggressions of
another kind. And well, if you ask me whether I was tortured—if it is
with picana, then no. But that is another kind of torture, it's the torture
of seeing your daughter tortured, it's the torture of suffering what one
suffers in there. That is also torture; not just the picana is torture. So I
tell that I cannot say that I was not tortured. They tortured me in many
ways. And the biggest torture is not having my daughter with me now."
Carmen's subjective experience of torture included not only what was
done to her physical body but pain stemming from her embodied emotional connection with her tortured daughter. The persisting wound that

her absence has represented points to a more extended temporality of torture. While a too broad definition of torture may dilute its meaning from a legal standpoint, it is still important to recognize the understandings that survivors offer, for they help to more accurately assess the enormity of the injury perpetrated against them.

The arbitrary and overwhelming state power that determined life and death in clandestine detention was also an important dimension of how some survivors articulated experiences of torture. This refers not only to discrete actions, but to the whole experience of being at the mercy of state officials who could do with them whatever they pleased. For instance, Alicia Morales embedded the meaning of torture within the larger context of arbitrary power and impunity, pointing to how the repressors presented themselves

> as greater than God, deciding who lives and who dies. And this was torture. I mean, the. . . . the rapes, all of these things, cannot be framed in relation to anything but . . . the perversity that the impunity of power means. Nothing else. So that's why I say that what is unacceptable from every point of view is . . . this thing . . . this thing that is torture, which is much more than the picana, much more than the blows, much more than all that. But it is to make you feel that you have absolutely no alternative, no value, and that you depend on . . . on power . . . let's say. . . . And how to overcome that?

These assessments point to more intangible dimensions of torture and the power relations that torture embodies. Survivors' insights push the contours of narrow definitions and show the depth, variety, and persistence of physical and emotional wounds inflicted by state terror. Torture becomes a signifier of broad forms of suffering, which can exceed even the boundaries and time of confinement. As Macarena Gómez-Barris (2009) points out, atrocious events have an "afterlife" that not only functions as a reminder of the original wound but can also be channeled toward social and political change.[19]

Some of the expansive notions of torture, which are grounded in historically specific understandings of how the CDCs operated, eventually found resonance in the judicial system.[20] "More or less recently, jurisprudence has introduced a more comprehensive perspective on the events: Besides the individual acts of torture, the idea was added that the general conditions of detention, taken as a whole, and independently of the concurrence of individual acts of violence, configure the crime of torture" (Felgueras and Filippini 2010, n.p.). This approach mirrors more closely the experiences narrated by various survivors, in the sense that torture exceeds the prototypical image of torments inflicted in order to extract a confession.[21] In other words, the subhuman conditions and extreme suffering that characterized the experience of clandestine detention have by now been recognized by different Argentine tribunals as constitutive of torture. In that sense, actions that in certain contexts (such as those of the CDC) can meet the criteria of torture include the following: forced physical exercise, the deliberate attempt to deny the person's identity through the assignment of codes, sensory deprivation and stress positions, the brutal conditions of abduction, mock executions and having to witness the torture of loved ones, forced nudity and sexual violence, and food and hygiene deprivation (Felgueras and Filippini 2010). Women in this study narrated virtually all of these situations.

As Nora Strejilevich noted, torture and other degrading treatment were integral parts of the process of turning detainees into "bare life" in Agamben's sense (1998). Detainees inhabited what Agamben called a "zone of indistinction," where they could be killed with impunity, with no recourse to the law or any of the protections afforded to citizens.[22] The very act of "disappearing" members of the citizenry with total impunity entailed the notion that these lives were not really "grievable," in Judith Butler's terms. The disappeared were deemed outside the frame of "[w]ho counts as human" (Butler 2004a, 20) in at least three senses. First, the ability to inflict torture and torments on detainees rested on their radical dehumanization. Second, the methodology of disappearance itself inhibited grieving rituals on the part of family and friends because there was no body to mourn. Third, the blatant assertion that the people abducted were "neither alive nor dead. [They were] disappeared"—as dictator Jorge Rafael Videla asserted at the time[23]—relied on the expectation that this explanation *could* and *would* be accepted by the public. The corollary of the repressors' discourse was the implicit assumption that most of the citizenry would not agitate for the people disappeared because they were a nonentity. They were not "dead or alive," they were in a zone of indistinction. From that perspective, they were barely human.

In taking stock of such experiences, women in this study not only addressed how detainees coped with, endured, and even resisted the conditions of the camps (more about this in later chapters), but also reflected on the meaning of the perpetrators' actions and what this suggests about the human condition. Rather than trying to establish the motivations or make sense of the perpetrators' actions, I am interested in how survivors grappled with these difficult questions so as to better understand another important dimension of these women's experiences.

"Could They Be Called Persons?" On Human Beings, Normal Monsters, and Crazy Enemies

Beyond all the forms of physical and psychological oppression inflicted on detainees, a more subtle form of suffering perhaps involves how these actions can shake core normative assumptions about what it means to be human. A sense of bewilderment, incredulity, and consternation emerged in different testimonies as these women recounted unimaginable acts of cruelty. As mentioned by a woman who offered testimony about atrocious state repression in Guatemala, "It was so horrible there are no words to describe it" (Vásquez 1991, 53). The question of how a person could treat another one in such indescribable ways haunted the testimonies and was sometimes explicitly stated. After narrating the forms of torment and humiliation she endured in clandestine detention, Tita Sacolsky expressed, "[T]hey were all those things that . . . that one cannot conceive in human beings. [. . .] [T]wenty-five years later I sometimes think and say, 'How could have something like this been this way?'" More than revealing some inherent characteristic about humans or what might disqualify a person as such, we can think of the dilemmas and questions expressed by these women as reflecting ethical and political standpoints. Survivors mobilized these frames in diverse ways at the moment of detention as well as in the reflections that the testimonies prompted.

Citing Nora Strejilevich, Ana Forcinito (2012, 19) notes that "the experience of detention [. . .] 'is perceived as unreal' not only for those who didn't go through it, but also for the survivors who try to understand it 'from everyday life in freedom.'" That feeling of unreality was apparent in the words and gestures of several interviewees who struggled to make sense of their experiences and what repressors did to them. However, their accounts are also stark reminders that for all the surreal dimensions of CDCs, these were places where very real suffering was inflicted. The mind-boggling events that survivors narrated challenge ordinary frames for meaning making—frames that are socially and politically constructed and emerge from experiences in particular communities and social settings. Yet the context of clandestine detention was so unfamiliar and unimaginable that it could drastically shake such frames. Ordinary ways of making sense of the world clashed with the lived experiences of state terrorism, creating multiple forms of dissonance, including assumptions regarding what a shared humanity might entail.

What seemed particularly daunting to different survivors was not only the broad state machinery of terror and disappearance—and the "banality of evil" (Arendt 1963) that such structure entailed—but concrete situations at the micro level of interaction with repressors. These painful circumstances threw into sharp relief human beings' ability to engage in extreme cruelty, raising questions about what it means to be human. These women responded in different ways to the horror they were subjected to and grappled with what this said about the perpetrators, and also about the human condition more generally. There is a spectrum of reactions ranging from the characterization of perpetrators as monsters to affirming a shared humanity even in the face of despicable acts committed by the repressors. In some cases, the human qualities of the perpetrators were cast in doubt, even if for a split second, as when Julia Ruiz recounted her efforts to remember the physical appearance of repressors: "And when we try to think or describe certain and specific . . . the persons who were there, the pers . . . the . . . the—Could they be called persons?—those who were in charge of standing guard, or who formed the *patota* [gang of repressors], eh . . . we did not remember their faces." Julia speculated that detainees' inability to remember the faces of perpetrators had to do with impaired perception due to blindfolding as well as the "fear factor." But what I want to emphasize here is the rhetorical question that Julia posed about the perpetrators: "Could they be called persons?" This question emerged almost as an afterthought, and yet it is so significant in flagging key ontological issues. What makes us human? Can a member of the human community be disqualified from such belonging? Offering an answer to these questions is not the focus of this work. Rather, what interests me here is to explore how the expression of these existential dilemmas may reflect a more hidden form of suffering; that is, suffering grounded in personally felt atrocious actions, but conveying a broader pain for humanity.

In describing her experience of torture, Norma Berti implicitly addressed the contradiction between the practice of torture and what might be expected of other human beings. This contradiction seemed especially hard to wrap the mind around at that moment of extreme suffering: "Let's say that torture, among other things, what it does to you, what most brings you down during torture—and from what I can remember—is on the one hand the physical pain, like even this feeling of . . . of burning flesh, that you feel emanating from your own body, all these sorts of things. But also the fact that it is the persons. . . . You cannot ask for help because it is the persons around you, the ones who are doing this damage, this enormous damage to you."

Norma started to point out how the suffering of torture is more than physical. The last part of the passage evokes a powerful and disturbing image: that of a human being reduced to utter vulnerability and subjected to a dehumanizing process, but who nevertheless seemed to retain some sense of the repressors around her as persons ("the fact that it is the persons . . ."). A subtext of the passage, expressed in the negative, is the implicit expectation that a person *would* help another person who is suffering—only for Norma to drastically realize the impossibility of such assistance in that context, as the intention of the people around her was precisely to cause her harm. The deep human betrayal that this scene constitutes could be said to be one dimension of the devastation that actions such as torture generate.

The surprise, incredulity, and confusion that various women narrated do not suggest that they had been naïve. Many of them were political activists and knowledgeable about the forces they were confronting, even if they did not anticipate the whole magnitude of atrocity. However, the values that had inflected the activism of so many, including the hope to create a better world with justice and equality, were anathema to the experience of the camps. The conditions in CDCs were radically opposed to the kind of world and human relations they envisioned.

As detainees interacted with or were acted upon by repressors, they tried to understand the motives and meaning of their actions. In addition to the duplicity that "bad cop/good cop" tactics entailed, there was the jarring contrast between repressors' brutal actions and the mundane activities they also undertook. Embedded in some of the narratives about such situations is again the question of what it means to be human. For example, Celeste Seydell, a seasoned political activist, narrated how a guard who seemed to have some compassion toward her after a severe torture session—offering her something to eat—immediately hit her on the head with the butt of a gun. She reflected on the sense of disbelief that this and other discordant behaviors generated, and how they challenged her usual frames for understanding:

> Because you cannot wrap your mind around it, it is something. . . . Imagine, like it happened to me, after [. . . a repressor] was doing to me all kinds of, you know, torturing me. A bit later I heard that same voice saying, "Okay, yes, bring me coffee." I mean, it was something that I could not link in my head, that that same guy could drink coffee. [. . .] Or another one who would say, "No, my son . . . yes, today is . . . the celebration at school, I will leave more. . . ." I would say, "It can't be, he has a son," you see? It is . . . it is like you get a *bollo* [confusion] in your head because you cannot understand that . . . that people—monsters, which for me would be monsters, you know?—that suddenly they would be normal, that they could drink coffee, have children. That's what bothered me the most. [. . .] It was like it created a rupture in my head [. . .] not being able to unite those two things. [. . .] I had that feeling during the whole detention, you see? [. . .] You cannot wrap your mind around it.

In Celeste's assessment, normal social activities—drinking coffee, participating in a celebration, caring for a child—seemed to be impossible in the lives of torturers. The notion of normal monsters seems a contradiction in terms, and Celeste oscillated between naming her torturers as "people" while also categorizing them as "monsters." The possibility of coexistence between the ordinary and the atrocious has been explored in other studies and analyses, showing or suggesting that perpetrators of human rights violations can be ordinary people (e.g., Arendt 1963; Milgram 1975; Conroy 2000). Studies in the field of social psychology, for example, show that contrary to the common belief that people behave consistently, in fact a person's behavior can vary widely, and even jarringly, from situation to situation. A person's actions are reflective not merely of stable personality traits but of the interaction between individual dispositions and concrete situations (Mischel 1968). In this case, Celeste describes a very slight change of scene, punctuated by a temporality shift: at one moment the repressor is busy torturing, a bit later he engages in mundane activities and talk. Still, what I would like to analyze here are not the characteristics of the perpetrators, but how women survivors interpreted perpetrators' actions, as this was an important facet of their experiences.

Taking into account the tactics of subjugation inflicted on these women, it is not surprising that the term "monsters" would emerge to describe perpetrators. Given that torture itself was a way of transforming detainees into "monstrous" bodies (disfigured, unrecognizable, and dehumanized), labeling repressors as monsters effectively reflected the image back from the tortured body onto perpetrators, revealing perpetrators' own deviant condition. At the same time, this label could fulfill other functions, such as helping to draw a sharp line between perpetrators and detainees, a distinction that some survivors said was important to remember. After all, this distinction could help detainees maintain their sense of self under conditions aimed at subjective disintegration.

The notion of "enemy," which in many cases preceded the moment of detention, could also help demarcate the difference between captives and repressors. For instance, Susana Caride explained that in order to maintain her dignity, she clung to the following reminder: "I am captive, this is the enemy, they have me imprisoned. I don't ask for anything." Though here the label used is "enemy" not "monster," it has a similar boundary-demarcating effect. This distinction could also implicitly help to preserve the worlds and values of the detainees, particularly as they were under intense pressure to give information about relatives, friends, or fellow activists. Iris Avellaneda reported how repeating the mantra of "never giving the enemy more than what is due" may have played a role in her forgetting and therefore not giving the information demanded of her during torture.

Since many of the torments inflicted on detainees had humiliating or stigmatizing qualities, labels such as "monster" could also be a way for survivors to redirect the stigma, to "reverse the shame," as Temma Kaplan (2002) argues. Kaplan explains this mechanism in her account of the ordeal suffered by Nieves Ayress, a woman who survived brutal detention under Chile's dictatorship: "The torture itself, designed both to exaggerate her sexuality and at the same time to make her feel unfeminine, could have caused her to feel ashamed, but she was able to reverse the shame. She still speaks of the torturers as monsters and herself as a political revolutionary who was fighting for social justice" (2002, 192). Here, too, the label "monsters" contributes to sharply separate worlds: the world of torture where repressors reign and that of social justice that the survivor strove to create.

The "reverse the shame" interpretation also echoes the narrative of another woman in this study, Graciela García. She expressed the sense of shame and guilt that sexual contact with repressors generated in women who were forced to endure this during clandestine detention. Referring to "Tigre" Acosta—a top officer at the ESMA who took her to an apartment for sexual purposes several times—she said: "This is something that at the moment, I believe that in order to survive, one . . . didn't dwelled much on it. [. . .] And only when we came out it was like [. . .] total clarity in saying 'this is a monster that abused me in this way.'" In this narrative, the construction of the perpetrator as a monster is linked to the exposure of his actions as entailing sexual abuse and not any kind of consensual sex. The discursive and spatial separation helps this revelation to emerge.

Another way in which some survivors resolved the contradictions and incredulity that events in CDCs generated was to label repressors or the situation itself as "crazy." After being hit in her head by the pseudo-compassionate repressor, Celeste Seydell screamed, "You are crazy! You are crazy! Very crazy!" Similarly, Susana Reyes explained that after a repressor gave her a mini (prisoner) hood for the baby she was expecting, she realized "the level of madness. [. . .] That is, someone sat down to sew that. I mean it is really something crazy." Marta Álvarez also defined as crazy the kind of (sexualized) double game played by repressors, particularly with respect to women who were captive but were sometimes taken out of the camps to accompany repressors on pseudo-dates, or to pay a visit to detainees' family (which could both provide relief to detainees and their loved ones, but also serve intimidation purposes):

And it was crazy, right?, because the same one that—at least from what I saw, or found out or was told about—that same one who tortured you, that same one . . . was the same who seduced you. Because there was also a seduction game, let's say; there was a thing like giving attention, the little flower, [. . .] the candy—it was something very crazy. There was a perverse game in that: to take you out to eat and then take you to see your family. I mean, the same person who . . . would make sexual use of you, would take you to see your parents, then would take you to the school. . . .

The label "crazy" in these examples seems to be a shorthand for these women to name situations that defied their meaning-making frameworks. They were events and interactions that were completely unintelligible from the standpoint of "normal" life.

While some guards or officers at times displayed relatively humane gestures, offering some relief to detainees, these actions could also be disconcerting to the persons in captivity, as they somewhat blurred the boundaries between repressors and captives—a boundary that some survivors articulated as essential to maintain their sense of self and to realistically assess the situation. At the same time, some survivors appealed to the possibility that repressors retained a shred of humanity—a hope tied to efforts to minimize suffering and secure their own survival and/or that of other captives. Munú Actis recounted: "Suddenly there were some [repressors] that were more accessible. One . . . one would try to make them more accessible, and to ask on behalf of someone who had fallen. [. . .] I don't know, maybe they didn't listen to me at all, but I want to believe, or need to believe, or needed to believe—each time I believe less—that that other had a side that was somewhat *humano* [human/humane]. And I don't know if this is due to . . . because I cannot think that everything was so Machiavellian."

At times, survivors' hopes were encouraged by situations somewhat reminiscent of more familiar forms of interaction. Yet it did not escape from survivors that the situation they were in was far from normal, and any act of "generosity" or "normal" gesture by repressors in the context of the camp was necessarily fraught. Said Munú:

Suddenly they would sit there and tell you things about . . . about their lives, overwhelmed, worried, telling you as if you were a friend. And I remember that I responded as if I were—I don't know if a friend—well, an interlocutor, someone valid with whom to talk. Then, of course, we were all the time in there, them and us. And ultimately you end up living together in daily life with the same person who tortured you, the same ones who [were] torturing you, but the same ones who tell you about what happens with the kid who goes to school [. . .] and the other who will take the Communion [Catholic ritual], and the wife, which I don't know what happens to her.

In her testimony, Munú mentioned that she did not recall the conversations with repressors as representing a "great effort" on her part. Perhaps, she said, this was the case because she dissociated from the situation as a survival strategy. And yet, despite the oppressive character of detention, it is also possible that seeing the repressors' more vulnerable and ordinary side was a reminder of their potential humanity and thus the possibility of survival. Drawing on Pilar Calveiro's (1998) work, Ana Longoni (2007, 99) stated that the "view of the other as an enemy was altered based on his daily proximity, which humanized him, and for that reason it enabled the relativization of the power of the abductor."

Survivors' humanization of the repressors could happen not only in the comparatively better moments, but also in relation to situations of heightened anguish, such as torture. Elena Lenhardtson described this facet of her suffering: "[T]here I learned what horror is, because horror is to find that there's another human being that is capable of that, and that one is human as he is. That means that there's something that one shares in that which is so terrible. I believe that that is like unbearable." Although the violence Elena experienced, including torture with electric shocks, can be categorized as monstrous, she described her torturers not as monsters but as human beings. Whereas her torturers aimed to dehumanize her—even by explicitly telling her that she would become *un despojo humano* (human waste)—she still humanized them. It is this gesture of looking herself into the mirror of her captors—individuals capable of committing atrocities—that appears unbearable. Elena's insight is deep and connotes multiple layers of meanings, but one possible interpretation is the following: the fact that Elena did not strip the human condition from her oppressors might have helped her retain her ethical standpoint and assert her own humanity—a condition that her torturers tried to snatch away from her unsuccessfully.

In recounting their clandestine detention experiences, women talked with more or less detail about the repressors involved in their kidnapping, torture, and/or captivity. The level of detail partly depended on the conditions and length of detention, the nature of the relationships generated in captivity, and even the possibility of seeing or not seeing guards or officers because of blindfolding. Given the atrocities that survivors narrated, it is not surprising that negative feelings and impressions about the perpetrators appear implicitly or explicitly in the testimonies. Perpetrators' brutal actions speak for themselves. Yet in remembering specific circumstances, some women also conveyed ambivalence, or even a hint of gratitude toward certain individuals in repressive roles. This, however, is contextualized as gestures that provided at least some relief amid horrific conditions. For instance, there is the story of a young guard who played the guitar for a crying woman in captivity; in another situation, a guard in a police station brought clean underwear for a woman held in that facility; and in another CDC, an officer stopped his colleague's brutal beating of a pregnant detainee. These narratives add nuance to our understanding of a system of terror designed to dehumanize captives, but that in the process also encouraged ordinary people in repressive roles to shed their own humanity in order to accomplish state goals. Survivors' complex emotions regarding gestures of compassion or vestiges of humanity on the part of individual members of the repressive apparatus point to some of the fissures in an overarching structure of state terror.

Conclusion

The dehumanizing conditions of clandestine detention aimed to silence the voices and bodies of detainees at the same time as the military regime imposed a rule of silence on the larger body politic, and particularly on political dissidents. In this chapter, I explored how women survivors came to assert embodied voice by sharing their "living testimonies" of state terror and survival. They offered their accounts despite the significant personal and social losses they endured and the difficulties that often surround the recounting of traumatic memories, including feelings of guilt and shame. Gender inflected not only the events in question, but also the narration of these events and the societal responses to such accounts. Additionally, gender influenced ascriptions of guilt for having survived and the challenges that women faced in expressing an authoritative voice that could be fully heard. The embodied voices of women survivors disrupt a gender order that deemed them voiceless or able to speak only from stereotypical gender positions.

As these women descended into their memories of terror, they not only exposed and conceptualized the conditions of atrocity during a disturbing chapter of Argentine history, but also interrogated the human condition more broadly. They problematized definitions of torture and exposed the extended temporality of the torments inflicted in the camps. Their testimonies also bring attention to more subtle dimensions of suffering, which implicitly call the listeners to deepen their investment in the story. After all, this is not just about what happened to these women in particular or to the disappeared in general. It is a story about events that have dramatically shaped Argentine society, and that interpellate each of us as members of the human community. In grappling with the repressors' actions and what these behaviors conveyed about the human condition, these women used various interpretative strategies that helped them to make meaning of the dehumanization processes they had been subjected to in clandestine detention.

Yet, as Pilar Calveiro points out, the fact that the repressors tried to dehumanize their victims—inside and outside the camps—does not mean that they succeeded (Lazzara, Olivera-Williams, and Szurmuk 2013, 328). The testimonies of these women and other survivors abundantly *counter* such systematic attempts at dehumanization. Through their testimonies, survivors have asserted their agency, conveyed their understanding of the events, and advanced their demand for justice. Additionally, many fellow activists, relatives, and friends of the disappeared, as well as others in human rights organizations, have continued asserting the humanity of the disappeared with a variety of strategies, such as displaying their photos in protests, telling their stories, engaging in "micro-commemorative practices," and refusing to forget them (Druliolle 2011, 32). As we shall see in the following chapters, the women in this study certainly "tell terror," speaking about embodied forms of suffering, but that is not the whole story they narrate.

3

Narrating the Body

The collective memory of the last military dictatorship in Argentina has frequently evoked the bodies of the people targeted by the regime. Photos, silhouettes, murals, sculptures, and other artistic and political performances have helped to bring the disappeared persons' "corporeality back," making their presence visible in the public sphere (Bergman and Szurmuk 2001, 390; see also Kaplan 2007). In the context of trials for crimes against humanity, some of the people disappeared have even been "sitting" on the chairs in the courtrooms, as large pictures of them occupied several rows of seats. These are significant examples of the connection between bodies and collective memory in Argentina; and they are particularly poignant given the last military regime's intention to vanish these people/bodies. However, and as important, there is also the embodied living memory of those who were subjected to practices of state terror and have survived to tell their stories.

The oral testimonies of survivors—including the ones that form the basis of this study—have contributed to build the collective memory of the period of state terrorism in Argentina. We can think of these oral testimonies as *body narratives*, which connect body and memory in at least two ways: (1) they are *embodied memories* in the sense of being grounded on, felt in, and expressed through the body, and (2) they are memories *about the body*, including references to the physical body's pain and scars as well as embodied resistance and resilience. These body narratives bring to the fore the lived meanings of human rights violations, moving past abstract declarations of rights and into the concrete and messy realm of individual and social suffering.

When addressing experiences of clandestine detention, it makes sense to talk about the body. After all, common practices in the secret prisons—torture, shackles, hoods, nakedness, deprivation of basic physiological needs, and other torments—took the body as a primary medium of suffering. However, the body can easily disappear from accounts of state terror. In terms of the people who survived, talking about the body could mean revisiting a kind of suffering that can be difficult to narrate both because of the "inexpressibility of physical pain" associated with torture and torments (Scarry 1985, 3)[1] and because narrating these events can lead to retraumatization unless appropriate listening conditions are in place to help give meaning or obtain redress (Agger 1989).[2] Furthermore, as Rebekah Park (2014) points out, after the initial need for denunciation, survivors may not want to focus on their tortured bodies, but highlight other dimensions of experience such as resistance and solidarity. For people who are sympathetic with the survivors' plight and wish to denounce and seek justice for the atrocities committed, centering the body on the public narration of events can be challenging, too. Scholars have noted the risks of making a spectacle—even a pornographic spectacle (Kaplan 2007; Forcinito 2012; Park 2014)—of experiences of subjection that violated the most intimate and private aspects of the detainees' selves (Jelin 2014). For those wishing to deny, downplay, or forget state-sponsored human rights violations, erasing the body can make it easier to achieve such goals. For instance, Peter Halewood (2012, 261) notes how contemporary torture debates tend to present "concerns about human dignity in a cryptic manner, often excluding a discussion of pain or the body's actual experience. The torture victim and his or her physical experience are oddly absent from the torture debate, or that physical experience is mischaracterized so as to lessen the moral impact of the torture."

If the body is to be made visible in discussions of torture and other torments, how can we account for the gendered body, for the concrete material bodies of people—in this case women—subjected to various forms of domination in clandestine detention? In what ways did gender hierarchies, ideologies, and identities play out in the infliction of bodily oppression, in the disavowal of the tortured body, and in embodied strategies of resistance and survival? Paying close attention to such dynamics helps to reconfigure how state power and human rights violations might be understood, even in relation to narrow notions of "human rights" associated mainly with freedom from political repression by the state. This characterization has traditionally not taken into account women's specific experiences of violence. In contrast, listening to women's body narratives of state terrorism helps to visualize the global women's movement's longtime claim that "women's rights are human rights." Laura Gioscia (2015) argues that attending to the materiality of the body is necessary to give substance to that claim and to counter overly universalistic constructions of human rights. She notes that such abstract notions of human rights tend to disengage from power relations and are ill equipped to address diverse experiences of inequality among women in concrete social locations, times, and places.

Notions of what constitutes reprehensible violence vary historically and culturally. Accordingly, some forms of torture and "cruel, inhuman, and degrading treatment" directed to the body have been more on the public radar than others in different locations and points in time. While societies might perceive certain types of violence as repulsive, other forms of violence might simultaneously be conceived as necessary. Talal Asad (1996) observes the double standards in the emergence of modern sensibilities toward cruelty, as permeated by the power relations of coloniality: "[I]n their attempt to outlaw customs the European rulers considered cruel it was not the concern with indigenous suffering that dominated their thinking, but the desire to impose what they considered civilized standards of justice and humanity on a subject population—that is, the desire to create new human subjects" (1091). In doing so, the pain that the colonial enterprise itself inflicted on colonized peoples, in order to "humanize" them, was often deemed necessary and therefore not reprehensible.

Regarding the practice of torture, Jared Del Rosso (2015, 28) notes the "illiberal" connotations associated with the term, and Asad (1996, 1095) states that "'torture' in our day functions not only to denote behavior actually prohibited by law, but also desired to be so prohibited in accordance with changing concepts of 'inhumane' treatment (for example, the public execution or flogging of criminals, and child abuse, as well as animal experiments, factory farming, and fox hunting)." Though this list is nonexhaustive, it is worth noting how the three categories pertaining to animals as well as the gender-unmarked categories of "criminal" and "child" can obscure common forms of violence targeted specifically at members of half of humanity: women. This raises the question about how socially salient and condemnable these actions have been. Whatever the answer, and whatever the variations from society to society, Asad's point still holds that torture has come to be seen as a broad signifier that is anathema to modern sensibilities. This has also meant that different constituencies could use this frame to denounce forms of violence similar to or constitutive of torture (Copelon 2008). Among these groups are feminists who have advocated for women's rights in the international activist and policy arenas as well as in the scholarly literature. An example of this approach can be found in analyses that define rape as torture (e.g., Card 2005; Copelon 2008; Gaer 2013).

For a long time, women's rights were hardly a concern or a priority for the international community. In fact, the now obsolete language of "Rights of Man" that emerged in late eighteenth-century Europe, and influenced later human rights formulations, excluded women rhetorically. Interestingly, according to Hannah Arendt (1958), advocates for the protection of the "Rights of Man" and for a new bill of human rights followed an overlapping trajectory with those wishing to protect animals: "The groups they formed, the declarations they issued, showed an uncanny similarity in language and composition to that of societies for the prevention of cruelty to animals" (292). Yet the types of human rights violations and violence especially likely to be experienced by women, both in war- and in peacetime (e.g., sexual violence and intimate partner violence condoned or ignored by the state), were not voiced as "human rights" issues until much more recently (Bunch and Frost 2000; Copelon 2008; Gaer 2013). In the late twentieth century, in the context of the lead-up to the United Nations World Conference on Human Rights in Vienna in 1993, members of the global women's movement still felt compelled to clearly assert that "women's right are human rights."

Discussions of torture that emphasize that the practice is more than an attack on individual bodies, but an affront against humanity or the body politic,[3] have often overlooked a critical feminist insight: the fact that what counts as a citizen or as human cannot be readily taken for granted (Pateman 1989; MacKinnon 2006). Women and categories of people marginalized by class, race, ethnicity, nation, or other intersecting axes of inequality have at different points in history been excluded from human or citizen status in different parts of the world—implicitly and/or explicitly. Thus while the modern repulsion toward torture asserts the universal dignity and humanity of all persons, some groups of people can fall out of the picture more easily than others in such accounts. In fact, feminists have advanced compelling arguments about how prevailing representations of torture and measures to prevent and punish the practice traditionally reflected a masculinist perspective, neglecting harmful acts that women are disproportionately likely to suffer (Bunster-Burotto 1994; Edwards 2006; Copelon 2008; Ibañez, Slattery, and Todd-Gher 2010; Sifris 2013). Libby Tata Arcel (2001, 328) points out that "the typical image of the torture victim is a male that is arrested or imprisoned, suspected of a crime or dissenting political activity, tortured and maltreated in custodial settings."

From a political perspective, if torture consists of "twisting and breaking of the body politic or of a community by way of the twisting and breaking of the bodies and minds of individual human beings" (Antaki 2007, 11), then it is important to ask: what might a focus on the torture of women reveal about the body politic, state power, and gender?

Torture, Gender Ideology, and Military Rule

Scholars and activists have pointed out that the military dictatorship in Argentina aimed to suppress highly politicized groups and organizations that were pushing for radical social transformations. While revolutionary and other activist movements of the sixties and seventies were not exempt from sexism, as Bacci et al. (2012) point out, these were still domains in which many women actively participated, developing a political voice and engaging in activities that defied or at least destabilized traditional gender norms (e.g., from transgressing dress codes and sexuality/reproduction expectations to participating in high-risk activism) (see Andújar et al. 2009; Martínez 2009; Grammático 2011; Oberti 2015). In a sense, in trying to squash these political communities, the regime was also targeting the societal openings that this activism represented for women's participation in the public sphere and for the defiance of gender relations.

Diana Taylor (1997, 77) points out that "the feminine—the *image* of Woman constructed in patriarchy—and women were vital parts of the drama" that the repressive military project constituted. The idealized representation of "the feminine" was embodied by the "good women" who abided by traditional gender norms as mothers, wives, and homemakers and who exhibited the traits associated with those tasks: nurturance, self-sacrifice, tenderness. An additional requisite in this particular context was that women "supported the military's mission" (78). While this image was glorified, "the feminine" was also viewed with contempt to the extent that it represented weakness, vulnerability, submission, and other traits against which men defined themselves. At the same time, the "bad women" who transgressed gender norms and engaged in political "subversion" had to be violently suppressed, particularly by attacking the bodily symbols of their womanhood. "Women were annihilated through a metonymic reduction to their sexual 'parts': wombs, vaginas, breasts" (84; see also Bunster-Burotto 1994; Hollander 1996).

Even though the military proceeded to permanently "disappear" most of the people abducted, the testimonies of survivors narrate how in some clandestine detention centers (CDCs) a minority of captives were funneled into varieties of "rehabilitation" or "recuperation" processes geared toward changing detainees' ideology and loyalties.[4] In the case of activist women, the apparent intention was also to suppress their politicized disposition and socialize them into "proper" femininity: motherhood, feminine dress, feminine interests (Actis et al. 2001; Bacci et al. 2012). From this perspective, being a woman *and* a political person was a contradiction in terms. By sexualizing women's bodies and directing them to adjust their behavior to gender appropriate conduct, *the political* (and not simply a particular political stance) was to be exorcized. The way that women were treated in clandestine detention mirrored and exaggerated the social and political subordination of women as a whole. In the repressive state's "fiction of power" (Scarry 1985, 18), women would have no political voice and their domesticated bodies would be sexually available and oriented toward the home.[5]

During the dictatorship, the military convoked women to play limited social roles, embodying conservative values and expectations. According to Nazareno Bravo (2003, 118), "[t]he few times that the military discourse is especially oriented toward women it does so in order to emphasize 'their place' within the family, in the roles of homemaker and wife, but, above all, as mothers." Mothers were called to contribute to the nation by caring for their families, and especially by raising children who would not be prone to adopt "subversive" ideas or actions. Conservative gendered expectations regarding women's place in society were disseminated through political speeches, media, and education channels (e.g., Laudano n.d. [1998]; Bravo 2003; Margulis 2006). The motherhood mandate, including women's duty to reproduce, was reinforced through policies aiming to restrict the availability of birth control (continuing policies initiated during the previous Peronist government). Ironically, a remarkable group of mothers—Mothers of the Plaza de Mayo—were able to turn the military ideology against the regime: in their roles of concerned and grieving mothers, they demanded information about their disappeared sons and daughters, and became central actors in the human rights movement in Argentina.

According to the social mores advanced by the military regime, women were to be subordinated to men's desires and projects. Even if the discourse at times allowed for some of the shifts in gender relations characteristic of "modernizing" societies, the figure of the mother continued to be central (Laudano n.d. [1998], 89). Women's place was the home, and their sexuality was to be expressed in the context of monogamous heterosexual relations and put in the service of reproduction. Women's sexual desire and autonomy had no place in the normative image of the "good woman." The military discourse associated women's "nature" with the following prominent traits: "sensitivity, politeness, cordiality, hospitality, patience, love and moral conditions" (Laudano n.d. [1998], 88).

The women disappeared had been catalogued as "subversive." Those who were part of political organizations or had exhibited any hint of having adhered to recent cultural transformations were seen as especially deviant: both politically and morally subversive (González 1992). In the testimony of actress and survivor Marta Bianchi, we see a glimpse of conservative gender ideologies held by members of the military. Before her kidnapping, Marta found herself barred from work. Thus she inquired with a military officer about what the accusations were against her. When in the course of this conversation she mentioned her "partner" (referring to her husband, also an actor), the military officer lashed out against her saying that people who used that kind of terminology were the ones destroying Western and Christian civilization. The gender order and morality advocated by the military regulated language as well as the embodied behaviors that such language represented. The word "partner" might have suggested a more egalitarian gender relation (whether this was true or not in practice) and was thus unacceptable to the member of a regime that, among other things, was to keep women in "their place."

Other indicators of subversion were sometimes read in physical appearance and demeanor that violated the conservative morality and norms of the military (Taylor 1997). Survivor Graciela García, who had been a political activist, remembered activist bodily aesthetics that in some ways blurred distinctions between men and women. She talked about the "activist couple" saying that the main "difference was height," but there were many similarities: "[W]e wore the same jackets, jeans, the same sweaters, sneakers, perhaps long hair. But, let's say, the genders did not differ that much, they were almost mimetic." This kind of clothing signified a contradiction to the mandate for women to engage in traditional feminine activities and to display a marked feminine appearance. In the book *Ese infierno*, Escuela de Mecánica de la Armada (ESMA) survivor Adriana Marcus mentioned that being well dressed and wearing makeup and feminine accessories were interpreted as signs of women's recuperation from the military perspective, in opposition to wearing jeans or moccasins (more gender-neutral items) (Actis et al. 2001, 169). Graciela García observed that it was at the ESMA that some women started wearing makeup and learned to wax their body hair. This type of activity can be hard to imagine in the context of a concentration camp, but some detainees—even those who had gone through the brutal treatment that was customary in CDCs—had access to beauty products at certain points. Elisa Tokar, also an ESMA survivor, mentioned that the repressors would sometimes bring perfume for women detainees to use: "I remember, in *Capucha*, the smell of rats and the aroma of French perfume" (Actis et al. 2001, 178).

As has been extensively documented, one salient aspect of many captives' experiences in clandestine detention was the infliction of torture. Much has been written about torture and its relation to state power in various international and historical contexts (e.g., Scarry 1985; Foucault 1989; Langbein 2006; Rejali 2007). What will be highlighted here is how such actions uphold a certain kind of gendered power that is integral to state power. If, as Lindsay DuBois (1990) argued, torture in Argentina was partly a method of creating an enemy (i.e., a constitutive act rather than just the branding of a person already defined as such), then one may wonder what kind of enemy the torture of women produces. One possible answer is that torture produces the abject woman, the "whore," the "bad mother," the woman who "does femininity" the wrong way.

For instance, in the context of state terror in Argentina, Elisa Tokar was called "Montonera bitch" while being tortured, underscoring a perceived feminine deviance. When Tita Sacolsky, an older woman, said to one of her repressors, "Ay, my son, I can't stand it anymore"—referring to the physical torments inflicted—the response was: "my mother was not a *turra* [bad woman, whore] like you, my mother was a saint." In both examples, a sexualized figure is invoked to represent a tainted feminin-ity as well as to constitute the tortured women into a particular kind of enemy.[6] In the case of Tita, the figure of the *turra* is associated with that of the "bad woman," defined in opposition with the "good mother" who was a saint. The enemy of the nation then was not just a generic "subver-sive" but the "bad woman" who transgresses the heteropatriarchal order. As González (1992, 181) pointed out, these women were conceived as *double transgressors.*

Gender matters not only in how captives were perceived and treated in clandestine detention, but also in terms of how the gender ideology and gender identity of the perpetrators shaped their actions. Given the masculinist character of institutions such as the military, the police, and other security forces, it is not surprising that when we talk about the dictatorship's repressors, we are largely talking about men in those roles. At the same time, it is also important to note that women who sympathized or were associated with the regime were not just passive spectators, and that in some cases women participated directly in re-pressive activities (for instance, Adriana Arce mentioned in her testi-mony a woman who integrated one of the repressive "task forces" in Rosario, and Celeste Seydell referred to a woman torturer in Córdoba, known as *La Tía* [The Aunt], who was notorious for her level of sadism). Débora D'Antonio (2003) explores a variety of levels of participation and complicities, including some women who participated in torture sessions or assisted with clandestine birthing arrangements, abusive women guards in the regular prison system, women judges and lawyers accused of participating in the appropriation of children and property of people disappeared, women who were the wives or romantic partners of repressors and supported their mission, and women who advanced their careers and helped to shore up the ideological underpinnings of the regime through social gatherings with repressors and by publicly endorsing their doctrine. D'Antonio (2003, 11) points out that many of these activities contradicted the military regime's gender discourse and the place it reserved for women—the private sphere of the family—but were still accepted for politically expedient and utilitarian reasons. In other words, the participation of women as accomplices did not detract from the overall masculinist imprint of the repressive enterprise.

When it comes to some of the most egregious acts in the secret prisons of the dictatorship, namely the brutal torture of detainees, the social construction of masculinity also played an important role. In her essay "Gender, Death, and Resistance," Jean Franco (1992) points out how the ability to exert pain—which was paramount in Latin America's Southern Cone torture camps—was culturally associated with being a manly man: "The military governments inherited a long tradition in which the power to inflict pain was taken as proof of masculinity. The rituals that bonded many male groups (whether boarding-school rites of passage, military drills, or group sexual experiences) traditionally reduced the other to the status of passive victim, to a body to be acted on or penetrated" (108). That is, there is a relationality between the feminization of tortured bodies constructed as passive—whether they are men's or women's bodies—and the bolstering of an aggressive masculinity constituted as all-powerful, and that was central to how the militarized state operated.

As will be discussed later, besides the most obvious actions through which the importance of gender is revealed in analyses of state terrorism—such as the infliction of sexualized violence or the treatment of pregnant women—there are perhaps less evident ways in which state terror practices drew on gender scripts. In the following sections, and based primarily on the body narratives of women who survived clandestine detention, I examine the production and disavowal of suffering bodies and how gender ideologies and hierarchies infused the experiences of women in captivity. I argue that even when not containing an explicit sexual dimension, the torture and torments inflicted in the camps subtly drew on and reproduced gendered cultural imaginaries and practices. I explore how a particular fiction of femininity is re-created through the tortured and tormented body.

Women's Body Narratives

Women as a group have been culturally marked as "body" in Western culture (Bordo 1993), especially as sexualized and reproductive bodies. Yet such representations frequently elide the women of flesh and blood (Sutton 2010). When it comes to women survivors of clandestine detention, their diverse, nuanced, and complex accounts of embodiment have been insufficiently taken into consideration in public discourse. Women in this study talk about their own bodies and those of other women in ways that include but go beyond the sexualized and reproductive bodies that appear in dominant representations of women.

While women have often been reduced to the body, women—like all human beings—are both their bodies and more than their bodies. In fact, there is a tension embedded in cultural understandings of bodies/people, body/self, and body/mind, which affects how we talk about "the body." Thus we could think about the self as *being* a body, *having* a body, being *more than* a body, feeling *connected* to the body, *using* the body, *experiencing* the body, and so on (Turner 1984; Lock 2001). When the body and the self are conceived in dichotomous ways, an overemphasis on the body can enact a form of dehumanization, in the sense of treating or representing the person as just a piece of flesh devoid of subjectivity. In focusing on women's body narratives and describing different modes of bodily oppression in captivity, I had to grapple with this tension.

My references to "the body of evidence," "the suffering body," "the sexualized body," "the pregnant body," and similar phrases are meant to highlight survivors' experiences in captivity *as they relate to embodiment and the social construction of bodies.* However, in a context in which repressors aimed to reduce prisoners to mere bodies robbed of their humanity, might a scholarly emphasis on "the body" re-create such dynamics? Throughout this study, I straddled the line between emphasizing *the body* while also making visible the experiences of concrete *persons*, with their own interpretations, subjectivities, aspirations, and agency.

Although women's body narratives are relevant in their own right, as I have argued in previous work, "the analysis of bodily experiences offers a particularly valuable location from which to understand social issues more deeply, partly because it encourages a closer approximation to social suffering" (Sutton 2010, 11). The notion of social suffering is intricately connected to the workings of power, as it stems from "what political, economic, and institutional power does to people, and, reciprocally, from how these forms of power themselves influence responses to social problems" (Kleinman, Das, and Lock 1996, xi). When it comes to the lived experiences of state terror, "power" and "suffering" can be readily detected particularly, though not exclusively, via the body. Indeed, embodied social suffering is abundant in the testimonies of the women I listened to. However, women survivors' body narratives also reveal multiple strategies of coping with and contesting power relations. Within the constraints imposed by the brutal enactment and display of state violence, detainees enlisted their bodies in more or less overt ways to dispute state control, stop aggression, express solidarity, and maintain dignity (see Bacci et al. 2012; chapter 4 of this volume). Furthermore, without minimizing the terrible conditions and aftereffects of captivity, the stories of these women are also living testimonies of embodied resilience and of the possibilities for transforming trauma in generative ways.

As women mobilized their memories of state repression, a multiplicity of stories about and from the body emerged: bodies in pain, dissociated bodies, bodies giving and receiving care, resilient and resistant bodies, bodies in the mass, dignified bodies, bodies expressing voice, and bodies carrying memory, among others. That is, there is more to tell beyond the maternal bodies and sexualized bodies that also appear in the testimonies. These narratives make visible women's specific experiences as well as a complex matrix of broader survival in the context of state terrorism.

Even though I pay central attention to gender dynamics in my analysis of these testimonies, these stories also hint, more or less explicitly, at the role of intersecting axes of inequality, including those based on age, class, race/ethnicity, religion, and disability. While in some cases these differences are explicitly articulated, for example, interviewees who recalled how they were specifically denigrated based on being Jewish, one can also wonder to what extent bodily markers associated with social inferiority in Argentina, such as darker skin tone or indigenous/mestiza heritage, also enabled particular forms of brutality and abuse (Bunster-Burotto 1994, 170). These threads are difficult to disentangle particularly given the atrocious treatment that captives of all social groups had to endure. Additionally, in the context of Argentina, certain forms of oppression and exclusion have been largely invisible, and the dearth of debate on such matters may mean fewer tools to articulate particular dynamics in terms of that which is silent. For instance, disadvantages and discrimination that can be linked to ethnoracial background or phenotypical characteristics such as darker skin tone have often been presented in public discourse as mainly a problem of class, even as people from the popular/working-class/impoverished sectors of society have been often denigrated through racist slurs. One can hypothesize, and in some cases demonstrate, that intersecting discriminatory discourses and practices were not left at the door of the camps but were integral to the operations of the CDCs. We need to keep in mind that the abuses that took place in the secret prisons of the dictatorship drew on broader repertoires of oppression already available in the society at large.

The Body of Evidence

The physicality of suffering is central to many narratives of captivity. Forced nudity; the lack of regular or sufficient food and water; denied access to bathrooms when needed; physical confinement with shackles and blindfolds; cold and/or wet spaces of detention; and all manners of torture and sexual violence were painfully experienced in the body. The narrative of survivor Fátima Cabrera illustrates general methods of embodied torment as well as the most overt gendered dimensions of the experience. Her testimony speaks of the production of a suffering body through state terrorist practices as well as the institutional disavowal of such experience, even in the face of a "body of evidence."

In the 1970s, Fátima, of humble socioeconomic background, was an activist with a Christian orientation who lived in a very poor neighborhood in Buenos Aires. She was abducted by police forces, taken to a police station, and then brought to the CDC "Garage Azopardo." She remained disappeared for ten days under brutal conditions:

> They tortured us. . . . Well, [in the case of] women, in the vagina, breasts. . . . Here, all over the eyes; one had the feeling that later on one would not be able to see again [sheds a tear and dries it with a handkerchief], because on top of that we were with a hood and a blindfold all the time [. . .] they tied it very hard. And then, they would take us to a place

that was like a big room that had some small windows with bars in the upper part. They had some numbers, and they had some kind of chains. They had us with our hands behind all the time. And we were semi-seated, as that was the position. It was very uncomfortable. Where one practically agonized, because we were not given anything to eat or drink.

Fátima also related that as a result of this cruel treatment she was left in a "deplorable state." Yet, as we shall see, the violence that her body evidenced was denied by institutional state power immediately upon her release from clandestine detention.

While the military regime largely vanished the traces of state-perpetrated human rights violations by resorting to the physical disappearance of people, Fátima narrated other ways in which the erasure of the "body of evidence" of state crimes was accomplished early on. In her case, this occurred right after her transfer to the regular prison system. Fátima recounted how upon entry to the prison she was examined by a medical doctor who wrote in his report that her general state was "normal"—something that Fátima contested. Not only had she told the doctor about the torture she endured, but her body also offered vivid proof of torture, as it was covered in stripes left by the picana. Fátima recalled that none of these facts were recorded in the doctor's report. "Official denial" (Cohen 2001) percolated through and was produced even at relatively low levels of the "legal" prison bureaucracy,[7] showing the continuum and interconnections between the clandestine and non-clandestine systems of imprisonment (D'Antonio 2009; Garaño 2010; Bacci et al. 2012). Another way by which the state minimized the bodily evidence of torture, mentioned by survivor Norma Berti, consisted of moving tortured prisoners from a CDC to another intermediate site, presumably for convalescent purposes, *before* transfer to the regular prison system.

These types of erasure tactics are a reminder of how important the body is as proof of human rights abuses—something on which human rights organization reports rely to denounce torture, though not in entirely unproblematic ways.[8] At the same time, they also suggest how even the "hard facts" of torture can be easily circumvented in the context of unchecked power. As different authors also point out, torture methods have become more sophisticated over time precisely to avoid marking the body (Cubilié 2005; Halewood 2012). Governments have developed a variety of so-called "clean" torture techniques to evade detection, criminal responsibility, and social condemnation (Rejali 2007). Of course, while the dictatorial government was concerned enough about its international image so as to try to conceal the human rights violations perpetrated,[9] its (illegitimate) sovereign power also meant that state officials could carry out atrocities with impunity, and that the direct victims did not have much recourse with authorities or key institutions in Argentina, even if they could produce embodied proof.

Furthermore, survivors' bodies cannot necessarily be taken as a transparent text of what occurred in the camps. Indeed, some survivors expressed concerns regarding how other people perceived their ordeal when their bodies did not fit preconceived assumptions. That is, bodily appearance could cast doubt or foster social denial of former detainees' experiences of state violence. Isabel Cerruti—who was a student activist held captive in El Banco and El Olimpo between 1978 and 1979—explained:

> Because when I left [the CDC], it was as if my family, many would look at me li[ke] . . . [facial gesture expressing a kind of doubt]. "Ah, how good you look." [. . .] Like they thought that I would come back from Biafra. [. . .] Everybody would lose weight. I gained weight, well, because I had a problem during all that time, practically in six months I did not menstruate. And according to the doctor, a gynecologist I saw later, he commented that in the Jewish concentration camps . . . in Germany, it happened. [. . .] And it is kind of . . . first because the stress is obviously . . . so great, and on the other hand is a kind of defense by women. And well, that caused me to gain a bit of weight, obviously. So, everyone . . . the fam . . . [would say] "how good" like saying "what a good time this girl had."

Amenorrhea and other menstrual disturbances are among the gendered conditions that have been documented in relation to traumatic situations such as armed conflict and confinement in concentration camps (Hannoun et al. 2007; Pasternak and Brooks 2007). Likewise, Isabel underwent a disruption of her menstrual cycle (this was also the case for other women who stopped menstruating during their captivity in the Argentine CDCs; see, e.g., CONADEP 1984; Actis et al. 2001). In the case of Isabel, and irrespective of the exact connection between amenorrhea and weight gain, what I would like to highlight here is people's reaction to a body that failed to produce "proper" evidence of captivity and suffering. Isabel's body did not live up to the expectation of famine (evoked by the reference to Biafra); she looked healthy enough. As mentioned before, survivors were often cast as suspect for surviving, and women could potentially be perceived as "bitches and traitors" (Longoni 2007, 155). The reactions that Isabel described seem to be consistent with those themes, to the point that her suffering could potentially be translated into "what a good time this girl had."

A similar concern about the responses of other people to her experience of repression emerged in the testimony of Eublogia "Rita" Cordero de Garnica, a survivor from a working-class family in Jujuy province. Rita was detained and held in the CDC known as El Guerrero, along with her two sons. She was later transferred to the regular prison system, but her sons remained disappeared. She joined the Mothers of the Plaza de Mayo-Ledesma-Jujuy. Her concerns regarding other people's perceptions bridge the past with more contemporary contexts: "Because there are many who perhaps do not believe, because they now see me fat. Because before I was thin. And well, it more or less seems that I . . . many believe that I am forgetting. No, it is just that I don't think [about it] as much as before, I don't work as much as before. So that's . . . that's why I'm gaining weight. But it is not because I have forgotten, but many do not believe that I was in prison." In this passage, Rita seemed to worry that her body weight and appearance decades after her detention would be used to cast doubt on two aspects of her experience: (1) her having been imprisoned and (2) her commitment to the memory of human rights abuses. The burden to produce embodied proof is then not limited to the past, but is also part of a perceived duty to remember. According to Rita, her slowing down her work affected her weight, which could then be taken as evidence either that she "forgot" or that the events she described had in fact never happened. The statement also evokes cultural associations between "excessive" body weight and character qualities such as laziness. In this case, the implicit concern seems to be that the state of the body would be problematically read as revealing a lack of commitment to the cause of human rights.

The narratives of Rita and Isabel bring to mind Anne Cubilié's (2005) warning to not overly rely on the body as *the* measure of truth of experiences of state terror, including the dangers that this presents from the perspective of survivors:

> [F]or the people who inhabit these bodies, truth is a much more complex negotiation than the seemingly transparent validation of "seeing it with one's own eyes" would suggest. The scar on the body both makes visible the "authentic" claim to experience of the survivor and obscures further seeing of the difficulties of such experience. The expectation that survivors' bodies are marked in some way by the experience of atrocity is a burden not just of the overly visible but of the expectation of the visible. Many survivors' bodies are not visibly marked by the experience of atrocity, but the lack of physical traces does not imply a lesser experience of atrocity. (153–54)

This pressure to produce embodied truth can be particularly pronounced in the context of judicial procedures, human rights violation reports, and survivors' quest for reparations. The body of the survivors becomes literally the body of evidence that atrocious crimes have been committed.

As will become apparent, women in this study carried both visible and invisible embodied marks of state violence. Some of these experiences could be explained by referring to body scars or describing ongoing physical health problems. Other experiences were much more difficult to articulate, as partially suggested by narrative false starts, efforts to search for the right words, and bodily gestures that denoted a sense of disbelief even for the affected women themselves. Survivors' narratives bring to the fore suffering bodies, whether visibly marked or not. Here the tension between bodies/selves emerges again. After all, it is not just "the body" per se that suffers but the whole embodied self, even as repressors inflicted much of that suffering through torments applied on the body.

The Suffering Body

Women shared multiple and overlapping accounts of embodied suffering in captivity, which included torture as a paradigmatic methodology of state terror. The repressors' apparent intent behind the use of torture was to produce bodily pain both as an interrogation strategy and as a ritual of degradation. "Then they grabbed my hands, they tied them up behind [my back] touching the metal of the chair. They took my blouse off and started to apply picana, from the get-go," said Elena Lenhardtson, who was detained in a secret detention center for two days (a middle-class psychologist, Elena had contracted poliomyelitis as a child, and in her testimony she was apparently referring to her wheelchair). Iris Avellaneda, from a working-class activist family, similarly recounted, "[F]irst they pour water on you, then they apply picana everywhere, armpits, breasts, mouth, neck, all the most sensitive spots, down on the feet and the genitals. In the midst of desperation, [it] seems like you are thinking 'earth swallow me.'" Laura Schachter—who had been a secondary school student activist—was taken to different CDCs, kept out in the open in cold weather and surrounded by guard dogs, and subjected to repeated torture: "And there they interrogate me again, they apply picana again. And at that point, I no longer had any idea of who I was, nor why I was there."

These testimonies, by women of different backgrounds, ages, and bodily abilities, coincide in their descriptions of the brutality of detention. Their words give a hint of how torture was geared toward shattering the tortured person's subjectivity, the "unmaking of the world" of the victims (Scarry 1985, 23): "earth swallow me," invoked Iris; "I no longer had any idea of who I was," recalled Laura. Elena also remembered the promise of her torturers: she would become "human waste." Yet as it becomes clear in many testimonies, repressive efforts to destroy these women's worlds and subjectivities were not successful on a variety of levels. Iris's testimony shows that she was able to endure brutal interrogations without giving information that could be used to harm others precisely by holding on to her world, specifically through the internalized advice of a comrade and lawyer: "never giving the enemy more than what is due." While Elena recounted the suffering produced by the application of picana, she also emphasized that though she screamed loudly, she "did not shed even one tear." Laura tried to resist the repeated torture sessions by "playing dumb," to make the repressors believe they had made a mistake. It is true that torture wreaked havoc—putting detainees in impossible situations—yet it is also important to note the multiple ways in which different detainees endured and/or resisted despite the devastation.

While torture with the infamous electric picana is emblematic of the dictatorship's tactics, many other methods of torture targeting the body were also reported by survivors. Celeste Seydell mentioned that though she was not tortured with picana, she experienced "the dry nylon bag, the submarine, cigarette burning, blows, *culatazos* [blows with a firearm]." A somewhat more subtle form of torture appears in Martha Díaz's testimony, as she narrated painful aggressions barely disguised as a health treatment: "Then they take me to the dentist, because supposedly . . . well, for a checkup, I don't know. And well, they take out a molar without anesthesia, so that 'Well, let's see, tell us something more. Tell us something more of what you know.'" These and many other examples drive home an observation of Adriana Arce about the "creativity" of the repressors when it came to devising suffering methods—the repertoire of oppression was as varied as cruel. However, at the same time, many of these methods were not original at all, but techniques also used in other national and historical contexts (see, e.g., Rejali 2007). These testimonies offer just a glimpse of how "the body in pain" (Scarry 1985) was produced in the context of state terrorism, as narrated by survivors. These instances concretely remind us of what being "disappeared" entailed in terms of embodied suffering. More extensive documentation of the atrocities committed can be found in various activist, scholarly, judicial, and official sources, including the report produced by the truth commission, CONADEP (1984).

I believe it is important to avoid assembling a "horror show" about what happened to the people held in clandestine detention, like the sensationalistic media coverage in the early transition to democracy (Feld 2002). However, it is also necessary to recognize how "sanitized" representations (Glover 2012, xvii) can diminish a sense of responsibility toward redressing the described events or preventing similar occurrences in the future. Even the repeated circulation and banalization of the label "torture"—which governments still try to eschew in relation to their own acts—can become devoid of the moral and emotional outrage that can be a basis for action against human rights abuses. Words often fail us in their ability to help us grasp, represent, and react appropriately in the face of atrocity.

Women survivors' narratives give an idea not only of what they endured at the moment of detention, but of the physical, emotional, and psychological consequences that they carried later on, which imply a more extended temporality of suffering.[10] Even though many survivors also showed a great deal of resiliency, the nature of the traumatic events affected many realms of their lives, and even their ability to recount aspects of the experience. For instance, Norma Berti expressed the challenge of addressing bodily topics such as torture: "Because I think that talking about the experiences of the body is among the most difficult things that exist. And I believe that torture is the exaltation of all these types of sensations of the body, right?, the exaltation of the body in a negative sense. One feels enormous pain, I don't know, I was never so gravely ill to feel atrocious pain, but sometimes it is very difficult to talk about pain. About physical pain."[11]

This magnified position of the body through torture is paradoxical. On the one hand, torture situates the body center stage—via the insistent production of physical pain—but it can also displace the body from speech in the difficulty to talk about the experience, as Norma relates.[12] Susana Jorgelina Ramus also emphasized the physical pain of torture while simultaneously struggling to explain it: "Well, it was something very. . . . Look, very intense physically because . . . of the pain, on the one hand, no? But above all, it is like it generates in you a kind of panic, because you don't know, it is such a strange pain, so unknown. Because I can tell you that it is like you get an electric shock, no? And it is not exactly like that because it is as if you would get several continued [shocks]. So, for example, your body arches." In her efforts to put in words what is indescribable, Susana outlined in this passage three dimensions of her experience of torture: the physical mechanical response (the arched body), the physical suffering (pain), and the embodied emotions associated with this unfamiliar pain (panic). And yet this categorization cannot even start to convey the experience. In this sense, Elaine Scarry's (1985) thesis about the inexpressibility of pain holds true in several accounts by survivors.

As we shall see later, the intensity of this type of embodied experience sometimes resulted in various forms of distancing from the body by detainees. The torturers centered the body, but some captives somewhat circumvented this attempt by leaving the body through different dissociation mechanisms (Bacci et al. 2012; chapter 4 of this volume). In some cases the physical pain was almost trumped by other dimensions of the experience. For example, Liliana Gardella remembered torture as "something very violent, probably torture is the most violent [act] of everything that was done during the process. I think that torture concentrates the violence of a lot of pressure, a lot of chaos, a lot of screams. I don't know how to explain it, even the physical pain gets diluted in the terror of the pressure, and of the screams, and of the *apriete* [intimidating demand], and of their demanding things of you, and of their asking and asking you again. It is something very confusing. It is very confusing." In this passage, the experience of physical pain seems to be somewhat overshadowed by the terror achieved by other means during the torture situation. Still, here we can also see how the connection between torture, bodily pain, and other emotions defies easy articulation ("I don't know how to explain it").

The level of pain inflicted was so extreme that various women expressed a sense of disbelief or surprise about their own ability to endure such conditions, and in some cases to even withstand without giving any information. Iris Avellaneda mentioned not knowing "from where one gets so much strength." Fátima Cabrera concluded: "I still cannot . . . understand how I went through that, or how could I withstand that, because [the tortures] were terrible." Rita Cordero de Garnica expressed: "I thought that . . . that I would die, but no." These experiences, which exemplify the surprising powers of the body beyond what the mind can predict or direct, remind of Spinoza's philosophical notion: "We do not know what the body can do" (Deleuze 1988, 17). In this sense, the suffering body is not merely a passive entity, but an active one in the face of a repressive state power that aimed for total subjugation. Of course, there are material limits to what the body can withstand, and these limits do not necessarily mean passivity. However, the point is that even extreme forms of oppression that cause excruciating bodily suffering may encounter bodies that endure well beyond what might be expected. The resilient bodies of women survivors also remind us of a kind of strength that is antithetical to pervasive notions of femininity that construct women as inherently weak. What is perhaps doubly surprising then are not only the unimaginable things that "the body" can do, but what a *woman's* body can do.

As we shall see, state power inscribed the heteropatriarchal order through the infliction of various forms of gendered bodily suffering, even as they met potent women's bodies. Women were to be returned to "their place" via sexual violence, through their treatment as mere reproductive entities, and through other forms of torments and torture that carried the social mark of normative femininity. Women coped with, negotiated, and responded to such situations in a variety of ways.

The Sexualized Body

In recent years, and in the context of the reopening of trials for crimes against humanity, feminist scholars and advocates have written works that document and analyze the extensive use of sexual violence in the Argentine CDCs.[13] Beyond the Argentine case, feminist scholarship and activism in the international arena have also denounced militarized rape as a gender-specific tactic for exerting power and control against people deemed as enemy (e.g., Bunster-Burotto 1994; Hollander 1996; Enloe 2000; Falcón 2006; Sonderéguer 2012). In the United Nations report "Sexual Violence and Armed Conflict: United Nations Response," the uses of and motivations behind sexual violence against women in armed contexts are summarized as follows:

> [A] commonly held view throughout history has been that women are part of the "spoils" of war to which soldiers are entitled. Deeply entrenched in this notion is the idea that women are property—chattel available to victorious warriors. Sexual violence may also be looked upon as a means of troop mollification. This is particularly the case where women are forced into military sexual slavery. Another reason that sexual violence occurs is to destroy male, and thereby community, pride. Men who have failed to "protect their women" are considered to be humiliated and weak. It can also be used as a form of punishment, particularly where women are politically active, or are associated with others who are politically active. Sexual violence can further be used as a means of inflicting terror upon the population at large. It can shatter communities and drive people out of their homes. Sexual violence can also be part of a genocidal strategy. It can inflict life-threatening bodily and mental harm, and form

part of the conditions imposed to bring about the ultimate destruction of an entire group of people. (United Nations 1998, n.p.)

As this extended passage reveals, culturally constructed notions of femininity and masculinity are integral to the perpetration of sexual violence in militarized contexts. Women are the disproportionate targets of this type of violence, and such actions reinforce stereotypical notions of what it means to be a woman in a sexual sense.

Yet men have also been victims of sexualized violence in the Argentine CDCs and elsewhere, but the meanings conveyed through such actions are not the same as when the violence is directed toward women. While sexual violence against women in armed contexts reproduces and magnifies the subordination that women as a group already experience in "normal" times, sexual violence against men is often a way to feminize men, making them feel like women. It can also be used to bolster their humiliation by drawing on homophobic scripts in contexts in which homosexuality and any attribute associated with femininity are constructed as diametrically opposed to being a real man. As femininity is constructed as a subordinated identity in patriarchal society, the feminization of men through sexual violence can be one of the tools used to subjugate men deemed as enemies. This can be seen in the case of the Argentine dictatorship, as well as in more contemporary militarized international settings (for example, in the case of sexualized violence perpetrated by U.S. military personnel against detainees in the Abu Ghraib prison in Iraq in the context of the "war on terror"). Dominant sex/gender/sexuality systems play an important role in the perpetration and meanings attached to such acts, often in intersection with other systems of inequality such as those based on race, ethnicity, and nation (e.g., Taylor 1997; Puar 2005; Philipose 2007).

Though information about sexual violence in the context of the dictatorship apparatus in Argentina was already available in the transition to democracy in the early eighties (e.g., in the CONADEP report), a number of obstacles undermined the possibility of judging those offenses as autonomous crimes that were nevertheless part of the overall repressive plan of the military regime. Balardini, Oberlin, and Sobredo (2011) mention that such obstacles have ranged from issues that are common to the investigation of these types of crimes—the sexist and gender discriminatory characteristics that the Judicial System reproduces, the lack of sensitivity from the operators in this system and the fact that these are considered "private instance" offenses [*delitos de instancia privada*]—to those linked to proof, the character of crimes against humanity, and the conception that is adopted with respect to authorship and criminal participation. Finally, there is the tendency to subsume the penal type of rape under that of the application of torments. (196; see also Duffy 2012)

Though sexual violence in clandestine detention has unique characteristics, at the same time it crosses the borders of the secret prisons and overlaps with other experiences of noncaptive women. This commonality can function as another obstacle to recognizing rape and other sexual violence that occurred in CDCs as crimes against humanity. After all, such actions implicitly appear to be in the spectrum of normalized violence that women are disproportionately likely to experience (and that enjoys a great deal of impunity). Sexual violence against women preceded and continued after the dictatorship, has occurred inside and outside state-run facilities, and has been perpetrated by state officials and private individuals. Given this situation, feminist advocates and scholars have worked hard to demonstrate the systematic, generalized, and context-related characteristics of state-sponsored sexual violence in CDCs, which qualify these actions as crimes against humanity (Aucía et al. 2011; Bacci et al. 2012; CLADEM n.d.). Developments in international jurisprudence with respect to the judgment of sexual violence perpetrated during armed conflict and genocide—particularly in the cases of Rwanda and the former Yugoslavia—as well as international treaties and jurisprudence related to crimes against humanity have helped support the prosecution of the sexual crimes of the dictatorship.[14] Furthermore, the cultural, legal, and institutional shifts propelled by the women's movement in Argentina with regard to gender violence more generally help create an environment more amenable to addressing the experiences of women who underwent clandestine detention.

In a book based on a collaborative and in-depth investigation of sexual violence in the context of state terrorism, Analía Aucía (2011, 36) defines sexual violence as "those behaviors and actions of sexual content or nature to which a person is subjected by force, threat of force, coercion, fear of violence, intimidation, psychological oppression or power abuse." She then gives examples of such violence and connects them to the experiences of detainees in the secret prisons of the dictatorship, including various forms of rape, sexual abuse by other means, forced pregnancies and abortions, forced nudity and exhibitionism, sexual serfdom and exploitation, and sexual humiliation and harassment, among others (36–37).

While both men and women experienced various forms of sexual violence in clandestine detention, women were key targets of a wide variety of sexualized aggressions, with different material and symbolic implications. At the same time, assessing sexual violence against men has been particularly challenging given the silence around these matters not only in Argentina, but in situations of armed conflict in other parts of the world too (Oosterhoff, Zwanikken, and Ketting 2004; Aucía et al. 2011). This is partly connected to gender and sexual ideologies that constitute such acts as particularly shameful for men, in the sense of "turning" men into women or homosexuals, both subordinated identities in heteropatriarchal societies. Inger Agger (1989, 313) points out the role the sexual torture of men plays on "the activation of castration anxiety and homosexual anxiety," that is, on the "fear of not being a 'real' man." Reflecting on the sexualized torture of Iraqi prisoners in the U.S.-run Abu Ghraib prison post-9/11, Jasbir Puar (2005, 28) analyzes the "feminizing"/"'faggotizing' of the male body" in relation to "racial, imperial, and economic matrices of power." She argues for the need to pay attention not only to "women as the victims of rape and pawns between men during wartime" but also to the role that "castrating the reproductive capacities of men" (in relation to the perpetuation of their kin) may have in the torture of men deemed terrorists (27).

Sexual violence has overlaps with torture in how it transforms the body into an object of suffering and degradation. However, there are differences between varieties of torture and varieties of sexual violence. For example, Susana Jorgelina Ramus pointed out that part of the panic she experienced in relation to torture with electric shocks was the feeling that the body would not be able to withstand such drastic attacks: "you feel like anything can happen to you, no? That with one [electric] discharge you can die." And yet she put other forms of (sexual) violence on a similar level, even when they might not produce death per se. Such is the case of sexual violation: "I think that the rapes can be sort of placed on the same level, no? Not because they carry mortal danger, but because of the feeling of *vejación* [humiliation, degradation] that one feels, no?—as much as with torture as with rape. But with torture, well, one thinks more that . . . it is more related to life endangerment, no? With rape, no." The commonalities between torture and rape reveal the atrocious dimensions of sexual crimes that have been taken less seriously than torture. At the same time, the differences between such actions speak to the importance of not necessarily subsuming rape under torture, for it would undermine the ability to understand the significantly unique factors and consequences of rape including its relation to broader social scripts regarding sexuality, guilt, and shame (see, e.g., Agger 1989).

The testimonies of women in this study reveal a broad repertoire of sexual violence, from rape to other tactics of sexualized denigration. The latter included the forced nudity of captives, their having to go to the bathroom in front of guards, obscene commentary about the captives' bodies, and other forms of sexual harassment. Susana Reyes, who was pregnant during her captivity, recounted: "when we bathed, the bathroom had no doors, and the *tipos* [men], you know, would take advantage, and. . . . They did not rape you but would start to tell you obscenities, you know? 'Clean yourself here' or 'Look how you have that,' you know? So, I did not take my clothes off to bathe."

Being able to clean oneself or bathe was not something that could be taken for granted in the context of the camps, and survivors from different CDCs referred both to the lack of privacy and to the discomfort that the lack of hygiene produced. Celeste Seydell remembered: "That adrenaline odor, you know? A metallic odor, disgusting, which. . . . They did not allow us to bathe . . . everything was disgusting, it was. . . . You know, it was surviving with your thoughts [she places her hands on her temple], with your mind, saying 'I have to live, I have to live.'" Other survivors recalled that detainees sometimes wetted or soiled themselves because they were not allowed to use the toilets when needed, because of fear of being tortured when asking to go to the bathroom, or as a physiological reaction to fear. These are forms of degradation that, as Alicia Morales pointed out, "are often not talked about." She recalled:

"The most mundane and common things, like going to the bathroom . . . how tormenting that can be in these circumstances. I mean, these are things that people never imagine, but they are things that a prisoner loses. That is, even the privacy to go to the bathroom." Lacking this type of privacy is anathema to cultural expectancies around basic body functions, particularly for adults. Furthermore, forcing adults to "regress" to bodies wetted or soiled could be more than physically unpleasant: it could produce shame. After all, the "command of the privacy of excretions" is learned in childhood (Fuchs 2003, 230) and culturally expected for adults. Thus silence around such themes is not surprising. Shame is a powerful social emotion that can operate as a form of social control (Scheff 2003) and is closely linked to the body both in how it manifests (e.g., blushing, clumsiness) and in terms of its source (e.g., temporary or permanent bodily characteristics that may be perceived as shameful [Fuchs 2003]).

As Cristina Zurutuza (2011) points out, this lack of privacy involved captive people's sexuality and violated basic cultural norms regarding contexts of body exposure. She further notes that these norms are gendered in the sense that, since childhood, men have traditionally been more used to having their bodies exposed to their peers in places such as locker rooms in sports or recreational facilities or during group urination or masturbation while growing up. In contrast, women have been encouraged to keep their bodies more private, to have a certain "modesty" regarding bodily functions. Given the general conditions of degradation in the camps, detainees sometimes had to "lose their shame" in exchange for gaining some measure of dignity or comfort in other ways, including being clean. This could also be thought of as one way of countering the symbolic construction of detainees' bodies/selves as dirty and disposable (Zurutuza 2011). Graciela García recalled that in the ESMA "the bathrooms were small, in general, you would bathe alone, but with the Green [low-level guard] watching you, right? And you couldn't care less, just for the chance to bathe—I couldn't care less. I was happy I could bathe. For a long time we did not bathe. So when you started to bathe it was . . . with the cost of the Greens [watching you], and with whatever clothing they give you." For many women in captivity the (rare) comfort of being able to clean themselves came with a very literal, voyeuristic male gaze imposed as the price for intimate bodily self-care.[15]

This male gaze was an integral part of the camps, for most of the people directly involved in the clandestine repressive enterprise were men. The male gaze was one dimension of gendered state power, often magnified by the fact that while guards and officers could look at detainees' bodies at will, people captive were often blindfolded.[16] Women were subjected to the voyeuristic gaze of officials and guards who could, and oftentimes did, sexually abuse them with impunity—both through overtly violent rapes (including in repeated instances of the same women, or through gang rape) as well as in situations in which the action mimicked consensual sexual relations but in which the women involved were in no position to refuse (Aucía et al. 2011). In some cases, detainees were able to resist or denounce particular instances of abuse, for instance, enlisting the help of other detainees through screams or more organized tactics, or by working the system of hierarchies in the camp (Bacci et al. 2012). Bacci et al. (2012) illustrate the latter point referring to the case of Munú Actis, who hit a guard back when he tried to grope her. She noted that she had some room to maneuver because the perpetrator in that case was not an officer. That is, she used the knowledge about the differential power of guards and officers in order to stop the abuse. However, the bottom line was the extreme vulnerability in which detainees were placed that generally precluded their ability to stop the perpetrators.

Furthermore, as survivor Mario Villani and other former detainees point out, one difference between the regular prison system and some of the CDCs was that in the latter, repressors often circulated and lived in closer proximity with detainees (Villani and Reati 2011). While this proximity often meant that detainees were acutely exposed to the torture and abuse of other detainees—Viviana Nardoni describes this situation as "promiscuous"—in some cases it also facilitated disparate types of relations between repressors and detainees. These relations included individual repressors offering some kind of "protection" to particular detainees (more akin to a sense of personal ownership) and moments of pseudo-friendly gestures (e.g., a food treat, a trip to see a family member) even when the same repressors were also capable of the worst types of atrocities. In the case of women, some of the twisted ways in which repressors treated them had sexual dimensions or constructed the women into objects of display, as in the case of officers in ESMA who took women for dinner or dancing, while having them wear feminine attire (Actis et al. 2001), or took them out to have sexual "relations" that the women were in no position to refuse.

Sexual violence against women detainees drew on gender ideologies that construct women's bodies as men's property and women's sexuality as men's rightful "spoils of war." While the military drew on Madonna/whore binaries, which construct the women in the latter category as sexually available and those in the former as deserving protection, no women who ended up in the camps were truly protected from the possibility of sexual abuse in one form or another. By virtue of their detention, no matter their age, political background, religion, race/ethnicity, or occupation, women in captivity could be easily labeled as whore, as many sorts of behavior were translated into immoral sexuality in the eyes of the military. Aspects of identity, however, could be used to stress sexual deviance. For instance, Elisa Tokar recalled the following about an interrogation with picana: "I was able to tell them that I was living somewhere else, in a *pension* [boarding house]. [. . .] So then they started to attack me, [saying] that I was a Montonera bitch, like all the Montonera bitches who live in boarding houses." Here Elisa's place of residence as well as her activism transformed her into a "bitch" from the repressors' perspective. The state policed not only citizens' political ideas but also women's personal choices and sexuality.

Furthermore, the arbitrary nature of how the camps operated, as well as the twisted and inconsistent ways in which repressors applied their moral compass, made it hard to predict which women would be subjected or spared from sexual violence. Some survivors conveyed that in particular contexts, or at particular times, repressors would deploy a sexually puritanical or chivalrous ideology that was supposed to restrain their abuse of women. Munú Actis remembered how despite the brutalities that took place at ESMA, repressors at that site still liked to portray themselves as the "knights of the sea" (*caballeros del mar*), an identity that was allegedly inconsistent with sexually abusive behavior. Laura Schachter, who had finished secondary school the year before her kidnapping, pointed out the double morality expressed by some of the repressors she encountered. Laura was captive in the CDC El Vesubio and in Campo de Mayo, and she dealt with different groups of repressors. She recalled that at one point during her captivity, her bra broke, which in turn elicited the following response from one group: "These *tipos* [men] were torturers but their great concern was to know whether someone had abused me. So I remember that they sewed the bra because it was something that worried them, because it seems that internally their moral sense was a bit peculiar—because that was frowned upon, but they could torture given that it was approved of."

Similarly, Celeste Seydell, who had experienced the threat of sexual violence while in clandestine detention in Córdoba, recalled how later on she had to hear an explanation about the morality of the military during a medical examination with a supposed physician who ordered her to undress:

> He takes the blindfold off and tells me, "You have to undress because I am a doctor, and what I need to do is see how you are and cure you," and so on. And I [respond], "No, no." [The supposed doctor says:] "But you have to undress because here the military . . . we would never do what happened to you in *Informaciones* [another detention facility] [. . .] because we have codes of honor. We will *never* touch even one of your hairs. We will torture you, kill you, but will never rape you. Let's be clear about that." He talked to me, you don't know for how long, about the morality of the military, and that they would never rape me.

In the cited cases, members of the repressive apparatus tried to portray a sexually appropriate veneer, perhaps deployed to enhance their self-image or to distinguish themselves and establish moral hierarchies in relation to other men. At the same time, as various testimonies attest, this type of ideology seemed to be rather lax and feeble, in the sense that it did not really prevent rampant sexual violence. In sum, women's bodies were sexualized in a variety of ways, though this dimension of violence has only recently been more fully addressed through research and at the judicial level.

The Pregnant Body

If there is a feminine status that is culturally glorified in Argentina and other parts of the world, it is the one represented by the mother. As the popular notion that *madre hay una sola* ("there's only one mother") suggests, motherhood is not only a celebrated identity, but also one that is naturalized.[17] However, this celebratory stance has not been uniformly applied to all women. Silvana Darré (2013, 12–13) explores how "maternal pedagogies" disseminated through state, charity, medical, and psychology discourses at different historical moments in Argentina produced "inappropriate motherhood" at the same time as they were geared toward "appropriate" maternal practices. The glorification of motherhood in Argentina and other parts of Latin America finds fertile ground in the Catholic religion—especially in the iconic image of the Virgin Mary and the exaltation of so-called "natural" family structures. Mónica Tarducci (2008b, 10–11) points out that although motherhood is often essentialized, it tends to be "lived as 'natural' only by those women who share dominant patterns about what a mother is expected to be." In the case of the ideology fostered by the last military dictatorship in Argentina, mothers were expected to fulfill a pivotal role by "properly" socializing their children so that they did not become "subversives" (Laudano n.d. [1998]; Bravo 2003).

What place did women who embodied "motherhood" through their pregnancies occupy in the CDCs? How does the pregnant body figure in this repressive context? While the overall treatment of pregnant women was utterly deplorable, especially taking into account that so many of these women were tortured and ultimately killed, it can also be argued that pregnant women occupied contradictory or ambivalent positions. On the one hand, pregnant women could be said to embody women's gender duty to procreate, and in some cases, the very image of the "good woman" who deserves special protection. On the other hand, pregnant women in captivity were still construed as subversive, partners of subversives, and/or mothers of future subversives who needed to be punished and whose lineage it was imperative to end (thus setting the stage for the appropriation of their children). In other words, the pregnant body posed a particular challenge to a repressive plan bent on the annihilation of groups of people deemed subversive (Duhalde 1999). The elimination of the women after giving birth and the placement of their children in "proper families" were essential to accomplish the goal of ending the "subversive" lineage, as the families linked to the regime were trusted to instill the right values. Tarducci (2008b, 12) notes a "[s]trange paradox" in this dynamic: "The same Catholic and conservative sectors, staunch defenders of the family, who claim blood ties as foundational of kinship, are the ones who appropriate children and raise them as their own, trusting the virtues of childrearing instead of biological ties."

With regard to the situation of pregnant women in CDCs, here too the repressors' inconsistent morality and discretionary power created room for both unspeakable abuse, as well as the granting of certain "privileges" to some pregnant women. For instance, Marta Álvarez, who was pregnant and gave birth during captivity, suggested that her pregnancy may have somewhat shielded her from certain forms of "sexual use" that repressors imposed on other women detainees: "I was the image of the mother, and the image of an immaculate thing," she said.[18] In the Madonna/whore imaginary the "immaculate" woman is sharply contrasted with the one who is sexually available. And yet, the degrading and harmful conditions that so many pregnant women experienced— including torture and sexual violence[19]—defy any stable notion of the pregnant body as a sort of insurance against abuse. Moreover, the systematic plan to steal babies and kill their mothers after giving birth shows that whatever the sacred status assigned to motherhood, it did not really protect pregnant captives who ended up dead, or the appropriated children separated from their mothers.[20] Bacci et al. (2012) point out that given the appalling plan to appropriate children, we might lose sight of the experiences of their disappeared mothers or "of those women who kept their children after having gone through pregnancy in captivity, those who lost their pregnancies as a result of ferocious torture sessions or who were subjected to forced abortions, in some cases, after having been raped by the repressors themselves" (Bacci et al. 2012, 53). This variety of configurations does not contradict the systematic nature of the overall repressive plan, of which the appropriation of children was a component (Regueiro 2008).

Pregnant women who gave birth during their captivity had to go through this vital experience in the oppressive conditions imposed by the regime with no control over what was done to their bodies before, during, and after giving birth. Some detainees gave birth in "maternities" set up in CDCs, while others were taken to medical centers where the procedure took place in irregular conditions, including not being officially registered (Regueiro 2008; Bacci et al. 2012). Bacci et al. (2012) mention some of the common ways in which the pregnant woman's body was treated around and during the moment of giving birth: captive women's eyes were covered, they often had to undergo cesarean sections, and they were given medications to stop the production of milk after birth since they would not have a chance to nurse.[21] Bacci et al. (2012, 61) and Regueiro (2008, 118) also refer to testimonies about doctors who expressed a desire to perform, on captive pregnant women, delivery procedures that were not commonly done at the time.[22]

The testimonies of surviving women who were pregnant during captivity, and those of other survivors who witnessed the treatment of pregnant women, show that the pregnant body was simultaneously or alternatively protected and deprecated, depending on the person and/or the specifics of the camps in question. The discretionary power that the regime enjoyed in determining who lived and died applied to the situation of pregnant women as well (Regueiro 2008). The testimony of Adriana Friszman, who was pregnant while captive in the ESMA, speaks of certain "privileges" afforded to pregnant women:

> I was staying in the place that they called *Capucha* [Hood], which was a big *galpón* [warehouse] with partitions, mattresses on the floor, and where they had people shackled, with chains, and in the first partitions closer to the door they put women and pregnant women. And pregnant women had privileges, they had beds. That is, in the partition there was a bed, and every week, rigorously, a navy guard would come and change the sheets—the sheets always impeccable. So that was the difference. And another difference was that pregnant women were given a plate of food, and the other people were given a sandwich to eat. So it was a minimal difference, but. . . . And they also had a room in which three or four pregnant women were living, who were in a more advanced stage of the pregnancy. And the rest of us could visit them, so during part of the day we could go to that room and stay there. And we were able to do things there.

While these relative privileges may be taken as evidence of some "sense of humanity" on the part of repressors—parallel to the decision to let some children live (Pilar Calveiro cited in Regueiro 2008, 124)—a more utilitarian logic might have been operative too. That is, the "pregnant body" needed to be somewhat cared for to the extent that it supported the development of a future baby to be appropriated. After delivery, the bodies of many of these women had no apparent value and could

therefore be disposed of. This utilitarian logic is conveyed in the testimony of Susana Reyes, who was pregnant and ultimately survived
and gave birth after her release. She recalled that during her pregnancy
there was a guard who seemed to take special interest in her, sometimes
bringing her a fruit or medicines when she was sick: "And then, when
he would perhaps bring me a mandarin he would say, 'Take care of
him [Susana's future child], because that one will be for me.' That is, he
would bring me those things because . . . because the boy would be for
him—he would say, no? You know, I thought it was a joke or something
like that."[23] At that point, Susana was not yet aware of the fate of so many
children born in captivity (and the women who gave birth to them),
something she started to figure out during her detention, particularly
when another pregnant woman—who ultimately disappeared—was
brought back to the camp without the baby, and without having even
seen the child or learning the sex of her baby (see also Bacci et al. 2012).

The utilitarian logic applied to the "pregnant body" reproduces and
magnifies (in extreme form) social practices and ideologies that deem
women's bodies as reproductive vessels. This kind of logic is enshrined
by state power in Argentina, for example, in the long-standing penal-
ization of abortion. This policy implicitly dictates that women must
be a "body-for-others" (Lagarde 2001, n.p.), mere "reproductive life"
(Deutscher 2008, 67). Ironically, while the ban on voluntary abortions
was in place during the dictatorship (with few exceptions), abortions
did take place in clandestine detention when repressors considered it
necessary or useful (Aucía et al. 2011; Bacci et al. 2012). From the "body-
for-others" construction, a pregnant woman's own life and desires do
not really matter.

While it is not my intention to equate pregnant women wishing to
perform an abortion in ordinary times with pregnant women in the
CDCs of the dictatorship, what I would like to underline here is how
the notion of women's bodily utility/disposability was already available
as part of more widespread gender ideologies. Obviously, everyone who
was killed in concentration camps was ultimately deemed "disposable."
However, the usefulness of the pregnant body as a body-for-others, even
at the expense of the woman's own life and desires, is part and parcel
of socially prevalent, oppressive gender scripts. In the case of pregnant
bodies—as in the utility/disposability inscribed through sexual violence

described in the previous section—we see how the gendered body is central to state power dynamics.

The pregnant body, which often evokes tenderness and mythical images of motherhood, was not immune to its association with degrading sexuality and gender-based violence. This was the case for Susana Reyes, who recalled an obscene comment made by a guard when he saw her: "'Ehh' he says. 'Che, and you? Who went through your *chabomba* [slang for panties]?'" This sexualized remark—which depicted Susana as a passive body penetrated by who knows which man's penis—was the last straw for Susana. She had already been enduring too much, and she responded to the comment by cursing and insulting the guard. Using the disproportionate power that he had in that situation, the guard then tied up Susana and brutally beat her, making use of a kind of baton: "I mean, the guy had beaten me ruthlessly. That is, besides the fact that I could not move, because I was tied up. [. . .] Hands tied up, so I could not cover myself." Obviously, Susana's pregnant body did not protect her from either a sexualized verbal aggression or vicious physical violence. In the case of other women, pregnancy did not protect them from rape either. Elena Alfaro, also a survivor of El Vesubio, mentioned that "sadism was to rape pregnant women" (cited in Vassallo 2011, 20).

As Bacci et al. (2012) documented, some of the survivors who were pregnant did not reach full term and/or had health problems from the torture and other maltreatment experienced. Gloria Enríquez, who was tortured and hit in her belly because "the son of a guerrilla did not deserve to live," lost her pregnancy. Adriana Arce was also tortured while pregnant, had suffered hemorrhages, and had an abortion practiced in the precarious conditions of captivity, including without the use of anesthetics (of course, this was not a context in which Adriana had "choice" in any real sense). Delia Bisutti, who was six months pregnant during her captivity and whose daughter was born with microcephaly, suspected that this condition was probably related to the harsh and stressful event of her detention. Later on, she commissioned medical studies—including in the United States—that showed no trace of any physical or genetic probable cause, so an environmental explanation might have been at root.[24]

Pregnancy constituted a distinctively gendered form of embodied vulnerability in the context of the camps, and in the case of pregnant activists it also revealed the ways in which prevailing models of activism failed to account for gender specificities. Referring to the situation of political prisoners in Uruguay, and particularly the cases of pregnant activist women, Ana Laura de Giorgi (2015, 212) describes the gendered challenges that these women faced, namely, the incompatibility between the duty to "fulfill the militant mandate to 'not sing' [not reveal information during torture] and the maternal mandate to protect the child in the womb." That is, pregnancy put activist women in an ethical and political bind that the politics of militant organizations, tailored after men's bodies and lives, were ill equipped to foresee.

There are also other issues to consider: pregnancy in captivity is often talked about as if the gestation of all pregnancies predated the moment of detention. However, as de Giorgi points out, other possibilities—such as pregnancies conceived in captivity—are more likely to be surrounded by silence. Some of these pregnancies are evidence of the specific embodied vulnerability of women of reproductive age. Certainly, rape during captivity could lead to pregnancy, and sometimes it did (Aucía et al. 2011). However, in this research I also heard about other types of pregnancies in captivity, such as the cases of women whose pregnancies were gestated with their romantic partners while detained in the same cell. This situation points to the affirmation of desire and a will to survive under conditions in which there seemed to be room only for despair and death. In the case of Uruguay, de Giorgi refers to a "girl conceived and born in prison" in the context of political repression, which confronts us with issues that, though hard to address, point to the possibility of "love, no doubt sexuality and a chosen motherhood that transgressed militant mandates and also those based on gender by utilizing motherhood as a political tool" (e.g., in that case apparently related to the opportunity to move from a hostage situation to inmate in a women's prison) (de Giorgi 2015, 219).

For some women, pregnancy could be a vehicle for resistance, a refusal to accept the end of their lineage, of their own lives, and of their political projects. In that sense, Cristina Comandé remembered a young fellow detainee who toyed with the idea of pregnancy: "[S]he said 'how I would love to be pregnant, and have a child.' And I told her, 'But you are crazy; what are you saying? To have a child in this situation?' And she said, 'Yes, yes, it would be like a *proyección* [a projection into the future], it would be . . . it would be great.' So despite the extreme situations, in fact, we thought that by having a child we would make a world . . . a better world for our children and for children who were not ours, but who would form our future country." Similarly, Isabel Fernández Blanco spoke of her pregnancy in captivity as "another *estrategia de vida* [life-affirming strategy]" in the sense that it required "keeping oneself alive for that," generating a sense of responsibility to survive. She also mentioned that although retrospectively she felt scared about "what could have happened," that was not how she felt during captivity as what prevailed was a "doing and living" (*hacer y vivir*) impulse.

The variety of situations described suggest that pregnancy could be both a specific *vulnerability* that some women experienced and also a unique *gendered power* that the state aimed to harness. Among the pregnant detainees, Susana Reyes was released before the time of giving birth. Though she was anemic, her son Juan was born healthy and of normal weight. Still she reflected on the oppressive context that shaped her overall pregnancy, with long-term consequences for her child (including the fact that his father remained disappeared). In the occasion of her giving birth, Susana was in a room at the hospital, where a curious phenomenon helped symbolize the adverse conditions in which her pregnancy developed: "The pigeons—the urban pigeons—had built a nest made of nails. [. . .] I mean, there was a nest on the window at the hospital—next to me, to the bed—made of rusty nails, you know? And there were eggs in the nest. So the nurse said, 'Look!' [. . .] [L]ater I remembered this as being spot-on, because Juan had been born into a reality of nails. Because that's how it was, no?"

* * *

In this and the previous section, I elaborated on some of the most direct ways in which gender ideologies and hierarchies infused the embodied experiences of women in captivity. As we will see, there are other perhaps less evident mechanisms by which gender is inscribed through torments and torture in clandestine detention, and which reveal the central role that gender played in the maintenance of a masculinist regime of state power and terror.

Re-creating "the Feminine" through the Tortured Body: Gender as an Implicit Script

There are at least three ways in which we can detect gender at play with respect to how detainees' bodies were treated in clandestine detention (the bulk of this section will be dedicated to the third one). First, some forms of violence inflicted on prisoners were gender-specific (e.g., the treatment of pregnant women) or particularly directed to one gender group (e.g., rape mainly directed to women). Second, even when torture and torments inflicted on men and women were similar, they could still hold different meanings for each group given their different location in the power structure and the traits ascribed to each group (e.g., rape often has different connotations when directed to men or women). Besides such forms of gender and sexual violence, I am also interested in a third, more hidden dynamic of gender inscription in CDCs. To the extent that torture does not happen in a vacuum but is embedded in broader social systems that subordinate some groups (for example, women), then one could argue that torture as a method of subjugation carries the broader social model as an implicit script. That is, in addition to the more direct ways in which gender systems infuse and are reproduced through militarized sexual violence, I argue that gender matters in relation to torture more subtly: even if not containing an explicit sexual component, such violence still incorporates cultural imaginaries associated with embodied experiences that are gendered.

As a practice that takes the body as an intense site of domination, torture overlaps with certain social constructs traditionally associated with femininity, which have been functional to securing women's subordinated place in society and marking them as deviant: (1) the conception of women as *just* bodies, (2) the expectation for women to be hyperaware of their bodies, (3) the construction of women as vulnerable, and (4) the association of women with monstrosity. To be clear, I consider none of these four dimensions as inherently "feminine" but the product of "processes of gender formation, the effects of modes of power that have as one of their aims the production of gender differences along lines of inequality" (Butler 2014, 112). Furthermore, in each case, we can think of gender in intersection with other regimes of power and inequality such as those based on class, race/ethnicity, nationality, sexuality, age, bodily ability/disability, and other social statuses.

While these insights derive from my reading of women survivors' testimonies in light of various feminist literatures, the arguments I advance are meant as a broader commentary on torture that is potentially relevant to people of different genders. I explore how prevailing gender ideologies and hierarchies are part and parcel of the practice of torture, even if as *an implicit script*. Regardless of the perpetrators' intentions, the tactics of bodily oppression implemented in CDCs can be said to re-create and mobilize socially constructed notions of "the feminine," gender scripts that sustain the social subordination of women. At the same time "the feminine" is itself a contested terrain, and the body-oppressive techniques inflicted on detainees were also the grounds for embodied resistance and resilience (this aspect will be analyzed in greater depth in chapter 4).

Just a Body

The construction of detainees in captivity as just bodies was one key method of dehumanization and degradation. The testimonies of survivors show multiple ways in which the persons in captivity were treated as mere things, just flesh at the disposal of repressors. According to feminist theorizing, the reduction of a person to the body or body parts is one important dimension of objectification (e.g., Langton 2005). Susana Jorgelina Ramus talked about the torture and sexual torments inflicted as "all mechanisms of degradation, right? Which somewhat convert you into an object. You are not a person, you are something that they found or something that they captured, and you have to do absolutely everything that they tell you to do, no? Otherwise . . . if you rebel a bit, they kill you, no? Because that was more or less how that worked."

Similarly, survivor Eva Orifici remembered how she and other detainees were treated as a mere pile of bodies when taken to one of the CDCs where she was held, located on a ship, the *Buque Murature*:

> And they transported us in [. . .] a large barge. [. . .] They were shouting [. . .] they had us lined up there. And they pulled you to get you to that

place [. . .] they pushed you. I honestly have images of something very much of . . . groups, no? Like a mass, no? Human beings like a mass that, well, were put there. And they made us lay down [. . .] in fact, we were all on top of each other [. . .] each body on top of the other. There were people who fell into the water there. The screams, the desperation of the one who falls, of the other one who realizes that, of those of us who didn't know what had happened, no?

Eva offered a vivid description of how captive people were treated as just bodies, as piled up things that fall into the water with no significant consequence. Treating prisoners as just bodies meant that their subjectivity, feelings, desires, and biography were to be completely obliterated. As we shall see in the next chapter, this is something that prisoners disrupted and contested in multiple ways, including through gestures of care and solidarity.

The reduction of persons to their bodies through torture and confinement in CDCs was not an exclusive feminine experience. However, being treated as *just* a body is reminiscent of long-standing cultural notions of femininity that conceive "woman as body" (Spelman 1982; Bartky 1990; Bordo 1993). The preeminence of the body (often in contradistinction to the mind) as the supposed definitional quality of women has often been used to suppress women's political voice as a group and as individuals. Furthermore, as feminist works demonstrate, women have been regularly constructed as just bodies, or just body parts, through cultural discourses and practices in various societies. We see this for example in mainstream and pornographic media that portray women as sexual objects, mere bodies for display, or bodies that can be harmed and violated at will. Women are treated as just bodies, or as just reproductive bodies, through laws that continue to criminalize abortion or impinge on contraception use. These are different ways in which women's subjectivity, desires, and self-determination can be shattered or alienated from their bodies.

If we intersect gender with other categories of social location—class, race, ethnicity, sexuality, nation, disability—we can gain a more precise view of which social groups have been particularly likely to be constructed as just bodies (Garland-Thomson 2002). Bodies for display, bodies for labor, bodies for sex, bodies for sale, bodies for rent—this is the stuff of subordinated groups. In various ways, the experience of being treated as just a body, a body with no voice, even a disposable body, overlaps with forms of oppression beyond torture and torments but that are culturally mobilized through the practice. As detainees in clandestine detention were loaded, unloaded, piled up, thrown, displayed, kicked, hanged, and subjected to multiple forms of torture, a form of feminized objectification, which overlaps with certain aspects of life outside the camps, was reinscribed with the specificity that characterized the extreme conditions of clandestine detention. Feminists and other critical scholars have made the connection between the objectification of women's bodies and the creation of a cultural climate amenable to the types of violence that women are disproportionately likely to experience (e.g., Kilbourne and Jhally 2000).

Hyperawareness of the Body

Conditions of torture and captivity can generate a hyperawareness of the body, ways in which the whole of existence becomes dominated by the corporeal. This heightened bodily awareness relates to some of the techniques rampant in the camps, including pain-producing torture that made it impossible for detainees to ignore their bodies as well as methods such as forced nudity that can produce a sense of shame and vulnerability. These circumstances echo Fuchs's (2003) explanation regarding the distinction between the *lived body*—which is the medium through which we experience the world without constant awareness of or reflection about the body itself—and the *corporeal body*, which "appears whenever a reaction or resistance arises to the primary performance of the lived-body; when the body loses its prereflective, automatic coherence with the surrounding world; when our spontaneous bodily expressions are disturbed, blocked, or objectified by an inversion of our attention upon ourselves" (225). Situations in which the corporeal comes into acute self-awareness include (1) "the experience of heaviness, fatigue, injury, or illness: i.e., whenever the lived-body loses its 'taken for granted' carrying role and becomes the sluggish, obstinate or fragile body which 'I have'" (224), and (2) "situations of exposure to the view of others when the body becomes an object for them" (224). These two modes of bringing the corporeal to the fore took place in CDCs through the various techniques of torment applied.

In her account of clandestine detention, Emilce Moler illustrates the centrality of the body during her clandestine detention. She narrates how this "minute to minute" experience was permeated by efforts "to see how to avoid pain from the mark [. . .] in the hand, to see how to make yourself comfortable, that this hurts. The body occupies a very strong place, then it is like you are very obsessed with and very attentive to the corporeal. You can't . . . project." Torture and other torments bind the body to a perpetual present. The constant preoccupation with the body interferes with the ability to plan, implying a reduced horizon of existence. This situation deeply contrasted with Emilce's biography as a lively young woman, an excellent student, and a political activist. Emilce's narrative about the relation between a heightened corporeality and the inability to project is consistent with Fuchs's (2003) assertion about "an alteration in temporality" that accompanies the passage from the *lived* to the *corporeal* body: "spontaneous life, always reaching out for the future, is interrupted, and the subject is suddenly fixed on the present moment or on a lost past" (225).

Emilce's comments about her "obsession" with the body during captivity are also reminiscent of gender differences in body awareness outside of secret prison contexts. Although her awareness was related to the pain of the torments inflicted, there are other ways in which many women are already "used to" being hyperaware of their bodies—be it because of fear of sexual violence, as a response to cultural mandates of femininity (e.g., body posture, appearance), or in relation to reproduction (e.g., menstruation, the possibility of pregnancy). Feminist literature has shown the myriad ways in which women are encouraged to keep track of changes in their bodies, monitor its outward appearance, and regulate its movements (Bartky 1990; Bordo 1993). Increased self-consciousness and reduced bodily satisfaction have also been found among women victims of sexual abuse (Kearney-Cooke and Ackard 2000). Jean Franco (1992, 109) noted this feminizing dimension of captivity in Latin America's Southern Cone clandestine camps of the seventies and eighties. Referring to male prisoners, she said: "[A]bjection often forced male prisoners to live as if they were women, so that, for the first time, they came to understand what it meant to *be constantly aware of their bodies*, to be ridiculed and battered, and to find comfort in everyday activities like washing clothes or talking to friends" (emphasis mine).

While painful torture could surely lead to bodily hyperawareness, simply forcing detainees to strip naked could produce such results in ways that enhanced their suffering. Given that cultural norms about attire and nakedness reserve disrobing for particular situations and settings, most of them intimate, the radical departure from the norm that forced nudity in front of strangers entails can be enough to create a heightened awareness of the body. This dimension also emerged in an interview I conducted for a different project (Sutton 2010) with "Nina," a woman who was held in a CDC in the period leading up to the coup. She emphasized the heightened bodily awareness that forced nudity induced: "I never thought that they would rape me, or anything like that. I did not think about that. Let's say that I didn't have the conscious fantasy, but being naked, it was like being unprotected, like something humiliating, awful, no? . . . It is like you had the whole awareness of your body. I was naked. [I thought], 'I'm here, naked. I'm here, naked.' I don't know how it is. I can't, I can't interpret it, it is the sense that you are there, you are naked, and you are at their mercy" (137).

Although Nina did not have the "conscious fantasy" that nudity could lead to sexual violence, the forced exposure of intimate body parts in front of men she could not see due to a blindfold, and who could do with her whatever they pleased, can be considered a form of sexualized violence in itself. In fact, her mentioning the possibility of rape (even if to say that she did not think about it at the moment of detention) brings to the fore the imagined association between forced nudity and rape. The linkage between forced bodily exposure and sexual degradation or violence was something that could also produce heightened body awareness and prompt prisoners to try to avoid such exposure when possible. Susana Reyes mentioned that she bathed while clothed given the guards' denigrating commentary on women bathing in a space without a door. Nina not only linked the imposition of nudity to an increased body awareness, but also implicitly connected that situation to my next point: the production of vulnerability.

Vulnerability

The whole power imbalance inherent to the dynamics of clandestine detention and the particular body techniques that repressors applied were designed to produce extreme vulnerability in the prisoners, as evidenced by Nina's reference to her being at her captors' mercy. Survivors' testimonies reveal a wide array of techniques designed to produce this effect. Blindfolds and hoods to disorient, shackles to impede movement, disabling torture, the clandestine status of the whole operation, and the arbitrary power that the military enjoyed contributed to the prisoners' sense and reality of being at the mercy of the repressors (even if detainees were sometimes able to leverage individual and collective resources to resist). Elena Lenhardtson, a survivor with a physical disability, recalled the augmented feelings of vulnerability associated with torture: "It is really a feeling of *vejación* [humiliation, mistreatment] and that one is in their hands. So all the time they would tell me, 'Not even Videla [de facto president] will get you out of here, so do not get your hopes up.'"

The vulnerability that Elena describes is the counterpart of the impunity with which repressors operated. This type of magnified vulnerability goes well beyond vulnerability understood as human susceptibility to being affected by others or the interdependence that characterizes social life, or the need for a social and environmental context that supports human existence in its diverse forms (Turner 2006; Butler 2014). The vulnerability that Elena and other former detainees described was, by design, a tool to produce submission and destruction.

The production of vulnerability in clandestine detention can be thought of as another form of feminization, regardless of the gender of the captive. This is the case not because women are inherently more vulnerable than men, but because different societies have discursively and materially placed women in vulnerable conditions. This is historically and culturally variable, and not some sort of essence. As Butler (2014, 111) has argued, "certain kinds of gender-defining attributes, like vulnerability and invulnerability, are distributed unequally under certain regimes of power, and precisely for the purpose of shoring up certain regimes of power that disenfranchise women." Women's bodies in particular have been socially constructed as particularly vulnerable, weak, and in need of protection. Gendered scripts regarding vulnerability have been reproduced through scientific discourse, crime prevention advice, interpersonal interactions and conversation, and the media, among others (Hollander 2001; Campbell 2005).

People in captivity were placed in situations of extreme vulnerability through torture, inadequate food, constraints on movement, and the general debilitation of the body that the conditions of detention generated. These techniques (re)produced attributes associated with femininity in a patriarchal society, such as weakness, helplessness, and vulnerability. Perhaps Elena Lenhardtson's already referenced comment about how she did not cry during her torture session points to one way in which she retained her sense of dignity in a deeply masculinist context, that is, by not showing any sign of so-called feminine weakness. The vulnerability produced in the camps incorporated the gender scripts widely available in society.

In recent years, feminist and other critical scholars have aimed to conceptualize vulnerability in tandem with forms of agency. They have looked at vulnerability as a flexible construct that can be attached to people of different genders and that can be used to define certain populations as particularly "injurable," but that can also be mobilized and be the grounds for resistance (Butler 2014). Marianne Hirsch (2014) notes that we need not contrast vulnerability with invulnerability, but rather could pair it with resilience. In that sense, the body stories of women in this study speak not only of imposed conditions of extreme vulnerability but also of the resilience necessary to survive as well as of concrete instances of resistance.

Monstrosity

Torture not only creates vulnerability, but can also radically transform bodies. It can produce bodies that do not conform to normative standards and that elicit shock and horror—in other words, bodies that may be socially perceived as monstrous. The effects of torture and captivity were sometimes evidenced in drastic signs of aging, rapid loss of weight, disfigurement, and more or less temporary disabilities (e.g., impairment of body parts or organs, inability to walk as a result of torture). In addition to almost losing a hand due to the brutal treatment she suffered, Rita Cordero de Garnica mentioned that in ten days of detention her hair had turned white. Similarly, Iris Avellaneda recounted how even though at the time of her detention she was thirty-eight years old, she ended up looking like *una vieja* (a hag) in a very short time. Fátima

Cabrera left clandestine detention with her "body full of stripes" as a result of the picana. Santina Mastinú remembered: "my face was there to be disfigured, the way they left it, you know?" Isabel Fernández Blanco narrated how another detainee described her appearance after having been severely beaten up: "you were a monster."

The figure of the monster has a long tradition in Western thought, bringing up sticky "questions of identity and membership" in a political community and about the boundaries between human/nonhuman (Shanks 2015, 455; see also Shildrick 2002). While writings in this tradition focus on people born with "physical or mental anomalies and disabilities" (Shanks 2015, 456), the case of torture raises questions about the social production of "monstrous" bodies through the infliction of deliberate harm. Here a question that arises is how to denounce these actions without reproducing an ableist stance or one that upholds only normative bodies. Focusing especially on disability, Rosemarie Garland-Thomson (2002, 8–9) analyzes how the monstrous body often intersects with categories of Otherness based on gender, race, class, sexuality, and disability: "The historical figure of the monster [. . .] invokes disability, often to serve racism and sexism. Although the term has expanded to encompass all forms of social and corporeal aberration, *monster* originally described people with congenital impairments. As departures from the normatively human, monsters were seen as category violations or grotesque hybrids." What does it mean that the military regime produced "grotesque" bodies through the brutal treatment of detainees? How did this practice relate to existing systems of power and inequality, and how did it contribute to upholding the boundaries between "us" and "them" that undergirded the dictatorship's annihilation enterprise?

Through the infliction of torture and torments, detainees' bodies could become monstrous, estranged, difficult to recognize. In an interview for the TV program *Historias Debidas* (2014), journalist and survivor Lila Pastoriza indirectly speaks to this point by recounting a disturbing dream she had: She was in some sort of surgery room or clinic with white artificial light; she saw herself in a mirror, and her face looked strange, with bruises and stains. She didn't look like herself, and this provoked great anguish in her. To her relief, a compañero firmly assured her, "You are Lila." While this was a dream, the story does point to the very real temporary or permanent bodily alterations that many detainees experienced because of torture as well as how these dramatic physical changes could produce a sense of estrangement: this monstrous body is not me (though it is me).

The production of "monstrosity" can be said to be one way in which Otherness was imprinted on the bodies of detainees, and this Otherness includes femininity as an implicit script. Feminist scholars point to the cultural association between the construction of femininity and the realm of the monstrous, of abjection (Shildrick 2002; Ussher 2006). Barbara Creed (1986) and Rosi Braidotti (1997) recount how women's sexual difference itself has been culturally conceived as monstrous, a deviation from the normative (male) body. Braidotti (1997) chronicles the linkage between femininity and monstrosity in Western science, literature, and philosophy, noting the persistent "*topos* of women as a sign of abnormality, and therefore of difference as a mark of inferiority" (63): "The theme of woman as devalued difference remained a constant in Western thought; in philosophy especially, 'she' is forever associated to unholy, disorderly, subhuman, and unsightly phenomena. It is as if 'she' carried within herself something that makes her prone to being an enemy of mankind, and outsider in her civilization, an 'other.' It is important to stress the light that psychoanalytic theory has cast upon this hatred for the feminine and the traditional patriarchal association of women with monstrosity" (64).

It is significant that the notions that Braidotti refers to include the construction of the deviant body/woman as the "enemy of mankind," someone in the outskirts of "civilization." Such attributes are often ascribed to political dissidents, and in the case of Argentina, the military regime articulated a systematic plan to eliminate the perceived enemies of the nation, the Others who threatened "Western and Christian Civilization." In a sense, the production of monstrous bodies through torture was one way of creating a dehumanized Other. While it may be argued that the military picked up people already seen as subversive Others, it can also be argued that torture branded monstrosity on the flesh, producing Others who did not belong to the body politic, a "grotesque enemy" who could be readily eliminated (Alexander 2005, 239). In the case of women, such actions reinscribed a monstrous femininity already in the margins or excluded from the body politic. In some ways women were even more "monstrous" than men in captivity, both in terms of the bodily effects of torture and in terms of their having been branded as subversives. Their "disfigured" bodies violated norms of feminine appearance and their "subversiveness" (engagement in political activities, raising "subversive" children, etc.) meant that they were disobedient of the gender order, that they embodied a particularly monstrous femininity in their deviation from the norm.

* * *

The four modes in which gender scripts are mobilized through torture—the production of just bodies, bodily hyperawareness, vulnerability, and monstrosity—are not discrete but discursively and materially interrelated. The repressive state power that aimed to reduce captive persons to mere bodies without voice used degradation techniques that made it difficult for the targeted persons to ignore their bodies. In turn, the conditions of detention generated extreme forms of vulnerability as well as "monstrous" bodies. In fact, while the figure of the monster elicits fear and a sense of threat, monstrosity can also be linked to vulnerability (Shildrick 2002). Monsters are liable to being harmed and having their bodies placed on display, prodded, scrutinized, and regulated by various institutions and discourses (including state, medical, and religious practices and ideas). The monster's radical Otherness is perceived as a sign of inferiority and is constituted as a threat, and as such it is crisscrossed by various axes of difference and inequality such as gender, race/ethnicity, and disability. The four dimensions of torture and torments I have discussed help reveal how social constructs associated with femininity are inscribed in these practices.

Conclusion

Following Cynthia Enloe's gender analysis in *Seriously!* (2013, 15), one may argue that paying attention to torture and other forms of violence against women in clandestine detention is vital for at least two reasons: (1) for these women's "own sake," as their lives are important in their own right, and (2) in terms of how such acts of violence reveal the centrality of gender—including cultural constructions of femininity and masculinity—to the operations of state power. We see how the repressive apparatus mobilized the utility and disposability of the gendered female body in order to achieve systematic state goals and to reproduce a broader regime of power in society that rested on heteropatriarchal norms. The narratives of women survivors illustrate how pervasive gender ideologies "gelled" with the military's political aims, contributing to victimizing women in gender-specific ways but also inscribing gender on a wide set of oppressive practices that could potentially "feminize" victims of all genders.

These operations of state power relied on raw forms of bodily control as a privileged tactic. In the age of "disciplinary power" (Foucault 1989), which characterizes various aspects of Argentine society, testimonies such as those in this study also call attention to the continued significance of repressive forms of power directed to the body in modernity. In the case of women, direct, repressive, and coercive attacks on the body have never been quite superseded by disciplinary regimes (as evidenced by sexual violence, domestic violence, and feminicide both during states of exception and in other times) (Sutton 2010). Not surprisingly, the kinds of normalized sexual violence that women have been disproportionately likely to experience—before, during, and after the dictatorship—were also widespread in CDCs.

In the following chapter, I continue my analysis of body narratives exploring how women deployed different embodied tactics and mechanisms to cope with and resist the conditions of captivity. While a number of these practices involved people of different genders, some of these acts entail distinctly gendered meanings and performances that include normative notions of femininity, sexuality, and motherhood.

4

Body, Survival, Resistance, and Memory

The bodies of women in captivity were not merely passive targets of torture, violation, and other forms of oppression. The very conditions of vulnerability generated in clandestine detention centers (CDCs) and the multiple ways in which detainees' bodies took center stage were also the grounds for embodied resilience, agency, and even outright resistance (see also Doyle 2001). The testimonies of the women in this study reveal various instances of embodied agency under conditions that would otherwise allow none. However, as Bacci et al. (2012, 14) note, underscoring these expressions of agency does not diminish in any way the recognition of the atrocities committed against women in captivity. Nor is it meant to suggest that detainees had control over their chances of survival. Instead, I draw on notions of agency that do not see it as the diametrical opposite of coercion, but that recognize the social constraints that characterize a person's ability to act (Madhok, Phillips, and Wilson 2013; see also Macón 2014). That is, agency can occur in the absence of the autonomous individual idealized in liberal conceptions of the self. Madhok, Phillips, and Wilson (2013, 7) remark "that agency is always exercised within constraints, that inequality is an ever-present component, and that the constraints relate to social, not just personal, power relations." Even those placed in situations of extreme vulnerability in the context of armed violence and war may exercise what Alcinda Honwana (2006) calls "tactical agency," a very limited form of agency, or "agency of the weak" (73).[1]

Furthermore, following scholars such as Saba Mahmood (2001) and Roberta Villalón (2010), a distinction can be made between agency and resistance, which becomes useful in trying to disentangle survivors' actions within the constraints of clandestine detention. Mahmood (2001, 203) defines agency as a "capacity for action" that is embedded within historically specific relations of power, and that may or may not be directed at challenging social hierarchies or structures of domination. Likewise, drawing on Mahmood's definition, Villalón (2010, 553) makes the case that "agency does not always equate resistance—that is, expressed by breaking free from oppressive conditions [. . .]—but may instead be compliant—that is, expressed by following norms, rules, regulations, ideals, and expectations. [. . .] Lastly, agency may be the result of conscious, strategic planning [. . .] but also, agency may be unintended." According to these conceptualizations, even if some actions may not be characterized as resistance, there may still be agency and not necessarily passivity.

Detainees' responses to the extreme conditions of captivity were rather complex and do not always fit into neat modes of classification. For instance, it is debatable whether all the detainees' actions that contributed to their survival were forms of resistance, or whether some may be better described, for example, as "compliant" forms of agency (Villalón 2010, 553) or "accommodation" (Weitz 2001, 670). Jocelyn Hollander and Rachel Einwohner's (2004) review of the literature on resistance shows the disparate kinds of behaviors that scholars have described as resistance, including those more or less coordinated; physical or symbolic; verbal or silent; and directed to individuals, institutions, or larger systems. They identify, however, two core dimensions of resistance: "action" (defined in a broad way) and "opposition" (in the sense of countering, challenging, transgressing, or disrupting the powers that be) (538). In contrast, "recognition" and "intent" were areas of disagreement in the literature (539).

Here, I use the term "resistance" as encompassing a variety of actions (visible or imperceptible; physical, verbal, or cognitive; individual or group-based) that were aimed at frustrating or disrupting the will of the captors, that purposely transgressed the norms of the camps, and/or that explicitly or implicitly countered the grip of the regime. Some of these actions were not necessarily recognized as transgressive by the captors, but still circumvented the rules and impositions of the camps. In fact, out of necessity, many of these actions had to be kept covert. Thus, a broad definition of resistance seems the most apt to characterize the range of oppositional and transgressive acts that detainees undertook. At the same time, as Hollander and Einwohner (2004) remind us, intent can be difficult to assess, as intent might not be easily inferred based on the nature of the act itself. Furthermore, we should also consider the possibility that ostensibly compliant agency (e.g., following the rules) may be used as a means toward a resistant end (e.g., surviving and denouncing the conditions of captivity).

Building on these concepts, this chapter highlights the role of the body in detainees' actions that resisted and/or accommodated to the rules of the camps in order to survive. The extremely coercive and violent context of the torture camps certainly limited detainees' capacity to act. Yet, under the concepts outlined above, the analysis of coercive conditions imposed on captive women's bodies need not impede detecting agency, and even outright resistance, as well. In an essay exploring vulnerability and resistance, Judith Butler (2014, 107) speaks to this tension: the "confined body does not always have the freedom to move, but can it still make use of its confinement to express resistance?" In a similar vein, Ewa Płonowska Ziarek (2008)—who engages Agamben's notion of "bare life" as a life "[s]tripped of political significance and exposed to murderous violence" (90)—asks "whether bare life itself can be mobilized by emancipatory movements" (89). These questions encourage us to examine how the vulnerability of the confined body might be mobilized to confront daunting power structures and how, even under regimes that treat prisoners as "bare life" (Agamben 1998), overt and almost imperceptible sites of resistance may still be carved out.

In the context of the Argentine torture camps, Bacci et al. (2012, 71) talk about the *resquicios para la resistencia*, or the small openings for resistance that women survivors narrated, including collective actions to impede sexual abuse. Given the tight control and severe forms of punishment that the repressive regime exerted in different secret prisons, detainees often had to struggle to create even minute spaces of transgression. While in very rare cases a few people managed to escape from CDCs, most captives had no chance of undertaking such feats.[2] More common were diverse forms of micro resistance: lifting one's hood to see the surroundings, lending a comforting hand to a fellow captive, making sounds to communicate with other detainees, sharing food and other objects that sometimes circulated in the camps, remembering the address or names of other detainees to be able to denounce their detention later, and many others. Any and all forms of micro resistance were liable to be met with brutal forms of retaliation and punishment, and thus entailed considerable risk.

Some expressions of agency and resistance in CDCs were very subtle and derived directly from the instruments designed to heighten detainees' embodied suffering. This is akin to what Laura Doyle (2001, 78) calls a "paradoxical carnal logic" in the sense that "bodily vulnerability founds resistance, weakness forms the ground of defiance." For instance, Marta García de Candeloro remembered her transgressive use of the hood—a paradigmatic instrument of dehumanization. The hood was meant to deprive detainees of sight, causing a sense of disorientation and isolation. Instead of conceptualizing the hood as a mere tool of oppression, Marta also experienced it as an object that afforded her a certain degree of freedom, the possibility to do what she wanted behind the hood without the control of the repressors: "[You could] shed tears, you could laugh, you could feel that it was you from there inward" (see also Bacci et al. 2012, 39). This usage of the hood contradicted the goal of total subjugation implemented by the regime. Marta pointed out that sometimes repressors and guards "perhaps could not stand not seeing your face, and they would take the hood off. They were the ones who could not bear it. Because in some way, I believe that [they] perceived the world that was built behind [the hood], based on a physical element like the hood." Marta also described the heightening of senses other than sight in response to the forced use of the hood (see also Salerno 2009). Given the restrictions on her ability to see, she started to rely on senses such as touch and sound to grasp her surroundings. She talked about how she "discovered the world of textures [rugosidades]" and how "voices became important." Later on, survivors drew on subtle sensory memories as a resource to identify or describe places of confinement—that is, these memories were incorporated into acts of denunciation, showing the extended temporality of some forms of resistance.

In CDCs, people sometimes coped and endured even despite themselves; the wish or resignation to die in the face of atrocious treatment did cross the mind of some survivors. At the same time, various forms of "clinging to life," as Marta García de Candeloro put it, were also described in the narratives. Raquel Odasso, who was captured by repressors in Uruguay,[3] spoke in ways that illustrate the coexistence between the resignation to die and the will to survive: "They would tell us, 'You'll be dead by Christmas.' [. . .] I felt that, yes, they could really do that. [. . .] It was like you accepted it, [. . .] there's no other way because you are in their hands." Yet, Raquel also spoke of tactics to hold on to life: "[I thought] of my family, I thought about what I believed in, about what we were seeking, about what we aspired to as well. All those things, I don't know, I don't know if we were a bit crazy [laughs], but they really gave us strength, they gave us strength."

As a whole, the testimonies show variation between camps, between the treatment of different people within the same camp, and in the experience of the same individuals at different points in time. Thus, detainees deployed tactics of survival adapting to particular contexts, which entailed finding ways to protect the physical body, preserve the psyche, deal with attacks to personal dignity and/or sexual integrity, and establish connections with other detainees when possible. In some cases, enduring the oppressive conditions meant "leaving the body," so to speak. That is, painful and degrading attacks on detainees' bodies through torments and torture prompted some people in captivity to "flee" the body during moments of extreme suffering (Calveiro 1998; Doyle 2001; Bacci et al. 2012). In this way, they were able to somewhat circumvent the pain inflicted or escape to "another dimension," as survivor Liliana Callizo put it, to evade from the horrific realities of clandestine detention.

The camps involved extreme situations of bodily vulnerability and destruction as well as repeated attacks on whatever psychological and emotional resources detainees might have had. In order to understand this heightened vulnerability and the significance of even minute forms of resistance, it is important to understand the body as always *in relation*. Judith Butler (2014, 103) elaborates on this relational dimension of bodily existence, which is critical to grasp notions of vulnerability— even in everyday life and beyond situations of extreme confinement: "[T]he body, despite its clear boundaries, or perhaps precisely by virtue of those very boundaries, is defined by the relations that makes its own life and action possible. [. . .] [W]e cannot understand bodily vulnerability outside of this conception of its constitutive relations to other humans, living processes, and inorganic conditions and vehicles for living." The vulnerability of people in CDCs was produced and augmented to the extreme through the severing of vital forms of human connection. Isolation, hooding, bans on communication and solidarity among detainees, and disconnection from the outside world were among the methods for breaking the relational ties that characterize social worlds and that are important for individual survival and development. Another marker of vulnerability is signified when survivors point out that they were completely *in the hands* of repressors. In the context of the camps, this bodily metaphor means to be at their mercy, with a strong possibility of being harmed. However, in a different context it could mean to be under someone's care, evoking the double meaning of vulnerability as the possibility of either support or harm.[4]

Detainees' survival tactics under such vulnerable conditions—including the extreme experience of bodily torture—cannot be placed into rigid categories, such as those pertaining to heroes or traitors, which have been used to either romanticize or blame various people (Calveiro 1998; Longoni 2007). As several survivors' testimonies show, the camps were full of complex responses to the conditions of captivity. Elena Lenhardtson recounted:

> [T]he *vejamen* [humiliation, mistreatment] of the body is something very hard—that *vejamen* of the self and the feeling that one has no way out, that one is completely in their hands, and that this can grow and grow. [. . .] People are so harsh with people who collaborated or broke down. . . . There I learned that I did not know whether I cou– . . . how much I would resist, which is something so personal, and so, I don't know, about the defenses that one has, beyond the convictions, the ideals, or what one is. I think there is a moment when one is so devoid of everything, of all . . . care, when one has the feeling that there's nothing that will offer protection, and one doesn't know how, what's going to happen to oneself, no? Or until when one will be able to resist. [. . .] I realized that I struggled for my dignity when I said [to the repressors], "Don't touch me, I will move myself." But I did not know for how long that would last, and for how long they would accept it.

Elena's words remind us that detainees were human beings with strengths, weaknesses, and resources and placed in impossible situations that hinged on radical forms of bodily degradation and suffering. When asked about how she was able to endure her torture without giving away any information, Haydée Fernández—a lawyer with a background as a political activist—responded that what sustained her was the commitment to prevent others from going through the torments to which she was subjected. However, she also explained that her experience in captivity led to a significant shift in her perspective: "Look, in the past I used to be very harsh with respect to torture and the people who sang [gave away information under torture]. [. . .] It was very difficult for me to change. How did I change? When I saw the magnitude of the tortures and when I saw that torture places you somewhere in the limits between reason and madness." The extreme forms of bodily and psychological vulnerability produced in clandestine detention are impossible to fathom for those who did not have such experience. It might also be difficult to understand detainees' reactions and responses. However, listening to these testimonies is still necessary both on ethical grounds and as an exercise of collective memory.

In this chapter, I analyze how women coped with, negotiated, and resisted different aspects of the coercive conditions they were in, paying particular attention to the role of the body in such dynamics. First, I explore various ways in which women left, split, and performed the body/self, including through evasion, dissociation, and tactical performances of femininity and emotions. I then turn to practices of care, solidarity, and resistance through the lens of the body—from micro and almost imperceptible gestures of embodied resistance to more overt or organized forms of embodied support among fellow captives. I note how the body often became a privileged conduit of solidarity, even in the absence of speech: a kiss, a feeding hand, a hand that stroked the shoulder, and a hand that literally held another body were all forms of embodied connection that helped assert the humanity of those involved. Indeed, a different meaning of *being in others' hands* emerges here, this time linked to embodied care and solidarity. These were small gestures but significant enough to be mentioned in the narratives survivors offered many years later. Finally, the body also functioned as a carrier of memory, both based on the specific sensory information generated in the camps and based on the more or less tangible bodily sequelae that detainees had to live with after their release. These sensory recollections and bodily marks became not just sources or reminders of suffering, but an opportunity to exercise agency and denounce state terror. Body memories served to narrate state repression in various spaces, blurring the private/public dichotomy (Bacci et al. 2014).

How did women survivors narrate embodied survival and resistance? What is the significance of these narratives to memory making? What is at stake in remembering even seemingly small gestures of care and solidarity? What role did gender play in various forms of embodied agency? In the following pages, I explore multiple ways in which women survivors inhabited and dis-inhabited the body/self, established "intercorporeal" connections with other detainees (Doyle 2001, 91), and mustered overt and covert tactics for enduring and confronting the power of the repressive apparatus. These were practices of both the possible and the impossible, situated within the confines of a system designed to impede any kind of opposition.

Leaving, Splitting, and Performing the Body/Self

The diverse forms of embodied survival and resistance narrated in the testimonies speak to the malleability of mind/body configurations in conditions of extreme violence and oppression. I analyze these situations in light of the feminist critique of the mind/body dualisms that have characterized hegemonic Western understandings of the self. According to Elizabeth Grosz, among dominant perspectives are conceptions of the body as "an instrument, a tool, or a machine at the disposal of consciousness, a vessel occupied by an animating, willful subjectivity" (Grosz 1994, 8).[5] Feminist scholars and activists have challenged dichotomies privileging the mind over the body, including as a source of knowledge (e.g., Jaggar and Bordo 1989; Grosz 1994; Tuana 2001). They also note that men have been culturally associated with the first term and women with the second one. In order to counter dichotomous understandings of mind and body, feminists developed alternative conceptualizations. Elizabeth Grosz (1994, xii), for example, offered the metaphor of the Möbius strip, "the inverted three dimensional figure eight," to argue that "[b]odies and minds are not two distinct substances or two kinds of attributes of a single substance but somewhere in between these two alternatives." Grosz adds that the Möbius strip helps to represent "the inflection of mind into body and body into mind, the ways in which, through a kind of twisting or inversion, one side becomes another" (xii).

While the challenge to binaries—including mind/body—has been a significant theoretical and epistemological intervention from feminist and other critical theorists, it is also important to note that extreme forms of oppression, in tandem with cultural assumptions about the mind/body divide, can encourage dichotomous understandings of the self, at least temporarily. In such contexts, the splitting of the mind from the body and the person's ability to locate the self in the mind can function as a mechanism of survival. Without intending to reinscribe the binary, I want to point out that this dualism operates in the way some survivors remember and describe their attempts to cope with and survive horror. Perhaps precisely because detainees were often treated as *just bodies* (as described in chapter 3), one way to counter this was some detainees' ability to "leave" the objectified, degraded, and suffering body and instead situate agency and subjectivity in the mind. In this way, they turned the repressors' strategy around. However, as Laura Doyle (2001, 82) argues, this might not be simply a reproduction of the Cartesian mind/body dichotomy. Referring to Jacobo Timerman—also a survivor of an Argentine CDC—Doyle describes a more complex dynamic in his withdrawal from the body and engagement in intense "mental labor" during his detention (82): "The very word 'with-drawal' indicates a pulling-with, a struggle *with* that assumes the countervailing presence of his body—a presence that must remain in order for him to return or, in other words, to survive the electric shocks and the blows. That is, to live *through* the torture he escapes into a mental elsewhere, but to effect this escape he implicitly counts on returning to himself 'here'" (83).

Leaving the body, so to speak, is not a complete detachment of the self from the body but a move that relates to the human power of the imagination to produce alternate worlds—even from the location of a body that has been terrorized and severely harmed. Bacci et al. (2012, 80) note that among the various coping and resistance practices by women in the CDCs in Argentina were those that involved splitting mind and body in order to dissociate from horrific experiences of clandestine detention. Citing survivor and scholar Pilar Calveiro, they suggest that these "modes of fleeing" the scene allowed detainees to create a somewhat protected space in the midst of horror. Julieta Lampasona (2015) points out that even though this type of phenomenon can be considered "'impossible,' that is, the separation of the subject from [her or his] own self, from [her or his] own body" (n.p.), "this splitting—even if it were imaginary—has the effect of truth: at the moment of torture it apparently helped to tolerate it, at the moment of evocation it merges in the configuration of the experience itself" (n.p.).

We can think of practices involving varying levels of detachment from the body or previous sense of self as a spectrum: from ways of "leaving" the body through evasion or dissociation to embodied performances of self. These tactical performances included the enactment of particular modes of femininity and displays of certain emotions/non-emotions in order to avoid the wrath of repressors and to maximize survival chances. Although these performances could be said to belong to a different category of action, I include them in the spectrum of survival mechanisms pertaining to malleable mind/body configurations because they also entailed a certain level of alienation or detachment from the embodied self, at least as previously lived and experienced by the person involved. These tactical performances entailed the creation of a character that suited the repressors' expectations, and as such, it meant inhabiting the body in ways that disengaged from the person which that body/self had been. However, this self-preservation tactic could be a double-edge sword. The repeated enactment of certain behaviors and emotions could become a kind of "deep acting" (Hochschild 2003, 35) that potentially made it difficult for the performers to ascertain the separation between performance and their own sense of authentic self.[6] Tactical performances, evasions, and dissociations are part of a complex repertoire of survival in the camps.

Evasions and Dissociations

Evasions and dissociations included a variety of voluntary and involuntary practices. One of the most direct attempts to leave the body, or at least to inhabit it from an altered state of consciousness, consisted in some detainees' efforts to sleep as much as possible. This evasion tactic was aimed at avoiding the horrific reality of the camp. Susana Caride—survivor of El Banco, El Olimpo, and Escuela de Mecánica de la Armada (ESMA)—mentioned the devastating effects of torture and how her emotional state during detention was dominated by wondering, "When is this going to end?" She reported how she "tried to sleep, and slept as much time as possible, so that time passed as fast as possible until the time they would come fetch you." Similarly, Graciela García recounted how sleeping was a common response among women who had been forced to have sexual contact with repressors including during the pseudo-dates arranged by ESMA officers in hotels or apartments:

> I remember that some compañeras returned from this type of situation, and they would get in bed and sleep the whole day. [. . .] You know, sleeping was something fairly important. I had insomnia at one time and that was distressing, because sleeping allowed you to evade. It was the only real, possible and certain, evasion that you had in there. So there were compañeras who slept the whole day. Because when you would open your eyes, you would again see the nightmare represented, to be there. When you were asleep, you would get out of there. So being asleep was one of the few situations that . . . [was] pleasurable, to put it in some way.

In Graciela's account, the nightmare was constituted by the waking hours while sleeping could provide a measure of relief. Therefore, insomnia deprived her from this coping tactic. To enable this resource, some detainees tried to exert whatever leverage they had based on their observations of how the camp functioned. Adriana Friszman reported how at the ESMA there were "guards who were very, very wicked, very violent, so when the guards were violent people resorted to sedatives. They took things to sleep, they asked the nurse" who did the rounds. In this way, detainees used this resource to temporarily leave the reality of the camp, leaving the body behind. At the same time, sleeping can be thought of not only as a form of escape, but as a way to take care of the self by restoring bodily balance and strength. In this sense, sophisticated forms of "clean" torture used in contemporary armed conflicts, such as sleep deprivation, deprive prisoners of not only a basic human physical need but also one possible coping mechanism in response to atrocious conditions.

Besides sleeping, there were other ways of transporting the self to a different space and time, which could also involve a more or less altered state of consciousness, but that relied on the human powers of the imagination and fantasy. For example, Viviana Nardoni narrated her experience in La Calamita, one of the detention camps where she was held, as follows: "I was sort of delirious in that place, right? I remember that in those long hours that I was lying on the mattress, waiting to see what happened to our lives, I thought about what I'd do when I got out of there. [...] And I thought, 'Oh, I would like to learn to play the guitar.' See how crazy. I needed to think about things absolutely removed from that reality that I did not understand, and that horrified me and that ... I needed to isolate myself from absolutely everything." In retrospect, Viviana seemed surprised about her thoughts while in detention ("See how crazy"). She tried to make sense of a world that was unintelligible to her during her captivity and afterward. Her body was forced to immobility, but in some way she could escape, and even dream with a space of learning and creativity. The brutal physical conditions of the camp often included immobilization through shackles and/or through isolated confinement of the body in small spaces. In such situations, a mind/body separation could be functional for prisoners to exercise a certain level of autonomy in a context meant to completely destroy it. Marta García de Candeloro expressed how in the absence of body movement, prisoners could still move through the mind: "So, if they block your view so you cannot handle yourself, so that you are totally disconcerted; if you cannot walk, if you cannot move—and besides, you can't move due to the effects of torture—you move mentally [makes hand gesture pointing to the temple]. Without realizing it, your exercise you own motility, mentally."

The women in this study also reported other body/mind mechanisms that resulted in seemingly strange or surprising configurations of the self at particular moments, including modes of dissociation. I am using the term "dissociation" broadly to include various forms of disengagement from or splitting of the self/body as a response to or defense against experiences of terror.[7] Among other things, these mechanisms point to how different parts of the body are culturally invested with meaning in particular sociohistorical contexts. For instance, when Marta Bianchi was taken to a CDC, another form of splitting of the body/self occurred as she interacted with a repressor:

My body was divided in two parts. From the waist up, I spoke very firmly, with much authority. I looked at him in the eye—something that irritated him a lot—and he started screaming, "Lower your gaze, *zurda de mierda* [fucking leftist]," and so on, "You are worse than the other." But I felt that I had to try to not show how afraid I was, and defend my dignity as much as I could. But from the waist down—it had also happened the first time

I gave birth—my body started shaking, and my legs were shaking. So I would hold my legs strongly so that they would not see it. And they were two . . . my body had dissociated in two [parts].

Marta's account reveals gendered dimensions to the splitting of the self/ body: the authoritative and outwardly fearless body speaks to the male repressor as an equal; the shaking and uncontrollable body evokes the eminently feminine experience of birth giving. We see here that the repressor tried to reduce Marta to her supposedly natural state of femininity, to a fearful body socially mandated to be submissive: "Lower your gaze," he said. Marta's bodily split was one way in which she responded to the power dynamics of the camp. Was she also implicitly resisting her imposed subordination as a woman?

In the context of talking with other survivors about physical pain and other disturbing sensations surrounding torture, Miriam Lewin (Actis et. al 2001, 74) recounted a different kind of splitting: "I would leave my body and look at it from outside. [. . .] It is a defense mechanism." Similarly, Liliana Callizo—who denounced torments including rape— recounted how she tried to protect her "head" despite the awful violence inflicted on her "body" (see also Bacci et al. 2012, 79). She mentioned how she was "completely disconnected" and had "separated head from body." Liliana explained: "'They cannot capture my head.' I mean, I was more concerned about the head than the body." Liliana's use of the word "head" points to how the head is culturally invested as the locus of the *mind*. The mind is in turn construed as a realm of freedom, a presence that may wander around and escape oppression. Liliana's "head"/mind was the space to which repressors had no access, and as such was important for preserving her own sense of self. While here head seems to signify mind (almost as a separate entity), the use of the term "head" throws into relief a corporeal organization that is culturally and historically inflected—the head is actually part of the body and socially endowed with particular meaning and value. Even as the head is invoked to signify an entity that can disconnect or separate, head—in its inseparability from the living body—defies the mind/body dichotomy, bringing the mind back to the body.

Situating the self in the head/mind seemingly allowed Liliana to somewhat escape from the painful reality of the place in which her body was situated. Still, she also recognized that this move could also carry costs: "I endured a long time like that. Even when I left [the CDC], it was very hard for me to land on reality, because as a self-defense, I decided to live in another dimension." In this and the previous passages, we see that Liliana tried to locate herself elsewhere—not in her mistreated body, not in the horrific place of clandestine detention. However, Liliana's narrative also suggests that the ability to *return* that Doyle (2001) mentions cannot be taken for granted, as there could be lingering effects to the "withdrawal" from the body, even if it constitutes a "withdrawal that for the terrorized body is survival, *is* resistance" (84).

Moments of extreme pain and terror, like those exerted during torture sessions, were especially ripe for the kinds of split of the body/self that some survivors reported. Norma Berti spoke of this in the context of reporting how during her torments she completely forgot sensitive information, for example, related to planned meetings with fellow activists.[8] She said, "I forgot everything, I forgot absolutely everything. I had a kind of schizophrenia, no? A split, I don't know, of things. . . . Between the fright, the tension, and the physical pain. Besides, at one moment I feel the smell of burnt flesh, and I realize that it was me the one being burnt practically." In the "split" that Norma reported, an underlying oppositional current can be detected in the sense that her "forgetting" ran counter to the intent of her captors to produce information. At the same time, another form of splitting seemed to take place: a momentary unawareness of what was happening to *her* body, a kind of disconnection between her bodily sensations and the practices that were producing the burnt smell, almost as if the odor came from elsewhere.

The numbing of physical sensations such as pain—which also implies a kind of detachment from what was happening to the body—was sometimes reported in relation to torture or other brutal treatment. In a way, this type of reaction frustrated or countered the repressors' intent: to cause pain as punishment or for information extraction. For instance, Isabel Fernández Blanco recounted:

> I think that at one moment I really stopped feeling. At one moment, my body could not withstand it. When the Turco Julián [a repressor] was hitting me—he hit me, hit me, hit me—I did not feel pain, right? What happened is that at one moment I could not get up from the floor. And I

stayed there on the floor, and he continued kicking me, hitting me, and I stayed there like . . . like dead, right? But I have no register of the pain. [. . .] [Another woman detainee] told me, "I can't understand how you did not feel the pain." I tell her, "No, no, I don't feel pain." And even today she continues remembering that image saying, "You were a monster, the way you were," no? I. . . . Luckily there were no mirrors [laughs], so I don't have the memory neither of the monstrosity of my face nor of pain.

In this case, the register of pain was blocked *at the time* in which the aggression was perpetrated, which in turn precluded memory of the pain.

However, other women seem to have blocked the *memory* of the act or of the pain that torture practices and other abusive conduct must have elicited. It is hard to know how the women felt at the moment of occurrence because they cannot remember. For example, Eva Orifici, who was badly hurt, reported: "[T]he compañeros told me that I was being hit on the head, [the repressors] grabbed me, lifted me, and *bang* the head against something. I do not remember, frankly, I do not remember." Here both the violence and the pain are blocked, though perhaps the reason for not remembering is a loss of consciousness at the moment of the events. In other cases the aggression on the body was remembered, but not the pain. For instance, in recalling the experience of torture, Munú Actis explained: "I mean, if I internalize what is an electric discharge on a body [she touches her head] and I can remember . . . I remember the arching of the body, but I cannot remember feeling the pain that that provokes. That is, I cannot experience the pain. I cannot experience the pain, I cannot experience the anguish, probably the *terror*—because it is not possible to feel otherwise—but these are all theoretical things, in some way. That is, I know that these things no doubt existed."

In Munú's narrative, dissociation appears as an ex post facto way of dealing with the traumatic situation experienced. Munú assumed that she had felt physical pain and terror during the episodes of torture, but could not fully remember: "I remember very little about the torture experience. I mean, it is not that I remember very little, I remember a lot, but I remember in the only way that I still can, no? [. . .] I remember in a very dissociated manner. [. . .] I mean, I cannot get myself inside that tortured body. [. . .] I am there in a confusing thing, inside, outside, because I have some sensation, but evidently not all." In blocking the memory of what were likely extremely painful sensations, the complex self/body relation is once again thrown into relief: Where is the self located in relation to the body, its sensations, its history? The tortured body is part of the history of those who had the experience, but perhaps the self cannot go on with the full embodied weight of that history.

Other forms of body/self splitting involved the numbing of emotions. If emotions are intricately linked to embodied experience, such emotional numbing also implies a deadened body housing a detached self. Susana Muñoz, however, asserted that this dissociation mechanism "saved" her. This is similar to other testimonies that referred to self-defense. In Susana's case, this consisted of emotional detachment from the brutalities she had experienced during her detention, and even from recognizing that her treatment was indeed atrocious. After her kidnapping and clandestine detention she was transferred to the legal prison system, where other prisoners encouraged her to reconnect with her experience of clandestine detention so as to help her process the trauma. After her emotionless response to the death of another prisoner, a small group of incarcerated women invited her to sit down and told her:

> "You see that you do not react, [...] you do not laugh, you do not cry ... nothing, you are not [present]." So they started to [...] give me a psychological treatment so that I would realize that I had been disconnected, which was a defense mechanism—which saved me. So, well, they forced me to recognize that I had been beaten up, which was another kind of torture but it was torture, that the isolation during fourteen days in a wet cell, alone, all that is torture. Not to me, because since it was not picana, it was not torture, see? They tried to bring me back, but I don't know where I was; really, I was very, very disconnected.

Here again we see a kind of split in the way Susana described her state of being: almost a body without self to the extent that the "I" had somewhat detached and needed to be brought back. The solidarity of other imprisoned women helped in the process.

The preceding narratives show a variety of ways of "splitting" or dissociating. Marta García de Candeloro, survivor and psychologist, articulated the following interpretation regarding the adaptive qualities of survivors' responses: "[I]t was an extreme situation that was unknown and where the human being [. . .] would start using defense mechanisms that in another context one may regard as sick, but which in that context were healthy mechanisms to avoid falling into illness." This was the case, for example, with dissociation mechanisms that somewhat helped detainees to "survive all that invasion of stimuli and all those contents that were so . . . so sinister."

While the psychological and medical literature on trauma can help to shed light on the short- and long-term effects of interrogation, torture, detention, and war on survivors (e.g., Becker et al. 1990; Punamäki et al. 2002; Brenner 2010; Putnam 2013), my interest has been to explore related themes from the perspective of body/mind dynamics and their relation to power structures. Attending to such dynamics has more than psychological salience; it has a political dimension in the sense that harnessing the bodies/minds of detainees was a central logic of oppression. How did malleable configurations of mind/body/self—which are more than individual, more than biological, more than psychological—allow detainees to endure and survive political repression? To the extent that the repressive state apparatus aimed at total subjugation—controlling the bodies, voices, and thoughts of captives—one can think of some of these survival mechanisms as not only ways of coping but also practices that helped counter the stranglehold of the regime.

Tactical Performances

Within the stark constraints of the camps, captive women sometimes engaged in *tactical performances* to soften harsh conditions and increase their possibilities of survival, even if they could not control such outcome. Following Honwana (2006)—who in turn draws on Michel de Certeau's work—I use the concept of *tactic* in reference to "complex actions that involve calculation of advantage but arise from vulnerability" (73). In the case of CDCs I examine two types of tactical performances that some women engaged in: performing the feminine body and performing embodied emotions. These are not necessarily discrete categories, but will be discussed separately for analytic purposes.

The notion of tactical performance evokes various connotations. First, it links the idea of "tactical agency" with notions of embodiment and performativity. Tactical agency focuses on the maneuvers by subordinated subjects in the context of oppressive circumstances, and includes things like "trickery and deception" (Honwana 2006, 71). Second, tactical performance has an affinity with theatrical acting, with putting on a performance for an audience. In fact, author, performer, and activist L. M. Bogad (2016, 2) uses the term "tactical performance" to refer to "the use of performance techniques, tactics, and aesthetics in social-movement campaigns." While I use the term in a different fashion and in relation to more individual acts, the tactics I describe here, like Bogad's activist/artistic examples, are in response to powerful forces of injustice and oppression. Finally, the term "tactical performance" is also associated with warfare, firearms, and militarized notions of security (for example, a number of commercial ventures that use the term "tactical performance" sell law enforcement and military gear). While the tactical performances by women in CDCs did not involve any militarized gear, guns, or the like, they were tactics that took place in militarized contexts and were aimed to survive state terror utilizing the "weapons of the weak" (Scott 1985).

Performing the Feminine Body

Women's tactical performances in CDCs included, in some cases, the enactment of normative femininity characteristics that differed from the performers' sense of authentic self. Here I focus on gendered tactical performances that entailed a variety of body dispositions and gestures as well as the expression of interests and concerns associated with the kind of womanhood expected by the military. While people "do gender" in everyday life as a matter of socialization and within the constraints of multiple forms of inequality,[9] I am characterizing certain performances of femininity in CDC as *tactical* to the extent that women enacted them for the purpose of maximizing chances of survival in a context of utter disempowerment. While these tactical performances occurred in an extreme context, it is also important to remember that in hierarchically structured societies, people frequently engage or are advised to engage in tactical performances of sorts in order to secure material or symbolic rewards (or even rights): from body presentation recommendations during a job interview to popular advice for heterosexual women to downplay their intelligence during dates with men.

According to some testimonial accounts, the performance of norma-tive femininity was important at the ESMA, where a process of "recuper-ation" was implemented in relation to a minority of detainees. This plan was supposedly meant to rehabilitate "subversives" back to society, and it entailed the expectation that detainees would renounce their previous political and ideological ways. For women, this included adherence to normative femininity. As a survival tactic some women tried to adjust, on the surface, to the military expectations. Referring to the process of recuperation, Marta Álvarez recounted her response to officers who were apparently testing whether the women were recuperating:

> So, for example, the questions were, "And what will you do when you get out of here?" [The response was] "Well, I am going to dedicate myself to my son. In fact, I would like to do Ikebana [flower arrangements], how nice" [laughs]. [. . .] "Ay, I like it so much . . . I heard that they bought that perfume, I like that perfume so much." The issue with recuperation was to turn you into a *pelotuda* [a stupid woman], which was what they were accustomed to, you see. Let's make an idiot who thinks about the af-ternoon soap opera. But they did not indoctrinate you saying, "From now on, the Argentine woman. . . ." No, no. You knew what kind of woman you needed to be, what kind of person—the less intelligent, the better, [someone who would] not question the family, religion. [. . .] [I]t was a good idea to demonstrate that one had discovered God, and that from now on it was the Sunday mass. [. . .] That you were never again going to get involved in anything, because politics was really for men. "How many years I wasted in this. Now I discovered what it means to be a woman and . . ."—that was what one had to convey, and we clearly knew that that was what they wanted to hear.

Although Marta did not make an explicit mention to the body, play-ing to these normative gender expectations entailed a particular type of embodied disposition: leaning toward a child, doing delicate handiwork, delighting in the scent of feminine perfume. Miriam Lewin, who also had been an activist and a detainee in ESMA, recounted how another woman in captivity who was "all fixed up, wearing makeup, [and] tidy" explained to her that, from the military perspective, being well dressed was "a symptom of *recuperation*" (Actis et al. 2001, 62). Similarly, women who were taken on pseudo-dates with the officers from ESMA were supposed to look elegant (178). As women survivors from ESMA recalled, the repressors even gave perfume to captive women and tried to enforce certain ideals of womanhood:

ADRIANA: They looked for the feminine characteristic.
ELISA: With shackles, dear! With shackles, but with French perfume!
MIRIAM: They wanted one to demonstrate to them . . .
ELISA: . . . that we were concerned about being very feminine women!
ADRIANA: They didn't forgive the shoes I was using.
MUNÚ: They made a compañera throw them off and buy others. (Actis et al. 2001, 178)

While there were variations among the different CDCs regarding the general policies and the specific treatment of different prisoners within the camps (and of the same prisoner at different points in time), efforts at so-called rehabilitation apparently occurred in camps other than the ESMA as well. Isabel Fernández Blanco, who was in the Olimpo, recounted:

And I think that at a certain moment, there was a sort of policy of rehabilitation [air quotes gesture] of the subversives. So on three or four times, they took us out of the cells and they brought us to an office that they had in the Olimpo. [. . .] So there it was for drinking mate; the women painted their nails, combed their hair. [. . .] I suppose that the compañeras who were in charge of taking us out and bringing us to the GT2 Office, were in charge of rehabilitating us, right? But nobody ever talked about politics either, or . . . anything. As I tell you, it was mere . . . nail painting.

Like Marta Álvarez's comments regarding recuperation expectations in ESMA, Isabel's words about the Olimpo also suggest that efforts to change women's behaviors and outlook did not need to rely on grandiloquent speeches about politics or about women's place in society. The process could be more oblique. In Isabel's narrative, it seemed to simply consist of the replacement of the (supposedly masculine) world of politics by the (supposedly feminine) world of nail polish and other bodily appearance concerns.

The abandonment of politics as proof of proper femininity is also apparent in Elisa Tokar's narrative. In trying to survive, Elisa performed a character that would fit military notions of proper depoliticized femininity. The performative nature of her actions is clear, but Elisa also exposed the dangers that such performances entailed, even if this acting started as a tactical maneuver. What happened when the tactical performances that Elisa and other detainees repeatedly enacted started to become entrenched in the body/self? Elisa reflected on this issue:

> So that character—which I thought they were looking for within me so that they could let me live—I developed it. So suddenly, I was the girl who had not been an activist, but rather the . . . the girl that, well, was there because I saw light and a movement, and I entered. So I developed that character, and you develop it to such an extent, in such a way that you come to believe it, no? And there comes the other part of the story, how do you get your life back? But that's how it is. You believe in it. So you put up with it, and your approach to life inside the camp is this: "I saw light and I entered." So it is all about talking about music, about fighting with the compañeros to hear rock music. And you don't even talk about the rest, nor do you touch upon it, nor can you. And it is better that you don't even think about it, no? You invent that character, you put yourself inside that character, and what is most terrible, is that in some cases you believe in that character—which is what happened to me, no?, that afterwards it is difficult to leave that character.

Elisa's narrative reveals, in extreme ways, the performative dimensions of gendered identities. From a performativity theory perspective (Butler 1990), there is no authentic or essential gender self or identity, but one constituted through citational and iterative performative acts (even though such performative acts are still grounded in material bodies and produce a certain solidity through their repetition over time). In this case, for the performance to be effective, it had to be convincing, it had to be drilled into body and psyche—as the captive woman's life was at stake. However, the danger was that the character could creep in and take over the performer's sense of authentic self, to the point that her former self might no longer exist, or would have to be reconstructed with great effort. Similar to Liliana Callizo, whose decision to leave in "another dimension" entailed difficulties adjusting to a different reality afterward, Elisa's performance of a particular kind of depoliticized femininity also carried its own costs.

As women detainees tried to preserve their lives, they played not just one but various types of femininity, adapting to preexisting cultural notions that might allow them to "get away" with certain behaviors. In constructing their personae, there was an interaction between the perceptions projected by the military and the social backgrounds and traits of different women. Marta Álvarez, who gave birth to a child during her time in captivity, recounted that the military gave her the role of "immaculate" mother. Munú Actis, a woman with artistic inclinations, talked about how she was seen as the "bohemian" or "the crazy one" (la loca). In particular situations, for example during paseos ("outings" in which repressors took detainees to identify other activists), Susana Jorgelina Ramus recounted how she "played dumb" (me hacía la boluda) in order to avoid giving information that might endanger others. Given stereotypical assumptions about women's inferior intelligence, one might wonder to what extent the role of la boluda (the dumb one) was more believable in the case of women. Similarly, Laura Schachter played on stereotypes associated with being just "a little girl who did not know anything," intersecting gender and age:

> And here they did torture me with electric picana, [and] with the submarine. [...] [M]y strategy was always to play dumb, very dumb, let's say. My age helped convince them that I was a little girl who did not know anything, about anything, or about anyone. Well, I think that this also helped me, because there it was enough to admit that one had done anything to make it so that you would never appear again. I was somewhat clear about that. So my strategy was to make them think that they made a mistake. [...] I somewhat maintained this discourse of knowing nothing about nothing, that I did nothing, nor knew anyone, nor. . . . I was the one going to school and asking to see my mom.

Laura did not explicitly mention the body, but age is often read on the body, and for her performance of innocent femininity to be convincing, certain bodily traits were probably helpful. Although the military did not spare very young or young-looking individuals, assertions of innocence were perhaps more believable in certain bodies than in others, as influenced by age and gender (conversely, presumptions of culpability could also be superimposed on the body.)

The dynamics of age, gender, and bodily appearance are illustrated by Emilce Moler's narrative of her abduction. Repressors' confusion about who they were supposed to snatch was related to Emilce's youthful look:

> Well, and they were looking for a fine arts student. [. . .] I show up, as you can see, very small—you can imagine seventeen years old with a little pajamas. I show up, and I looked like ten years old. And I say, "Well, I am from fine arts." "No, but this is a little girl" [laughs], they said, you know? So my sister, who was older, was there. And they tell her, "And you, what do you study?" "Philosophy" [replies the sister]. "No, but it was from fine arts" [a repressor says]. "Well. Well, let's take both of them," they said. "Well, both of you put on your clothes, we'll take the two of you."

Due to lack of space in the car, the repressors ultimately took only Emilce given her academic background and despite her young-looking appearance. However, the moment of confusion narrated shows the way that stereotypical notions and bodily appearance could play a role in shaping the repressors' assumptions. These notions could in turn be played up by detainees in order to buy themselves some time or to steer repressors away from exerting harm. Even so, the fact that people from various ages, genders, sexual orientations, religions, and ethnic and class backgrounds were tortured also shows that there were serious limitations to the potential effectiveness of survival tactics based on identity performances.

All in all, women's tactical performances parodied, enacted, and played on cultural notions of femininity deemed appropriate or expected by the military. These performances varied in terms of their length and ability to seep into the performers' deeper sense of self. Some of the examples presented here occurred in relatively discrete and short-term situations, while others extended over time, also influenced by the conditions and length of captivity.

Performing Embodied Emotions

Another tactical performance in the camps involved detainees' active management of emotions, including the performance of emotional detachment. To understand these survival practices it is useful to draw on the concepts of "surface acting" and "deep acting," which apply to bodily demeanors that display emotions required by a situational context. Sociologist Arlie Hochschild explains:

> We all do a certain amount of acting. But we may act in two ways. In the first way, we try to change how we outwardly appear. As it is for the people observed by Erving Goffman, the action is in the body language, the put-on sneer, the posed shrug, the controlled sigh. This is surface acting. The other way is deep acting. Here, display is a natural result of working on feeling; the actor does not try to *seem* happy or sad but rather expresses spontaneously, as the Russian director Constantin Stanislavski urged, a real feeling that has been self-induced. (2003, 35)

In the narratives of some survivors, we see that being able to effectively do at least surface acting was an important survival mechanism. However, some of the long-term consequences of such acting suggest that these performances could potentially veer into the terrain of deep acting. If under more common circumstances of everyday life people engage in both surface and deep acting, for example, as part of their job requirements (Grandey 2003; Hochschild 2003), one can imagine how high the stakes were in delivering an effective performance of certain emotions in the extreme conditions of the camps, where not doing so could mean death.

A number of survivors report that in the perilous context of CDCs, detainees had to guess and beware of behavioral and emotional displays that could provoke anger and retaliation on the part of the repressors. Elisa Tokar explained that at the ESMA, showing any sign of caring about other detainees was among the behaviors to be avoided, including exhibiting concern for pregnant women or grieving the death of fellow detainees and activists. In this way, it was necessary for those in captivity to domesticate the body to show the "right" type of emotions (or nonemotions) and to hide their true ones. Munú Actis, survivor of the

ESMA, called this embodied performance *cara de ní* (*ní* face)—*ní* being an invented word that combines *no* (no) and *sí* (yes). That is, *ní* is a contradiction in terms, as it can mean one thing and its opposite simultaneously. Munú explained that a *ní* face is "when you are told something terrible and you put a face that . . . that keeps the other from knowing what you are feeling, no?—to the extent possible." A *ní* face is a kind of poker face.

Elisa Tokar illustrated this point referring to situations in which detainees were taken in cars to participate in the operations that repressors conducted to identify and kidnap other people. These "outings" were very stressful not only because of the expectation that detainees should point to people they knew, but also given that these were circumstances in which they were exposed to the twisted conversations of repressors:

> And well, that's how these outings were, no? It was a horrible thing because, well, let's say that they forced you to . . . into a situation, first to be in the streets, [and also] have close contact with them [the repressors], no? They would be in the car talking, with complete freedom and impunity, and would comment on how they killed Fulana, how they killed Mengano. [. . .] Well, they were nonchalantly commenting on those stories among themselves, and even chatting with us, no? That is, it was hard, due to the situation, we . . . I don't know, perhaps it is difficult to understand very well the situation we were in, and the blank look [*cara de nada*] that we would have to put on in order to endure those stories, no? And . . . or the look of surprise [*cara de asombro*], or I don't know, a face that, let's say, didn't reveal to them our true feelings, no? That became very difficult, very difficult. And well, and apart from all the tension that one of those outings involved, because one knew, let's say . . . one perhaps was thinking that even if one recognized someone, one would look the other way, but did not know what the nearby compañero would do, how he would react.

In this passage we can get a glimpse of the extremely stressful circumstances to which detainees were subjected: trying to preserve their own lives, trying to protect the lives of potential abductees by faking ignorance, and trying to not react with expressions of horror to the tales of atrocity narrated by the repressors. Managing facial expression was part of the embodied emotional management required to survive. A *ní* face could be a handy tactic to endure such situations.

Similarly, Elisa also remembered the terrible scene of the "transfers"—when detainees were taken out of the detention centers to be killed—and the fact that the remaining detainees had to refrain from expressing anguish when confronted with such situations:

> One of the things that I remember as . . . as very terrible was in . . . in those transfers, in those transfers that they did, the issue was that you could not cry, no? As crying implied that you were also being concerned with the other, no? Eh . . . and I remember that in the first transfer that . . . that I experienced. [. . .] I was overtaken, let's say, by a . . . a terrible anguish; I started to cry, and two compañeras come and tell me, "No, no, don't cry. You cannot cry." And I say that, well, it was a stigma that marked me for life, let's say, because till this day it is hard for me . . . for me to cry, no?

This pedagogy of survival passed on by detainees entailed an effort to decode the imperatives of the camp and maximize avoidance of harm through the management of body and emotions. While detainees could not predict what determined survival, what might gain them one more day alive, or what exactly could trigger the repressors' rage, this did not prevent detainees from trying to ensure their chances of leaving the camp alive. However, the embodied performance that this necessitated was difficult to achieve. It required extreme emotional management in the face of extreme circumstances. While such performances can be conceptualized as a kind of "surface acting" (in which the expression of emotions does not match inner feelings), the persisting "stigma" associated with crying that Elisa reported suggests that the proper emotion rules of the camp could become more deeply and permanently entrenched in the body. However, it is unclear whether what had been suppressed through the long-term stigma of crying was the *display* of emotion (i.e., crying) or whether this had been accomplished through the numbing of emotion *itself* (i.e., suppressing sadness). In any case, it is worth asking to what extent surface acting turned into deep acting—with long-term consequences—due its repetition in the context of the camps. Furthermore, to what extent does the distinction between surface and depth work? The distance between surface and depth might narrow as the performer is compelled to repeat the act over and over as a condition for survival.

The kinds of emotional performances described here are not unique to CDCs. For instance, referring to a different oppressive context—the history of slavery in the United States—feminist author bell hooks (2015, 99–100) writes about black people's repression of emotions as a survival mechanism:

> Slavery socialized black people to contain and repress a range of emotions. Witnessing one another being daily subjected to all manner of physical abuse, the pain of over-work, the pain of brutal punishment, the pain of near-starvation, enslaved black people could rarely show sympathy or solidarity with one another just at that moment when sympathy and solace was most needed. They rightly feared reprisal. It was only in carefully cultivated spaces of social resistance, that slaves could give vent to repressed feelings. Hence, they learned to check the impulse to give care when it was most needed and learned to wait for a "safe" moment when feelings could be expressed.

The need to repress emotions, says hooks, had long-term implications in the sense that the descendants of enslaved people also learned to keep certain emotions at bay and to find value in "the ability to mask, hide, and contain feelings" (100). At root was the institution of slavery, but hooks refers to lingering and intergenerational effects of this utterly oppressive institution.

In his work with sons and daughters of Holocaust survivors, Simon Gottschalk (2003) draws on the concept of deep acting to explore another type of emotional management that can also be considered as a long-term consequence of atrocity with intergenerational dimensions. Gottschalk examines how members of the Holocaust's "second generation" engaged in various forms of deep acting, such as the suppression of seemingly inappropriate emotions (e.g., joy and pleasure) and the production of expected emotions (e.g., mourning and sadness) in light of their parents' trauma and suffering. While the performances of emotion described in this chapter are different from those analyzed by Gottschalk—particularly since here the focus is on the experiences of survivors of atrocity themselves—the idea that there can be more than time- and space-bound dimensions to emotional management is relevant to this work. To what extent did the embodied emotional management required in the camps overflow its spatial and temporal confines? How might these emotional legacies carry into the future?

Finally, it is important to note that some kinds of emotion performances—particularly when there is a strong incongruence between inner feeling and what a person might be compelled to display in response to situational factors—have been found to be associated with emotional tension and exhaustion (Grandey 2003). Furthermore, as emotions have social and political dimensions,[10] one may wonder whether the tension derived from certain emotional performances also had more than individual components. For example, while it would be emotionally difficult for any person with a shred of empathy to witness without betraying emotion the kinds of violence that were rampant in the camps, the demand to suppress feelings and displays of care might have been particularly taxing for people who were socialized into a strong ethos of solidarity. This included members of social justice and political organizations that encouraged such an outward orientation as well as loyalty toward compañeros/as. In other words, the demand to literally embody individualism through the suppression of emotional displays of care or acts of solidarity was yet another layer of political repression in the camps that gripped the bodies and emotions of detainees. In this sense, the performance of emotion/nonemotion can be characterized as a tactic of adaptation and survival, but one that bears the imprint of the very conditions of oppression from which they emerged.

Embodied Care, Solidarity, and Resistance

Despite the strong mandate to not care, the testimonies of survivors also show that many detainees did care and expressed multiple forms of solidarity when they could. In the oppressive conditions of the camps, such solidarity can be characterized as a form of resistance, which operated in tandem with other expressions of agency. Micro and almost imperceptible forms of embodied resistance coexisted with more overt or organized efforts on detainees' part (though the latter were practically impossible in the conditions imposed in some CDCs).[11] Bacci et al. (2012, 71–72) explain:

It is known that in clandestine detention centers the persons abducted generated ties of solidarity and a type of sociability that allowed them to sustain within certain limits their integrity as persons. Some testimonies also show that sexual violence or the threat of violence by the repressors mobilized collective strategies of resistance and gestures of solidarity that managed to stop the threat or at least suspend it at a given moment. Screams, bangs, and alerting signs among fellow captives who did not know each other, who could not even see each other, improvised actions that restricted, at least temporarily, the intentions of their captors.

Descriptions of micro resistance and embodied solidarity appear repeatedly in the testimonies, as "weapons of the weak" that could be deployed to survive and undermine the stranglehold of the system (Scott 1985). Survivor Ana Di Salvo referred to the "little tricks" (*trampitas*) that detainees performed, for example, saying "let's lift the hood to see each other's faces." Graciela García remembered how a fellow captive taught her how to breathe in order to calm the anguish. Marta García de Candeloro constructed an interior world behind her hood where repressors could not go. Susana Reyes, who was pregnant, spent her days intensely focused on her growing belly, constantly touching it, observing its movements. Her body, that was two, offered some relief from the brutal conditions of detention.

Other forms of embodied resistance were more overt. For example, Lelia Ferrarese remembered her response during torture: "There they do the submarine to me. [. . .] I kick, *las mil y una* [make a lot of trouble]. In truth it was not easy for them to do that to me [smiles]. And, [one repressor said] 'Fine, fine, leave her alone' [imitates the repressor's voice]." In this description, we see how Lelia's actions interfered with the repressors' aims, as well as a certain pride in her ability to resist. Similarly, Munú Actis struck a guard who had started to fondle her and stopped the aggressor's action, and Fátima Cabrera obtained help from fellow detainees to avert sexual violence.[12] Whatever the tactic that captives used to contest different manifestations of power and oppression, these efforts often involved very high risks. The possibility of harsh retaliation, including death, was ever present even as a response to minimal gestures of transgression.

Some forms of resistance that detainees deployed entailed implicit or explicit efforts to maintain dignity (Bacci et al. 2012), and enlisted the body as a resource to accomplish this goal. This was the already alluded case of Marta Bianchi, who described the authoritative posture of her upper body when speaking with repressors, even while fear was her true emotion (evidenced in uncontrollable shaking in the lower part of her body): "I felt I had to try to not demonstrate how afraid I was, and defend my dignity to the extent possible." Sometimes this claim on dignity was evidenced in the refusal of some women to receive any help from repressors, even when their bodies after torture would have benefitted from assistance. This is the case in Elena Lenhardtson's recollection, mentioned earlier: "I realized that I struggled for my dignity when I said [to the repressors], 'Don't touch me, I will move myself.'" Similarly, Rita Cordero de Garnica related the following interaction with a younger guard after she was tortured:

> I even had the satisfaction that they didn't [have to] hold me. I had to go to wash myself alone, and so on. The policeman who took this off [points toward wrist]—the ropes—[. . .] was trembling and crying. And I tell him, "Why do you cry?" [. . .] He was [standing] against me, but I saw him far away because [. . .] blood was coming out of my eyes. "I," he says, "You remind me of my mom" he said. [. . .] "Why," he says, "are you involved in this?" "What do you know about what I'm involved in?" I tell him. "You do not know who I am, you do not know me." That's what I told him. "And leave me alone as I can manage myself." And I couldn't, but I managed to avoid them washing me. I had to wash my face. And then they took pictures of us and everything. And I already had, you see, in ten days my hair turned white.

Despite the evident deterioration of Rita's body post-torture—including bleeding eyes, the sudden whitening of her hair, and other body injuries—she still tried to maintain a sense of autonomy in a context that was meant to do away with it. She recalled this episode with a certain pride, and in the narrative, we can detect a reversal of roles: the captive woman assumes a position of authority, questioning the male guard, even as she is vulnerable; and the guard cries, even as he accuses her of wrongdoing. This reversal between guard and captive is accomplished via the intersection of gender and age. Rita is figuratively positioned as a "mother"—a normative gender identity—who can question and reprimand the inappropriate remarks of the younger guard, who in turn positioned himself in the role of "son," needing caretaking. The crying and shaking body of the man contradicts normative conceptions of masculinity, particularly militarized masculinities. However, this gendered social status seems to be trumped by a more complex intersection of gender and age that plays out in the relational construction between captive and guard. Rita implicitly reclaimed a measure of dignity through this reversal of roles and through her refusal to show dependence on her oppressors despite the terrible state of her body.

Another form of resistance to the conditions of the camps was embodied care and solidarity. Despite the strong mandate for detainees to keep to themselves and not care about other people in the camps, several testimonies reveal how people in captivity still engaged in various forms of solidarity that involved a use of the body that was different from what the military regime prescribed. While the isolated body—the body turned inward that is exemplified by the figure of the hooded prisoner—certainly appears in the narratives of survivors, their testimonies also speak of bodies in solidarity, bodies that connected through words or gesture when possible. These "intercorporeal" forms of connectivity (Doyle 2001, 91) subverted the repressors' imposed mores and expectations and aided detainees' survival. Drawing on Tzvetan Todorov's notion of "everyday virtues"—such as individual acts of care that may not have been readily apparent except to the beneficiaries—Pilar Calveiro (1998, 132–33) argued that "survival would have been simply impossible without the circulation of these everyday virtues." These acts of care can be conceptualized as forms of resistance to the extent that they defied the rules of the camps and helped sustain detainees.

Embodied gestures of care not only had the value of concretely aiding in the sustenance of people's physical bodies, but also helped to assert ethical values that had been paramount for many of the people held captive, both as an individual ethic and as a political philosophy. Indeed, a number of the women in this study remembered the ethos of solidarity that imbued their political activism, and some of this transpired in the camps as well. Still, it is important to note that gestures of solidarity took place among people with varied political and ideological backgrounds, who in the process reaffirmed basic forms of humanity and connectivity. One cannot assert whether acts of care were expressions of political and/

or social identities. At the same time, it is hard to disentangle the different threads (biographical, political, social) that constitute a person's behavior and orientation in particular situations. Though the opportunities to engage in mutual help varied from camp to camp (and in different spaces and periods of time in specific camps), a number of survivors remember gestures of transgression and solidarity—sometimes almost invisible, sometimes more evident and organized.

"There were a thousand forms of everyday resistance, minute [forms]," said survivor Marta Vassallo who was captive in El Atlético. She narrated acts that broke with the isolationist and dehumanizing organization of the camps. She remembered "the young man who helped the older man eat" or how "[w]hen we were forming a line, someone squeezed my shoulders—the one behind me—and I felt it . . . he was a young man. I felt it . . . I felt his desperation, but I also felt it as a gesture of friendship, no?, like saying 'we are in the same [boat].'" The subtle touch between bodies conveyed meaning, a secret code of solidarity in opposition to the military regime's code. Ana Di Salvo, held in El Vesubio, also recalled embodied sharing and caring practices amid situations of imposed scarcity: "There was another *piba* [young woman] [laughs] who was thin, very thin. [. . .] And she liked the interior of the bread, and since they gave us bread, we would then take the interior and give it to her. She was thin with a belly. A belly from bread. There . . . we all ended up thin. I think I was never thinner than when I left there." Food, as bodily nourishment and as a token of love, was part of the economy of embodied solidarity narrated in this passage, and it was particularly significant in a context in which provisions did not abound or were frequently spoiled.

Graciela García, who was held at the ESMA for an extended period (from 1976 to 1981), remembered the critical support she received from a fellow captive woman, underscoring the emotional dimensions of bodily care:

They brought me to what they called a *camarote* [ship's cabin], which was a room where there was a compañera. During the day I was there, and at night I went to sleep in *Capucha* [another sector of the CDC nicknamed Hood]. That compañera . . . was . . . yes . . . each time that I tal- . . . [her voice cracks, as if about to cry; the recording stops]. Well, Norita [the compañera] was a lot younger than me and I believe she had less activist experience, but in truth, she was the one who taught me how to survive at the beginning, no? She pushed around the *Verdes* ["Greens," low-level guards], she had a way of treating them, like almost. . . . For me it was . . . I was impressed when I saw her telling them, "Caniche, bring me water," "Fulanito, bring me bread." And . . . and I saw that distinct treatment, and moreover . . . well, I was choking. I was choking, literally, I couldn't . . . couldn't get air. And she helped me to breathe. She taught me to breathe, to stop anxiety, anguish. She taught me to survive. And afterwards they transferred her.

As in the examples provided by Marta and Ana above, Graciela's testimony highlights both the nurturance of the physical body as well as the emotional connection between detainees through embodied gestures that, though small, were vital to endure the conditions of the camps. In the vignette above, we see how Norita provided essential assistance to help Graciela survive. Sadly, Norita's own life was prematurely and brutally ended.

Tender bodily connection between detainees sometimes happened as a by-product of oppressive techniques themselves, which detainees sometimes managed to turn around. For example, Eva Orifici—who, among other sites, was held in a CDC that functioned on a ship (*Buque Murature*)—remembered the support she received from a fellow detainee while being transported on a barge along with other people. As recounted earlier, repressors threw the detainees onto the barge in a pile, as if they were objects. Yet the momentary interaction that Eva narrated shows not only detainees' efforts to comfort each other, but how in the process they implicitly contested their objectification and asserted their mutual humanity:

I was there . . . lying there, and well, they throw another compañero on top of me . . . and so [. . .] it was one of those little moments in which you can talk with someone, no? [. . .] Well, and then this compañero asks me, "Who are you?," something like that. I tell him my name, and he tells me his. We didn't know each other. And I was crying a lot because I thought, "Well, they will throw us into the water." And then he asks me whether I had children. And I said, "Yes, I have . . . a little boy . . . he is two years old, his name is Martín, and he was left alone." [. . .] Then the compañero tells me that he also has a girl, but she had been left with her compañera, no? So at one point he says, "Look," he says, "I do not know what's going to happen but I will give you. . . ." He gives me a kiss, like that, on the cheek, and he tells me that it is [. . .] in the name of Martín and in the name of his daughter.

The harrowing image of human beings piled up on top of each other as disposed objects—who could fall in the water at any time and just die due to arbitrary state power and impunity—is modulated by the interaction between the two captives. They engaged in an act of affective and embodied connection, defying the anonymity and objectification imposed on them. The regime's attempt to transform prisoners into just bodies, with no name or biography, was subverted in the described scene. Though torturers' efforts to transform each detainee into a "body with no voice" (Scarry 1985, 57) were integral to repression, this fleeting interaction between two prisoners who did not know each other shows how the perpetrators' attempts did not go without contestation. In the interaction above, the detainees asserted their names, biography, and lineage as well as values such as embodied solidarity and care.

During moments of heightened fear, detainees' expressions of embodied care made a significant difference. The terror that detainees experienced in the camps, as Graciela García's difficulty to breath illustrates, often manifested in the body. Such feelings and symptoms were sometimes attenuated through the support of other captives. Isabel Cerruti recalled how in situations in which she thought she would surely be killed, her body was overtaken by the *tembleques*, the shakes. In her narrative, she underscored the helpful hand of another detainee: "A young guy from the Council held me—a great guy—who held me because I was falling. But I was not falling because of . . . of weakness. I was falling because [I would] say, 'I prefer to faint,'—well, unconsciously, no? I . . . all the time when those things happened I thought that they would kill me. I would get the . . . the shakes, like that." In this and in previous examples, the body became a privileged conduit of solidarity. It was through embodied gestures of care that the material body was sustained and detainees could assert their own and other detainees' humanity. The interdependence that bodily vulnerability breeds is part and parcel of being human (Butler 2014). In that sense, it is more than the material body that is sustained, but a more holistic embodied "self" and a social body that rests upon interdependency.

Sometimes acts of care were aimed at healing the body. Celeste Seydell—who had been brutally treated during her clandestine detention—remembered the big wound on her head and the infection in her blindfolded eyes that such mistreatment generated. Yet she also recalled in detail the care she received from another detainee who helped clean and disinfect her wounds, providing a basis for recovery:

> [There was] a compañera who was a nurse, who was an activist with us. [. . .] She washed me with white soap, she put a lot of white soap, and she told me "Anything in this wound, you should always apply white soap, because it is aseptic, because it heals, because. . . . And if you can get an aspirin where you go, apply the aspirin, as a powder," she said, "that will also . . . will relieve you . . . it is anti-inflamma[tory]." [. . .] She put a very aseptic bandage, she put drops, some ointment, a bandage—bandage-bandage, let's say, not rags, you know? And then, well, they take me, they make me lay down on a mat, and I start coughing and another cough answers back, and [someone] tells me, "Are you there?" says, "I'm el Paco." "Yes, yes" I say, "Are you here?" "Yes, yes, we are very close," something like that. Well, "And where are we?" "In La Perla," [he] says. "We are in La Perla." "Uuuy," I say.

Celeste's body was nurtured by another woman detainee, and as her body started to recover, other forms of solidarity were also set in motion: Celeste did not waste time; and as soon as she laid down after receiving some care, she tried to get a fresh grasp of her situation and break the imposed isolation. She coughed with the intention to reach out and communicate with fellow detainees. She connected with someone she knew and obtained important—though not comforting—information. She found out that she was in a particularly notorious CDC.

Another dimension of solidarity and resistance involving the body was related to the use of clothing. As Salerno (2009) points out, clothing is an important marker of culture and identity denied to detainees by forcing them to disrobe or by compelling them to wear clothing other than their own. She also mentioned that repressors would sometimes transform detainees' own clothing into repressive instruments, for example, by using detainees' own garments to tie their hands or as ad hoc blindfolds. References to clothing appear in various testimonies in this study. For instance, Nora Strejilevich talked about the process of depersonalization in clandestine detention, which included detainees having to wear clothing that "belongs to someone who no longer needs it," presumably because that person was already dead or in route to be killed. Graciela García mentioned that guards at the ESMA would give detainees any clothing they found, and as a result detainees seemed *disfrazados* (as if wearing costumes). Some of the clothing available in the CDCs was the result of looting by the repressors (Salerno 2009, 93), which was another layer of the criminal operations of the regime. Yet the testimonies of survivors also speak of resistance through clothing.

In some cases, detainees used clothing in creative or playful ways, or made clothing for each other as a gesture of solidarity that helped sustain body and soul. Ana Di Salvo, for example, kept a scarf that Martha Brea—a fellow detainee who did not survive—knitted for her while they both were captive in El Vesubio. Ana also remembered an anecdote that shows how detainees sometimes generated spaces to laugh, including through playful bodily performances and use of clothing:

> One time it was the birthday of one of the *chicas* [young women] who was there. So the ones who went to headquarters, the ones who had access to clothing—there was a wardrobe with clothes in one of the rooms of headquarters—brought a dress. And we gave it to her as a gift. And since it was her birthday, the guards let her show off her dress. Then she did a kind of fashion show, walking among the *cuchas* [prisoner cubicles; literally kennels]. And then she said, "Ask me where I get my clothes." So we said, "Where do you get your clothes?" [and she answered] "In the 'Fuck Elegance Boutique'" [Boutique Me Cago en la Elegancia] [smiles]. And she walked, coming and going. Her name was Ofelia Casano, she was a medical doctor. When I left, she stayed, but did not survive.

In this scene, women detainees expressed solidarity through the gift of clothing in a way that resisted the oppressive relation between clothing and the body that the regime had established. If one way of shattering the identities of detainees was by having them wear clothing that belonged to other people, here we see how detainees turned this dynamic around by appropriating clothing for their own goals—in this case to make a fellow detainee feel appreciated on her birthday. In addition to this display of solidarity, another dimension of resistance was embodied through detainees' "laughter out of place," the use of laughter as an oppositional practice within a system that imposed suffering (Goldstein 2003; see also Calveiro 1998). The birthday woman's sense of humor and creative use of her body parodied rituals of normative upper-class femininity (the fashion show, the boutique), opening a release valve from the conditions in the camp. Here again, a detainee—Ofelia Casano—engaged in actions that helped somewhat to alleviate the oppressive context. Ultimately, though, her own life was not spared.

Sometimes the acts of solidarity that nurtured body and soul came from extremely stigmatized individuals, including those persecuted by state and paramilitary forces in the name of "morality." People abducted by the state under the frame of political subversion sometimes coincided in places of detention, such as police stations, with people detained for minor infractions related to sexuality—offenses enshrined in local police edicts or targeted by "morality brigades" (Insausti 2015, 67). In the province of Mendoza, the Comando Moralizador Pío XII (Moralizing Commando Pío XII), which started its repressive operations before the 1976 coup, targeted women in prostitution. These women were sometimes "kidnapped, tortured, sexually abused and assassinated, [and] their bodies were thrown out in mountainous zones" (Agüero 2009, 109). Alicia Morales, who was clandestinely detained in Mendoza, was at some point transferred to a space under police authority where there were also women targeted as "prostitutes." These women were very helpful to Alicia, feeding her and enacting other forms of solidarity:

The prostitutes were the first ones who gave us something to eat. They opened the cell and they fed us. One of them—she said, "my name is María," I never heard anything about her again—was the one who took the blindfold off and untied my hands, and gave me a cup of coffee with milk and some pastries and a pack of cigarettes, after who knows how many days without eating, without being taken to the bathroom, nothing. [. . .] And well, the prostitutes even called my home to say that I was alive and I was imprisoned there. [. . .] They fought . . . fought *a brazo partido* [tooth and nail] with the police. Every night, 60 or 70 came in, something like that, it was an incredible number. They were all shouting, making a terrible commotion. And in the middle of that commotion, they took advantage [of the opportunity] to open the spyhole and give us things. [. . .] With all the commotion that they created, the *milicos* [pejorative for military] chased them to one side, and they [the women] ran to the other, making fun of them.

Similarly, Gloria Enríquez remembered the solidarity of "travestis" detained in the police station where she was held in Buenos Aires province. These persons—arguably among the most stigmatized members of the population—offered Gloria clean underwear and also helped avert sexual violence against her, by starting "a ruckus, revolutionizing everything" even at their own risk of punishment (see also Bacci et al. 2012, 82). Gloria recounted that besides having to clean the whole police station in retaliation, they might have also been raped by police officers (see also Bacci et al. 2012; Insausti 2015). Individuals whose gender identity/expression does not match societal expectations, such as travestis, are among the categories of people often constituted as *just bodies* (as outlined in chapter 3) and whose humanity is denied in many societies. In the cases narrated, we see that despite conditions of oppression that they themselves faced, members of groups stigmatized in relation to their gender and sexuality practiced an ethic of care that helped sustain other people they crossed paths with while in detention facilities.[13]

Whereas in the context of judicial testimonies the memories of torture and other crimes have special relevance, it is apparent that many survivors also want to remember experiences that may not have juridical value but that are still highly significant both for them as individuals and for social memory. Bacci et al. (2012) remark that survivors still remember with gratitude and emotion other detainees' gestures of solidarity and care in the camps. Park's (2014) study of former political prisoners of the dictatorship also shows that they emphasize memories of solidarity and resistance, and that their accounts of agency are tied to activist identities. However, as Park (2014) notes, this reclamation of agency puts survivors in a bind in the sense that it may convey the impression that they had control over their fates, raising thorny questions about why they and not others survived: "Yet, the reality is that the political prisoners were dependent on their captors for food, water, space, light, and air. What the political prisoners did, however, was find points of agency amid the repression" (Park 2014, 21–22).

In an interview with Ana Cacopardo for *Historias Debidas* (2014), scholar and survivor Pilar Calveiro disputes the repeated notion that those who survived atrocity were the "worst ones" and those who died were "the best ones," or that those who survived did it at the expense of the people who died. Instead, she argues that a diversity of individuals— who engaged in varied levels and forms of solidarity during detention— were among both those who died and those who survived. At the same time, she concludes the following with regard to survivors: "We all lived thanks to the help of others." That is, even though the repressors had ultimate control, gestures of care among detainees did take place in the camps, providing essential emotional, spiritual, and physical support and sustenance.

Embodied Memory as Voice

As the testimonies of survivors abundantly show, many of the experiences of former detainees were stored in the body. They remained not only in the form of thoughts, but also as embodied feelings, bodily scars, and sensory recollections. Many of these embodied memories extend the temporality not only of suffering but of resistance as well. Among other things, these embodied memories have been important as resources for denunciation and redress during the post-dictatorship period. The testimonies of survivors have been essential to identify CDCs, to reconstruct the scenes of crimes against humanity, and to trace back the fate of people disappeared or appropriated by the military regime. Survivors have had to rely on memory, sometimes going back to experiences that took place decades earlier, in order to provide the information.

Some of the survivors' memories are subtle and rely on a variety of bodily stimuli in the absence of sight, as detainees were often blindfolded or hooded. Salerno (2009, 94) suggests that resorting to other senses as sources of information was a crucial way to counter the denial of knowledge/power that the deprivation of sight entailed: "From this perspective, [the sense of sight/vision] represents a necessary tool to gain knowledge through experience. If knowledge is power, then the gaze is part of its dynamic." The blindfolds and hoods were tools in the arsenal that repressors used to suppress the knowledge/power of detainees and turn them into "passive and observed entities" (94). However, testimonies show that this goal was not necessarily accomplished, as detainees resorted to other senses to grasp their surroundings, including in very subtle ways. For instance, Ana María Cacabelos remembered her arrival to the CDC: "When we arrived [. . .] they made me get out of the car; I was wearing cork platform [shoes], more or less this high [gestures with fingers indicating several centimeters], so it was fairly difficult . . . I have full awareness that it was a cobbled street because I found it very hard to walk there, no? And especially since I was hooded." Although Ana María could not see, other embodied cues—in this case difficulty walking—provided information about the terrain and were retained in the memory of this survivor. As the body is never neutral or universal, it can be argued that it is from a particular location in a matrix of power relations and social signifiers that this form of knowledge emerged.[14] The information that Ana María produced can be conceived as individually based or idiosyncratic; however, it actually emerged from a gendered bodily experience and positioning at a particular historical moment. It is the interaction between a specific form of gendered apparel that was popular in the seventies—high cork platform shoes—and the materiality of the built environment that produces one salient hint about the place of the detention. As in this case, other forms of knowledge about the camps also emerged from gendered selves/bodies and became embodied memories that later on took the shape of testimonies.

The repressive apparatus aimed at total and absolute reign over detainees, but survivors' embodied recording of events and later recounting show some of the fissures in such a formidable structure. For instance, subtle pieces of sensory memory became important as survivors denounced their ordeal and tried to identify sites of captivity. Susana Caride drew on such memories when she and others returned to the sites where former CDCs operated, in order to help identify the place where she had been illegally held: "We entered with the car [. . .] and I closed my eyes, and it made a movement in one of the curves in the entrance [she makes a wavy motion with hand], I said, 'It is the same.' But once we were there, like a chorus [. . .] we said, 'The tank continues leaking'—the tank with which they tortured you with the leaking water. And [. . .] even though certain things had changed, we remembered perfectly." The leaking tank and the memory of the car's movement when entering the camp were certainly subtle clues, but important enough to be registered at an embodied level, as sensory input that now fulfilled a testimonial function.

In addition to phenomenological memories rooted in the senses, women in this study also spoke of body memories in the form of scars. Body scars from the camps can be likened to how different societies have violently branded bodies constituted as dangerous or deviant: from the imposition of identification tattoos to the marks of corporal punishment such as whipping. As DeMello (2014) points out, these types of practices produce literal body markings. Many survivors of clandestine detention also carry more or less visible but enduring brandings on their bodies. These have taken the form of physical health problems and disturbing emotions experienced in the body (see also Park 2014). These visible and invisible scars constitute vivid forms of embodied memory of state terror. However, as much as the scar remits to the original injury and to the intent of the captors, women also tell a more complex story that includes elements of resistance, resilience, and survival. Their embodied marks speak; their bodies are voice.

The bodily scars of the camps are fleshly reminders of the state's "fiction of power" that produced them (Scarry 1985, 18). According to Scarry, in the torture scene, "ultimate domination requires that the prisoner's ground become increasingly physical and the torturer's increasingly verbal, that the prisoner become a colossal body with no voice and the torturer a colossal voice (a voice composed of two voices) with no body" (57). How does this relationship between body and voice fare over time as mediated by the bodily scars of these events? The embodied effects of captivity manifest a tension between body and voice beyond the torture room. Even if torturers aimed to turn detainees into bodies without voice, we can see in various testimonies how this intention failed, particularly if one takes a longer-term perspective. Women survivors sometimes turned the scars of torture and torments into vehicles or channels for voice.

For some survivors, the bodily scars of captivity have been rather severe and with long-term consequences. Ledda Barreiro described the state of her body after her clandestine detention in La Cueva as follows:

"They operate on me six times after . . . captivity . . . the kidneys. They operate on me several times because I was in very bad shape. They take my uterus out. So it took me a while to rejoin the struggle, because I could not walk. And well, later I continued, and later I entered Grandmothers [of the Plaza de Mayo]." In this case, the effects of captivity on the material body—including tangible wounds—temporarily impinged upon this survivor's ability to fully exert her political agency. At the same time, the state's brutal branding of Ledda's body was not successful in squashing her political voice or in imprinting passivity. She joined other women in protest to confront the dictatorship: "I went out all broken, as I was. We went out and screamed." Indeed, Ledda continued her activism for decades after her captivity, denouncing the disappearance of her daughter who was pregnant and searching for her grandchild.

The state's inscriptions of the body appear not only in the form of actual scars, loss of body parts, or permanent impairment but also through the more intangible yet potent experience of pain (Vilar 2009). According to Nietzsche, cited in Antaki (2007, 6), "pain is the most powerful aid to mnemonics." The bodies of women survivors sometimes recalled the experience of captivity in the form of lingering pain. For instance, Rita Cordero de Garnica—a survivor from a working-class family who was detained in El Guerrero—described the enduring marks of torture:

> I have problems [. . .] sometimes this hurts, all this [touches the top of her hand] and it is as if the [electric] current got me. [. . .] All of this was scarred [points from her chest to the neck]. [. . .] All this part is sagging [points to part of her face]. [. . .] Because they hit me a lot. And this . . . I used to have it all broken [points to part of her face]. [. . .] And there they knocked my teeth out. [. . .] In truth, all this, I have scars over here [points to her back, at the level of her waist]. I thought that . . . that I would die, but no. I got out of there weighing forty-five kilos. I couldn't even walk.

While many of Rita's wounds eventually healed, the memory of torture continued to be embodied through visible and invisible marks as living evidence that such state violence was indeed inflicted. Similarly, other survivors mentioned other enduring health effects of captivity. For instance, Eva Orifici and Celeste Seydell referred to problems in the back or shoulders as a result of being left hanging for extended periods. Through these types of bodily markings the memory of state violence can be reactualized but also used for denunciation of atrocity.

Scholars of "social suffering" have explored how the language of physical symptoms can be interpreted as more than individual experiences but as the merging of "bodily memory, biography, and social history" (Kleinman and Kleinman 1994, 714). These symptoms can serve to give voice to personal suffering and to tell a broader story. In the Argentine case, one of the salient stories that survivors narrate is that of state terror, including its various dimensions and responses. Kleinman and Kleinman (1994, 716–17) argue that "bodies transformed by political processes not only *represent* those processes, they *experience* them as the lived memory of transformed worlds. The experience is of memory processes sedimented in gait, posture, movement, and all the other corporal components which together realize cultural code and social dynamics in everyday practices. The memorialized experience merges subjectivity and social world." In this vein, ESMA survivor Graciela García opined that the person who "lived in a concentration camp cannot get rid of it ever again." While there is variation in how different survivors processed the experience, it is not surprising to hear testimonies suggesting that the memory of captivity can settle on the most *intimate* nooks and crannies of the self even though the embodiment of trauma also tells a more *public* story. In the words of Graciela, "I am going to carry this mark on my body, on my soul, till the last of my days. I have an immediate response to situations where I have . . . [when] fear, anxiety, and depression sprout up. I know it is going to be like that until the end. And I believe that this serves as testimony because . . . it is something that . . . is a direct consequence [*hijo directo*] of the concentration camp." In this description, persistent symptoms are evidence of the military regime's oppressive branding of the body and at the same time function as "testimony" denouncing practices of state terror. In articulating these embodied experiences, various survivors used their body memories as the grounds for denunciation of human rights violations.

Besides observable bodily traits or reported physical ailments, women survivors sometimes referred to shifts in how they have felt about their bodies or how they expected other people to relate to them. Elena Lenhardtson spoke of this type of shift as an enduring "mark" of captivity.

She referred to "a before and after in one's life, no? And above all, I think that it marked my body the most." She recalled a time when, though she had to go through multiple surgeries due to health issues, she had generally felt that these constituted "fantastic" solutions. However, in the aftermath of torture and captivity her previous outlook changed: "[N]ow anything that happens to my body causes me anguish. And I wonder why is it that I have such anguish. Until I realize that I have a headache, or I have, I don't know, I have a stomachache. Anything that happens to me is as if the body had registered it and had stored it, because I think that the resistance that one exerts at that moment—to resist—remains very much imprinted on the body." Interestingly, in this passage, the bodily marks of captivity speak of not just a body acted upon, but a resisting body. In this sense, though the branding of state terror involves the amplification of the suffering body across time, an important aspect of this marking is also a memory of resistance.

In different ways, more or less tangible bodily effects became not just sources or reminders of horror but an opportunity to exercise agency and speak out. Munú Actis recalled that the launch of *Ese infierno*—a book she co-authored with other women who survived ESMA (Actis et al. 2001)—was attended by perhaps surprising guests, namely, her dentist and her gastroenterologist:

> I mean, all people to whom—in order for me to accept that they touch me, that they get in my body—I have had to first tell them, "Stop [makes a stop gesture with the hands]. My history is this." [. . .] Or I meet someone who takes care of me . . . but I say, "My history is this, I don't have to put up with. . . ." So [that person] knows that I'm putting him in that place. [There's people] to whom I had to apologize later, because well, I put [them] in that place, as the one who will come to hurt me. It is a whole mental process to realize that [they come] to cure me, not hurt me, no? But, well, I end up talking to them. I speak.

In this way, body memories served to narrate a story of state repression to a variety of interlocutors. In doing so, memory became not something strictly "private" (personal) or "public" (pertaining to judicial proceedings, official reports, or public protest) (Bacci et al. 2014), but something alive in everyday interactions and spaces where survivors circulate, creating ripple effects in the process of memory making. In circulating these memories, Munú used her embodied emotions as a platform to give voice to her experience of state violence, squarely defying the state terrorist regime's attempts to turn her into a body without voice: "I speak," she said.

These stories echo aspects of Cecilia Macón's (2014) analysis of "metatestimonies" of women who survived the CDCs of the dictatorship, namely her challenge to traditional victim/agent dichotomies. In Macón's work, metatestimonies refer to "what the victims express as their own affective experiences on the fact of giving testimony, primarily through their own words, but also through their bodies and actions" (38). In paying attention to these dimensions, Macón argues that even "negative" affects such as shame can be performatively productive, and not mere impediments to agency. In publicly displaying affects—for example, in the contexts of trials for crimes against humanity—women survivors' embodied testimonies, including narratives of sexual violence, "may also help to resignify the injury and empower the victim[s]" (26). In a similar way, the stories about embodied pain and scars narrated here straddle the borders between victimhood and agency. Women survivors drew on stories of embodied suffering to signify their memories of captivity beyond horror, including dimensions such as dignity, courage, resistance, solidarity, and creativity. They used these embodied memories to denounce atrocity in multiple social spheres.

These embodied memories of horror, survival, and resistance also alert us to the fact that memory is not something that is frozen in time, but is a socially lived and living construction. It is the memory that is lived in the body; it circulates among family, friends, and acquaintances; it erupts in the judicial testimony and in the metatestimony; and it is stored in the archive with a projection toward the future. Even in the seemingly congealed form of the archive, these memories continue to breathe and live as long as there are people willing to listen to, learn from, interact with, and be affected by the stories.

Conclusion

In her work on memorialization of human rights violations and atrocity, Marianne Hirsch (2015) advances a critique of "monumental" memory projects, as illustrated by certain outsized buildings and larger-than-life monuments that are often used to prop up ethnonationalisms. Hirsch encourages us to pay attention to "small acts" that memorialize events in ways that reveal neglected dimensions of experience, and that may also create room for hope and the imagination of different futures.[15] The memories of embodied survival and resistance narrated here are "small acts" in at least two senses. First, the articulation of these memories is generally not in the form of grandiloquent political manifestos. Although these oral testimonies tell a more than individual story, they often draw on personal memories, family anecdotes, and relationships with friends and fellow activists. Second, many of the acts of survival and resistance that these narratives refer to are "small": they were not spectacular; they did not result in escape from captivity; they did not overthrow the regime; they were not always collectively coordinated (see also Bacci et al. 2012). Many of these accounts are narratives of the subtle and even the imperceptible. They tell of hidden and fleeting embodied connections among human beings who asserted their humanity in a dehumanizing milieu: a kiss, a banned conversation, the circulation of bread, a healing hand, the gift of a piece of clothing. Many of these minute embodied acts of solidarity and resistance helped to counter, erode, or cushion the power of an overwhelming structure of oppression, disrupting the military regime's definition of detainees' realities and identities (Calveiro 1998; Bacci et al. 2012).

These small acts remind us that, as Butler (2014) suggests, vulnerability is not the opposite of agency, and that agency can take multiple forms. From a long-term perspective, we can also see the cumulative and public impact of small acts that helped sustain detainees during captivity, in the sense of enabling the *possibility* of testimony and denunciation later on. That is, survival was a necessary, though insufficient, condition for many former detainees to be able to denounce the regime and help bring perpetrators to justice. Of course, the survival of the people in captivity has intrinsic value—whether they chose to testify or not. Yet, the broader and public significance of survival is highlighted here because the idea of surviving to tell the story also appears in various testimonies.[16]

Small acts might not be readily recognized as important, and there is often a gender bias with respect to the seemingly minimal stories that also make history. Women's "small stories," particularly those from marginalized social locations, may be "obscured by more important public figures, by large-scale events deemed more significant than those that frame their lives, and by grand narratives that may touch on contexts of significance to them but that effectively brush by them" (Burton 2010, vii). In narrating her participation in Mothers of the Plaza de Mayo, Ilda Micucci—who was also a survivor of clandestine detention—remembered:

> We, women, were in the streets doing things, and men not so much. Because once they did everything [they could] in that first moment, it was as if there was not much more that was left for them, that they could do. Those things that we did were women's things. [. . .] Men have other ways of . . . of fighting, no? Or I think that . . . that they aim more for the big things, the most important things. And those small things, a bit . . . sometimes sort of silly, the ones we did, were only women's [smiles].

In the case of Mothers of the Plaza de Mayo, history in the making is already recognizing that the supposedly small things, silly things, unimportant things that women and other marginalized individuals may do can indeed change the course of events, particularly when these actions become coordinated and ignite larger movements. How many important stories might we miss when we neglect women's "small acts," women's worlds and perspectives?

Though I heard the testimonies only of women, through their stories I also learned secondhand about some of the detained men's "small acts" of solidarity and resistance (e.g., a man sneaking poems to a woman detainee in response to her gesture of solidarity, a young man feeding an older one, and yet another man giving emotional support to a woman during transportation to a CDC). Jean Franco (1992) mentioned some of the "feminizing" aspects of captivity in the Latin American secret prisons—might this feminizing also breed forms of survival and transgression associated with women? Or perhaps these are simply acts of humanity that are not the exclusive province of any gender. Still, it is possible that gender influences what becomes salient in a particular testimony, what deserves to be remembered and narrated. In her work with testimonies of political prisoners of the dictatorship, Rebekah Park

(2013) detected gendered differences in how they narrated resistance and political commitment (*compromiso*): women tended to highlight "their resistance and solidarity within the prison walls," while men tended to connect "their own lives to Argentina's longer history of social change, reasserting their assumed role in history-at-large" (90). While narratives of solidarity, mutual care, and support within CDCs are important dimensions of women's testimonies in the present study,[17] many did also talk about their activism and how their lives connected to broader historical and political events.

Part of the value of the Memoria Abierta testimonies lies in the possibility of acknowledging the importance—for the protagonists themselves and for collective memory—of overlooked dimensions of political resistance and captivity. The small stories about embodied acts of survival and resistance, which include people of various genders, deserve to be registered, heard, and shared as part of historical memory. While instances of resistance must be remembered, I also believe they should not be romanticized, particularly given the high costs that many people paid for their transgression, and since the results of these types of actions are never guaranteed. And yet, testimonies of resistance, solidarity, and survival also encourage us to think about the lessons that these actions offer for today's world and for the construction of a tomorrow with social justice and full respect of human rights. This forward-looking perspective animates the next chapter.

5

Transmitting Memory, Reclaiming Utopia

> Speaking about memories means speaking about the pres-
> ent. In truth, memory is not the past, but the *way in which*
> *subjects construct a sense of the past*, a past that becomes
> meaningful in connection with the present through the act
> of remembering/forgetting; as well as based on a desired
> future. The present contains and constructs past experience
> and future expectations.
> —Jelin (2013, 79, emphasis original)

Past, present, and future interweave in survivors' narratives about the
recent history of state terrorism in Argentina. As scholars of collective
memory remind us, memories of the past are also formulations of and
from the present (e.g., Jelin 2004; Traverso 2007). Current concerns influence how societies remember the past, and memories of the past also
shape present events and future options. Even when orienting the narrative toward the future, it is easy to be thrown back to the past, as the range
of possibilities for the future is demarcated by prior experiences. Our collective and personal memories, the opportunities and challenges we face
as members of particular societies, and the lessons learned and unlearned
during specific historical periods are already traces of the future—a future
that nevertheless is not already determined but susceptible to change.
Gabriela Fried Amilivia (2016, 23) considers memory "not as grounded in
the past or present, but in the future, working as a compass, providing orientation and guidance to individuals, communities, nations, and regions."
In light of these considerations, this chapter explores the following questions: How did memories of state terrorism relate to the ways women
survivors conceptualized more contemporary social problems? How did
they construct a sense of futurity based on personal and political memories, including activist histories? What insights about social change do they
offer, and what messages did they wish to transmit to future generations?

These questions expand the scope of inquiry beyond survivors' time in clandestine detention. While certainly drawing on these past experiences, women survivors also offered poignant political commentary and insights that are relevant for today's social and political issues. These analyses were anchored not only in their experiences of captivity but, in the case of several women, in a history of political involvement and participation before, during, and/or after the dictatorship. In this chapter, I aim to emphasize women's *political* voices, not only referring to their past activism but also foregrounding their political assessments and visions for justice, democracy, and human rights in the contemporary world. Their testimonies also shed light on important aspects of activism such as the role of bodies and emotions and an ethics of solidarity and perseverance. These women shared their political perspectives with an eye toward transmitting their memories to future generations, particularly since their archived testimonies would transcend the moment in which they told their stories.

In order to listen fully to women survivors' political voices, it is important to recognize their historical and political agency and not just cast them as victims of violence (Fried 2006; Macón 2014; MacManus 2015). In the early years of the democratic transition, the political identities of the people held in clandestine centers were minimized or silenced (Otero 2010; Crenzel 2011a; Jelin 2013). This silence was related partly to the installation of the human rights paradigm, which was central to the denunciation and judgment of the military atrocities. As Jelin (2013, 87) points out, there was a shift from political discourse that underscored "class struggle" and "national revolutions" to a discourse of human rights; and this meant "putting the emphasis on the violation and suffering of the victim (passive), over [that person's] commitment (active) to a politically significant project or action." It was as if recognizing the political background and activities of the people disappeared or of the survivors meant yielding to the frame of the state's repressive apparatus, which used blanket labels such as "subversive delinquents" or "terrorist delinquents" to characterize the people targeted.[1] In this context, while many survivors contributed their testimonies to the report by the CONADEP (1984) and/or to the trial of the military juntas (1985) (Bacci 2015), the human rights organizations formed by family members of the disappeared took center stage in public discourse and visibility.[2]

In the discourse of the democratic transition, the status of *victims* was attributed not only to women but to other survivors and people disappeared. In denouncing the atrocities of the dictatorship, the notion of "innocence" was often invoked and particularly applied to some sectors of the population, such as very young victims and people not involved in the armed political organizations. Kathryn Sikkink (2011, 73) narrates that in the 1985 trial of the military juntas the cases considered especially compelling and thus presented first included "those victims who had no connection to the guerrilla movements." One of these cases included high school students tortured and disappeared (one of the survivors who testified at the trial had been kidnapped at age sixteen).[3] In addition to children, women as a group are more likely than men to be placed in the "innocent victim" category in the context of political violence, armed conflict, and repression. Cynthia Enloe (1991) refers to this socially constructed notion of innocence through the term "womenandchildren," which points to women's infantilization and the conflation of groups who are deemed to need special protection. This conflation is often based on women's association with noncombatant status, as opposed to adult men who are more likely assumed to be combatants/not innocent.

Traditional gender stereotypes and general assumptions depicting women as apolitical, or as mere victims of violence, obscure women's participation in revolutionary movements and armed struggles around the world (Gómez-Barris 2009; Melzer 2015). In the Argentine case, these notions also undermine recognition of the significant activist experience and accumulated political knowledge of many women taken to clandestine detention centers (CDCs). Although a detailed analysis of the activist trajectories of individual women is beyond the scope of this work, I argue that we can learn a great deal from listening to women survivors' voices in political terms, from a perspective that does not relegate them to passive roles, but recognizes them as history makers. The relevance of women survivors' political voices might be more readily appreciated if we also remember the wealth of political experiences that many of these women have drawn on, based on personal and collective histories of activism. These activist dimensions of experience are intricately connected to the social memory of state terrorism, for it was precisely the wave of mobilization for radical social change that the military regime aimed to crush.

The large majority of the fifty-two women in this study had activist experiences before the dictatorship (71 percent were members of various political, community, labor, rural, religious, student, and armed organizations that mobilized to bring about social and political transformations). Even some women who were unaffiliated with specific political organizations still participated in discrete actions, such as marches and political debates, or supported the efforts of political organizations. Some women who had not been activists before the dictatorship joined or helped found human rights organizations later on in response to the political situation in the country and its concrete impact on their lives. Additionally, a number of survivors who had been activists before the dictatorship also became involved in human rights activism, among other forms of social and political organizing over the years.

The political voices of survivors of state terror have contemporary significance, even when many of the insights they offer are based on past events. For one thing, in order to interrogate the present and envision a future, it is often necessary to return to the past. However, this means not remaining stuck in a previous era, but learning from it. Through her notion of "revolutionary time," feminist philosopher Fanny Söderbäck (2012) argues for an understanding of time and social change that allows subjects to be grounded in history while also able to break from the past. In many cases, this means avoiding both oblivion as well as the recurrence of marginalization, exclusion, and ultimately atrocity against people deemed different, dangerous, or expendable. This approach also entails a recognition that the future is open-ended and susceptible to change. The model that Söderbäck proposes differs from models of linear and cyclical time, and refers to "a temporal movement that neither forgets nor repeats the past, a model of time that allows us to redeem the past and the present without instrumentalizing them in the name of a future always already defined in advance" (304). It is in the spirit of revolutionary time that I juggle various temporalities in this chapter, looking to the past while traversing the present and orienting the gaze toward the future.

Women's histories of activism are part of a past that Argentine society is still grappling with and that reactualizes itself in current social and political conflicts: be it around the appropriate economic model for the country, the state response to political protest, or the role of state armed and police forces in ensuring "security." As gains in the human rights field cannot be taken for granted and because many of the promises of democracy remain unfulfilled, visions of transformation from past social movements continue to be relevant. Based on their activist experiences, several women survivors reclaimed utopia, even after the extreme suffering they went through. A number of these women continued their involvement in social justice projects, human rights work, and politically significant initiatives. They recognized the changes in the political landscape and in their own biographies, but often held on to hard-fought visions for a more just world. According to survivor Alicia Morales, who was a political activist in the seventies and the chairperson of a human rights organization in the post-dictatorship period, "If we don't have utopias there is no tomorrow."

Reclaiming utopia and working toward a better present and future demand taking stock of the past. In this sense, examining the shortcomings of and deriving insights from previous social change efforts—including past revolutionary projects—are important for the transmission of memory. Among the issues that remain relevant today are gender inequality and violence against women as well as women's struggles to assert their political voices and demands. Hence, the first part of this chapter returns to the past with the aim to highlight, along with other feminist scholars and activists, women's historical and political agency, despite significant obstacles. Keeping in mind women activists' experiences, particularly in revolutionary and other movements for social change, I then turn to women survivors' perspectives on contemporary issues, addressing what they wished to transmit through their testimonies.

Reclaiming Women's Political Agency

Feminist scholars investigating the recent history of state and political violence in Latin America have drawn attention to women in the context of male-dominated narratives. Some have also challenged accounts—both mainstream and feminist—that emphasize mainly the victimization of women. For instance, in her assessment of the limitations of the women's human rights discourse and its tendency to focus on women as victims, Viviana MacManus (2015, 42) argues for "ways of retaining women's political subjectivities." In response to the common depoliticization of the testimonies of women who survived human rights violations in Latin America, including Argentina, MacManus states: "I insist that we not allow the mainstreaming of human rights discourse to efface histories of women's activism in anti-capitalist, anti-racist and anti-misogynist resistance movements in Latin America (and globally). We cannot separate the political and economic history of violence from the history of gender violence that is exhibited in these testimonies" (54).

In a similar vein, Rebekah Park's (2013) work with former political prisoners of the dictatorship in Argentina reveals that these survivors did not want to focus on their victimization through torture and instead preferred to emphasize their political identities and agency. However, Park's findings also suggest that the available (gendered) frameworks to interpret politics in Argentina have likely influenced how men and women narrate their political resistance and what they choose to emphasize. Park found gender differences in the accounts of men and women members of the Association of Former Political Prisoners of Córdoba, Argentina: "Women defined their compromiso [political commitment] in their personal acts of resistance in prison; they resisted the oppressive conditions, they say, by refusing to give up information or to collaborate. The men, instead of talking about their personal experiences in prison, saw their compromiso located in these large-scale movements of which they were a part, that they played a role in this larger history" (2013, 107).

These findings raise questions about why women who had been political activists would deemphasize their experiential connections to "major historical events as the backdrop to their personal narratives" (96) while men would choose to highlight those linkages. Park suggests that women who were formerly imprisoned had a limited set of available narratives in which to insert themselves. In the post-dictatorship period, Mothers of the Plaza de Mayo figured prominently as embodying gendered forms of resistance to the dictatorship. The struggles of Grandmothers of the Plaza de Mayo also gained national and international visibility. Yet these roles did not readily fit the trajectories of a wide range of women survivors (though as discussed earlier, among the people taken to CDCs were also some women who became Mothers or Grandmothers of Plaza de Mayo). Furthermore, given the history of gender hierarchies in social movements and political organizations (despite the iconic status of political figures like former First Lady Eva Perón),[4] the experiences of women who were political prisoners during the period of state terrorism might not have readily fit "the male-dominated historical narratives of labour unions and university movements" (Park 2013, 109).

Feminist and other critical works during the past decade have shed further light on women's experiences in recent history, as well as on gender/sexuality dynamics, beyond the more common focus on Mothers of the Plaza de Mayo.[5] It is clear that countless women participated in the "great events" of recent history—and not just women fitting traditional gender expectations as wives, mothers, or grandmothers—but telling these stories has generally not been a priority. From participation in multiple social and political organizations before the coup to resistance to the dictatorship in Argentina and abroad, women were more than mere spectators. While the role of Mothers and Grandmothers of Plaza de Mayo has been visible and recognized in relation to the history of the dictatorship, the stories of other women who suffered the brunt of state terrorism also deserve attention. As was the case in various Latin American countries, many women in Argentina were killed, tortured, raped, disappeared, or imprisoned during the period of state terrorism precisely because they were politically active in various revolutionary organizations or other groups considered "subversive."[6]

The history of women's political participation becomes evident in many of Memoria Abierta's interviews with women survivors, particularly as they situated their personal biographies within the major movements, events, and organizations of the sixties and seventies.[7] For instance, some of these women spoke about the student and labor uprising known as the Cordobazo, the emergence of guerrilla organizations and their affiliated groups, the return from exile of former president Juan D. Perón, and the influence of Peronism in Argentina's history. Though there is variation to the depth and breadth of the political narratives in the testimonies, through these interviews one gets a sense of the intense political organizing that characterized the period, including in high schools, universities, labor unions, working-class neighborhoods, shantytowns, and rural communities, among others. Women's testimonies also addressed linkages between grassroots organizations, the political movements of the time, and the international dimensions of social conflict and political turmoil. Anecdotes about women's political involvement abound in the various testimonies I listened to in Memoria

Abierta. To contextualize these women's experiences and perspectives, I first draw on existing works on women's political participation in the sixties and seventies. Later in the chapter, I develop analyses based on Memoria Abierta's testimonies as I consider activist legacies and insights relevant to social movement theory and practice.

Women's narratives are at the center of some of the books that recount activist experiences in recent history, including in armed political organizations and their mass political fronts. An early contribution is *Mujeres guerrilleras* (Guerrilla Women) by journalist Marta Diana (1996). This book gathers the testimonies of women who were part of guerrilla organizations, regardless of whether they participated or not in concrete armed political actions. Already in this work, a number of stories show that even when having similar political commitments and involvement, "a woman [was] not as equal as a man" (28). The testimony of "Frida" is illustrative in this regard (see also Oberti 2015). A hardcore activist, Frida found herself confined in the home after having two children; meanwhile, her partner—father of the children and a committed activist himself—continued his political activities. One day, tired of the situation, Frida arranged for a babysitter to watch their children. She was criticized by men in her political organization, for they saw such solution as petit bourgeois. In a meeting with men leaders, she was confronted about her decision while her partner observed nervously. At some point, Frida recounted, her partner went to the kitchen to fetch coffee for the meeting participants: "But he returns right away and he asks me: 'Where is the sugar?' I looked at the compañeros who had come to 'judge' my attitude and I said: 'I think that the problem is already presented, because if in a household where there are two babies with the parents, one of the adults doesn't know where the sugar is, [then] it is very clear that the debate here is not with me but with the compañero who does not know where the sugar is in his house'" (60–61).

According to Frida, this anecdote exemplified the gender inequality that pervaded aspects of activism and the difficulty to tackle the *machismo* that characterized the attitudes of men and even some women in revolutionary movements (but which negatively affected women in particular). Frida pushed back and her response gave way to a discussion of domestic conflicts between men and women in the organization. Various other stories in *Mujeres guerrilleras* relate the particular challenges that women faced, even as they participated side by side with men in their efforts to create the revolution.

In the past decade, new historiographical studies and sociological works have analyzed Argentine recent history and the emergence of the "new left" through a gender lens, in ways that both make visible women's experiences and also problematize male-dominated narratives and assumptions.[8] For instance, in *Género, política y revolución en los años setenta* (Gender, Politics and Revolution in the Seventies), Paola Martínez (2009) examines the participation of women in the Workers' Revolutionary Party–People's Revolutionary Army (Partido Revolucionario de los Trabajadores–Ejército Revolucionario del Pueblo, PRT-ERP). She argues that political participation by many women had not been primarily driven by romantic partnership or other relationships with militant men, but by these women's own political commitments and convictions. They "entered the PRT-ERP convinced about their ideas, as a result of having made incursions into other political experiences at the university, in high school, in parties of the traditional left (socialist and communist) in labor union or syndical activism and parties of the new left, as well as other armed political organizations or of the revolutionary Christianity" (Martínez 2009, 158).

Yet, as anticipated in Diana's book (1996), women encountered gender-specific obstacles to their activism. These challenges were based not only on revolutionary organizations' ideals around the *Hombre Nuevo* ("New Man") in the style of the iconic revolutionary Che Guevara—which were ill-suited to account for various aspects of women's lives—but also on gender-discriminatory practices and attitudes (Martínez 2009). These asymmetries included women's disproportionate domestic responsibilities in practice (despite the organization's promotion of a more equitable division of labor) as well as barriers to achieve the highest levels of leadership within political organizations (see also Oberti 2015). Some of the testimonies by women who participated in revolutionary organizations, including in the Memoria Abierta testimonies, advance a gender-based critique, noting patterns of gender inequality. In her study about the Montoneros-affiliated women's organization Agrupación Evita, Karin Grammático (2011) asserts that in this context some women started to develop an "incipient questioning of the roles that they performed both in the home and the political spheres" (86). Interestingly, some women activists initially viewed their organization's assignment to work in a women's-only political group as a kind of demotion, a site separate from where the supposed real action was. Thus they joined Agrupación Evita reluctantly, even if they eventually came to appreciate the value of this work (Grammático 2011; Oberti 2015).

In her book *Las revolucionarias* (The Women Revolutionaries), Alejandra Oberti (2015) also explores the experiences of women in the armed political organizations of the seventies in Argentina, notably the People's Revolutionary Army (ERP) and Montoneros. From the subordination of women in the structure of organizations and during specific missions to the failure to arrange adequate support for women who had to give birth in the midst of political repression and the pre-eminence of a militarized orientation that was more in sync with men's socialization, women faced gender-specific challenges. Still, as Oberti observes, women's participation in revolutionary movements also enabled them to visualize themselves outside of normative gender expectations: not only as mothers, but as workers, activists, and fighters. A different mode of feminine embodiment, linked to high-risk activism, was also entertained: for example, "a new way of imagining the body (*carrying backpacks, going out on missions*) in a radically extra-domestic situation" (Oberti 2015, 90, emphasis original). Women's political voices found a space during this period in which women increasingly joined the political sphere of activism. Oberti suggests that even though there was already an emerging feminist presence and critique in the Argentine cultural and political scene of the time, feminism was not the main venue through which activist women tended to channel "their yearnings for liberty, equality and participation in public life" (180).

Many of the gender-mixed leftist organizations, including the revolutionary ones, provided such a space for women—but with limitations: while "some activists emphatically proposed that it was necessary to consider other forms of subordination and tried ways of combining activism in [revolutionary] organizations with feminist demands and a politics specifically directed to women, these positions have not been the majoritarian ones. The hegemonic version of the radicalized left consisted in subordinating the demands for equality to the practice of political activism and with that, to the universal and sexless character (that is, masculine) of the subject of politics" (Oberti 2015, 180). While these organizations combined a rhetoric of equality and an openness to women's participation, women's testimonies suggest that they generally failed to create a truly equal space for women or to recognize the specificity of women's embodied experiences in ways that did not result in their subordination (Oberti 2015).

From a feminist perspective, the already referenced gender conflicts around child care that Frida narrated in *Mujeres Guerrilleras* (Diana 1996) would be understood as not merely personal, but political—in the sense of being part of a societal pattern of gender inequality. Yet Frida's anecdote illustrates how the men in her organization had already politicized the issue, but in a different sense: by making Frida's child care arrangements their organization's business. This particular form of politicization is consistent with how, in armed groups such as Montoneros and ERP, "the personal became political within a collectivity that sought to build new moral foundations with the aim of banishing capitalist values (including individualism) from social relations but also from family and romantic relationships" (Cosse 2014, 447). In fact, the boundaries between personal and political were blurred, to the point that important aspects of everyday life and personal relationships were subsumed under the political (see also Peller 2013). All in all, the organizations had a say about "personal" matters such as romantic relations, infidelity, cohabitation, and separations among activists and their partners (see, e.g., Carnovale 2008; Martínez 2009; Felitti 2010; Cosse 2014; Oberti 2015).

The politicization of life within the most prominent revolutionary organizations had gender and sexuality implications, which included the delimitation of sexual expression and procreation within a monogamous and heterosexual norm, along with other rules on sexuality, which if violated could lead to punishment of both men and women (Felitti 2010; Cosse 2014). Yet, as Karina Felitti (2010) points out, women's punishment was likely to be compounded by societal stereotypes, for instance, around the construction of the "whore." Homophobia also played a role: "According to the logic of armed organizations, the *maricas* [pejorative for homosexual] were *flojos* [weak], that is, too *feminine* to act in the operatives, to resist torture, and not become informers" to the enemy (Felitti 2010, 81, emphasis original). That is, gender and sexuality inequalities were entwined in organizational logic, despite rhetoric on equality.

The reproduction of gender inequality within revolutionary organizations in Argentina has some overlaps with those of other revolutionary movements in Latin America. In her analysis of the Cuban and Nicaraguan revolutions, Lorraine Bayard de Volo (2012, 414) argues that "[a]lthough these revolutions were officially committed to the liberation of women, the devaluation and rejection of the feminine worked to maintain gender hierarchy." She states that gender asymmetries persisted even as the figure of "tough but tender guerrillas" was advanced (419). In the case of women, this figure was reflected in the idealized representation of the "woman with a baby at her breast and a rifle slung over her shoulder" as emblematic of the "New Woman" (421). Yet Volo points out that the combination of toughness and tenderness (toughness frequently associated with masculinity and tenderness usually linked to femininity and maternal love) still re-created gender inequality. This was evidenced by the militarized and gender hierarchies in various revolutionary organizations, and in the need to selectively suppress emotions such as tenderness in order to effectively become "cold killing machines" (422) for the sake of achieving specific revolutionary objectives.

In her work about El Salvador's prominent guerrilla organization FMLN (Farabundo Martí National Liberation Front), Jocelyn Viterna (2013, 117) also notes that despite former participants' "shared narrative of gender equality," which posited that "jobs were assigned to the most qualified individual" regardless of gender, this narrative was "in sharp contrast to the reality of a strikingly gendered system of stratification in the guerrilla camps." In the case of Guatemala, Emilie Smith-Ayala (1991, 208) noted that although revolutionary organizations incorporated women in various capacities, they failed to include "women's oppression [. . .] as an integral part of the struggle for social justice." The testimony of Yolanda Colom (1998) about her participation in a guerrilla organization in Guatemala spoke of pervasive machismo in Guatemalan society, which also percolated into practices and attitudes in revolutionary organizations. In Daphne Patai's book (1993), the testimony of "Célia," who was an activist in a leftist organization in Brazil during the seventies, highlighted the contradiction between proclaimed ideals and actual practice: "The organization had a line, actually a very good line, on women. [. . .] The men in the organization are totally in favor of the emancipation of women—on the 'woman problem,' the document is terrific. It's great for women, other women, but not in my house!" (239).

Interestingly, women's feminist consciousness sometimes emerged in relation to their revolutionary political participation as they questioned, at the time or later on, the gender logics that shaped such involvement. (In some cases, it took exile for revolutionary women to make sense of their experiences within a feminist frame [Felitti 2010].) Karen Kampwirth's comparison of insurgent movements in El Salvador, Nicaragua, and, more recently, Chiapas (Mexico, 1990s) shows the unintended consequences of mobilizations that did not start as a quest for gender equality. According to Kampwirth (2004, 165), "in all three cases, many of the women who were mobilized for one agenda came to rethink those political goals, and the best way to carry them out, after the original crisis had passed. In both Nicaragua and El Salvador vibrant autonomous feminist movements emerged after the wars. In Chiapas, before the war had even ended, women's rights activities grew and consolidated both in women's organizations and within the nationwide indigenous rights movement." A feminist lens can be useful not only to reclaim women's political participation, but to constructively critique the functioning of gender-mixed political organizations that welcomed women and created significant spaces for their participation yet failed to radically transform gender hierarchies.

In the Memoria Abierta testimonies, some women offer a critique of the political organizations to which they belonged, including top-down authority structures, limited space to express dissent about certain decisions, increasing disconnection from the masses, the lack of women in the most senior leadership positions, and other sexist characteristics. For instance, Marta Álvarez, who had been a political activist and survived extended captivity at the Escuela de Mecánica de la Armada, mentioned that for a long time it was hard to question the ways in which *militancia* (activism/militancy) functioned, including the authoritarian and machista facets of the revolutionary organization she joined. Marta talked about how there was often a prioritization and valorization of men's activist work while women were assigned to secondary tasks even when included in high-risk missions (e.g., being the *campana*, lookout person). She also observed a tendency of activist women to *masculinizarse* (adopt masculinist traits) in terms of clothing, modes of expression, and avoidance of emotional displays associated with weakness, such as crying. Revolutionary organizations' critiques of class relations also filtered into the realm of activist women's physical appearance: Marta recounted how displays of normative femininity, such as wearing makeup or dressing up, were considered petit bourgeois (see similarity with the testimony of "Célia" who participated in a leftist organization in Brazil [Patai 1993]). In fact, activist women sometimes deployed conventional feminine behavior or appearance (e.g., wearing makeup and miniskirts) as a political strategy, including to avoid suspicion about their activities (Oberti 2005). These examples offer a glimpse of how women's political participation demanded that they grapple with or negotiate new ways of inhabiting gendered bodies, including rejecting and strategically deploying normative femininity.

While women in Argentina participated in political life in significant numbers during the sixties and seventies, including in revolutionary organizations, their stories have traditionally not been the most salient. And yet, as in the case of men, numerous women paid for their activism with state and parastatal repression. They were not spared from extreme violence because of their gender. In fact, as already analyzed in previous chapters, aspects of their identities as women compounded their oppression in the torture centers. In the following sections, and starting with the recognition of the accumulated activist experience of many women survivors, I focus on what messages and memories they wanted to pass on through their testimonies, particularly to future generations. As we shall see, and akin to Park's (2014) findings from her interviews with former political prisoners in Argentina, it is not just pain and horror that many of these women remember. In fact, they also recover other dimensions of experience such as personal and political commitment, collective organization, and the pursuit of utopias.

Dreams and Activisms

In listening to the testimonies of survivors, it becomes evident that the living memory of the seventies is a memory not only of tragedy but also of the ideals and commitments that inspired the lives, work, and activism of those targeted by state repression. Survivors remind us that many of the people held in CDCs had turned to certain political and social projects with the intention of changing the world, of creating more equitable societies. Survivor Cristina Guillén, who was an activist in the province of Córdoba, pointed out that it was a "unique histori- cal moment" and a "unique generation" whose "drive toward *el hacer* [action], toward commitment, cannot be objected." The field of activ- ism that Cristina was implicitly alluding to was not a homogeneous camp, but formed by diverse "social and political forces that decisively contributed to produce an intense process of social protest and political radicalization, ranging from spontaneous outbreaks and cultural revolts to guerrilla actions" (Tortti 2006, 22).

The testimonies of Memoria Abierta recover the activist, political, and social commitments of many survivors of state terrorism, helping to deconstruct the victimhood/agency dichotomy. In the testimonies analyzed, women talked about their experiences in ways that reveal the articulation of individual biographies and political events in the country, even before the coup, often narrating intense political activity. Thus, we can hear the echoes of the utopias and dreams that propelled the ac- tions of so many. For example, Patricia Erb—who was a political activist before her abduction at age nineteen—remembers people of her genera- tion who had "a conception of an utopia that was much closer than what it really was, but which generated the possibility of very beautiful human beings." In her testimony, Patricia mentioned the difficulty of transmit- ting a full account of these experiences to younger interlocutors (her own children). However, she also posited that "those people's energy"— the ones who were activists in the seventies—can nourish the present: "[O]ne picks it up, and I believe that ahead is a period when people will once again try to think how we can organize ourselves better in the world. That's how I feel it, I feel that southern winds are blowing now." She offered her testimony in 2007, during the decade when various Latin American countries were governed by left or center-left governments, known as the Pink Tide.[9] Patricia was working on development issues in Bolivia, a Pink Tide country under President Evo Morales. As progres- sive or leftist politics became embattled and the tide turned to the right in Argentina and other parts of Latin America, the question of how to organize for a more equitable society became particularly relevant.

Continuity and Change

While uniform descriptions can hardly encompass the diversity and complexity of the vast group of people disappeared by state terrorism—and the risk of idealization or demonization is ever present—it is still possible to think about what aspects of a generation's dreams and forms of knowledge can be recovered and projected into the future. This legacy does not belong only to the disappeared, but continues alive in many of the people who survived. For several survivors, there was a connecting thread between their past activism and their work at the time of their interviews. Julia Ruiz, who was a political activist in her youth, commented, "it is not a coincidence that I continue my human rights activism." She also mentioned that many other survivors "continue working on social issues" and "doing activism, acting in politics." Even though the political project that in the seventies motivated many of these women was brutally interrupted, that does not necessarily mean that their views and actions toward social change were dismantled. Adriana Friszman—an activist in the seventies and college professor living in Brazil at the time of her testimony (2004)—explained: "That which once upon a time led me to activism continues to be present, unmovable, despite that we lost, that they crushed us. But the reasons that led to that [activism] continue to exist, and the will to contribute so that we might have a *mundo mejorcito* [a world that is a little better], to the extent possible, remains. What has changed? What's changed is the perspective. It doesn't need to be here, it doesn't need to be in this political site. It is a way of life, let's say." In various testimonies, we see that, through changing political and historical circumstances, survivors adapted to and adopted new ways of intervening in the political realm, trying to make a difference: in public office, through education, in the media, in sites of memory, as part of human rights organizations, and through community and social welfare work, among others.

For some women, activism became an engine of their own lives. Carmen Lapacó, survivor of clandestine detention and also a Mother of Plaza de Mayo, articulated the deep existential meaning that her activist journey had for her: "It has served me to continue living. [. . .] I had to go out to struggle. And that struggle and the company of the people who were by my side was very good for me. It helped me to go on, and as I say, I will keep going even if with two canes, walking with that walker [laughs] but I will continue as long as my mind allows me to."

While a number of women survivors continued (or started) their activism post-detention—in new forms and spaces—it would be a mistake to simply advance heroic interpretations. Recognizing the resilience, forms of resistance, and commitment of these women does not contradict the possibility of recognizing the profound marks that state terror left in their lives, to the point that some women who had histories of committed activism prior to their kidnappings did not participate again in political organizations. Not only did the dictatorship decimate the political organizations to which many belonged, but also the disruptive and traumatic experiences of clandestine detention, persecution, and/or exile conditioned their participation even after the end of the dictatorship.

The reclamation of activism was not a uniform response in the testimonies, and thus it is important to also hear such perspectives, particularly since there may be many more women who withdrew from politics, but whose stories may not be publicly available (women who perhaps are less likely to participate in a project like Memoria Abierta's Oral Archive). Liliana Gardella was a political activist in the seventies and at the time of the interview an anthropologist and co-author of the book *Ese infierno* (Actis et al. 2001). While taking stock of her experience, during the interview with Memoria Abierta, Liliana related: "No, on balance, things did not turn out well. I suffered and suffer a lot. I don't have a good life. It would've . . . it would've been better not to do activism. I wouldn't have suffered what I suffered. Now, how does this get resolved? How does one improve the world around us? I don't know." The high personal cost of political activities in the context of brutal repression, and particularly the painful sequelae of experiences of clandestine detention appear in different testimonies. The modes in which pain was processed are diverse, and in various cases compounded by the loss of other family members and loved ones.

Furthermore, the different life trajectories and backgrounds of different women also shape responses. In contrast with the military discourse, not all people targeted by the regime were involved in political activities, let alone armed struggle. For example, Luisa Blanco de Amarilla mentioned that she had not been interested in politics and had led a life dedicated to her three children before the dictatorship. She had also worked in a factory, where she met her husband, and at home as a seamstress. She defined herself as someone who went from her "home to work and from work to home." During the dictatorship, she was kidnapped along with her husband and one of her sons, and held in captivity for about a week. Another son, Fernando, was also targeted by state forces and his body was disappeared. Fernando's partner was kidnapped and disappeared while pregnant, so Luisa may have had a grandchild. From the interview, one may infer that Fernando was involved in high-risk activism. However, this is somewhat implied, for instance, in a statement in which Luisa mentioned that though she did not know much about his activities, she had never seen a firearm in the house.[10] When asked about the message she wished to convey to those who might listen to her testimony, she recommended that young people

> tell their parents everything that happens to them, everything that they do, so that one can give them advice, whether it is good or bad what they do. That they have faith in God, that God helps everyone. I don't know what else. That they be good students, that they work. That it is very sad that a kid who studies, who works, who has led a nice life, gets killed, taken away because of something. So that's why I tell them to have trust in their parents, that they tell them about what's going on. Not that they do . . . I don't know. . . . That they realize that it is a mother who is talking, who did not . . . never left the eggshell, so to speak, no? That I was always . . . I've never gone out to dances, those kinds of things.

Unlike other survivors who had more of a message of transgression and rebellion for young people, here we see the implicit advice to go by the rules, by what is expected—study and work—under the guidance of family and God. The reference to the possibility of being killed or taken away because of "something" is ambiguous; as if that "something" could still not be named or talked about (e.g., political activities) or as if "something" pointed to the sheer arbitrariness of state power (e.g., "anything" could trigger a brutal response). In contrast to the radical change in subjectivity that some mothers of the disappeared experienced— illustrated by the Mothers of Plaza de Mayo's repeated notion that "our children gave birth to us" (*Nuestros hijos nos parieron*)—Luisa spoke as a mother who "never left the eggshell." While epic narratives about activism and changing the world are perhaps comforting or inspirational, the diversity of life experiences and ways of accounting for the past denote a more complex texture of the reach of suffering and the ways to continue living.

The testimonies also evidence political differences, points of tension, and issues that appear ambiguous or unsaid—about both certain dimensions of activism, particularly armed struggle, as well as situations within CDCs that can be painful to remember or recount (see also Davidovich 2014). Independently of their past activism, and whether they continued or not with political activities, the fact that these women decided to give testimony shows their commitment to intervene in the public realm and their desire to contribute to issues that are related to, though not exhaustive of, politics. However, it is also important to remember those women who survived but perhaps abstained from giving public testimony. How did they process trauma? How might the passage through clandestine detention have affected practices of citizenship in the context of democracy? How did these experiences influence (or fail to influence) the desire to participate in groups with an impact upon the political life of the country? As Macón points out (2015a), the silence of women who decided not to publicly testify may be driven by various motives, related not necessarily to passivity or denial, but to an active desire to process the experience in a manner independent of the frames established by the judiciary, human rights organizations, or the media.

Today, survivors who might retain a desire to participate politically are facing a very different scenario from the one of the seventies. Not only have the times changed, but some of those who survived the dictatorship no longer live in the country. Perhaps due to their experiences during and after captivity, as well as the more recent political context, one can see that along with the continuity of ideals, some shifts in perspective took place in terms of the conceptualization of paths to social transformation. Instead of the more overarching or revolutionary activism of the seventies, which included the notion of "taking over power," the ability to make small but significant changes from the position of each person was contemplated at the time of the testimonies. For instance, Adriana Friszman's desire to contribute to create a "world that is a little better" implies a smaller scale intervention, but which in some ways still links everyday activity to politics. As a university professor, she said: "That's activism, too, no?—to do research, disseminate knowledge, to generate knowledge to the extent possible, to teach. [. . .] I have no pretension to save people, or to illuminate. No. But there's so much to do everywhere, there's so much . . . so much to do." Adriana saw academic practice as one mode of intervention, and yet she pointed out: "Of course, it is not the same to do activism than to be a professor. It's not the same. But that's what I do now." We see in this perspective that everyday activities can be politically inflected and at the same time different from political participation in an activist organization with more overarching aims. The testimony of Raquel Odasso also echoes that sentiment. Raquel was a student movement participant and labor activist before her kidnapping. Later on, she became a member of human rights organizations. She said: "Before, perhaps we had grand ambitions, or we believed that it was possible to take over power and do the revolution. Well, maybe we are now more humble and think that, well, we can contribute a bit to the transformation."

These types of statements should not necessarily be read as a retreat to an individual or depoliticized realm (although in some cases there is a striking contrast between a vibrant activist life before the dictatorship and what appears to be a marked departure from politics later on). Collective matters and the need to organize politically emerge in several testimonies, even as different options for change and intervention are considered. The significance of past struggles for today is also mentioned. Survivor Marta Vassallo, a political activist in the seventies and a feminist journalist today, said that recognizing the value of her generation's past activism "is totally compatible with the will to revise the mistaken premises, with the will to turn activism into something that is perhaps more modest but more precise. Where what one says never exceeds that which a human being can really do; and that it should be compatible with stopping to think that one needs an absolutely closed vision of the world in order to act. I believe that closed visions are harmful and one has to know how to maintain that capacity of openness of vision, and of immediate action, of concrete action."

Marta's reflection creates a space for a critical, though not demonizing, assessment of past struggles; and in doing so it generates the possibility to build on the basis of such experience. In this vein, and referring to her generation's activism in the seventies, Liliana Callizo added: "Perhaps we were betting all or nothing, you know, perhaps that should be revisited. Life or death. Perhaps that's not. . . . At that moment, it was [like that] because we were product of an era, of a history—also international, right?" Liliana contextualized the experience of revolutionary movements while retrospectively questioning some of its premises. She was not discarding the experience altogether, but encouraging a critical assessment of past certainties.

The mobilization and activism of the seventies included various strategies, such as the armed struggle of revolutionary organizations. Some survivors who belonged to these organizations explored controversial issues, such as the role of violence to achieve political goals and as a means of social transformation. While the responsibility for the actions of state terrorism firmly rests on those who planned, organized, and executed these atrocities—and so is articulated in the testimonies—some survivors also encourage us to consider the social and political context that surrounded the repression. The need to think more deeply about the role of armed struggle by political organizations emerges in the testimony of Liliana Gardella. In her message to future generations and other people who might access her testimony, Liliana wished for them to

> learn to find in the everyday life of society the things that end up sustaining a repressive structure. That's it. Because everything else is relative, debatable, and fixable. That is not fixable. And if it is useful to know how a [concentration] camp functioned, or if it is useful to know how is it that an organization of activists ends up trapped in a repressive logic and is not able to change the course of things, I think that we must go deeper. I mean, what happened to us that we handed to the military on a platter the possibility of eliminating thirty thousand people from this country? Would they have done it anyway if we had left aside the armed struggle? I don't know. But I think that that's what we need to ask, because if that has to do with the growth and sustenance of a repressive structure—because ultimately this is how these *tipos* [men] make a living, otherwise they need to make a living from something else—well, then evidently it must not be done. Besides the violence and the generic pacifism that one may have developed with the years. But I think that there are options that facilitate certain processes, no? It seems to me that what we must achieve is to dismantle that.

Liliana's narrative poses a number of questions to consider when evaluating social change strategies, though such assessments should take into account the relevant historical contexts. For instance, with regard to the emergence of armed organizations, scholar of art and politics Ana Longoni (2016) encourages us to consider the context of the various coup d'états that characterized Argentine political life since the 1930s, the proscription of Peronism since 1955, and the repressive cultural and political measures of the military regime in power during the 1960s. Furthermore, she argues that in assessing "the radicalization of a sizable part of society" in Argentina, it is also important to keep in mind the international context, including events such as

> the Vietnam war, the U.S. invasion of Santo Domingo, the assassination of Che Guevara in Bolivia, of Martin Luther King in the United States, the massacre of Tlatelolco in Mexico, and so many other pieces of evidence about the systematic application of repressive violence, which convinced many—even Jean-Paul Sartre—that the only legitimate and effective solution was to respond with insurgent violence. This does not mean defending Montoneros or ERP [People's Revolutionary Army], or their methods or actions, but to approach that extreme experience from a situated perspective, incorporating the theoretical and political discussions that took place then, considering that era with less prejudice, and more willingness to understand and elucidate. (Longoni 2016, n.p.)

In terms of the current implications of analyses of insurgent violence, Daniel Feierstein (2011) points out that in contemporary Argentina there are no political groups that present revolutionary armed struggle as a viable method of social transformation, and on the other hand, that it is necessary "to make visible the social reorganization caused by terror as relatively independent of the extent to which different political or cultural groups adhered to insurgent violence" (583). Nevertheless Liliana's call to reflect on the role of violence as a method to achieve social and political changes is important, as past experiences can still inform dimensions of our present and future, even if not as exact replicas of the past. Without excusing state atrocities or adhering to the theory of the "two demons" popularized in the early democratic transition, survivor Pilar Calveiro (2005) undertook such reflection in the book

Política y/o violencia (Politics and/or Violence). She critically analyzed the contexts and practices of guerrilla organizations that emerged "as a response to and a continuation of the violent logic that prevailed in Argentine politics throughout the XX century," particularly the power of the state military apparatus, manifested in successive military coups and through previous terror practices (2005, 97). Calveiro points to the high costs of the displacement of politics by a militarized logic, even within revolutionary organizations aiming to create a more just world.

Some women who were directly involved in guerrilla organizations, or were part of their mass political fronts in the seventies, refer to the political and personal changes that have taken place since those years when armed political organizations challenged the state's monopoly of violence (Calveiro 2005). After their activist experiences, the horror of dictatorship, and decades of (an imperfect) democracy, several continuities and changes are evident in the visions and methods of the past. For instance, Celeste Seydell, who was a political activist in the seventies, asserted during her testimony in the 2000s that she continued fighting for "the well-being of the human being" but in a different form:

My mother said, one starts from [a place] of love, and because of love for [someone or something] one has to do certain things. In that sense, I assumed the armed struggle, it was my turn to fight against people who were subjugating, crushing mankind, who set themselves as the masters of . . . of life and death. It was my turn to do that. But my starting point was love for these [people], not hate toward these others. [. . .] That's all I can say, that love moves the world, and that with love everything can be achieved, in different ways.

In other words, similar ethical commitments guided Celeste's past activism and her more contemporary work with single mothers and adolescents at risk, whom she saw as the "most hurt of society." At the time of the interview, Celeste worked as part of a municipal program on gender violence.

Other survivors also reflected on the past and connected it to more current ideals and activism, from participating in human rights organizations to occupying related positions in the government, working with marginalized populations, and participating in contemporary social movements. Isabel Fernández Blanco—who was a political activist in the seventies and state functionary in the area of human rights at the time of the interview—wanted her audience to know the following:

> I experienced everything that I did in life with much joy, with a zest for life. [. . .] I wanted and want a better world, a more just society. That the ideals continue as strong as when I was a teenager. That the forms change—now being more than fifty years old—the ways of doing politics changed. The context in which we move also changed. That in that moment, even though I was not as convinced that the way to reach power and change the world was through armed struggle, I understood that there was no other way, that it was the only path. Today I believe there are other paths and [. . .] I remain convinced of [the need to] remain politically engaged, to continue fighting for human rights, to continue fighting for a more just society.

A different political landscape along with the passing of time and aging marked a shift in strategy for Isabel, even as her core commitments persisted. Isabel also highlighted the joy associated with the activities she undertook, a theme that appears in a number of other interviews. This raises questions about the role of emotions in activism as well as their relation to activist embodiment and ethics. What insights do survivors of state terror provide that might be relevant today, even as tactics and strategies to intervene in new political and social scenarios change?

Activist Embodiment, Emotions, and Ethics

Women survivors who participated in movements before, during, and/or after the dictatorship narrated forms of activism that involved specific emotions and embodied practices as well as ethical stances. Their reflections are not merely about the past but raise questions that resonate today. They prompt us to consider the relationship between bodies, emotions, and social movement participation. They also advance the value of an ethics of solidarity and perseverance. Women's stories expose the complex facets of political engagement and reveal both the difficult dimensions as well as the rewarding aspects of activism.

Bodies and emotions are an integral part of political action. Emotions often help to motivate and maintain participation in social movements, from moral outrage in the face of injustice to affective ties among movement participants (Goodwin, Jasper, and Polletta 2001; Juris 2008). While everything we do involves our bodies, the role of the body sometimes becomes especially prominent in politics, for example, when activists put their bodies on the line in situations of risk or engage in spectacular and performative protest actions (Parkins 2000; Peterson 2001). Activists may also use their bodies as the text and material grounding of their political message (e.g., DeLuca 1999; Sutton 2007a; Alaimo 2010; O'Keefe 2014). Additionally, movement participants routinely connect with other bodies through everyday actions of embodied care, solidarity, and organizational sustenance. This embodied activist work helps keep movements alive, reflecting organizational principles and commitments and/or societal implicit scripts on the expected division of labor among different groups of people (Sutton 2007b). From physical presence in meetings that may extend for many hours to leafleting or walking door to door to deliver a political message, carrying supplies for a political event or protest, and preparing meals that nourish and sustain the bodies of activists, activism demands embodied presence and work. In Argentina, the phrase *poner el cuerpo* encapsulates the embodied dimensions of activism, including embodied presence and commitment, coherence between words and actions, sacrifice and risk, and activist work (Sutton 2007b).

The embodied and emotional dimensions of political activity and risk are evident in the case of activists taken to CDCs. The torments they endured are extreme examples of the centrality of the body as a target of political repression. While a number of the people disappeared were part of the structure of armed political organizations, which entailed a heightened level of risk, survivor Marta Álvarez pointed out that, in a repressive context, even relatively minor actions of political propaganda, such as graffiti painting, meant risking one's life. This is a theme that continues to this day, as scores of social movement leaders and participants are summarily executed, tortured, or disappeared around the world.[11] Even if not as extreme, other forms of political repression that target the physical body—e.g., the use of Tasers, tear gas, rubber bullets, and batons, if not lethal force—are still part of the arsenal of many police and security forces with which activists have to contend. In the testimonies of women survivors, the embodied consequences of political repression were apparent in the narratives about their time in captivity. Emotions associated with the spread of political repression, such as fear, also emerged in the testimonies, particularly as more and more people in survivors' circle of friends, relatives, and fellow activists started to disappear. Emotions, such as sorrow or outrage, were also integral to the movements denouncing state terrorism, which tried to elicit emotions such as empathy, and hopefully solidarity, from the public (Wolff 2015).

Although many types of political organizing represent demanding embodied work (Sutton 2010), this seems to have been particularly the case for many activists who participated in the radical movements of the sixties and seventies. Women's testimonies of such activism mention its intense pace as well as its all-consuming and seemingly inexorable quality (see also Oberti 2015). This had to do not only with the strong political commitments of a generation of activists, but also with the belief that radical transformation was within reach, for example, as illustrated by Cuba's revolution. As various Memoria Abierta interviewees mentioned, activist immersion also meant that affective relations, including friendship and romantic attachments, tended to form among fellow activists, and that all other projects were touched or subsumed by activism. In her study of armed organizations of the sixties and seventies in Argentina, historian Isabella Cosse (2014, 427) noted how politics "tied together all aspects of life, including social, romantic, and sexual relations." Munú Actis, survivor and artist, reflected on these overarching dimensions of activism: "The activist project was an absolutely comprehensive project, which did not leave anything outside. The partner was inside, the project of how I want to raise my child was inside, the project of my studies was inside, and the image of my mural was inside. And everything . . . everything was part of that project."

Munú also recalled the passion associated with activism and the significance of feeling connected to something larger than the self. One of the implications of this, Munú mentioned, was the acceptance of the possibility of one's death for the cause, given that the revolutionary project transcended individual lives. In other words, for many participants in revolutionary movements, activism could entail the ultimate embodied sacrifice: the loss of one's life. On the one hand, passion—with all its lively connotations—surrounded activism, and on the other, passion and life itself were threatened by repressive forces (and concentration camps in particular). Referring to passion, which according to Munú is needed to produce artwork, she recounted, "I feel that this is one of the things that were mutilated from me, and that I think that I am slowly recovering, no?"

In listening to women's testimonies about activism before the last dictatorship, one can almost feel the strong sweep of history. Laura Schachter, who was part of a high school student organization before the coup, spoke about the speedy unfolding of events, how it seemed virtually impossible not to become politically involved, and how activists' whole life was imbued by the experience. Isabel Cerruti, also a political activist, spoke about how political participation appeared as practically unavoidable, and how there was a very strong emphasis on doing, on action, which shaped activist work. This compelling pull of activism also had embodied costs. While interviewees did not always articulate the embodied toll of activist practices, it is implicit in statements signifying bodily exhaustion and burnout (although at times it is difficult to disentangle the tiredness intrinsic to dedicated political participation from the context of increasing repression that forced many people to be constantly on the run). For instance, Marta Álvarez talked about her activism before her abduction as an all-encompassing, full-time practice that left little room for anything else. She was constantly on the move, and would often sleep while riding public transportation.

Even as they recognized the political context that made possible such intensity, in hindsight some of the women who had been activists raise questions about the costs of a practice that demanded endless dedication and unconditional commitment. These costs included activists' personal exhaustion, lack of time to reflect upon their own activist practices or question the decisions of activists higher in the ranks, and a certain rigidity in their perspectives (see also Oberti 2015). In other words, while key political organizations of the time were vertically structured, some women's reflections point to how not only the structure, but the mode and context of activism (e.g., focus on constant action, no time to think) can also create little space for critique and/or dissent. The expectations of total commitment and the intense pace of participation in tandem with gender expectations (for instance, assigning child care and domestic work to women) created specific challenges for activist women, as their responsibilities were not always compatible (Oberti 2015). These gender expectations started to be questioned in conjunction with or as a result of women's political participation.

At the same time, several women mentioned the rewarding aspects of their activist experiences, including the sense of joy that imbued their political participation before the intensification of repression. Nora Strejilevich spoke about how, for many young people at the time, it seemed impossible not to participate in some form of political activity. Though she did not formally join a political party or organization, she participated in political demonstrations and debates. She mentioned the joyful feelings that surrounded such participation. Emilce Moler, who was a student activist in secondary school, also recalled the joy, commitment, and dignity that young people's activism embodied. Cristina Guillén recounted that though the memory of the period is imprinted with pain—given how state terrorism wrought havoc in the lives of so many people—she also remembered the deep sense of joy and fulfillment involved in active engagement with transformative projects. References to joy also emerged in the testimony of Susana Muñoz, who contrasted this positive affect with early experiences of repression during political protest when she started to realize that state forces were truly capable of beating up and strongly repressing protesters. The sense of joy that these women referred to points to the possibility of deriving deep meaning from agentic, collective, and transformative engagements with the world.

The joy that permeated activist practices is very different from the individualistic, consumer-oriented, personal-responsibility kind of happiness advertised in late capitalist societies or promised to women who fulfill normative gender roles (Ahmed 2010; Vacarezza 2015). In many social and historical contexts, dominant ideologies have often translated in expectations for women and members of subordinated groups to be happy, smile, be pleasant, and make others feel comfortable (Frye 1983; Ahmed 2010). Sara Ahmed (2010) gives examples such as the myth of the "happy housewife" that Betty Friedan and other feminists challenged in the United States during the sixties (572) or how black lesbian feminist Audre Lorde confronted the politics of happiness through her critique of "a medical discourse that attributes cancer to unhappiness and survival or coping to being happy or optimistic" (590). The oppressive expectation of happiness embedded in normative practices and ideologies differs from the kind of joy referred to by women survivors who were activists in Argentina during the sixties and seventies. This was joy that broke away from traditional gender expectations: it was born in rebellion, sustained through solidarity, and expressed in actions that aimed to challenge the structural causes of unhappiness for large sectors of the population. While the joy associated with social movement participation is not something that only women may experience, it is worth considering the deep meaning that it might have had for members of a group socially expected to follow a radically different path, such as centering their lives on marriage and motherhood.

Activist women's references to joy remind us that emotions matter to social movements, and not only in the form of anger or outrage about injustice—which might trigger participation in collective action—but also in the form of positive affect. According to Jasper (2011, 296): "The satisfactions of action[—]from the joy of fusion to the assertion of dignity—become a motivation every bit as important as a movement's stated goals." Survivors' narratives about the joy of activism need not be used to romanticize an activist past that sometimes appears as almost mythical. Yet this dimension of experience is part of the memory of the period, and an important reminder for present and future movements. Liliana Callizo mentioned that it is important "to recognize that history is built with memory, and it is built with truth, and it is built with the crude reality, too. And with joy, no?" Despite having experienced the brutalities of repression and captivity in her own flesh, Liliana concluded with a note of hope, mentioning that activist "struggle is joy, is changing things." She then added that a good ending is possible. This raises the question of how to effectively generate the possibility of a good ending, and how to remain hopeful, when the analysis of reality can easily lead to pessimism, cynicism, or paralysis. Recovering the positive emotions associated with collective action and activists' capacity to change the course of society, Liliana reminds us that the future is not already determined, that different outcomes are possible, and that political participation is worthwhile.

Believing in the possibility of change and exerting energy and dedication toward that end have been key to the trajectories of a number of women who survived clandestine detention and political imprisonment, particularly those who continued with some sort of activism after the dictatorship. In these cases, an ethics of perseverance emerged repeatedly as essential to achieving objectives and overcoming obstacles, even those that seem intractable. Several survivors spoke about the need to stay true to one's convictions, to not relinquish dreams, to have determination, and continue the struggle. Soledad García, who was a political and social activist in the seventies, commented: "I am told, 'you continue fighting at sixty as if you were thirty [years old].' I don't know, I think we have to apply the mind and body to the will and need to change this. And well, it is done in different ways."

The achievements of human rights organizations such as Mothers and Grandmothers of the Plaza de Mayo have already demonstrated the value of perseverance. The testimony of survivor Carmen Lapacó, who was kidnapped along with her daughter Alejandra (still disappeared), is illustrative in this regard. Carmen became a Mother of Plaza de Mayo and a member of other human rights organizations. She pushed for her right to know the truth about what happened to her daughter when the impunity laws were in full force during the 1990s. She went through the domestic courts, reaching the Supreme Court without satisfactory results. She then turned to the Inter-American Commission on Human Rights. In the context of these international proceedings, the Argentine state reached a "friendly settlement" with Lapacó to establish institutional mechanisms to guarantee the right to truth about what happened to the disappeared (CIDH 2000). During the mid- to late 1990s, the Truth Trials were one of the mechanisms that some human rights organizations pushed for given the conditions of impunity generated by laws and presidential decrees (Filippini 2011; Romanin 2013). While perpetrators could not be criminally prosecuted and punished, the Truth Trials still helped maintain the issues alive in the judicial system, and later on the information gathered in the Truth Trials served as evidence to support criminal prosecutions (Lorenzetti and Kraut 2011). The struggle to achieve a measure of justice for crimes against humanity involved multiple actors—including human rights organizations, lawyers, survivors, and relatives of the disappeared—who refused to accept the status quo and persevered in their actions at the national and interventional levels.

These persistent activist efforts are not merely individual or voluntaristic—as the common advice to "never give up" might be understood. This is not a story of individual might, even as remarkable individuals emerge in the history of human rights struggles, but a story imbued by an ethics of solidarity and collective organizing. The words of survivor Ilda Micucci highlight both perseverance as well as collective efforts.[12] In addition to her own abduction, Ilda's son and daughter disappeared, which led her to become a member of different human rights organizations. In her testimony she articulated the importance of

> not getting hung up on the problem, and thinking "I can't do anything," accepting. No, look for a way. There's always some way. And . . . and try getting together. In unity. . . . When we say "unity makes strength," it is true, in every sense. And well, to give your all to what you set out to do and fight for that, looking for ways—novel or otherwise, or others that have borne fruit in other cases. But imagination is big, no? That is, when there is a need, there appear ways of fighting and achieving what you set out to do.

As various survivors chronicle the long, winding, and bumpy road in the struggle for "Memory, Truth, and Justice," the influence of historical contingencies as well as the persistence necessary to exert change become apparent. These activist legacies suggest that when a path is blocked, a different one can still be pursued. In this sense, Ilda's comments point to the variety of strategies available to activists—or what social movements scholars refer to collective action "repertoires" (Tilly 1978; 1995; Taylor and Van Dyke 2004)—including tried and true modes of intervention as well as the need for more innovative tactics. As Ilda mentioned, imagination can be bountiful; and we can think of a social movement as the possibility to collectively imagine otherwise. Yet, as social movement scholars have observed, it is also common for movements to deploy a "recurrent, predictable, and fairly narrow 'toolkit' of specific protest tactics" for social change (Taylor, Rupp, and Gamson 2004, 111). What new strategies might be needed in our current world to create more just societies? What are some of the contemporary challenges to thinking big and imagining otherwise? What are the practical and embodied constraints associated with specific strategies?

Whatever the answers, the legacies of activism in Argentina and other parts of the world suggest that an ethics of solidarity continues to be relevant, especially in a world that encourages ever more individualism. While the idea that "unity makes strength" might be considered cliché, Ilda points out that this is not just a saying. It is, in fact, a lived experience for members of countless movement organizations. In reflecting on their journey, a number of women who survived clandestine detention reclaimed solidarity and the value of collective organizing as modes of social transformation. These values are opposed to the individualism, fragmentation, and commercial culture that characterize many aspects of today's capitalist societies. In Argentina, the neoliberal economic model—promoted by the dictatorship, applied in full force in the nineties, and currently enjoying new momentum—embodies these capitalist values. Isabel Cerruti,[13] whose interview took place in 2002, during a severe economic crisis after years of neoliberal policies, spoke of the recurring need for collective organization: "This globalization ultimately seems to unite, but it ultimately fragmented and fragment us every day more. And in light of what happened to us, we have to learn just that, there are *redes* [nets/networks] that can be laid; we should not be afraid. We should not be afraid of that supposed enemy that tramples you. We should be careful. We should be the monster of a thousand heads. We should not put only one head [on the line]."

Here the figure of the monster appears once again, but this time not as the dehumanized and despised Other that the torturers tried to imprint on the bodies of detainees (as discussed in chapter 3). Rather, Isabel evoked the monster as a powerful and humanized creature that embodies unity in diversity as well as strength. Instead of risking the lives of individual people, the thousand-headed monster can most effectively confront or disrupt seemingly formidable forces in the era of globalization. From this perspective, solidarity and collective organization continue to be relevant as a defense against oppression, but also as the means to achieve political goals.

Bodies, emotions, solidarity, perseverance, and resistance are part and parcel of social movement organizing. Many of the women in this study shared stories that speak to these issues from the perspective of people who experienced political repression aimed at erasing their personhood, destroying their bodies, and crushing their dreams for social change. Fear was the emotion that was supposed to reign supreme. A sense of defeat was to replace activists' will and actions for social change. While women's testimonies certainly shed light on the high costs of activism in the context of repressive governments, their activist memories recover collective and resistive experiences that feed the social memory of the period and that are worth transmitting, problematizing, and learning from.

Testimony and Transmission: Passing on Memories

By recording their testimonies with Memoria Abierta, women survivors committed to pass on their memories to a broader public beyond their circle of family or friends. The testimonies are aimed at a more or less diffuse audience that includes not only people with their own memories of the dictatorship, but also generations further removed from the events. The possibility of transmission across generations is embedded in one of the last interview questions by Memoria Abierta. Variants of this question encouraged interviewees to summarize their thoughts about their journeys and/or articulate the messages they wished to transmit to people who might listen to their testimonies, including people with diverse perspectives and future generations. Although this question already brings to the fore the presence of "future generations," there is also an interest in memory transmission that emerges from the interviewees themselves.

For some of these women, communicating to young people what happened in the past was vital. After all, young people are often regarded as the key to the future. This does not mean, however, that these women abandoned their own participation, leaving to the youth the work of social transformation. As mentioned, many women have continued their activism, and in some cases their work has put them in contact with younger generations. This is the case, for example, of some women who in addition to having survived clandestine detention themselves also embarked on the search for loved ones. These efforts led these women to participate in organizations that elicited the interest and support of younger people, such as Mothers and Grandmothers of the Plaza de Mayo. The testimony of Ledda Barreiro, a member of Grandmothers and a political activist before the dictatorship, is illustrative in this regard:

So I am addressing the youths, who are the bold ones, the ones . . . the ones who *ponen el cuerpo* [literally "put their body"], the ones who make mistakes and start over again, because that's how they've got to be, because their imagination is in full bloom, because . . . because they dream. [. . .] Because a youth without a project and without dreams is a walking dead and is a product in service of a system that wants to stupefy [them]. [. . .] Then I tell them that if the Grandmothers' [experience] serves for anything, it is about the determination that one needs to have. And if we, the elders, have it, then how are the kids not going to have it, no? So just that: to be bold, to be bold—in the arts, at work, in demanding and not requesting what they are entitled to. That they should never ask; [but] demand their rights. And they shouldn't let up. That's the only thing I can tell them.

While sharing her message of courage, perseverance, and participation, Ledda also recognized the vitality that she herself derived from her contact with young people who project themselves to the future, who learn from Grandmothers, but who also reciprocate in the shape of a present in which "you don't talk about illnesses, you don't talk about ailments [. . .] because with the kids you have life. Life is there." That is, intergenerational transmission is a practice that can enrich members of different age groups and entails creative potentialities—even as it may also involve complex and conflictive intersubjective negotiations (Achugar 2016; Fried Amilivia 2016). It is one way of collectively processing a traumatic past, with eyes on the future.

In the case of survivors with disappeared sons and/or daughters, there is a particular poignancy to intergenerational transmission, in the sense that the younger generations could be construed as potential peers of the missing children, albeit separated by several decades. Among the people recorded as disappeared in the *Nunca Más* report (CONADEP 1984), the large majority were young (69 percent were between sixteen and thirty years old; the largest group was between twenty-one and twenty-five). We can situate against this backdrop the testimonies of women such as Lilia Amparo Jons de Orfanó, who spoke from a position as an activist, survivor of captivity, and mother of two disappeared sons who were also activists.[14] She referred to her involvement in decades of "very hard struggle," stating: "It continues to be hard because we did

not find the kids, but we continue our activism so that it doesn't happen to other kids. So that they can think and dissent. So that they have
rights." The struggle that Lilia referred to was anchored in the past, but
projected into the future through connection with new generations of
young people. A restitution of sorts might be achieved—though nothing
can compensate for the violent absence of the disappeared—if the new
generations can be spared the fate of the young people of yesteryear.
Referring to the disappeared youth, survivor and Mother of the Plaza de
Mayo Susana Martínez de Scala recalled the ideals of her disappeared
daughter—who was a union activist—for a "just society, a more equitable society, in which everyone is employed." She remarked: "I don't
want for their struggle to have been in vain."

Cristina Comandé, who was herself a young activist in the seventies,
also wanted to direct her message to young people, and in so doing exhibited not only a will to convey the experience of her own generation
but also the need to be open to the contributions and ways of seeing the
world that the new generations offer:

> In fact, today, we are pinning our hopes on the kids. We can accompany
> them, we can support them, we can talk to them, we can tell them about
> our experiences, about what we were thinking, what we were saying. But
> nowadays I think we have to listen to the kids, as many times we get stuck
> in the seventies, and today's kids have a different vision, which we have the
> duty to listen to. [. . .] And today, the ones who will continue the struggle
> are them. So, [they have] all my respect, and my affection, and my pride,
> because they do what they have to do with all the love and commitment,
> and with all the seriousness that they deserve. So . . . it is for the kids.

In this passage, one can appreciate Cristina's valorization of a bidirectional form of political communication across generations. Even if
the older generation's firsthand experiences of "living history" provide
essential perspectives, older people are not the only ones who have
knowledge to share. In this vein, the transmission of memory is neither a one-way street, nor a dogmatic exercise of passing down a given
knowledge. According to French psychoanalyst Jacques Hassoun (1996,
17), "successful transmission offers [the person] who receives it a space

of freedom and a foundation that allows [that person] *to abandon (the past) in order to (better) reencounter it"* (emphasis original).

In her study *Discursive Processes of Intergenerational Transmission of Recent History*, Mariana Achugar (2016) shows that memory transmission across generations involves varied and complex dynamics: While sometimes members of the older generation may transmit their interpretations to the younger generation in a top-down manner, meaning making about the past can also be cooperative between the generations; and it can even be conflictive. In some cases, the younger generation did not experience the issues remembered by the older ones, and yet the traces and controversies from the past are part of the contemporary public discourses in which young people are embedded. In other cases, the younger generation may have experienced that past, but from a different positionality, for example, as children more or less affected by the events in question. Thus, they have access to that past beyond memories passed down to them by the older generations (Levey 2014; Llobet 2015; Fried Amilivia 2016). Another dimension to consider is how the younger generation's understanding of the past may also be shaped by fresh political developments in which they are protagonists, for example, as activists or as members of society who bear the current consequences of past political decisions they had no chance to influence.[15] Thus, intergenerational conversations and exchange are crucial to meaning making with regard to the recent past and to the transmission of memory.

In several testimonies a sense of hope appears laced with the gesture of transmission: the possibility that future generations will be able to learn from the past and contribute to build a better future. But for this initiative to come to fruition, it is necessary to not only learn about state terrorism, but also recuperate the memory of the activism that the dictatorship tried to suppress. Marta Vassallo remembered the dreams and struggles of her generation, and connected them with the present:

> [M]any times the country is spoken about as something of the past, no?, as an unviable country. . . . We desperately wanted for it to be viable [seems moved]. . . . But I believe that now such viability is in the hands of other people, of other generations, who could think about it in a different way, with other parameters and with other options. But I believe that for

that viability [to happen] it is vital to know that. . . . It is, at least, vital to know that there were those who knew it was viable, and fought for that.

Legacies for the Present and Future

Taking their past experiences as a point of departure, these women's testimonies start to open a panorama of the current repercussions of the recent history of state terrorism and its implications for the future. What type of society is worth building? With what tools and methods? What lessons could be extracted from a past plagued by pain and horror?

Justice Aspirations

Building on their experiences, many survivors continued looking for ways to transform reality. Central to many of these women's social change visions were justice aspirations. In the testimonies, justice has different connotations, referring to distinct but interrelated phenomena. Similarly, in the article "Variations on Justice," Noa Vaisman (2017) analyzes different meanings of justice in the activism of HIJOS, the Argentine human rights organization initiated by sons and daughters of victims of state terrorism. Vaisman distinguishes three types of justice in the work of HIJOS: *historical justice, social justice*, and *judicial justice*. These categories are relevant to the analysis of women survivors' testimonies as well, with some overlaps with and distinctions from Vaisman's analysis:

Historical Justice: Setting the Record Straight

Survivors presented interpretations of the past from the standpoint of people who suffered the brunt of state violence. Their testimonies contradicted the version of events issued by the military regime, challenging repressors' power to shape the historical record. The activism of human rights organizations contributed to discrediting the military's account of the past moving in the direction of *historical justice*. In Vaisman's study, historical justice refers to HIJOS's work educating neighbors about silenced aspects of the dictatorship's history and about the reasons surrounding impunity in subsequent years. In the present study, the desire for setting the historical record straight emerges in the work of many women active in human rights and memory organizations, and who strongly countered the narrative offered by the military and their supporters. The contributions of many survivors as witnesses in trials for crimes against humanity are also ways of establishing a historical truth that turns the tables against those who held the upper hand in CDCs.

A yearning for justice in its historical dimensions is illustrated by survivor Ledda Barreiro's comment regarding the process of Truth Trials (Juicios por la Verdad) that took place in the nineties when the impunity laws impeded criminal prosecutions and convictions. Ledda argued that, despite its limitations, this process still helped to demonstrate that not only the "victors" can write history. Acknowledging the irreversible losses that she and other people targeted by state repression experienced, Ledda contended that some of the successes of human rights organizations—such as the state's holding Truth Trials in a legal and political context that had foreclosed crucial institutional routes to truth and justice—still showed that the "defeated" can strongly influence the historical record: "Because in the future a historian will not come and tell the history of the victors."

Social Justice: Ending Inequality

Another connotation of justice that emerges in the testimonies of women survivors is *social justice* in relation to social and economic inequalities, that is, as an indictment of the continuities of conditions of marginalization and deprivation that large sectors of the population have experienced in democracy. This meaning of social justice is broader than the definition that Vaisman (2017) provides in relation to HIJOS's activism and embodied by the *escraches* (shaming practices) performed by the group. In that specific context, social justice is defined as a kind of justice "from below" (382), by which the community engages in acts of shunning against the perpetrators of human rights abuses who live in the neighborhood, "socially ostracizing the criminal and symbolically marking his deeds" (374). While the label is the same, the type of social justice that I elaborate here refers not to such forms of accountability by the people, but to the general conditions of inequality and exclusion in society. This notion of social justice connects with the activist trajectories of many survivors, which entailed efforts to dismantle unfair social structures.

The visions of a better world that appeared again and again in the testimonies centrally require a sensitivity to social injustice. Democracy did not do away with poverty and inequality, and these problems were even exacerbated in the context of neoliberalism during the post-dictatorship period. The political and economic crisis of 2001 is a paradigmatic illustration (e.g., De Riz, Acosta, and Clucellas 2002; Svampa 2005; Sutton 2010; Felder and Patroni 2011). In the context of an electoral democracy that retained exclusionary economic policies, Emilce Moler argued that "an unequal society, with injustices, is not good for anyone. One cannot be happy in a society where there are so many inequalities, one suffers or at least should suffer when seeing the suffering of others. So then one has to see, in the political and economic contexts of the time, how to contribute to help with that. There are no recipes, it is not necessary to replicate events, but one must pay attention to see what can be done."

As in the case of Emilce, a concern with injustice and the structural violence that permeates contemporary societies also emerges in other testimonies. This is in line with the ideals that animated the political, labor, student, and social projects in which many survivors participated. In this sense, the invocation of justice refers to a more inclusive and equitable society without misery and poverty, and where people are treated with the dignity that any human being deserves—that is, a yearning for social justice is articulated. The hope and the commitment expressed by Raúl R. Alfonsín, the first elected president post-dictatorship, that "democracy feeds, cures and educates" suffered major setbacks. The entrenchment of neoliberalism in the nineties—including privatization, the disciplining of the labor sector, the restructuring of the role of the state, and the liberalization of the economy—was associated with declining social conditions in Argentina. At the dawn of the new millennium, the balance of such economic policies included the rise of unemployment, underemployment, and precarious work as well as historical increases in poverty rates, with over half of the population living under the poverty line by May 2002 (De Riz, Acosta, and Clucellas 2002; Felder and Patroni 2011). In a testimony recorded in 2003, Julia Ruiz said: "We are in the presence of a society, like the one we have at the moment, where probably there is not systematic torture, but where we are condemning generations and human groups to live like animals. And then we get scared when they react as such, and not like persons. Then, this continues affecting me, it continues hurting, and I believe that each of us has to do something to improve society, but on a fundamentally fair basis."

Julia's reference to systematic torture evokes the experience of state terrorism (even though cases of torture in legal prisons and police stations have continued to be documented in democracy [e.g., CELS 2015b]). As her testimony illustrates, the experience of violence in CDCs was sometimes juxtaposed with the violence imposed by an economic system that extends to the post-dictatorship period. Thus, paralleling the emblematic figure of the thirty thousand estimated disappeared by state terrorism, Susana Caride, who had a history of political activism and whose interview was a few months before the crisis of December 2001, expressed the need to "avoid having thirty thousand dead or so many dead because of hunger, and misery, and illnesses when the authorities do absolutely nothing." Similarly, Susana Reyes—who had a trajectory working with marginalized children—associated vulnerable kids with the disappeared. She pointed out these children's precarious conditions: "And I get off at the station and see them, I have seen them sleeping on the floor, you know? And the image comes to me, no? Because they are also as if . . . as if they were not there, you know? They are disappeared for this system, because nobody cares." Susana's reflection remits to the violence that multiple forms of not seeing, of excluding from the frame of "grievable life" (Butler 2004a, 34), those people whose rights and humanity are trampled by different systems of oppression—both state and economic violence.

Judicial Justice: Ending Impunity

Another meaning of justice that emerged in women's testimonies relates to justice in the *judicial* sense. As in the case of Vaisman's work, this notion of justice refers to obtaining redress in criminal courts for massive human rights violations. In a deeper way, this notion of justice also relates to survivors' yearning for these types of crimes to never again take place. The progress made through the trials of the military juntas in 1985 (Juicio a las Juntas), which convicted some of the top military officers responsible for human rights violations, was later stunted by the Full Stop Law of 1986 and the Due Obedience Law of 1987, also known as the "impunity laws."[16] Furthermore, the presidential pardons (*indultos*) of 1989 and 1990 furthered impunity, including the pardon of the high military officers convicted in the Juicio a las Juntas. Still, efforts to bring perpetrators to justice, locally and in other countries, never stopped (Yanzon 2011). In the 2000s, the impunity laws were annulled and declared unconstitutional (CELS 2005), and a new wave of trials ensued.

Women in this study generally decried the impunity that those responsible for crimes against humanity enjoyed for so many years. This, in turn, was associated with harmful ramifications for the present and the future of the country. One of the interviewees who spoke about this issue was Adriana Arce, who was a teachers' union activist at the time of her kidnapping and a member of the National Secretary of Human Rights in Argentina when she was interviewed in 2006. She gave her testimony a year after the Supreme Court declared the Full Stop and Due Obedience laws unconstitutional. Adriana saw a clear link between impunity and corruption, themes that have continued in public discourse (see, e.g., Faulk 2013):

> [W]e are witnessing how impunity has gotten into all levels of society, in all state structures, in any activity you do in this country you keep finding impunity, impunity, impunity. And that impunity is installed, why? Well because it is like in the collective unconscious what remains at the end is that there were people who killed others, who appropriated their patrimony, who stole their children, who tortured, who did . . . the most savage things, and nothing happened to them. Then everything is lawful. And when society sees that all that is not condemnable, is not punishable, then it is an open hand for all corruptions.

Justice is at the core of the human rights movement's demands. In Adriana's narrative, the articulation of this notion appears not as an expression of hatred or a desire for revenge but as the very foundation for the rule of law and social coexistence to flourish. Adriana demanded a fair trial for the repressors, with all the rights that that entails— something that was denied to her and to so many people kidnapped, tortured, and finally disappeared by the state itself. Some of that impunity was dismantled with the reopening of trials. It remains to be seen to what extent justice in relation to state terrorism also translates into redressing other forms of impunity plaguing Argentine society today.

Ending impunity for crimes against humanity in Argentina is part of a "justice cascade" in various regions of the world (Lutz and Sikkink 2001; Sikkink and Kim 2013), with Argentina as a "global protagonist" (Sikkink 2011, 60). Survivors of human rights violations have been central to this process of justice. Their judicial testimonies have been crucial evidence in various trials, including in those held decades later (Kaiser 2015). The new wave of trials has already yielded convictions. From 2006 through March 18, 2016, the Center of Legal and Social Studies recorded "155 sentences, which convicted 666 persons for crimes against humanity and acquitted 59" (CELS n.d. [2016]). At the time of this writing, trials across the country have been ongoing, including in Buenos Aires, La Plata, Mar del Plata, Santa Fe, Salta, Córdoba, La Rioja, Mendoza, Jujuy, and Neuquén (CELS n.d. [2016]).

Bringing perpetrators to justice has been an arduous process, involving a number of procedural, juridical, and political obstacles that human rights activists, families, survivors, and lawyers had to overcome, taking advantage of and creating openings at the national and international levels (Andreozzi 2011a; CELS and ICTJ 2011; Sikkink 2011; Balardini and Varsky 2015). Progress has been made not only in delivering justice locally, but also in holding accountable some of the participants in a regional system of coordinated repression. In this regard, the trials for Operation Condor that were held in Buenos Aires (with verdict read on May 27, 2016) judicially demonstrated the transnational dimensions of state terrorist activities. These included the disappearance of political prisoners across national borders, orchestrated by the repressive regimes of Argentina, Bolivia, Brazil, Chile, Paraguay, and Uruguay (CELS 2016; Lessa 2015). This trial served in the way of accountability even if justice delivered so late can hardly exhaust justice aspirations.

Ana María Cacabelos, whose family suffered state repression in full force,[17] articulated the linkages between justice aspirations and other values such as truth, peace, and memory. In other words, it is not a simple desire for retribution that has motivated the demand for accountability:

There are so many who ask you why keep stirring things up, why continue talking, why continue thinking, why always go back to that topic, that it must end. [. . .] If there's no memory there is no future. When you don't have memory, when you don't remember, when you have nothing, the future is not possible. And . . . and it is necessary to recover peace. And peace can't be recovered if there is no justice. And there is no justice without truth. And regarding this issue there is no truth. Because the only ones who have not spoken up to now are those . . . those who really should talk, and not shield themselves with laws that they themselves made it their business to trample at the time.[18]

For Ana María, the need to find out the truth and achieve a measure of justice for the state crimes committed against her family and so many others was an integral part of achieving a peaceful coexistence and making "Never Again" a reality.

Human Rights, Democratic Culture, and Social Change

The notions of justice, memory, and truth that appear time and again in survivors' testimonies are intimately connected with the construction of democratic cultures and institutions that foster the respect for human rights. The idea that a government should "never again" impose itself and commit atrocities emerges in more than one testimony. As Tita Sacolsky said, "[N]o human being deserves something like this. [. . .] We have to say it so that all generations know that it should never happen again."[19] This "never again," however, encompasses not only actions of the state. Testimonies also highlight a concern about the role that ordinary people need to fulfill in order to avoid such a power grab by an authoritarian government. Liliana Gardella referred to the need to dig into the everyday roots that sustain a repressive matrix. One of the questions that haunted her, "How is a torturer made?," is timely and urgent not only because the world has continued confronting situations of torture on smaller or larger scales but because the answer is not to be found on spaces drastically separated from common society, nor simply within the scope of the armed forces.

Inquiring about the quotidian dimensions that underpin a repressive matrix also raises questions about the institutions, common sense, intimate spaces, discourses, and power relations in societies that coexist with governments responsible for systematic human rights violations. In that sense, and in Argentina's concrete case, works such as those by Mariana Caviglia (2006), Sebastián Carassai (2013), and Valeria Llobet (2015) explore the imaginaries and practices of "ordinary people," such as sectors of the middle class who did not participate in political movements or did not occupy prominent spaces in the power structure (i.e., groups that have generally not been assumed or studied as protagonists of the history of state terrorism). Additionally, the responsibility of powerful groups, including those holding economic power, has emerged in recent research projects exploring the role of civilians (Verbitsky and Bohoslavsky 2013). The expansion of trials to civilians who enabled or collaborated with the repression is perhaps one of the most controversial issues, for it threatens to reach many more people than those directly participating in the armed and security forces.

Based on their own readings of current and historical realities, the interviewees also offered interpretations of various social practices and discourses that are antithetical to democratic cultures. Viviana Nardoni—an activist and worker at the Museum of Memory in Rosario—warned about everyday expressions of authoritarianism, especially the dangers of

> always seeing in front of you the other, the different one, with whom I can have no dialogue or agreement about anything, because it is always the other, the barbarian [. . .] and the other is my enemy. That has always condemned us as a society. Beyond variations in historical processes. [. . .] Then you sometimes discover yourself saying "those should be killed." And that's not a saying. There is [something] in your constitution as a person and as a society that moves you to use that expression. [. . .] And such things that shape us as a society [. . .] is what I would like to work to dilute.

Similarly, Norma Morello—an educator and activist with a history of participation in peasant movements—argued for the need to establish a genuine dialogue with people who might have a different perspective. She underscored the value of "the question" in the tradition of popular educator Paulo Freire. Instead of constructing the other as the enemy or holding on to dogmatic positions, Norma said that "we need to work asking ourselves whether what the other does is right or wrong, because oftentimes we start with the idea that the other is mistaken, and that one possesses the truth, no? So always have the doubt that the other is the one who is correct, and be open to discussion, no?"

Then, in addition to the critique of authoritarianism and the raw violence of a repressive state system, several interviewees also articulated more general values for society as a whole, including genuine dialogue, respect for others, and coexistence in democracy. Marta Bianchi, an actress and cofounder of the association Women and Cinema, summarized:

> I very much think that one has to be respectful of the other, that there is not one way of thinking, or feeling, or living, or inhabiting the world. And that there is space for everyone in the world. That what is important is tolerance and respect, and that violence has to be eradicated, and that words and negotiation are the ways of coexistence. [. . .] We should very much pay attention to violence, and to the defense of democracy, and to not be silent. And not be silent. And get together when we are afraid, and express ourselves, and defend what we believe, with the best arms—let's say, the arms of persuasion, and good coexistence. Those.

Marta articulated her vision with an awareness of social or political contexts when fear might reign. She spoke of fear not from an abstract perspective, but from the standpoint of someone who had the experience of being politically persecuted.[20] Susana Muñoz, who was a political activist and later joined human rights and memory organizations, offered a similar assessment of the need for respect, but was critical of the notion of tolerance: "One has to eradicate the language of tolerance, one has to be respectful." From this perspective, "tolerance" is insufficient to honor the difference and humanity of other people.

With these words women weaved in not only their ideals but also certain criteria for action in their defense, including collective organizing as an antidote to fear and as a limit to oppression. Again, these discussions were not mere theoretical exercises but based on these women's lived experiences. For instance, Marta Bianchi was part of Teatro Abierto (Open Theater), a famous challenge to the censorship of cultural expressions and the persecution of artists during the dictatorship.[21] Also with the goal of creating a more just society, Fátima Cabrera—who was an activist in a shantytown before her kidnapping and later participated in human rights organizations internationally—asserted the need to "know how to set limits when abuse comes." This insight emerged not only from her history of activism, but also from the concrete experience of solidarity among prisoners who helped her avert sexual violence through a coordinated act of resistance (see also Bacci et al. 2012).

Experiences from the recent history of state terror were then translated into lessons for the present, in line with a disposition to questioning, rethinking, and transforming current social relations and arrangements. Odila Casella reflected on how various human rights organizations expanded their foci and started both "concerning themselves with other issues" related to social justice and adopting a conception of human rights violations that includes but transcends state terrorism: "Today human rights organizations are not only talking about what happened in the seventies, but are also talking about trigger-happy [police], talking about what's happening today, about hunger, about . . . you understand? Today they are more involved with current affairs; without leaving aside the previous history, but it has to do with this, with what's happing today, because obviously if we get hung up on what happened . . . it is a disaster. That is, a human rights organization has to defend the rights of the people. That is, today, yesterday, and always."

Odila told an anecdote that illustrates how lessons from recent history can be rearticulated in the present in ways that foster a democratic culture. This is the case, for example, in relation to pervasive societal concerns with "security"—a notion that in public discourse in Argentina mainly refers to freedom from property crimes and related violent crimes. Odila talked about a debate in her neighborhood about this problem and how a number of people favored installing a *garita* (sentry box) as a solution. Tough-on-crime approaches—even at the expense of basic human rights guarantees—and the provision of private security have been favored by a sizable sector of the population. Odila did not agree with this type of response and was active in trying to implement alternatives, including the coordination of phone "chains" among neighbors, organization of alarm and code systems, and installation of street lights. But above all, developing a sense of solidarity and community in the neighborhood was an integral aspect of the response to security issues. Among other things, neighbors envisioned the occupation of the public space in ways that fostered community: organizing a carnival dance on the streets, blocking certain streets so that children could ride their bikes, planning to screen movies, and other proposals, which also became a model for other neighborhoods. Here we see how someone who experienced firsthand the lack of security produced by state violence decided not to rely on the punitive arm of the state or on private security guards as the primary solution to insecurity. Instead, she drew on values such as solidarity and collective organizing, which she associated with the seventies activist generation, and which she reclaimed for the present.

Soledad García, a survivor with an extensive trajectory in the labor movement, also envisioned activism as a response to contemporary problems. She referred to pervasive violence in the post-dictatorship period. This violence differs from the most evident forms of political and state violence of the past, but is nevertheless debilitating and destructive of the social fabric. This observation is consistent with Auyero and Berti's (2015) in-depth analysis of interpersonal and collective forms of violence in marginalized communities in Argentina, contextualized within "the recent skyrocketing of brutality" in many Latin American countries (8). Giving her testimony in 2008, Soledad stated:

> I think that today the kids face a world that is very torn apart in some sense, with a lot of risk, no? Violence—which is not precisely revolutionary violence, or violence aimed at a positive change, right? With the dictatorship project installed, the destruction and fragmentation [engendered by] neoliberalism wrought very serious consequences. Then, I believe that today's challenges are different, different *códigos* [codes/norms]. But what I really would tell today's youth is that be it through music, through poetry, through literature, through cinema, through the arts, everything is possible within a framework of an activism on behalf of life. And that life is worthwhile living in a different way. My freedom and your freedom, and the freedom of you all, of young people, is also the future that is possible and different.

Soledad and a number of other survivors advanced notions of entwined and interdependent futures, rather than narrow or individual solutions to social problems. She affirmed life, but conceived as more than mere survival. Instead, her narrative points to the construction of a society in which it is possible to thrive, play, create, and be free. It is no coincidence that many of these women—who had a history as political, social, and community organizers—should emphasize collective projects. Yet, what is perhaps remarkable is how their activist dreams survived the horrors of the torture and disappearance camps; even if in different forms, even if adapting to the times.

In reflecting about the functions of memory and lessons drawn from recent history, survivors established linkages with current issues such as the environment, cultural diversity, drug-related problems, police violence, gender violence, destitute youth, poverty and hunger, and others. In these narratives, memory does not appear as something frozen in time or circumscribed to state terrorism, but becomes alive and can be applied to the present in transformational ways (see also Perera 2016). Liliana Callizo asked: "What's memory like in the present, no? How do I see it? It is a social memory. It's everyone's memory. That is, it is not mine." She then linked this memory to action, to answer the question, "What should we do?" Liliana was particularly interested in the denunciation of sexual violence and using awareness of these experiences to dig deeper into questions of gender inequality. Soledad García derived hope from grassroots organizing, from the collective actions of groups fighting "for a hospital, for a school, for education, for social rights." She added, "I think that this won't change unless we all join." Among other things, she alluded to concerns that have not been as prominent in public discussion, such as environmental issues. She underscored the need to "gain consciousness that our patrimony is being expropriated, given away." She concluded: "I advocate for a different kind of society, and like me, many people continue thinking that some sort of revolution is possible [laughs]." While the idea of revolution might be perceived as passé or impossible—as Soledad's laughter hints—her statement shows that hope and work for radical social change have not disappeared.

Conclusion

The history of state terrorism in Argentina is composed of many experiences, including those of women survivors of clandestine detention.

However, the experiences and perspectives of these women have generally received insufficient public attention except for those speaking from the position of mothers or grandmothers of people targeted by the military regime. In some cases, the statuses of *survivors* of clandestine detention and *mothers of the disappeared* coincide in the same women. And yet, the former status—particularly if associated with a history of activism that preceded the dictatorship—has tended to recede in the picture. Many women survivors do not hold this double status, but their perspectives still need to be heard. This chapter advances the position that it is important to listen to women survivors in political terms, not only because the experiences they relate are eminently political but also because of the activist trajectories of many of the women taken to CDCs.

As political contexts change, as new forms of social and political organization emerge, as women gain new spaces in politics, and as feminists continue to raise awareness of gender injustice, the experiences and insights offered by women survivors need to be part of the conversation (whether they are also mothers of the disappeared or not). Furthermore, rather than regarding women survivors as mere victims of state terror, acknowledging their political and historical agency is an important step in constructing an inclusive social memory for the present and the future. Although these women had different experiences and degrees of political participation, overall they shared important insights for thinking about enduring questions related to justice, democracy, and human rights. The memories of collective resistance, political organizing, confronting oppression, and speaking truth to power are part of the legacy that many women survivors offer to new generations.

6

Conclusions and Implications

State terrorism in Argentina was not a gender-neutral phenomenon, but a process in which gendered bodies, oppressive gender ideologies and practices, and gendered strategies of survival and resistance played significant roles. The testimonies of women survivors provide one—though not the only—entryway to understanding these dynamics. Listening to their voices is essential both to collective memory making and to the development of nuanced understandings of human rights. I approached the analysis of women survivors' testimonies from a sociological perspective, enriched by interdisciplinary literatures on memory and human rights, gender and militarization, bodies and embodiment, and women's agency and activism. While the focus of the study is on Argentina, many of the issues addressed are relevant to other countries in Latin America that have undergone similar processes of political violence and state repression. These countries, too, have struggled to come to terms with their traumatic histories through a variety of transitional justice measures.

The feminist orientation of this book helps to reveal gender dynamics in relation to the embodied forms of state violence that women endured as well as to recognize their political and historical agency. Based on these women's poignant narratives, the study connects past, present, and future. It draws on the urgent lessons that women survivors offer to a world that continues to grapple with torture and other human rights violations, and when collective organizing remains a key path to social transformation. In what follows, I present some conclusions and implications of the study with respect to recent political and scholarly developments in these areas: (1) human rights, transitional justice, and collective memory; (2) gender and state power; and (3) bodies, vulnerability, and agency.

Human Rights, Transitional Justice, and Collective Memory

March 24, 2016, marked the fortieth anniversary of the last military coup d'état in Argentina. The anniversary carried a strong symbolic and political meaning, particularly in the context of the electoral victory of the center-right coalition Cambiemos (Let's Change), led by the newly elected president, Mauricio Macri. Beside the discontent expressed by a sizable sector of the population regarding new governmental measures,[1] there was also uncertainty about the fate of various human rights and transitional justice initiatives that had enjoyed governmental support in the previous decade. Given the right-leaning tendencies of the new elected government and many of the decidedly conservative sectors backing Macri's election, the new political landscape was cause for concern, mobilization, and resistance among those who had worked hard to create accountability for the crimes of a right-wing dictatorship. Would the trials for crimes against humanity continue? Would the new government fund important human rights institutions and programs? What would become of the sites of memory?

Adding to an already tense political environment, and in the context of Macri's efforts to establish closer relations with the United States, U.S. president Barack Obama visited Argentina during the fortieth anniversary of the coup. In light of the support that some U.S. administrations lent to counterinsurgency operations and military regimes that perpetrated massive human rights violations in Latin America, the timing of the U.S. president's trip to Argentina was decried by many in the human rights movement and broader society. Still, human rights groups used Obama's visit as an opportunity to renew the push for declassification of secret U.S. military and intelligence documents pertaining to the period of state terrorism in Argentina—something that President Obama agreed to do (Mochkofsky 2016; Osorio and Kornbluh 2016). On the anniversary, both presidents visited the Parque de la Memoria (Park of Memory, a site commemorating the victims of state terrorism), and during their speeches asserted the importance of human rights (White House 2016). However, the main action on March 24 was not in the Parque de la Memoria but in the symbolic Plaza de Mayo, where large crowds gathered to demonstrate and commemorate the National Day of Memory for Truth and Justice (Dandan 2016).

While in the world of national and international politics there is often a large gap between words and action, promises and actual policies, symbolic gesture and genuine commitment, it is not irrelevant that a trove of U.S. secret documents were slated for declassification on the occasion of Obama's visit. Also, that a politician like Macri—not known for his sympathy with the cause of human rights organizations in Argentina—decided to go to the Parque de la Memoria with his U.S. counterpart is evidence of the international significance of the Argentine human rights movement. The struggles of human rights organizations have crossed international borders, and their cause cannot be simply ignored. Indeed, President Obama's speech referred to the victims of the military dictatorship and recognized the "bravery and tenacity of the parents, the spouses, siblings, and the children who love and remember them, and who refuse to give up until they get the truth and the justice they deserve" (White House 2016, n.p.).

Although remaining within the often ambiguous language of diplomacy, Obama's brief speech still suggested the need for a greater level of introspection in the United States regarding these events: "There's been controversy about the policies of the United States early in those dark days, and the United States, when it reflects on what happened here, has to examine its own policies as well, and its own past. Democracies have to have the courage to acknowledge when we don't live up to the ideals that we stand for; when we've been slow to speak out for human rights. And that was the case here" (White House 2016, n.p.). These notions apply not only to the United States' role with respect to Argentina, but in relation to many other countries in Latin America and around the world where extreme violence either resulted from or was enabled by U.S. military and/or political interventions. Furthermore, the need for both a critical examination of and accountability for human rights violations holds for contemporary U.S. foreign policy and actions by U.S. state personnel, especially in the context of the U.S.-led "war on terror." In this regard, lessons from the past are meaningful to the extent that human rights in the present are more than hollow words. These connections between past and present, and across various countries, indicate that the lessons from this book are more than temporally and geographically bound.

The process of dealing with the consequences of massive human rights violations is far from easy, but the persistence of organizations demanding "Memory, Truth, and Justice" in Argentina shows that trau-matic histories do not just go away. They do not fade because of govern-mental mandates to "reconcile," "forgive," or "move on." More likely, the issues remain alive, repeatedly emerging, and coming back to "haunt" individuals and societies (Gordon 2008). Their continued significance is illustrated by the variety of transitional justice initiatives that have flourished in the past decades. Despite the short time span that the word "transition" may suggest, transitional justice can be a long pro-cess, taking many years, even decades. Over time, more than a dozen Latin American countries have developed transitional justice mecha-nisms such as truth commissions and/or prosecution of perpetrators of gross human rights violations in specific national contexts (Sikkink 2011; Skaar, García-Godos, and Collins 2016). In the case of the Opera-tion Condor trials, we see an effort to account for the coordinated and transnational dimensions of state-sponsored torture, disappearance, and political assassinations in the region. As Kathryn Sikkink (2011) points out, there is nothing inevitable or overdetermined about these types of accountability measures, which are also part of a more global "jus-tice cascade." Sikkink shows that the human rights movement played a major role spearheading the cascade, aided by the end of the Cold War and international democratization trends (24).

The human rights movement has not only pushed for justice, but has also helped to generate knowledge about state terrorism and the devas-tating effects of this violence for individuals, families, communities, and nations. This knowledge continues to unfold. In that sense, this book builds on the work of human rights organizations, activists, and archi-vists in an effort to examine relatively understudied experiential, social, and political dimensions of state terrorism and its aftermath. Specifically, the book contributes to knowledge on the embodied experiences, politi-cal voices, and agency of women survivors, beyond the more common focus on mothers of the disappeared or grandmothers of appropriated children. The production of archives with testimonies of people directly affected by political repression has been key to this task. The existence of these archives is important to historical memory, and their preservation and expansion are especially needed as political winds change and as certain truths may be pushed to oblivion. The testimonies of survivors are stark reminders that in Argentina a repressive state implemented a systematic plan of torture, disappearance, and persecution with the support, acquiescence, and/or indifference of various sectors of society. They remind us that it is incumbent on society at large to learn from the past to not repeat such atrocities.

While many of the testimonies in Memoria Abierta were collected during a period in which the demands of human rights organizations were gaining new political and judicial momentum, toward the end of this project the political scenario had shifted with the election of President Mauricio Macri in November 2015. Although the new president promised to not interfere with the continuation of trials for crimes against humanity ("Los juicios" 2015), his election apparently enabled a sense of empowerment among sectors sympathetic with the position of repressors judged or convicted for crimes against humanity. While the core ideologies supporting the military never really went away—though in many cases justificatory viewpoints were reframed or ameliorated (Sutton 2015)—the new political context encouraged conservative sectors of society to more openly question the validity of the trials and the wisdom of sending convicted perpetrators to prison.

Indicative of the new political landscape in Argentina was the editorial titled "No More Revenge," published in the conservative newspaper La Nación ("No más venganza" 2015) not even twenty-four hours after the announcement of the electoral victory of Mauricio Macri as new president. This editorial strongly questioned aspects of the transitional justice process that had been taking place in Argentina during the 2000s. The timing of the newspaper editorial piece was not coincidental. According to the article, "The election of a new government is a favorable moment to end with the lies about the 70s and the current human rights violations" ("No más venganza" 2015). While the term "state terrorism" appears twice in the article, the condemnation of such violence was not the main concern in the editorial. Rather, the authors of La Nación's editorial seemed more interested in questioning the judicial treatment of former repressors sent to prison for crimes against humanity, including the denial of the benefit of home detention to older convicts. As signaled by the editorial's title, the overall message seems to be that the prosecution and conviction of perpetrators of such crimes constitutes "revenge" not justice.

Besides critiquing the transitional justice process as embodied in the trials, the editorial also resignified the political violence of the seventies through the lens of contemporary security concerns such as those linked to international terrorism (concerns that different countries have used to justify states of exception, mass surveillance, growing militarization, harsh interrogation techniques, and even torture). *La Nación*'s piece puts on the same plane the Argentine armed political organizations of the seventies and the people responsible for the coordinated terrorists attacks carried out in Paris on November 13, 2015. This comparison, presented in the editorial a few days after the latter events, spoke to current fears regarding terrorism at the same time as it decried the contemporary judicial treatment of Argentine repressors who operated under a military dictatorship that claimed to be protecting society from terrorists.

What is noteworthy about this editorial is not just its content, but the immediate repudiation it generated from various sectors of society, including *La Nación*'s own employees. A large number of staff members of various ranks in this major newspaper staged an assembly and issued a public statement to express their vehement disagreement with their employer's official position. In a picture showing a room packed with people, several newspaper workers are seen holding signs reading "I repudiate the editorial," "#Never Again," and other statements ("Fuertes repercusiones" 2015). This swift reaction shows that the hard-won achievements of the human rights movement, which many in Argentine society have come to embrace, are not to be challenged without consequence. Furthermore, the newspaper workers' response also evokes a collective memory of resistance and the determination of a people who refuse to be silenced. This type of response does not come out of nowhere but should be understood in light of the human rights activism that started during the dictatorship and continued through democracy, with ties to various social movements in Argentina.

The commitment to sustain the collective memory of Argentina's recent history appears in many different forms, including academic studies, artistic performances and exhibits, journalistic accounts, and novels and films that explore the silences and complexities that still need to be untangled. The Memoria Abierta archives upon which this study is based are a critical contribution to this process. It is my hope that this book's focus on gender dynamics and women survivors' experiences sheds new light on the workings of state terrorism as well as on the complex embodied responses and resistance that this extreme form of violence generated. Yet, additional questions remain: What other silences and invisibilities do prevalent analyses of state violence authorize? What accounts still need to be heard, and why we have not heard them yet? Whose testimonies are still missing from collective memory archives, from truth commissions, and from other transitional justice initiatives?

A number of feminist studies of political violence, armed conflict, and state repression around the world pay particular attention to the voices of women and/or use a gender lens as central to the analysis. However, attention to gender—particularly in conjunction with sexuality and other categories of difference and inequality—can also open up spaces to dig deeper into how gender binaries and heteronormativity have shaped violence against members of the population whose experiences have also been largely invisible, namely, members of queer, trans, and gender-nonconforming communities. While contemporary political and identity categories might not be readily apt to describe the experiences of the seventies, the point remains that the stories of people who did not squarely fit normative gender and sexuality categories are still largely unheard or not understood. Recent scholarly works take us in this direction, for example, interrogating the invisibility of gender and sexual minorities' experiences in truth commissions (Fobear 2014) and how cis privilege structures contemporary technologies of security in the midst of "discourses that pair danger/terrorism and queer bodies/sexualities" (Shepherd and Sjoberg 2012, 13).

In the Argentine context, some recent academic contributions have drawn attention to dissident genders and sexualities in relation to the history of state repression during the sixties and seventies (see, e.g., D'Antonio 2015). The need to address these issues has also been raised in the activist front. For example, on the occasion of the fortieth anniversary of the last military coup d'état in Argentina, a social media post by the Coordinadora Antirrepresiva LGBTTTIQP (Antirepressive Coordination LGBTTTIQP) called for participation in the day's demonstrations, stating that "Memory is not a cis-heterosexual privilege" (2016; see also Máximo 2015). Additionally, the campaign Reconocer es Reparar (To Recognize Is to Repair) seeks "historical reparations for travesti [and] trans victims of institutional violence promoted by security forces," highlighting the linkages between past and present state violence and human rights violations (AWID 2016).

Other silenced histories about activism and repression during the period of state terrorism in Argentina have started to be traced and reconstructed, too. These histories include the forced disappearance of activists from indigenous communities who were involved in a variety of social and political causes, from land claims specific to indigenous peoples to more general labor rights (Lenton 2014; ENDEPA 2016). Anthropologist Diana Lenton (2014) discusses the invisibility of memories of repression against members of indigenous communities in Argentina, pointing out that the lists of the disappeared compiled by "Human Rights organizations or state agencies, do not state ethnic identity or of other kind (e.g., sexual orientation), and do not allow to distinguish the incidence of identity-affirming movements among the groups persecuted by state terrorism. This information void was based on, and in turn sustained, the widely disseminated hypothesis that the indigenous movements were 'prepolitical,' had no relation with 'real politics' and were not repressed" (193).

While in countries like Guatemala massive numbers of state-sponsored executions and disappearances of indigenous peoples have been amply documented,[2] in Argentina the information deficit alluded above is consistent with long-term trends of invisibilization of indigenous people's existence, experiences, and demands. Although Argentina's indigenous population is smaller than that of Guatemala (World Bank 2015), this only serves to compound a general tendency to discount the violence committed against indigenous people in Argentina. The dominant national narrative that "we Argentines descend from the ships" (from Europe) elides the impact of nation-building projects that violently targeted indigenous communities and aimed to erase indigenous cultures (see, e.g., Quijada, Bernand, and Schneider 2000; Viñas 2002). An example of such projects is the so-called Conquest of the Desert of the late nineteenth century—a military campaign aimed at expanding the country's southern frontier—which continues to be denounced by indigenous groups and allies. Significantly, relatively recent political and artistic interventions have drawn on the human rights discourse that emerged in response to the last military dictatorship to challenge the hegemonic narrative regarding the Conquest of the Desert (Masotta 2006). Some human rights activists and organizations have made connections between state terror in different historical periods and in turn supported the contemporary struggles of indigenous communities.

New research has also started to identify and examine the cases of Afro-Argentines who were kidnapped and disappeared during the last military dictatorship. According to anthropologist Pablo Cirio—who has led one such research project[3]—these experiences need to be understood in the context of the "historical disappearance of this group, [given that] its members had first been disappeared from Africa and then from the official history of our country [Argentina]" (cited in Spinola 2014). That is, the dominant national narrative has long asserted that "there are no Blacks in Argentina," though historiographical works such as George Reid Andrews's (1980) demonstrate the influence of Afro-Argentines while also analyzing processes of erasure. Advocates have sometimes drawn on the language of "disappearance" to raise awareness of the continued invisibility and exclusion of people of African descent (Sutton 2008). Claiming the position as *los primeros desaparecidos* ("the first disappeared") (Baig 2002; Spinola 2014) has particular poignancy in the Argentine context, where the term *desaparecidos* is largely associated with the human rights violations perpetrated by the last military dictatorship. Studies that examine the situation of Afro-Argentines during the period of state terrorism can shed new light by juxtaposing the "disappearance" of Afro-Argentines from a long-standing and dominant national narrative associating Argentina with white Europeanness and the political project of extermination that the military dictatorship implemented in the late twentieth century.

Scholarly and activist interventions that draw attention to the experiences of state terror of people marginalized based on ethnoracial identities, sexual orientation, and/or gender identity and expression beg the question about whose voices, bodies, and perspectives are still missing in the human rights archives and in prevalent understandings of the period. Archives are important to collective memory and to transitional justice, but they are neither complete nor static. Archives can be described as *living archives* to the extent that they change, grow, and develop. They become animated with life as long as someone is interested in listening, viewing, reading, inquiring, interacting with, and adding to their contents. A diversity of voices and experiences can be incorporated into the archives, and fresh perspectives can help detect hitherto invisible dynamics in existing materials. Thanks to the labor of human rights activists, archivists, survivors, family members of the disappeared, and others committed to keeping the memory of the period of state terrorism alive, we can start hearing more varied narratives and posing new questions for analysis.

Gender and State Power

This study addressed significant questions about gender and state power, focusing on the actions of the state's armed branch—the military, police, and security forces in Argentina—in a context of dictatorship. However, we need to consider that the lines separating violent state practices in dictatorships and democracies are sometimes rather thin, even if recognizing that a de facto government's power grab amplifies the possibility of exerting unchecked violence. As numerous cases of human rights violations in both dictatorships and democracies demonstrate, people deemed deviant, subversive, or enemies of the nation-state are particularly likely to bear the brunt of state violence. This book shows that attention to gender is required to more fully understand such forces at work. This entails not only noticing the gender of perpetrators and targets of state violence, but also examining how gender ideologies and practices structure the power of the state and its modes of regulation and subjection.

One of the ways in which gender matters to state power has to do with the state apparatus's regulation of sexuality and reproduction, mostly through policies but also through the use of the state's punitive arm. The regulatory role of the state sometimes turns into outright control, and the state's ability to inflict brute force is the most salient expression of this passage. In the clandestine detention centers (CDCs), we see a dramatization of these dynamics, as the physical control and abuse of detainees took place with total impunity. Feminist analyses of armed conflicts, war, and political and state violence have paid particular attention to rape and other forms of sexual violence as weapons of war, ethnic "cleansing," and political repression. This type of violence, however, is hardly exceptional or circumscribed to contexts of armed violence. In fact, the ubiquitous presence of sexual and gender violence and the impunity that perpetrators enjoy in peacetimes and in democracy fuel and are consistent with what happens in contexts viewed as exceptional, for example, due to armed conflict, states of emergency, or breaks in the constitutional order (e.g., INCITE! 2006; Fregoso and Bejarano 2010; Segato 2014).[4] In the Argentine case, the long and arduous path to obtain justice for the sexual violence of state terrorism as crimes against humanity mirrors the general difficulty that survivors of sexual and gender violence have experienced in ordinary situations.

The connections and overlaps between past and present, dictatorship and democracy, states of exception and "normal" times throw into relief the contemporary significance of the experiences of women survivors of CDCs. In this vein, lessons from these experiences can serve as interventions in current realities. Though women who suffered sexual violence in the context of state terrorism have dealt with the experience in varied ways, some of these women were actively interested in becoming complainants, in denouncing these crimes and hoping that this would help—in the words of survivor Liliana Callizo—"to go deeper into today's issues." These current issues include persistent sexual violence, feminicides, the sexualization of women as a means to shatter their voices, and law enforcement and judiciary systems that have a long way to go in terms of shedding their authoritarian and patriarchal legacies (even though some progress has been made in terms of increased awareness of and societal mobilization against gender violence).[5]

While the embodied violence that detainees experienced in the camps was extreme and had its own specificity, overlapping tactics continue in the present, including in police stations, prisons, and other institutions of confinement in democracy. After all, human rights abuses perpetrated by law enforcement still take place, against people of various genders. In Argentina and other countries in the region, institutional violence against transgender people is a persistent problem. As stated in a REDLACTRANS report (2012, 15): "transgender human rights defenders and other transgender women in Latin America are subjected to police brutality and cruel, inhuman and degrading treatment, which take place in both police stations and patrol cars as well as on the street." In Argentina, reports about the ill treatment of women in prisons have documented the authorities' continued reliance on degrading intrusions on women's bodies, including abusive pat-downs, forced nudity, and forced examination of vaginal and anal areas (known as *requisas vejatorias* or "humiliating searches") (CELS, Ministerio Público de la Defensa de la Nación, and Procuración Penitenciaria de la Nación, 2011). Similarly, the public revelation of disturbing images taken in a prison in the province of San Luis in 2013 vividly showed to the public the persistence of cruel and humiliating forms of bodily control in contemporary prisons: the pictures depict a group of young male inmates reclined on the floor, with their bodies completely naked, their heads and knees down, their hands behind their backs, and their buttocks upwardly exposed. They were flanked by prison guards, some seemingly relaxed, and at least one of them with a large dog (see "Denuncia del CELS" 2014). These acts were denounced by the human rights organization CELS as one example of "torture practices and inhumane treatment that are widespread in places of confinement across the country" (CELS 2014, n.p.). In this sense, we can see some continuities between dictatorship and democracy through the lens of state violence against people under the direct power of state authorities.

This book elaborates and furthers the discussion of gender and state power by looking at gender as an implicit script of torture, beyond the perpetration of evident forms of sexual violence. I have examined how normative notions of "the feminine" are re-created through torture and torments constructing human beings as just bodies, fostering hyperawareness of the body, heightening vulnerability, and producing monstrosity. In these dynamics we can see how gendered cultural imaginaries and practices in intersection with other systems of inequality shape torture as a radical form of bodily subjection and a means to enforce subordination. The power of the state—in this case manifested in the bodily control and suffering of detainees—does not happen in a vacuum. On the contrary, state power constitutes and is constituted by social hierarchies and discourses that help sustain its policies and practices. In extreme ways, torture gives concrete expression to and feeds ideologies that are already culturally available in particular historical times and places, while also bearing the traces of tactics with a longer transnational history.

Attending to gender is important to understanding both state violence in specific contexts as well as how the languages and techniques of violence move across dissimilar situations. In doing so, they blur the line between supposedly exceptional abuse and the realm of the "normal." What does it say about "normal" gender regulations, and cis privilege, that tactical performances of femininity were perceived as necessary for survival by some women in captivity? Why should state officers bother with the bodily appearance of women captives? To what extent did this interest exceed repressors' individual sexual desires and preferences to reflect broader state interests in enforcing particular gender roles, ensuring women knew their (subordinated) place in society? What does it say about "normal" heterosexual relationships that the coerced sexual contact and pseudo-dates that some women survivors experienced during captivity could pass as consensual sex or dates to uncritical eyes?

Subtle and not so subtle enforcement of dominant gender norms occurred inside and outside of CDCs, reproducing the hierarchies and heteropatriarchal ideals that the regime aimed to uphold (at the same time, it is important to note that women sometimes strategically deployed such norms, using them in agentic ways). Within the camps, repressors had the power of the state at their disposal, and impunity helped to not only re-create but dramatize asymmetrical gender relations. This study shows how women's bodies became a site where repressors could impose gender norms and exercise their presumed sexual birthright over women. Similarly, albeit not the focus of this study, a gender analysis can also contribute to deepen understandings of state repression against men and gender-nonconforming individuals. In addition to inquiry into masculinity, captivity, and embodiment through a feminist lens, or studies on the experiences of queer and trans detainees targets of state terror, a comparative analysis of body narratives of captivity *across* genders holds significant promise. In that sense, factors that can enrich the analysis include attention to gender ideology and the enforcement of gender binaries; class, ethnoracial, and sexuality-based hierarchies among men; homophobia, heteronormativity, and the devaluation of the feminine; and the cultural connections between masculinity, power, and violence.

These types of analyses are particularly relevant given the continued glorification of masculinist violence in societies around the world. Pervasive notions of militarized security are often associated with aggressive heteromasculinity and with the use of arms and lethal violence. In which ways do the militarized security tactics of the past transfer to the present? How is security defined, whose security is given priority, and at the expense of whom? What is the relation between dominant security measures and sexism, racism, class inequalities, and violence against members of queer and gender-nonconforming communities? Feminist scholars have productively addressed these types of questions in historical and contemporary perspective, showing the injustices and social costs associated with militarized and masculinist approaches to security.[6] In Argentina during the seventies, the military regime applied notions of national security that targeted a broad swath of people characterized as enemies, those whose human rights evidently meant nothing to the state. What similarities and differences emerge in contemporary societies, for example, in the context of the global "war on terror" or dehumanizing prisons construed as solutions to insecurity? Who can be presently dehumanized, tortured, maimed, dispossessed, violated, and killed with no consequences? How might these practices fuel more violence, from many directions?

As military, police, and security forces in various countries have started to include more diverse people across their ranks, new complexities have emerged. In the case of the last military regime in Argentina, even if women cannot be characterized solely as victims or as completely unconnected to the perpetration of atrocities (see, e.g., D'Antonio 2003), the top leaders of the dictatorship as well as most members of the military, security, and police forces were men. Yet in the new millennium, women are increasingly incorporated in state militaries and their perpetration of human rights violations has received public—sometimes sensational—media attention. For instance, in the context of the "war on terror," the participation of U.S. military women in the sexualized violence against detainees in the Abu Ghraib prison in Iraq shows the need for fine-grained gender analyses—beyond the men-perpetrator/women-victim model—incorporating intersecting axes of inequality (e.g., Puar 2004; Fusco 2008; Mann 2008). In the Abu Ghraib case, we can also see the connections between the normal and supposedly exceptional violence alluded to earlier (Puar 2004). Although in an uncritical way, one of the women participants in these human rights violations, Lynndie England, compared the violence that took place in the Iraqi prison to similar practices in colleges or military boot camps ("US Woman Soldier" 2009). While these types of comparisons trivialize torture and abuse in prisons and detention centers, they also raise questions about the construction of the "normal" in societies rife with sexist, racist, and homophobic ideologies and practices. To what extent do these problems persist even as the demographics of military and security forces in different parts of the world change and become more "inclusive"?

In addition to the role of sexuality and sexual violence as important to gender analyses of state power, another issue to consider is reproduction. State policies around the world are known to regulate reproduction in more or less coercive ways—from abortion restrictions and sterilization campaigns to "incentives" to achieve the fertility rate that the state considers optimal. State regulation of reproduction has often been linked to racial, nationalistic, religious, and eugenic ideas; norms on what supposedly constitutes a "proper" family; the sexual orientation and gender identity of the parents; the class and race status of mothers and families; and ableist discourses about who is fit or not fit to procreate and raise children (e.g., Hartmann 1995; Roberts 1997; Ross 2006; Spade 2013). In the case of the CDCs in Argentina, repressors' appropriation of babies born to women in captivity highlights the state's ability to seize women's reproductive capacities. Repressors were able to capitalize on women's reproductive powers for their own ends, deciding on matters such as birth giving and lactation for hundreds of detained pregnant women. What's more, judging by the repressors' actions, many of these women did not deserve to continue living, let alone raise their children. Their bodies had merely reproductive value, for the benefit of others. These women's lineage and influence were to be terminated by giving the appropriated children to families deemed more suitable. Many of these women were apparently considered unfit mothers, for they had failed to conform to prevailing gender expectations and had challenged the political project of the military regime. They were considered political and gender "subversives." In this context, the cases of women who gestated their pregnancies with romantic partners while in captivity, or fantasized about the idea of pregnancy, can be interpreted as resisting death, disappearance, and the termination of their family and political lineages. In other words, they subverted the aims of a regime bent on extermination.

Testimonies by women who were pregnant during their captivity also touch on other disturbing situations such as forced abortions and miscarriages due to torture. These events demonstrate state representatives' total disregard for women's ability to decide about their reproduction. Of course, in the context of the camps, detainees' ability to make choices about *any* aspect of their bodies and lives was severely restricted, when not completely shattered (regardless of gender or pregnancy status). However, the materiality of the gendered body—in this case, of pregnant women's bodies—influenced the personal and social implications of the violence and restrictions inflicted under the state's auspices. Despite the regime's pronatalist policies (e.g., Decree 3938/77 on population), some of the women detained were excepted from the implicit mandate to procreate—through abortions and preventable miscarriages—but not by their own choice. While many pregnant women's bodies became instrumental as a means to generate children for others, other pregnancies seem not to have been even worth the trouble. The torture, beatings, and rapes of pregnant women show the little value that the cultural glorification of motherhood had in relation to these women. That the violence inflicted could lead to miscarriage was something that could surely be anticipated; yet preventing miscarriage was clearly not a priority for repressors in such cases. Furthermore, the clandestine abortions performed on women under the control of the regime open up another set of questions about the differences and overlaps with other types of clandestine abortions that continue to take place in democracy.

Similarly to the cases of sexual violence, considering abortions within and outside CDCs side by side can productively shed light on the problems of the present. In that sense, attending to the notion of *clandestinity* is relevant for thinking about contemporary abortions in democracy (Sutton 2017). Specifically, I am referring to the hundreds of thousands of pregnant women forced into clandestinity each year in Argentina in order to have an abortion—to have a say on their reproductive bodies and life projects—in the context of abortion criminalization.[7] Many of these women, especially those who are socially and economically marginalized, have routinely risked their physical integrity and life in clandestine abortions performed in dangerous or substandard conditions. What does the figure of clandestinity—and clandestine abortion in particular—tell us about how state power is upheld in modern democracies? How is state violence implicated in producing hidden (women's) bodies exposed to danger and which may be "killed" with impunity? I say "killed" instead of "die" because I consider these deaths not the result of benign neglect but a product of a violent law that helps produce these deaths.

In Argentina, the notion of clandestinity carries special weight given the history of state terrorism. There is a relationship between the hiddenness and stigma of the zone of clandestinity and the violence produced in such spaces. There is also a point of contact, though not an equation, between the limbo of the disappeared by state terrorism—and the governmental refusal to acknowledge them as dead or alive—and the non-"grievable" lives (Butler 2004a) of the women who die because of dangerous clandestine abortions in "normal" times. The invisibility of violence produced in the zone of clandestinity has been denounced by the human rights movement in the case of the dictatorship and by the abortion rights movement with respect to clandestine abortions. Current abortion rights activism is nourished by multiple ideological and experiential strands, but includes a collective memory of state terror (Sutton and Borland 2013; Morgan 2015; Sutton and Borland 2015)—a memory that knows all too well the costs of clandestinity, silence, and political erasure of certain lives.

Writing about the dictatorship in Argentina, scholar and survivor Pilar Calveiro (1998, 25) argued that "power shows and hides, and it reveals itself as much in that which it exhibits as in that which it hides." Applying this idea to present forms of state power, we might want to think deeper about persistent forms of injustice that depend on hidden zones; or that are relatively apparent but seem to be under the mandate to be ignored, not talked about, and "disappeared" from public discussion. What does the figure of clandestinity tell us about the edifice of state power? For certain power structures to remain in place, it is as though we are required to sustain clandestinity, to uphold what Michael Taussig (1999) calls "public secrets." Argentine society had considerable training in this, judging by the pervasive forms of denial that characterized the dictatorship experience. With regard to clandestine abortion, many people know first- or secondhand of women who had a clandestine abortion, but—as was the case in relation to the "disappeared"—we are not supposed to know, ask, or talk about it. Social movements have broken the silence about various zones of clandestinity (in dictatorship and democracy), exposing the contours of invisibility, and contesting the violent erasure of lives constructed as Other.

Placing reproduction, sexuality, and the social construction of gender at the center of analyses of state power helps reveal key dimensions of its workings. Furthermore, a focus on CDCs shows that in the age of "disciplinary power" (Foucault 1989), the coercive centralized power of the state has continued to be a critical instrument of social control and of enforcing dominant social values. The people held in CDCs bore the brunt of this type of power, but it would be a mistake to assume that its pernicious effects stayed contained within these walls. Rather, the ideological apparatus that helped justify the spectral existence of the camps was diffused throughout society, and the spread of fear modeled concrete lives outside the camps prompting silence and other coping mechanisms. Likewise, the gendered hierarchies and discourses that repressors enforced within the camps traveled across the boundaries of places of confinement, feeding from society at large but also shaping institutions and influencing the lives of individuals under the "operational control" of the armed forces. As stated in the military junta's first communiqué, the whole country was to be under such "operational control" (Memoria Abierta n.d.-a).

In the contemporary world, sexual and gender violence continues to be common currency. According to the World Health Organization (2013, 35), "more than one in three women (35.6%) globally report having experienced physical and/or sexual partner violence, or sexual violence by a non-partner." This staggering figure does not include many other forms of violence that women experience. The resort to militarized and sexualized violence by states, parastatal groups, and private individuals; the persistent human rights violations perpetrated by state authorities in places of confinement and in the course of daily policing; the violent regulation of women's reproduction and the emergence of deadly zones of clandestinity; and the treatment of women's bodies as the text and material grounds for asserting heteropatriarchal norms suggest that the questions raised in this book demand continued attention.

Bodies, Vulnerability, and Agency

In the testimonies of women survivors of state terrorism, "the body" appears in multiple ways. It is the body that endures torture, gives birth, or experiences the pain of a forced abortion. It is the body that

nurses a child in captivity and the one that parodies or enacts normative femininity. It is also the body that sings and laughs and lends a
hand to alleviate the effects of oppression. It is the raped and sexually
humiliated body and the body that kicks and screams against repressors intent on harm. In the testimonies, the body emerges not only as
a discourse or a text but as a material presence and the site of powerful
emotions and extreme lived experiences. Paying attention to the body
in terms of gender differences and similarities can help provide more
adequate societal responses to the effects of state terror and significantly
account for the long-term bodily and psychological effects of torture,
sexual abuse, and other forms of degradation in contexts of repression
and confinement. Thus, a central approach in this project has been to
listen to survivors' testimonies of clandestine detention as *body narratives*, including embodied memories and memories about the body. In
doing so, I grappled with the tension, interactions, and entanglements
between discourse and materiality, the power of social construction, and
the material characteristics of fleshly bodies.

While the body is a social fact, and social discourses produce concrete
effects on the body, a sole emphasis on discourse or social construction
is insufficient to understand corporeal experiences such as torture and
other forms of bodily violence. Here I would like to emphasize the significance of the body's materiality. Maimed bodies, bodies burnt by the
electric picana, bodies unable to breathe during waterboarding, bodies disfigured by brutal beatings, and bodies with disabled limbs or organs as a result of torture constitute an imposing material reality that a
focus on language, discourse, and representation cannot fully account
for. Attention to such experiences need not be the sole business of the
health sciences and medical professions. They also belong to the realm
of social theories that conceive bodies as having cultural, historical, discursive, as well as material existence. Yet, as scholars of new materialisms and material feminisms point out, the "linguistic turn" or "cultural
turn" in theories of the body and society have meant that the material
body sometimes recedes in importance in contemporary body studies
(Alaimo 2008; Coole and Frost 2010).

The materiality of the body is central in situations of captivity; they
are concrete sites of oppression, resiliency, and resistance. In these and
other cases, it is not just the disciplining power of discourse that models

individual lives and bodies. Rather the violent physical actions of individuals and institutions exert a very direct grip on the material body. In other words, while discourses define and classify particular persons or groups as deviant, abnormal, or dangerous, understanding social control and regulation requires more than an analysis of violent speech or cruel norms. The use of torture as a radical technique of bodily subjection is a case in point. Such methods overlap with other physical acts of violence, usually against socially subordinated populations. Women survivors' narratives of torture and sexual violence offer a glimpse of what it means for power to operate through brutal attacks on the material body, even if such violence is infused by discourses and social relations that give such experiences particular meanings.

At the same time, even when the aim is to center the material body in the analysis of power, it is important to remember that the body may not always produce "evidence" of the exercise of power through physical violence—in this case torture. This may be due to the passage of time or simply because some thoroughly physical methods of torture leave no visible or tangible traces. Thus, an exclusive reliance on the material body can occlude or hide certain truths. Paradoxically, access to knowledge on what happened to the body is often through language. Yet, language is often incapable of reflecting what the experience actually entails. (This is also true with other representational strategies [Kaplan 2007, 13].) Words like "rape" and "torture" point to aberrant attacks on a person's material body and subjectivity, and yet the banal circulation of these words in everyday life gets in the way of fully apprehending what the victims of such attacks went through. Sometimes these words are used as metaphors of something else, and even when they are used as a label for the actions they are meant to name, the way these terms summarize a range of aggressions on the body falls short in conveying the severity of the injury—bodily, psychological, emotional, and social wounds. Phrases such as "I was tortured" or "I was raped" likely fail to adequately represent the events they are supposed to invoke, let alone their personal and social implications.

Presuming that a person's material body by itself can reveal truths is also problematic. This assumption can lead to misplaced conclusions as it excludes the voice and subjectivity of the person in question (a human being who has/is a body, but is also more than flesh). An overreliance on the material body can also constitute another form of violence, not only in the epistemic sense, but as already violated and tortured bodies are examined, prodded, and photographed to secure evidence, to produce truths. How, then, to account for the suffering of the person in terms of injuries on material fleshly bodies—as well as on subjectivity and social relations—without reproducing violence? How to recognize the concreteness of the bodily injury and the causes of these fleshly and subjective wounds without creating a voyeuristic spectacle? These questions need to be taken into account not only in acts of denunciation but also in the formulation of social supports for survivors. Such supports need to attend to the lasting impacts of embodied injuries and trauma, even after visible scars heal and only the pain of the victim is the reminder of the violence perpetrated.

Another important dimension of this study's attention to "the body" in the narratives of survivors of state terrorism has been the analysis of women's embodied agency and resistance. Here we see a multiplicity of embodied responses to conditions of extreme oppression, showing the complexity of human behavior in the face of sheer terror. The narratives counter the notion that there is one right way to act as a response to such abuse, or that it is easy to predict what one would do in such unfathomable situations. We do know, however, that many forms of embodied agency and resistance were set in motion in the camps, when none seemed possible. Women in this study elaborated on some subtle responses that involved the body—for example, some kinds of mind/body split—as forms of protection or self-defense. Although not necessarily intended and not exempt of personal costs, some of these complex responses contradicted the aim of the regime in sheltering the self from the brutalization of the body, in numbing pain despite outright violence, or in wiping out sensitive information from consciousness during interrogation. While there are surely physiological and psychological dimensions to these responses, analyzing them in terms of social relations of power shows their political implications, in the sense that they countered the grip of power in the camps and to some extent frustrated the goals of the perpetrators.

Similarly, the variety of minute, almost imperceptible, embodied gestures of care and solidarity by detainees acquire enormous political meaning. A kiss, a burst of laughter, or a comforting stroke on the shoulder can be mundane acts, but can be acts of resistance in a context of oppression. In addition, detainees' sharing food or tending to wounds implicitly helped to counter a regime of bodily and psychological, as well as political, destruction. While small acts of care could not guarantee survival, they powerfully contributed to sustaining mind, body, and soul and to confirming detainees' denied humanity. Some testimonies reveal that in specific camps or situations, detainees plotted, strategized, and sometimes carried out forms of collective resistance, yet in many cases the structure and conditions of detention precluded such possibilities. Thus forms of embodied agency through touch, body signs, and bodily noises became forms of resistance that detainees carved out at considerable risk. In these examples we see not only "oppressed bodies," but embodied human beings with agency despite a formidable structure of oppression.

Embodied solidarity was also an opportunity for some detainees to enact political values, even as repressors aimed to destroy such ethical and political orientations. Many people in captivity, including many women, were targeted precisely because of their political involvement in organizations that challenged the power of the state and that fought for a different kind of societal and economic structure. In the testimonies of captivity, we sometimes see women drawing on, hiding, and strategically managing their political subjectivities and knowledge in efforts to survive. The political identities and experiences of the disappeared and survivors were silenced in the early democratic transition in favor of a human rights discourse that left little room for thinking about victimhood and political agency as part of the same frame. Recognizing the embodied activism of women—before, during, and after the dictatorship—and the perspectives and insights that such political experiences have yielded has been another important goal of this book. Accounting for bodies in protest and the embodied emotions that infused political participation during the seventies in Argentina is critical to a nuanced understanding of the radical movements of the period and the experiences of repression that targeted such political organizing.

Survivors' testimonies also show the possibility of an extended temporality of embodied resistance. This is apparent in the ways in which women survivors pointed to the bodily marks of captivity or drew on sensory memories to reconstruct and denounce the events and conditions in the camps. Significantly, we see in these body memories how women were able to use their oppressed bodies in agentic ways, for example, to demand redress and advance justice. Rather than mere bodies without political significance, a number of survivors drew on their body memories as testimony of state violence, bringing their experiences to the very realm of politics. In doing so they enacted a claim on voice and membership in the body politic, a condition that (heteropatriarchal) state terrorism aimed to vanish. The individual body memories of survivors also feed into a more collective memory, expressed both in the public realm of testimony as well as in more intimate spaces where survivors have gone about their lives. Whether these body memories are perceived only as memories of victimized bodies, or whether we can also detect the political agency that such testimonies entail, may be partly dependent on the context of listening and on the historical and political conjuncture. Deploying the body as a tool of resistance and a way to assert voice has a long history in political protest and activism but has not always been deemed worthy of academic attention.[8]

Many of the survivors' bodily memories are memories of trauma and horror, but as we fine-tune our ears to listen to these accounts, we can also hear stories about embodied perseverance, resilience, and resistance. Though memory can be fragile, bodily memories are powerful reminders for individuals and societies. The memories inscribed on the body are not uniform but reflect the materiality of diverse bodies, the social arrangements that have shaped them, and the discourses that have helped to give them meaning. Constructing a social memory of state terror that serves to advance a democratic culture requires listening to a variety of embodied stories, not all of which have had the chance to fully emerge. In heeding these stories, we need to keep in mind that acknowledging the vulnerability and unmet needs of survivors is not contradictory with recognizing their resilience and agency. In line with conceptualizations of vulnerability as relational, we can think of survivors' psychological, emotional, and bodily resources as relational too. This means that societies should respond in ways that bolster and complement, as opposed to squash or ignore, survivors' own vital resources.

The lessons from the past are not only about stopping abuse or confronting the powers that be, but also about believing that things can be changed, and drawing strength from what it means to be human at its best. In the testimonies of women who survived state terror, one can detect both efforts to advance an antiauthoritarian project as well as ethical positions regarding the human condition. It may seem naïve to hold on to dreams that seem impossible, it may seem impossible to survive the situations these women were subjected to; and yet resilience, courage, vision, and concrete achievements are part of the narrative that these women as a whole offer. Theirs are stories not only of survival in the physical sense, but also of the survival of their dignity and, in many cases, hope. Ilda Micucci, who survived captivity but whose son and daughter remain disappeared, expressed:

> I recognize that in every circumstance I hold the memories of the good things that happened to me, and I cling to that firmly, and it is very important to me. And, well, it works for me. When I was there in captivity, one of the things that I remember is that at some point, someone came and put a little piece of chocolate in my hand. "Take it, take it" [this person] told me, and gave me the chocolate, which was kind of melted, all sticky. But, well, in the midst of all that—how awful it was to be there, in that situation—that someone would bring me a piece of chocolate, it was like . . . like a little light. [. . .] I say that in all situations no matter how awful they are, there's always something [. . .] a little light, or a window that opens and lets the sun come in.

This hopeful "something" that Ilda alluded to—grounded in the embodied memory of a sticky chocolate given by another human being—challenges us as members of the human community to meet the expectation to act in solidarity and not turn away from the suffering of others. Ilda illustrates this ethical stance through her experience in captivity, but also as someone with a significant trajectory in human rights organizations, including as a member of Memoria Abierta.

This book highlights the testimonies of women survivors in an attempt to contribute to academic and activist conversations concerning gender, politics, social memory, and state violence. It presents a glimpse of the richness of insights that these women offered while acknowledging women's political agency and the messages they wished to transmit to future generations. Hearing women's embodied voices in this way is not only a matter of gender justice, but also involves the possibility of nourishing the present and the future with the contributions of people who are much more than "carriers of the memory of horror" (Daleo 2010, 71). These women carry memories about social change, valuable political perspectives, and, in various cases, knowledge that emerged from the critical examination of their experiences as women. They also carry memories of survival and resistance (Daleo 2010; see also Park 2014)—a critical legacy to imagine and build a country with full re-spect for human rights. In that sense, I conclude with the words of Delia Bisutti, a survivor with a history of activism in a teachers' union, who became a legislator in the city of Buenos Aires in the post-dictatorship period: "The dictatorship left a strong mark. It left a very strong mark. But well, what I do feel is that we were not defeated individually or so-cially [. . .] or at least they have not crushed us. They have defeated us in many battles, in many. . . . But we continue gathering strength to con-tinue fighting, and I believe that that is what's important, what we have to capitalize upon for the construction of a society that needs to learn to live without fear."

ACKNOWLEDGMENTS

This book owes its existence primarily to women who survived clandestine detention centers and came forward to tell their stories. My deepest gratitude goes to them. The vision and dedication of members of the organization Memoria Abierta were also essential to this project, for they collected, archived, and made available the testimonies on which this book is based. I particularly thank Alejandra Oberti, coordinator of Memoria Abierta's Oral Archive, and Evangelina Sánchez, Nancy Lucero, Celina Flores, and Guillermina Zampieri for their helpful assistance making the public consultation of the testimonies possible. I thank Susana Skura and Claudia Bacci, who also worked in Memoria Abierta, for their constructive feedback on sections of this book. Other Argentine scholars have generously shared their input and perceptive comments on aspects of this project, including Eugenia Tarzibachi, Mónica Szurmuk, Valeria Llobet, Cecilia Macón, Ruth Felder, Guillermina Seri, and Verónica Perera. A special thanks goes to Nayla Vacarezza who thoughtfully read and offered feedback on virtually the whole manuscript.

I am fortunate to be part of a long-standing community of scholars whose encouragement as well as insightful critique have helped me develop my research and writing over the years. Friends from my times in graduate school, now established scholars, have continued to engage with my work: Kari Norgaard has been a constant presence, invaluable listener, and constructive critic. Thank you Hava Gordon and Sandra Ezquerra for reading and commenting on my work. Elizabeth Borland, whom I met while doing fieldwork in Argentina, has also been a continued source of ideas and support. One of my mentors, Linda Fuller, gave me detailed suggestions in this new project, and remains interested in my work over a decade after graduation. Sandi Morgen (1950–2016), also my mentor, has left an indelible imprint on my life and work: She shared with me her wisdom, warmth, sense of humor, and witty commentary. She modeled a form of critical and inclusive feminism in which theory and practice were inextricably linked; where serious intellectual engagement did not exclude enjoyment and pleasure; where analyses of gender inequality were inseparable from a denunciation of racism, class inequality, and other injustices.

A network of interdisciplinary U.S.-based scholars at the University at Albany and beyond has nourished my academic work through stimulating conversations and concrete engagement with my project. I am thankful for written and oral commentary on different facets of this study (from conceptualization to working papers, book prospectus, and specific chapters) offered by Patricia Richards, Sudarat Musikawong, Mitch Aso, Torrey Shanks, Julie Novkov, Kristen Hessler, Aaron Benavot, and Julie Shayne. I am especially grateful to Ron Friedman, editor extraordinaire and incisive interlocutor, who has helped me improve my writing and deepen my arguments. I thank him for his ongoing encouragement, support, and engagement with my ideas. I am also fortunate to be part of the Department of Women's, Gender, and Sexuality Studies, which has allowed me great freedom to develop scholarship that matters, and to have colleagues who have taught me in various ways the meaning of critical, intersectional, and engaged feminist inquiry and pedagogy. I particularly thank Rajani Bhatia, Virginia Eubanks, Janell Hobson, and Vivien Ng.

I developed parts of this book initially as conference presentations and/or shorter article publications. I presented portions of this project and received fruitful feedback at meetings of the Hemispheric Institute of Performance and Politics, Latin American Studies Association, National Women's Studies Association, Sociologists for Women in Society, Jornadas Nacionales de Historia de las Mujeres/Congreso Iberoamericano de Estudios de Género, and Women's Worlds/Fazendo Gênero. I am also grateful to Virginia Vecchioli for inviting me to share my research at the Seminario Permanente de Estudios sobre Política y Activismo. Sections of this work were first published in the following articles and have been adapted and reprinted here with permission: "Collective Memory and the Language of Human Rights: Attitudes toward Torture in Contemporary Argentina," *Latin American Perspectives* 42, no. 3 (2015); "Terror, testimonio, y transmisión: Voces de mujeres sobrevivientes de centros clandestinos de detención en Argentina (1976–1983)," *Mora* 21, no. 1 (2015); "Zonas de clandestinidad y 'nuda vida': Mujeres, cuerpo y aborto," *Estudos Feministas* 25, no. 2 (2017); "Beauty in Places of Horror: Testimonies of Women Survivors of Clandestine Detention Centers in Argentina," *ReVista: Harvard Review of Latin America* 16, no. 3 (Spring 2017). Reviewers and editors for these various venues, as well as for NYU Press, have provided invaluable suggestions. Ilene Kalish, executive editor at NYU Press, has been an enthusiastic supporter of my scholarship, encouraging me even before I knew I had a book project in the making. I also thank Joseph Dahm for his careful copyediting of my manuscript. Finally, this project received funding from an Initiatives for Women Award and the College of Arts and Sciences at the University at Albany, SUNY. For the many people who encouraged me with this project, I hope this book honors their faith and interest in my work.

NOTES

CHAPTER 1. WOMEN, STATE TERROR, AND COLLECTIVE MEMORY

1 See Kleinman, Das, and Lock (1996) for an introduction to the notion of "social suffering," which connects subjective experiences of suffering with the power structures of society, thus demanding more than individual responses.

2 See, e.g., Connerton (1989); Kleinman and Kleinman (1994); Dossa (2003); Spillman and Conway (2007); Gómez-Barris (2009).

3 In this book I use the terms "detainee," "captive," and "prisoner" interchangeably to refer to people illegally held in clandestine detention centers (that is, "detained-disappeared"), though I realize that each term can also have different connotations regarding conditions of confinement and the status of the person deprived of liberty.

4 Disappearance consisted of state officials kidnapping people and taking them to clandestine detention centers, but denying knowledge of their whereabouts (and eventually assassinating massive numbers of people). While there is no doubt about the large scale of repression, the exact number of missing people has been complicated to determine (Brysk 1994). In 1984 the CONADEP (National Commission on the Disappearance of Persons) registered at least 8,960 cases in its *Nunca Más* report, clarifying that the list did not reflect all the disappearances. Human rights organizations have repeatedly invoked the estimated figure of 30,000 disappeared, a number that has gained strong symbolic and political force. According to *Nunca Más*, among the people disappeared 30 percent were women.

5 This and all other testimonies viewed in Memoria Abierta and cited here are listed in the "Cited Testimonies" section at the end of the book. Some of the transcribed passages have been slightly edited (e.g., smoothing out oral speech disfluencies) to increase readability, while respecting the words, content, and tone in the original interviews. This and all quotes extracted from Memoria Abierta's testimonies and from texts published in the Spanish language are my own translation.

6 See, e.g., Ledda Barreiro's April 15, 2015, interview in the radio show *Un Día Perfecto* conducted by Valentín Belza and Julia Paiz (Belza 2015).

7 See, e.g., "El horror" (2015); Municipalidad General Pueyrredón (2015); "Se entregaron ejemplares" (2016).

8 For example, repression was exerted by paramilitary and vigilante organizations such as the Argentine Anti-Communist Alliance, the Comando Lib-

erators of America in the province of Córdoba (Duhalde 1999), the Anti-Communist Comando of Mendoza, and the Moralizing Comando Pío XII in the same province (Agüero 2009). Historiographical works such as Marina Franco's (2012, 17) demonstrate that the 1976 coup was part of a longer process of "institutional deterioration" of Argentina's constitutional democracy. Franco analyzes the gradual construction of the notion of the "internal enemy" since 1973.

9 Created in 1999, Memoria Abierta comprised the following organizations at the time of my research: Asamblea Permanente por los Derechos Humanos (APDH), Centro de Estudios Legales y Sociales (CELS), Comisión de Homenaje a las Víctimas de Vesubio y Protobanco, Familiares de Desaparecidos y Detenidos por Razones Políticas, Fundación Memoria Histórica y Social Argentina, and Madres de Plaza de Mayo–Línea Fundadora.

10 CONADEP is the acronym for the Comisión Nacional sobre la Desaparición de Personas.

11 See, e.g., Aucía et al. (2011); Balardini, Oberlin, and Sobredo (2011); Bacci et al. (2012); Forcinito (2012); Sonderéguer (2012).

12 For an elaboration of the concept of "bare life," see Agamben (1998).

13 The Juicio a las Juntas took place in 1985 and was presided over by a civilian criminal court. The court judged the members of the three military juntas that ruled the country from 1976 through 1983 for actions considered crimes in the Penal Code at the time of the events. The following sentences were imposed: life imprisonment (*reclusión perpetua*) for Jorge Rafael Videla and Emilio Eduardo Massera, seventeen years of prison for Roberto Eduardo Viola, eight years of prison to Armando Lambruschini, and four years and six months of prison for Orlando Ramón Agosti. Omar Domingo Rubens Graffigna, Leopoldo Fortunato Galtieri, Basilio Lami Dozo, and Jorge Isaac Anaya were absolved. The audiovisual records of the trial and other relevant documentation can be consulted in Memoria Abierta (n.d. [2016]).

14 The interim presidents were Federico Ramón Puerta (2001), Adolfo Rodríguez Saá (2001), Eduardo Oscar Caamaño (2001), and Eduardo Alberto Duhalde (2002–3) (Casa Rosada n.d.).

15 Among the international treaties that are particularly relevant to the kinds of events addressed in this book are the Convention against Torture and Other Cruel, Inhuman or Degrading Treatment or Punishment; the Inter-American Convention to Prevent and Punish Torture; the Inter-American Convention on the Forced Disappearance of Persons; and the Convention on the Non-Applicability of Statutory Limitations to War Crimes and Crimes against Humanity.

16 HIJOS is an acronym for Hijos por la Identidad y la Justicia contra el Olvido y el Silencio (Children for Identity and Justice and against Forgetting and Silence).

17 For analyses of narratives about the Tlatelolco massacre and related events, and how they are associated with broader processes of memory and reckoning with human rights violations in Latin America, see, e.g., Allier-Montaño (2009); Harris

(2005); MacManus (2015). The National Security Archive has also posted declassi-fied U.S. documents regarding this event (Doyle 2003).

18 In recent years, a number of scholarly works have gathered regional experiences and lessons related to collective memory and transitional justice in Latin America (see, e.g., Allier-Montaño and Crenzel 2015; Skaar, García-Godos, and Collins 2016).

19 See Payne (2008) on the "unsettling accounts" of some confessed perpetrators of human rights violations, including from the Argentine dictatorship.

20 The Mothers made their first public appearance as a group in the Plaza de Mayo in 1977, and in 1986 they split into two different organizations: Madres de Plaza de Mayo-Línea Fundadora (Mothers of the Plaza de Mayo-Founding Line) and Asociación Madres de Plaza de Mayo (Mothers of the Plaza de Mayo Association) (Miller 2008).

21 See, e.g., Fisher (1993); Bouvard (1994); Arditti (1999); Bellucci (2000); Borland (2006).

22 Importantly, in recent years scholars, activists, and journalists—including survivors—have published works that address sexual violence and other forms of gendered violence in clandestine detention centers (see, e.g., Aucía et al. 2011; Balardini, Oberlin, and Sobredo 2011; Bacci et al. 2012; Forcinito 2012; Sonderé-guer 2012; Lewin and Wornat 2014; Macón 2014). Earlier writings on the experi-ences of women survivors include works by feminist historians, literary scholars, and survivors themselves (see, e.g., Partnoy 1986; Treacy 1996; Strejilevich 1997; Actis et al. 2001; Ramus 2000). Ximena Bunster-Burotto (1994) published an early analysis of sexual violence under the Latin American Southern Cone military regimes.

23 Of course, for many women the death of a loved one, particularly a son or daugh-ter, felt intricately linked to their own experiences, not as something separate. Yet the point remains that women's *own* experiences of captivity seem to recede in the background as their role as mothers of people disappeared takes center stage.

24 The brutality detained women were subjected to, and the fact that some members of the Mothers of the Plaza de Mayo joined the ranks of the disappeared, shows that gender was of little protection for a number of these women.

25 A recent example is that of former president Cristina Fernández de Kirchner, of-ten referred to by political opponents with derogatory and sexualized labels such as *yegua* (mare).

26 The notion that "women's rights are human rights" was popularized internation-ally especially in the lead-up to the United Nations Conference on Human Rights in Vienna in 1993 (Bunch and Frost 2000). In Argentina the extensive language of human rights, linked to the history of state terrorism, helps to create resonance for the idea of women's human rights.

27 Examples of such initiatives include campaigns to raise awareness of violence against women (e.g., the campaign Ni Una Menos [Not One Less]), some of which enjoyed international support (e.g., UNDP 2010; CECYM 2014). Also

important is the passage of law 26485, "Integral Protection to Prevent, Punish, and Eradicate Violence against Women in the Realms in Which They Develop Their Interpersonal Relations." The feminist civil society organization La Casa del Encuentro (n.d.) has periodically disseminated the results collected by its Observatory of Femicides, which records the frequency of such crimes annually, and the National Council on Women has an Observatory on Violence against Women more broadly. Numerous organizations, both nongovernmental and run by the state, were formed to provide assistance to women who have experienced gender violence (see, e.g., MEI n.d.).

28 For instance, the feminist organizations CLADEM (Comité de América Latina y el Caribe para la Defensa de los Derechos de la Mujer-Argentina) and INS-GENAR (Instituto de Género, Derecho y Desarrollo) filed amicus curiae ("friend of the court") briefs to explain the dynamics of sexual violence in the context of clandestine detention centers and to encourage their judgment as crimes against humanity (CLADEM n.d.). Books such as CLADEM's *Grietas en el silencio* (Aucía et al. 2011) and Memoria Abierta's *Y nadie quería saber* (Bacci et al. 2012) provide useful tools to interpret these crimes.

29 See a discussion of judicial and legal obstacles in Balardini, Oberlin, and Sobredo (2011); Bacci et al. (2012); and Duffy (2012).

30 Besides the sexualized connotations that might be associated with a woman's painted lips, *Boquitas pintadas* is also the title of Manuel Puig's 1969 novel, which later became a film.

31 See, for example, CELS, Ministerio Público de la Defensa de la Nación, and Procuración Penitenciaria de la Nación (2011) and CELS (2015a).

32 The details of this case can be found at www.cels.org.ar.

33 The field of women's, gender, and sexuality studies has grown and developed, and the literature dealing with gender goes well beyond the "add women and stir" approach. Scholars have analyzed gender as a central organizing principle of society, involving social relations, structures of inequality, institutions, practices, identities, interactions, bodies, and subjectivities. See, for example, Scott (1986); Connell (1987); West and Zimmerman (1987); Acker (1990); Butler (1990; 2004b); Lorber (1994); Connell and Pearse (2015).

34 These ideas emerge from contributions to the field from activists and scholars who have advanced intersectional analyses of women's oppression and structures of inequality. See, e.g., Combahee River Collective (1979); Moraga and Anzaldúa (1983); Glenn (1985); Mohanty (1988); Crenshaw (1989); McCall (2005); May (2014); Collins (2015).

35 In light of these debates, I should mention that all of the testimonies in this study were initially identified based on gendered names that denoted identities as "women"; and as I watched the testimonies, none of the interviewees suggested they identified as otherwise. Even though they presented as women, it is still possible that unacknowledged variations exist in terms of how strongly interviewees attached to such gender identity.

36 Memoria Abierta has a policy of making documentation available to researchers, though at the time of my research it had recently instituted a consultation fee to help support the work of the organization. Those who visit Memoria Abierta can count on meeting a group of helpful and committed staff members.

37 Through my preliminary search of the Memoria Abierta's database, I identified seventy-four testimonies of women who were in the category of survivors; however, not all of them were included in my sample given restrictions of use, time of detention that preceded 1976, or very young age at the time of captivity (e.g., toddlers). Regarding my research interests, I wanted to gain a sense of women's embodied experiences under conditions of detention in different sites. The clandestine detention centers in question were located in various parts of Argentina, except for one case (a woman who went to Uruguay because of political persecution in Argentina, was then captured by Uruguayan repressive forces, and was taken to a CDC in that country, apparently in cooperation with Argentine armed forces). In terms of the period delimited, all of the women were held captive sometime between 1976 and 1983 (all of them were detained after the military coup of March 24, 1976, except for three women who were taken to CDCs in the days preceding the coup). Besides the general conditions established by Memoria Abierta, some of the people interviewed required a special permission or stipulated that the testimony could not be used in certain ways (e.g., mass media dissemination, audiovisual works, or any other use besides public consultation at Memoria Abierta). The large majority of the interviews I viewed had no special restrictions.

38 In a first stage of the project I prioritized interviews that appeared especially relevant to my research interests. Although it seemed I had reached a saturation of themes and categories after about forty interviews, given the uneven characteristics of the summaries, I decided also to watch testimonies that had more general or synthetic written summaries, and in one case no summary description. This last round of testimonies contributed to further illuminate the themes that had already been emerging, totaling the final fifty-two testimonies that composed my sample.

39 The political developments addressed in the testimonies varied; these examples offer an idea of the range of issues addressed.

40 I used a split-page approach. On the right-hand side I recorded the interview content, and on the left I recorded the time in which different interview parts or topics appeared. I would also mark sections I wanted to return to, usually a particularly poignant passage and/or items directly related to my specific research interests. After watching the whole interview and taking extensive notes, I would then transcribe the passages that seemed particularly relevant (for example, narratives about the body, or passages related to the question of transmission). I manually coded my notebook information and the transcripts. I classified content by emerging categories, for example, those relating to silence, fear, body, parodies of legality, resistance strategies, utopian dreams, notions of time, repertoires of

oppression, and many others. I also created summary sheets of the main themes in individual interviews and my general impressions of them. I wrote memos to reflect on particular topics and worked with matrices to organize basic information about the interviews.

41 I recognize this decision is based on my own assumptions. Perhaps specific women would not mind, or would actively welcome, the opportunity to talk with me about such issues. Yet I felt that they had already given testimonies for other people to hear, and that I could and should work with such already existing materials. Unlike previous work with my own interviews, I do not use pseudonyms here as the interviews are available for public consultation and as Memoria Abierta stipulates a specific citation format (see also Einwohner 2011). Thus, each testimony cited includes the real name of the interviewed woman and the location and year of the testimony (see "Cited Testimonies").

42 See Theidon (2014) on similar difficulties and for a discussion of possible corporeal and emotional effects of doing research and writing about extreme forms of violence.

43 See Llobet (2015) for a scholarly analysis of the memory narratives of Argentines of my generation who were children during the dictatorship and belonged to families that were neither direct targets nor perpetrators of the repression.

CHAPTER 2. TELLING TERROR

1 After the annulment of impunity laws and in the context of the trials for crimes against humanity, Jorge Julio López testified against Miguel Etchecolatz, ex–chief of investigations of the Buenos Aires provincial police during the dictatorship. Etchecolatz was sentenced to life in prison ("Los fundamentos" 2010). The fate of Jorge Julio López remains unknown.

2 The audio recording of this communiqué is available in Memoria Abierta (n.d.-a).

3 See Decree 261/75 (February 5, 1975).

4 Among the organizations mentioned are UES (Unión de Estudiantes Secundarios/Union of Secondary School Students), JP (Juventud Peronista/Peronist Youth), JTP (Juventud de Trabajadores Peronistas/Peronist Workers Youth), JUP (Juventud Universitaria Peronista/Peronist University Youth), Movimiento Villero Peronista (Peronist Shantytown Movement), Agrupación Evita (Evita Group), Fuerzas Armadas Peronistas (Armed Revolutionary Forces), Montoneros, PRT-ERP (Partido Revolucionario de los Trabajadores/Workers' Revolutionary Party–Ejército Revolucionario del Pueblo/Revolutionary People's Army), TERS (Tendencia Estudiantil Revolucionaria Socialista/Revolutionary Socialist Student Tendency), OCPO (Organización Comunista Poder Obrero/Communist Organization Labor Power), Partido Comunista (Communist Party), Partido Auténtico (Authentic Party), Partido Socialista Popular (Popular Socialist Party), Movimiento de Estudiantes por la Liberación (Student Movement for Liberation), Confederación de Trabajadores de la Educación de la República Argentina (Education Workers Confederation of the Argentine Republic), as well as other labor unions.

5 Forced labor varied from site to site, but it ranged from cleaning or cooking to clerical and intellectual work (e.g., news analysis and writing political reports). Though the context of the camp precluded any form of true consent—thus the notion of forced or slave labor—this work also provided different detainees with the possibility to break away from the strictest confinement and immobility as well as to gain information about the space and operations of the camp.

6 For testimonies, letters, drawings, and perspectives of women who were political prisoners in the argentine jails from 1974 to 1983, see Beguán (2006).

7 In the legal prison system, many political prisoners were nevertheless held under extraordinary statuses—such as being at the disposition of the National Executive Power (Poder Ejecutivo Nacional, PEN)—which made it uncertain when they would be released.

8 See Longoni (2007) for an analysis and critique of such narratives.

9 These women narrate a whole array of arbitrary acts: from Adriana Arce, who was told that she was lucky because her name was the same as the daughter of a high-ranking officer, to Viviana Nardoni, who was first liberated by one state force only to be immediately recaptured by another group. The impossibility of knowing the criteria that repressors used in their decisions to murder or let live emerges in various testimonies.

10 The context of the camps precluded any sort of "free" choice with regard to sexual "relations," yet even if there were cases of constrained agency related to sexuality, this would not entitle other people to judge the women involved.

11 See also Alcoff (1991) on "The Problem of Speaking for Others."

12 Picana refers to an electric torture device commonly used in clandestine detention centers.

13 *Poner el cuerpo*, literally meaning "to put the body," is an expression commonly used in Argentina in a variety of contexts, including in social movement circles (see Sutton 2010 for a discussion of such meanings). Poner el cuerpo has connotations associated with putting the body on the line or giving one's body and efforts to a cause. It entails a bodily investment in the actions in which one is partaking. For example, it could mean taking a physical risk, showing coherence between what is said and done, being present and involved in a task, and giving the whole self to a specific cause or endeavor.

14 See, e.g., Smith-Ayala (1991); Patai (1993); Colom (1998); Randall (2003). See also Bernardita Llanos's (2016) analysis of documentaries directed by daughters of former guerrillas or activists.

15 See also Menjívar (2011) on women in Guatemala and their relativization and minimization of acts of violence in everyday life.

16 Office of the United Nations High Commissioner for Human Rights (n.d.).

17 The continued significance of contested (and often politically motivated) interpretations of torture can be seen in more recent events, including in U.S. debates on whether "enhanced interrogation techniques," such as waterboarding, are indeed torture.

18 "Submarine" refers to a method of torture relying on asphyxiation (e.g., with water or a bag).

19 Gómez-Barris defines the "afterlife" of atrocious violence as "the continuing and persistent symbolic and material effects of the original event of violence on people's daily lives, their social and psychic identities, and their ongoing wrestling with the past in the present" (2009, 6).

20 In the context of trials for crimes against humanity, testimonial accounts have constituted central evidence and have provided key elements in cases where torture was part of the crimes being indicted.

21 Felgueras and Filippini (2010) note some problematic effects, in practice, related to the more expansive approach to torture: a number of judicial resolutions subsume all individual episodes of torture under the umbrella of the conditions of detention, treating them all as part of a singular event. This has implications in terms of the penalties assigned, for example.

22 See Downey (2009) for a discussion of various "zones of indistinction," beyond the concentration camp, and their representation through art.

23 Dictator Jorge Rafael Videla expressed these words during a press conference in 1979 (Pigna 2013).

CHAPTER 3. NARRATING THE BODY

1 Scarry (1985) argues that extremely painful acts on the body, such as torture, take the person to a prelinguistic state and can hardly be transmitted to other people. The incommunicability of pain and the world-destroying nature of torture work against the possibility of fully relating the experience.

2 Retraumatization is a concern especially given pervasive cultural norms that either blame women for bringing sexual violence upon themselves or construe abusive events as consensual sexual acts.

3 See Antaki (2007) for a discussion of humanitarian versus political accounts of torture.

4 Testimonies of a more systematized "process of recuperation" generally refer to the ESMA, where the repressors implemented a project that had "as its objective the 'recuperation' of some abductees in order to reintegrate them to 'Western and Christian values.' In order to materialize the project they combine[d] psychological action operations with the use of the prisoners' capacities as slave labor to cover the tasks in the concentration camp" (CELS 2009, n.p.). However, some survivors from other camps also spoke of repressors' attempts to indoctrinate or "rehabilitate" detainees. For instance, survivor Isabel Fernández Blanco, who was in the CDC El Olimpo, spoke of a presumed "policy of 'rehabilitation' of subversives" that might have taken place at a certain point in the camp.

5 See, e.g., Actis et al. (2001) on the repressors' expectations that women in the process of "recuperation" at the ESMA wear feminine clothing and accessories. See Laudano (n.d. [1998]) and Bravo (2003) on the place of women and normative gender roles in military discourse.

6 Given the actual persecution of women in prostitution by state and paramilitary groups already before the coup (Agüero 2009), the "enemy whore" is not just a symbolic figure.

7 I refer to the "legal" prison system with quotation marks because even though the prisons were nonclandestine and were part of the established criminal justice system, many political prisoners were held there for extended periods, even years, without normal judicial procedures.

8 Juan Pablo Aranguren Romero (2015) discusses how human rights violation reports that denounce torture may end up reinscribing the logic of the perpetrators through representational techniques that erase the human subjects who experienced the violence.

9 The government's denial efforts included propaganda campaigns and alterations of the ESMA detentions center before the visit of the Inter-American Commission on Human Rights (Actis et al. 2001).

10 See Park (2014) on the unaddressed health problems of former political prisoners/ survivors and the need for reparations in that regard.

11 A longer version of this passage can be found in Bacci et al. (2012, 85–86). See also how the testimony relates to the authors' analyses of survivors' difficulties to speak and be listened to.

12 See Scarry (1985) on the relationship between body and voice with regard to torture.

13 See, e.g., Aucía et al. (2011); Balardini, Oberlin, and Sobredo (2011); Bacci et al. (2012); Sonderéguer (2012). A more recent addition is the book *Putas y guerrilleras* (2014) by journalist and survivor Miriam Lewin and journalist Olga Wornat, who recount the experiences of women sexually abused in the context of the military regime's overall repressive apparatus. See also earlier works by Bunster-Burotto (1994) and Hollander (1996) on state terror, gender, torture, and sexual violence against women in Latin America.

14 For a more detailed explanation of the evolution of jurisprudence and judicial approaches to the judgment of sexual violence in the context of state terrorism, see Aucía et al. (2011); Bacci et al. (2012); Duffy (2012).

15 See also Laura Mulvey's (1975) influential work for a discussion of the "male gaze" in a different context (narrative cinema).

16 However, as we shall see in the next chapter, the blindfold could also be used to create a space of resistance.

17 See Menjívar (2011) on how the naturalization of motherhood expectations can operate as a form of symbolic violence.

18 Extended passages of Marta's testimony and related analyses can also be found in Bacci et al. (2012, 52, 63).

19 On the treatment of pregnant women in captivity, see Arditti (1999); Regueiro (2008); Aucía et al. (2011); Bacci et al. (2012).

20 It is estimated that 500 children were appropriated (Bacci et al. 2012, 38). As of October 2016, 121 formerly appropriated children, now adults, were restituted and reunited with their families of origin (Abuelas de Plaza de Mayo 2016).

21 One may wonder whether the forced suppression of lactation, a sign of mother-hood, could be another way in which captive women were further dehumanized, facilitating their elimination.

22 Regueiro (2008, 118) points out that this approach is reminiscent of other atro-cious situations, such as the "Mengelian tradition of experimentation on the bod-ies of subjects not considered as persons."

23 An extended quote about this episode can be found in Bacci et al. (2012, 57–58). See also the authors' useful analyses and information about pregnancies in the context of clandestine detention and regular prisons.

24 Extended passages and analyses related to these women's pregnancies can be found in Bacci et al. (2012).

CHAPTER 4. BODY, SURVIVAL, RESISTANCE, AND MEMORY

1 Honwana (2006) elaborated the concept of "tactical agency" drawing on Michel de Certeau's (1984) distinction between tactic and strategy, and applied it to the analysis of children and armed conflict in Mozambique and Angola. See also Mama and Okazawa-Rey's (2012) application of this notion to the discussion of women's experiences of armed conflict in Liberia, Sierra Leone, and Nigeria.

2 One emblematic case—depicted in the feature film *Crónica de una fuga* (Caetano 2006)—was the escape of four detainees from the clandestine detention center Mansión Seré. In a number of cases, even if there had been an opportunity to flee, threats to and control of detainees' loved ones outside the camps could contribute to the sense that there was no place to hide and be safe without risking others' lives. The outside became a mere extension of the interior of the camps.

3 Raquel had been a university activist in Argentina but left the country after the military coup due to the climate of political persecution. She went to Uruguay, but she was not safe there either as she was abducted in apparent coordination with the Argentine repressive forces.

4 I thank Nayla Vacarezza for her insightful comments on this matter.

5 Mind/body dichotomies and the subordination of the body relative to the mind are well ingrained in Western thought, dating back to classic philosophers, such as Plato, who according to feminist scholar Elizabeth Spelman (1982, 118) held the body "as the source of all the undesirable traits a human being could have." Feminists also point out how in the Cartesian tradition, the mind is conceived as the supreme tool for knowing, and conceptualized in dualistic terms with respect to corporeality (Bordo 1993; Grosz 1994).

6 Calveiro (1998, 133) notes a similar dynamic in relation to the dangers of simula-tion of collaboration, in the sense that "the never-ending repetition of a lie can convert it in a truth."

7 Works in the psychology tradition distinguish and define multiple forms of dis-sociation (see, e.g., Cardeña's [1994] mapping of the "Domain of Dissociation"). My intention here is to present not a psychological analysis but one that charts how women survivors narrated and interpreted their embodied responses to the

conditions of captivity, putting these narratives in conversation with feminist literatures on the body, resistance, and survival. However, I should note that the extensive influence of the "psy culture" in Argentina (Balán 1991; Plotkin 2001) has possibly filtered into survivors' ways of making sense of their responses to terror in the camps, including the explicit use of the term "dissociation" or related words.

8 Similar forms of forgetting emerge in other cases as well. For example, Ledda Barreiro related that the will to not identify anyone was so strong that the last names of other people were virtually erased from her memory in the context of torture. (In fact, she had repeated to herself from the moment of her capture: "I don't know any last name, I don't know any last name, I don't know any last name." She mentioned that even later she had a hard time remembering last names.)

9 West and Zimmerman (1987). See also a symposium on West and Zimmerman's "Doing Gender" in the journal *Gender & Society* (Jurik and Siemsen 2009).

10 See, e.g., Goodwin, Jasper, and Polletta (2001); Ahmed (2004); Eyerman (2005); Juris (2008).

11 Other works note the different possibilities of resistance arising in different contexts, for example, that of the clandestine detention center versus the regular prison system where several disappeared people later "reappeared" (Guglielmucci 2007; Garaño 2010; Bacci et al. 2012).

12 See Bacci et al. (2012) for a more detailed discussion of these instances of resistance, as well as of other detainees' responses to sexual violence.

13 Santiago Joaquín Insausti (2015) argues that the detention of people for political reasons and for sexuality-related misdemeanors (e.g., targeting homosexuals, people in prostitution) obeyed different logics, even if the places of detention sometimes overlapped, and even if among the disappeared were political activists who were also sexually dissident. Insausti charts a longer history of persecution against homosexuals and women in prostitution, enabled by police edicts well before the last military dictatorship. Police edicts penalized things such as "scandal and the offer of sex in the streets" and were used as tools for sexual disciplining (64).

14 On broader debates about the importance of social location and embodiment in the generation of knowledge, see, e.g., Haraway (1988); Harding (1993); Collins (2000).

15 See also Druliolle's (2011) discussion of places of memory in post-dictatorship Argentina, particularly "'micro'-memory projects" (16).

16 For instance, Isabel Fernández Blanco recounted a fellow detainee who kept telling her that she would probably be released, and how this hope related to her ability to denounce later on: "And I think that that was one of the . . . of the reasons why I also memorized so many names and last names, right? When 20 years later I read again my testimony at the CONADEP, I myself was surprised [laughs]—'How did I manage to remember all this?'" Small acts of communication among detainees and of remembering key pieces information enabled many survivors to testify against the regime and/or help search for the disappeared.

17 See also Bacci et al. (2012) for women's narratives of resistance both in CDCs and in the legal prisons.

CHAPTER 5. TRANSMITTING MEMORY, RECLAIMING UTOPIA

1 See Funes (2007) for a historical account of the use of these types of labels in the intelligence services in relation to the construction of an "internal enemy." As Funes documents, this labeling process preceded the last military dictatorship. Débora D'Antonio (2008) also notes that already in 1974, before the last military dictatorship, and in the context of increasing repression, the Federal Penitentiary System decided to "refer to all political detainees as 'terrorist delinquents' (DT)" (n.p.).

2 The emergence of public testimonies and discussion about the activism of many of the disappeared and survivors had to wait. In addition to the predominant human rights framing during the democratic transition, the legal context affected public narratives. Claudia Bacci (2015, 36) notes: "The Decree 157/83 [which ordered the criminal prosecution of the leaders of guerrilla organizations] was effective until the *indultos* [pardons] of the 90s; in addition to social stigmatization, this presented a limit to the narratives about the revolutionary activism and armed actions of the 70s." With changes in the political milieu, the figure of the activist was later reclaimed, including by mothers and sons and daughters of the disappeared (Cueto Rúa 2010; Jelin 2013). During the administrations of former presidents Néstor Kirchner (2003–7) and Cristina Fernández de Kirchner (2007–15), the activism of many people targeted by the military dictatorship—and the seventies generation more broadly—was also publicly recognized and extolled in tandem with a politics that supported several historical demands by the human rights organizations. Yet, Jelin points out (2013) that the reclamation of this history of activism still often silenced the most controversial aspects of past movements, namely those related to armed struggle. (For reflexive and critical examinations of revolutionary movements, which raise questions about the responsibility of armed political organizations without claiming equivalency with state terrorist violence, see, e.g., Calveiro [2005] and Vezzetti [2013].)

3 A 1986 film by Héctor Olivera, *La noche de los lápices* (The Night of the Pencils), contrasts state atrocities and innocent victims through the focus on the repression of high schoolers who had organized to demand a bus ticket discount for students.

4 See, for example, Macón's (2015b) discussion of the myth "Santa Evita Montonera" as central to the Peronist armed organization Montoneros.

5 See, e.g., Andújar et al. (2005); Andújar et al. (2009); Martínez (2009); Gramático (2011); D'Antonio (2015); Oberti (2015).

6 See, e.g., Beguán (2006) on Argentina; Fried (2006) on Uruguay; Kaplan (2002) on Chile; Randall (2003) on Honduras; Smith-Ayala (1991) on Guatemala; and Bunster-Burotto (1994) on Argentina, Chile, and Uruguay.

7 Although this apparently contrasts with Park's (2013) findings about how women defined their political commitment (*compromiso*), it can be tricky to compare findings between this and Park's study, especially given that Park's results show

relative differences between men's and women's narratives, while the present work analyzes only women's testimonies. Also, while this study is based on already recorded and archived testimonies, Park's study was based on ethnographic observations of former political prisoners and interviews that she conducted with them. The structure and focus of interviews may also influence what stories are elicited in each study. For instance, the questions and structure of the Memoria Abierta interviews enabled the women to elaborate on their political histories, and some of the interviews were conducted by scholars who have been writing about the recent history of revolutionary movements in Argentina, including women's roles in revolutionary organizations.

8 See Tortti (2006) for an overview discussion of the "new left" in Argentina during the sixties and seventies.

9 For a discussion of the gender implications and effects on women of Latin America's turn to the left or Pink Tide during the 2000s, see, for example, the cluster of articles by Christina Ewig, Jocelyn Viterna, Amy Lind, and Patricia Richards in the journal *Politics & Gender*, on the theme "Gender and Latin America's Pink Tide" (2012).

10 The written summary of the testimony of Luisa's husband, Francisco Amarilla, in Memoria Abierta (2002) recounts that Francisco referred "with emotion [to] the attitude of his son, whose activism he knows little about," and to his son's generation of activists.

11 In the contemporary Latin American context, two high-profile cases that immediately come to mind—among many others—are the murder of environmental activist Berta Cáceres in March 2016 in Honduras and the forty-three students from Ayotzinapa Normal School disappeared in México in September 2014.

12 At the time of the interview Ilda was a member of the Centro de Estudios Legales y Sociales (CELS), Fundación Memoria Histórica y Social Argentina, and Memoria Abierta.

13 Isabel was an activist in the student movement at the university. At the time of the interview she was a history professor.

14 Lilia was a political activist before the dictatorship and a member of Familiares de Desaparecidos y Detenidos por Razones Políticas from its inception in 1976.

15 For instance, Steve Stern (2016) refers to how the contemporary student movement in Chile has resignified the Pinochet dictatorship's disastrous legacy to include the restructuring of education.

16 The appropriation of children and rape cases were exempted from impunity provisions. According to Rodolfo Yanzon (2011), only the appropriation of children was prosecuted in practice, and very slowly during the period of impunity. In 1998 criminal complaints were filed against foreign nationals accused of participating in Operation Condor as they were not protected by the impunity laws or pardons (Yanzon 2011, 144).

17 In addition to her kidnapping and captivity for some hours in ESMA, one of Ana María's sisters and her brother disappeared and another sister was killed along with her spouse.

18 While perpetrators and accomplices could still provide key information to find out what happened, see Payne (2008) on the "unsettling" effects of such confessions.

19 Tita was an activist and helped people who were being politically persecuted. In her interview, she also described how repressors displayed particular cruelty toward her for being Jewish.

20 During the dictatorship, Marta was kidnapped by a state "task force" along with her then husband Luis Brandoni, who was a leader in the labor union of actors.

21 See Perera (2016) for a discussion of Teatro Abierto, including a critical perspective on certain dimensions of memorialization of the experience.

CHAPTER 6. CONCLUSIONS AND IMPLICATIONS

1 As soon as he took office, President Macri moved swiftly to implement deep political and economic changes: massive layoffs of state employees, an attempt to appoint two Supreme Court judges bypassing the regular process, harsh repression of street protestors, measures to undo key provisions of the *ley de medios* (a law on audiovisual communications) passed during the previous administration, the withdrawal of state subsidies to energy accompanied by dramatic increases in natural gas and electricity bills (known as *tarifazo*), payment of billions of dollars to international creditors, including prominent U.S.-based hedge funds (commonly referred in Argentina as *fondos vuitres* [vulture funds] to highlight their rapacious nature).

2 For example, the Commission for Historical Clarification (CEH 1999) found that among the identified victims of massive human rights violations (largely committed by the state during the period of "internal armed conflict" starting in the 1960s) 83 percent were Mayas (21). The commission also concluded that state representatives committed "acts of genocide" against Maya communities "in the context of counterinsurgency operations performed between the years 1981 and 1983" (51).

3 At the time of this writing, in July 2016, Pablo Cirio's research project was still a work in progress.

4 Of course, "normal" and "exceptional" are relative terms, constructions that vary from society to society and in specific historical periods. Also, the notion of "democracy" and "peace" as some sort of default condition cannot be assumed when looking at particular histories. The meanings of these terms themselves need to be deconstructed to assess to whom they apply or do not apply in practice.

5 An example of a growing movement to raise awareness of and end ongoing gender violence is the campaign Ni Una Menos (Not One Less) that brought together women and allies in a massive and historical protest against feminicide and other forms of gender and sexual violence in Argentina on June 3, 2015 (see Bidaseca et al. 2015) and that promoted other mega demonstrations, including a "women's strike" on October 19, 2016.

6 See, e.g., Enloe (1989; 2000; 2016); Cockburn (2007); Riley, Mohanty, and Pratt (2008); Sutton, Morgen, and Novkov (2008); Sjoberg and Via (2010).

7 While the clandestinity and illegality of the practice prevent an exact counting of induced abortions in Argentina, scientific estimates show that the annual numbers of induced abortions may be as high as 446,998 or 522,000, depending on the estimation method (Mario and Pantelides 2009).

8 See, e.g., Parkins (2000); Peterson (2001); Sasson-Levy and Rapoport (2003); Alexandre (2006); Sutton (2007a; 2007b). See also the "*Comparative Perspectives Symposium*: Gendered Bodies in the Protest Sphere" in *Signs*, edited by Miranda Outman-Kramer and Susana Galán (2014).

CITED TESTIMONIES

1. Memoria Abierta, testimonio de Nilda Actis Goretta (Munú), Buenos Aires, 2001
2. Memoria Abierta, testimonio de Marta Álvarez, La Lucila, Buenos Aires, 2007
3. Memoria Abierta, testimonio de Adriana Arce, Buenos Aires, 2006
4. Memoria Abierta, testimonio de Iris Avellaneda, Buenos Aires, 2010
5. Memoria Abierta, testimonio de Ledda Barreiro, Mar del Plata, Buenos Aires, 2007
6. Memoria Abierta, testimonio de Norma Berti, Buenos Aires, 2007
7. Memoria Abierta, testimonio de Marta Bianchi, Buenos Aires, 2006
8. Memoria Abierta, testimonio de Delia Bisutti, Buenos Aires, 2001
9. Memoria Abierta, testimonio de Luisa Blanco de Amarilla, Buenos Aires, 2002
10. Memoria Abierta, testimonio de Fátima Cabrera, Buenos Aires, 2002
11. Memoria Abierta, testimonio de Ana María Cacabelos, Buenos Aires, 2004
12. Memoria Abierta, testimonio de Liliana Callizo, Córdoba, 2009
13. Memoria Abierta, testimonio de Susana Caride, Buenos Aires, 2001
14. Memoria Abierta, testimonio de Odila Casella, Buenos Aires, 2003
15. Memoria Abierta, testimonio de Isabel Cerruti, Buenos Aires, 2002
16. Memoria Abierta, testimonio de Cristina Comandé, Buenos Aires, 2005
17. Memoria Abierta, testimonio de Eublogia "Rita" Cordero de Garnica, San Salvador de Jujuy, 2002
18. Memoria Abierta, testimonio de Martha Díaz, Rosario, Santa Fe, 2010

19. Memoria Abierta, testimonio de Ana Di Salvo, Buenos Aires, 2003
20. Memoria Abierta, testimonio de Gloria Enríquez, Buenos Aires, 2003
21. Memoria Abierta, testimonio de Patricia Erb, Buenos Aires, 2007
22. Memoria Abierta, testimonio de Haydée Fernández, Mendoza, 2008
23. Memoria Abierta, testimonio de Isabel Fernández Blanco, Buenos Aires, 2005
24. Memoria Abierta, testimonio de Lelia Ferrarese, Rosario, Santa Fe, 2010
25. Memoria Abierta, testimonio de Adriana Friszman, Buenos Aires, 2004
26. Memoria Abierta, testimonio de Graciela García, Buenos Aires, 2007
27. Memoria Abierta, testimonio de Soledad García, Córdoba, 2008
28. Memoria Abierta, testimonio de Marta García de Candeloro, Mar del Plata, Buenos Aires, 2007
29. Memoria Abierta, testimonio de Liliana Gardella, Buenos Aires, 2001
30. Memoria Abierta, testimonio de Cristina Guillén, Mar del Plata, Buenos Aires, 2007
31. Memoria Abierta, testimonio de Lilia Amparo Jons de Orfanó, Buenos Aires, 2001
32. Memoria Abierta, testimonio de Carmen Lapacó, Buenos Aires, 2001
33. Memoria Abierta, testimonio de Elena Lenhardtson, Buenos Aires, 2006
34. Memoria Abierta, testimonio de Susana Martínez de Scala, Buenos Aires, 2001
35. Memoria Abierta, testimonio de Santina Mastinú, Buenos Aires, 2003
36. Memoria Abierta, testimonio de Ilda Micucci, Buenos Aires, 2001
37. Memoria Abierta, testimonio de Emilce Moler, Buenos Aires, 2006
38. Memoria Abierta, testimonio de Alicia Morales, Mendoza, 2008
39. Memoria Abierta, testimonio de Norma Morello, Buenos Aires, 2004
40. Memoria Abierta, testimonio de Susana Muñoz, Mendoza, 2007

41. Memoria Abierta, testimonio de Viviana Nardoni, Rosario, Santa Fe, 2010
42. Memoria Abierta, testimonio de Raquel Odasso, Mendoza, 2007
43. Memoria Abierta, testimonio de Eva Orifici, Buenos Aires, 2007
44. Memoria Abierta, testimonio de Susana Jorgelina Ramus, Buenos Aires, 2001
45. Memoria Abierta, testimonio de Susana Reyes, Buenos Aires, 2003
46. Memoria Abierta, testimonio de Julia Ruiz, Buenos Aires, 2003
47. Memoria Abierta, testimonio de Rebeca "Tita" Sacolsky, Buenos Aires, 2001
48. Memoria Abierta, testimonio de Laura Schachter, Buenos Aires, 2011
49. Memoria Abierta, testimonio de María Celeste Seydell, Córdoba, 2008
50. Memoria Abierta, testimonio de Nora Strejilevich, Buenos Aires, 2008
51. Memoria Abierta, testimonio de Elisa Tokar, Buenos Aires, 2001
52. Memoria Abierta, testimonio de Marta Vassallo, Buenos Aires, 2002

REFERENCES

Abuelas de Plaza de Mayo. 2016. "Encontramos al hijo de Ana María Lanzillotto y Domingo 'El Gringo' Menna, El Nieto 121." www.abuelas.org.

Achugar, Mariana. 2016. *Discursive Processes of Intergenerational Transmission of Recent History: (Re)making Our Past.* New York: Palgrave Macmillan.

Acker, Joan. 1990. "Hierarchies, Jobs, Bodies: A Theory of Gendered Organizations." *Gender & Society* 4 (2): 139–58.

Actis, Munú, Cristina Aldini, Liliana Gardella, Miriam Lewin, and Elisa Tokar. 2001. *Ese infierno: Conversaciones de cinco mujeres sobrevivientes de la ESMA.* Buenos Aires: Sudamericana.

Agamben, Giorgio. 1998. *Sovereign Power and Bare Life.* Stanford, CA: Stanford University Press.

———. 1999. *Remnants of Auschwitz: The Witness and the Archive.* Translated by Daniel Heller-Roazen. New York: Zone Books.

Agger, Inger. 1989. "Sexual Torture of Political Prisoners: An Overview." *Journal of Traumatic Stress* 2 (3): 305–18.

Agüero, Laura Rodríguez. 2009. "Mujeres en situación de prostitución como blanco del accionar represivo: El caso del Comando Moralizador Pío XII, Mendoza, 1974–1976." In Andújar et al., *De minifaldas, militancias y revoluciones,* 109–26.

Águila, Gabriela. 2008. *Dictadura, represión y sociedad en Rosario, 1976–1983: Un estudio sobre la represión y los comportamientos y actitudes sociales en dictadura.* Buenos Aires: Prometeo.

Ahmed, Sara. 2004. "Affective Economies." *Social Text* 22 (2): 117–39.

———. 2010. "Killing Joy: Feminism and the History of Happiness." *Signs* 35 (3): 571–94.

Alaimo, Stacy. 2008. "Trans-corporeal Feminisms and the Ethical Space of Nature." In *Material Feminisms,* ed. Stacy Alaimo and Susan Hekman, 237–64. Bloomington: Indiana University Press.

———. 2010. "The Naked Word: The Trans-corporeal Ethics of the Protesting Body." *Women & Performance* 20 (1): 15–36.

Alcoff, Linda. 1991. "The Problem of Speaking for Others." *Cultural Critique* 20 (Winter 1991–92): 5–32.

Alexander, M. Jacqui. 2005. *Pedagogies of Crossing: Meditations on Feminism, Sexual Politics, Memory, and the Sacred.* Durham, NC: Duke University Press.

Alexandre, Michele. 2006. "Dance Halls, Masquerades, Body Protest and the Law: The Female Body as a Redemptive Tool against Trinidad's Gender-Biased Laws." *Duke Journal of Gender Law & Policy* 13 (1): 177–202.

Allier-Montaño, Eugenia. 2009. "Presentes-pasados del 68 Mexicano: Una historización de las memorias públicas del movimiento estudiantil, 1968–2007." *Revista Mexicana de Sociología* 71 (2): 287–317.

Allier-Montaño, Eugenia, and Emilio Crenzel, eds. 2015. *The Struggle for Memory in Latin America: Recent History and Political Violence*. New York: Palgrave Macmillan.

Alonso, Luciano. 2009. "Memorias sociales y estado en Santa Fe, Argentina, 2003–2008." *Política y Cultura* 31: 27–47.

Amnesty International. 2004. *Colombia: Scarred Bodies, Hidden Crimes*. London: International Secretariat.

Andreozzi, Gabriele. 2011a. "Introducción." In Andreozzi, *Juicios por crímenes*, 11–30.

———, ed. 2011b. *Juicios por crímenes de lesa humanidad en Argentina*. Buenos Aires: Atuel.

Andrews, George Reid. 1980. *The Afro-Argentines of Buenos Aires, 1800–1900*. Madison: University of Wisconsin Press.

Andújar, Andrea, Débora D'Antonio, Nora Domínguez, Karin Grammático, Fernanda Gil Lozano, Valeria Pita, María Inés Rodríguez, and Alejandra Vassallo, eds. 2005. *Historia, género y política en los '70*. Buenos Aires: Universidad Nacional de Buenos Aires, Facultad de Filosofía y Letras; Feminaria.

Andújar, Andrea, Débora D'Antonio, Fernanda Gil Lozano, Karin Grammático, and María Laura Rosa, eds. 2009. *De minifaldas, militancias y revoluciones*. Buenos Aires: Luxemburg.

Antaki, Mark. 2007. "The Politics and Inhumanity of Torture." *Law, Culture and the Humanities* 3 (1): 3–17.

Aranguren Romero, Juan Pablo. 2015. "Ante el cuerpo sufriente: Reflexiones sobre tortura y fotografía." Paper presented in "Precariedades, Exclusiones, Emergencias," Latin American Studies Association Conference, San Juan de Puerto Rico, May 27–30.

Arcel, Libby Tata. 2001. "Torture, Cruel, Inhuman and Degrading Treatment of Women—Psychological Consequences." *Psyke & Logos* 22 (1): 322–51.

Arditti, Rita. 1999. *Searching for Life: The Grandmothers of the Plaza de Mayo and the Disappeared Children of Argentina*. Berkeley: University of California Press.

Arendt, Hannah. 1958. *The Origins of Totalitarianism*. Cleveland: Meridian.

———. 1963. *Eichmann in Jerusalem: A Report on the Banality of Evil*. New York: Viking.

Asad, Talal. 1996. "On Torture, or Cruel, Inhuman, and Degrading Treatment." *Social Research* 63 (4): 1081–109.

Aucía, Analía. 2011. "Género, violencia sexual y contextos represivos." In Aucía et al., *Grietas en el silencio*, 27–67.

Aucía, Analía, Florencia Barrera, Celina Berterame, Susana Chiarotti, Alejandra Paolini, Cristina Zurutuza, and Marta Vassallo. 2011. *Grietas en el silencio: Una investigación sobre la violencia sexual en el marco del terrorismo de Estado*. Rosario: CLADEM.

Auyero, Javier, and María Fernanda Berti. 2015. *In Harm's Way: The Dynamics of Urban Violence*. Princeton, NJ: Princeton University Press.

AWID. 2016. "Campaña Reconocer es Reparar." September 27. www.awid.org.

Bacci, Claudia. 2015. "Testimonios en democracia: El Juicio a las Juntas Militares en Argentina." *kult-ur* 2 (4): 29–50.

Bacci, Claudia, María Capurro Robles, Alejandra Oberti, and Susana Skura. 2012. *Y nadie quería saber: Relatos sobre violencia contra las mujeres en el terrorismo de estado en Argentina*. Buenos Aires: Memoria Abierta.

———. 2014. "Entre lo público y lo privado: Los testimonios sobre la violencia contra las mujeres en el terrorismo de estado." *Clepsidra* 1 (1): 122–39.

Baig, José. 2002. "En Argentina 'no hay negros.'" *BBC Mundo*, September 28. http://news.bbc.co.uk.

Balán, Jorge. 1991. *Cuéntame tu vida: Una biografía colectiva del psicoanálisis argentino*. Buenos Aires: Planeta.

Balardini, Lorena, Ana Oberlin, and Laura Sobredo. 2011. "Violencia de género y abusos sexuales en los centros clandestinos de detención." In Centro de Estudios Legales y Sociales and Centro Internacional para la Justicia Transicional, *Hacer Justicia*, 167–226.

Balardini, Lorena, and Carolina Varsky. 2015. "El 'blindaje' judicial: Obstáculos a la investigación de crímenes de lesa humanidad." In *¿Usted también doctor? Complicidad de jueces, fiscales y abogados durante la dictadura*, ed. Juan Pablo Bohoslavsky, 345–63. Buenos Aires: Siglo Veintiuno.

Barrancos, Dora. 2008. *Mujeres, entre la casa y la plaza*. Buenos Aires: Sudamericana.

Bartky, Sandra Lee. 1990. *Femininity and Domination: Studies in the Phenomenology of Oppression*. New York: Routledge.

Becker, David, Elizabeth Lira, María Isabel Castillo, Elena Gómez, and Juana Kovalskys. 1990. "Therapy with Victims of Political Repression in Chile: The Challenge of Social Reparation." *Journal of Social Issues* 46 (3): 133–49.

Beguán, Viviana, ed. 2006. *Nosotras, presas políticas*. Buenos Aires: Nuestra América.

Bejarano, Cynthia L. 2002. "Las Super Madres de Latino America: Transforming Motherhood by Challenging Violence in Mexico, Argentina, and El Salvador." *Frontiers* 23 (1): 126–50.

Bellucci, Mabel. 2000. "El movimiento de Madres de Plaza de Mayo." In Lozano, Pita, and Ini, *Historia de las mujeres en la Argentina*, 267–87.

Belza, Valentín. 2015. "Leda [sic] Barreiro de Muñoz en 'Un Día Perfecto' sobre el libro 'Marimosa y Las Hormigas.'" *Facebook*, April 16. www.facebook.com.

Bergman, Marcelo, and Mónica Szurmuk. 2001. "Gender, Citizenship, and Social Protest: The New Social Movements in Argentina." In *The Latin American Subaltern Studies Reader*, ed. Ileana Rodríguez, 383–401. Durham, NC: Duke University Press.

Beverley, John. 1987. "Anatomía del testimonio." *Revista de Crítica Literaria Latinoamericana* 13 (25): 7–16.

Bidaseca, Karina, et al., eds. 2015. *#NiUnaMenos: Vivxs nos queremos*. Buenos Aires: Milena Caserola.

Biglieri, Paula. 2013. "Emancipaciones. Acerca de la aprobación de la ley del matrimonio igualitario en Argentina." *Íconos* 46: 145–60.

Bogad, L. M. 2016. *Tactical Performance: Serious Play and Social Movements*. New York: Routledge.

Bonner, Michelle D. 2014. "'Never Again': Transitional Justice and Persistent Police Violence in Argentina." *International Journal of Transitional Justice* 8 (2): 235–55.

Bordo, Susan. 1993. *Unbearable Weight: Feminism, Western Culture, and the Body*. Berkeley: University of California Press.

Borland, Elizabeth. 2006. "The Mature Resistance of Argentina's Madres de Plaza de Mayo." In *Latin American Social Movements: Globalization, Democratization, and Transnational Networks*, ed. Hank Johnston and Paul Almeida, 115–30. Lanham, MD: Rowman & Littlefield.

Bouvard, Marguerite Guzman. 1994. *Revolutionizing Motherhood: The Mothers of the Plaza de Mayo*. Wilmington, DE: Scholarly Resources.

Braidotti, Rosi. 1997. "Mothers, Monsters, and Machines." In *Writing on the Body: Female Embodiment and Feminist Theory*, ed. Katie Conboy, Nadia Medina, and Sarah Stanbury, 59–79. New York: Columbia University Press.

Brands, Hal. 2010. *Latin America's Cold War*. Cambridge, MA: Harvard University Press.

Bravo, Nazareno. 2003. "El discurso de la dictadura militar argentina (1976–1983). Definición del opositor político y confinamiento–'valorización' del papel de la mujer en el espacio privado." *Utopía y Praxis Latinoamericana* 8 (22): 107–23.

Brenner, Grant Hilary. 2010. "The Expected Psychiatric Impact of Detention in Guantanamo Bay, Cuba, and Related Considerations." *Journal of Trauma & Dissociation* 11 (4): 469–87.

Brysk, Alison. 1994. "The Politics of Measurement: The Contested Count of the Disappeared in Argentina." *Human Rights Quarterly* 16 (4): 676–92.

Bunch, Charlotte, and Samantha Frost. 2000. "Human Rights." In *Routledge International Encyclopedia of Women: Global Women's Issues and Knowledge*, vol. 2, ed. Cheris Kramarae and Dale Spender, 1078–83. New York: Routledge.

Bunster-Burotto, Ximena. 1994. "Surviving Beyond Fear: Women and Torture in Latin America." In *Women and Violence*, ed. Miranda Davies, 156–76. London: Zed Books.

Burt, Jo-Marie. 2016. "Military Officers Convicted in Landmark Sepur Zarco Sexual Violence Case." *International Justice Monitor*, March 4. www.ijmonitor.org.

Burton, Antoinette. 2010. "Foreword: 'Small Stories' and the Promise of New Narratives." In *Contesting Archives: Finding Women in the Sources*, ed. Nupur Chaudhuri, Sherry J. Katz, and Mary Elizabeth Perry, vii–x. Urbana: University of Illinois Press.

Butler, Judith. 1990. *Gender Trouble*. New York: Routledge.

———. 1995. "Contingent Foundations." In *Feminist Contentions: A Philosophical Exchange*, by Seyla Benhabib, Judith Butler, Drucilla Cornell, and Nancy Fraser, 35–57. New York: Routledge.

———. 2004a. *Precarious Life: The Powers of Mourning and Violence*. London: Verso.

———. 2004b. *Undoing Gender*. New York: Routledge.

———. 2014. "Bodily Vulnerability, Coalitions, and Street Politics." In *Differences in Common: Gender, Vulnerability and Community*, ed. Joana Sabadell-Nieto and Marta Segarra, 99–119. Amsterdam: Rodopi.

Caetano, Adrián, dir. 2006. *Crónica de una fuga*. Film.

Calveiro, Pilar. 1998. *Poder y desaparición: Los campos de concentración en Argentina*. Buenos Aires: Colihue.

———. 2005. *Política y/o violencia: Una aproximación a la guerrilla de los años 70*. Buenos Aires: Norma.

Campbell, Alex. 2005. "Keeping the 'Lady' Safe: The Regulation of Femininity through Crime Prevention Literature." *Critical Criminology* 13 (2): 119–40.

Carassai, Sebastián. 2010. "Antes de que anochezca: Derechos humanos y clases medias en la Argentina antes y en los inicios del golpe de Estado de 1976." *América Latina Hoy* 54: 69–96.

———. 2013. *Los años setenta de la gente común: La naturalización de la violencia*. Buenos Aires: Siglo Veintiuno.

Card, Claudia. 2005. *The Atrocity Paradigm: A Theory of Evil*. New York: Oxford University Press.

Cardeña, Etzel. 1994. "The Domain of Dissociation." In *Dissociation: Clinical and Theoretical Perspectives*, ed. Steven J. Lynn and Judith W. Rhue, 15–31. New York: Guilford.

Carnovale, Vera. 2008. "Moral y disciplinamiento interno en el PRT-ERP." *Nuevo Mundo Mundos Nuevos*, July 12. http://nuevomundo.revues.org.

Caruth, Cathy, ed. 1995. *Trauma: Explorations in Memory*. Baltimore: Johns Hopkins University Press.

Casa Rosada. n.d. "Galería de los presidentes." www.presidencia.gob.ar.

Caviglia, Mariana. 2006. *Dictadura, vida cotidiana y clases medias: Una sociedad fracturada*. Buenos Aires: Prometeo.

Centro de Encuentros Cultura y Mujer (CECYM). 2014. "Campañas." www.cecym.org.ar.

Centro de Estudios Legales y Sociales (CELS). 2005. "Las leyes de Punto Final y Obediencia Debida son inconstitucionales." June 14. www.cels.org.ar.

———. 2009. "ESMA: Qué fue la ESMA?" www.cels.org.ar.

———. 2013. "Situación de los juicios por crímenes de lesa humanidad en la Argentina." March 21. www.cels.org.ar.

———. 2014. "Las violaciones estructurales a los derechos humanos en los lugares de encierro exigen políticas enérgicas." June 18. www.cels.org.ar.

———. 2015a. *Aportes del CELS a los debates legislativos sobre derechos sexuales y reproductivos*. Buenos Aires: CELS. www.cels.org.ar.

———. 2015b. *Derechos humanos en Argentina: Informe 2015*. Buenos Aires: Siglo Veintiuno.

———. 2016. "Plan Cóndor: Por primera vez el poder judicial de un país dio por probada la asociación ilícita." May 27. www.cels.org.ar.

———. n.d. [2016]. "Estadísticas. Juicios: Proceso de justicia por crímenes de lesa humanidad." www.cels.org.ar.

Centro de Estudios Legales y Sociales (CELS) and Centro Internacional para la Justicia Transicional (ICTJ), eds. 2011. *Hacer justicia: Nuevos debates sobre el juzgamiento de crímenes de lesa humanidad en Argentina*. Buenos Aires: Siglo Veintiuno.

Centro de Estudios Legales y Sociales (CELS), Ministerio Público de la Defensa de la Nación, and Procuración Penitenciaria de la Nación. 2011. *Mujeres en prisión: Los alcances del castigo*. Buenos Aires: Siglo Veintiuno.

Cepeda, Agustina. 2013. "Narrativas familiares y memoria de la pos-dictadura en Argentina: el caso de HIJOS de desaparecidos." *Asian Journal of Latin American Studies* 26 (1): 25–45.

Cockburn, Cynthia. 2007. *From Where We Stand: War, Women's Activism and Feminist Analysis*. London: Zed Books.

Cohen, Stanley. 2001. *States of Denial: Knowing about Atrocities and Suffering*. Cambridge: Polity.

Collins, Patricia Hill. 2000. "Black Feminist Epistemology." In *Black Feminist Thought: Knowledge, Consciousness, and the Politics of Empowerment*, 251–71. New York: Routledge.

———. 2015. "Intersectionality's Definitional Dilemmas." *Annual Review of Sociology* 41 (1): 1–20.

Colom, Yolanda. 1998. *Mujeres en la alborada: Guerrilla y participación femenina en Guatemala 1973–1978. Testimonio*. Guatemala: Artemis & Edinter.

Combahee River Collective. 1979. "A Black Feminist Statement." In *Capitalist Patriarchy and the Case for Socialist Feminism*, ed. Zillah R. Eisenstein, 362–72. New York: Monthly Review.

Comisión para el Esclarecimiento Histórico (CEH). 1999. *Guatemala: Memoria del silencio. Conclusiones y recomendaciones*. Guatemala: Oficina de Servicios para Proyectos de las Naciones Unidas (UNOPS). www.undp.org.

Comisión Interamericana de Derechos Humanos (CIDH). 2000. "Informe N° 21/00 CASO 12.059. Carmen Aguiar De Lapacó Argentina. 29 de febrero de 2000." www.cidh.oas.org.

Comisión Nacional Sobre la Desaparición de Personas (CONADEP). 1984. *Nunca más: Informe de la Comisión Nacional sobre la Desaparición de Personas*. Buenos Aires: EUDEBA.

Comité de América Latina y el Caribe para la Defensa de los Derechos de la Mujer (CLADEM). n.d. "Amicus Curiae." www.cladem.org.

Connell, Raewyn, and Rebecca Pearse. 2015. *Gender: In World Perspective*. Cambridge: Polity.

Connell, R. W. 1987. *Gender and Power: Society, the Person, and Sexual Politics*. Stanford, CA: Stanford University Press.

Connerton, Paul. 1989. *How Societies Remember*. New York: Cambridge University Press.

Conroy, John. 2000. *Unspeakable Acts, Ordinary People: The Dynamics of Torture*. New York: Knopf.

Constitution Project. 2013. *The Report of the Constitution Project's Task Force on Detainee Treatment*. Washington, DC: Constitution Project.

Coole, Diana, and Samantha Frost. 2010. "Introducing the New Materialisms." In *New Materialisms: Ontology, Agency, and Politics*, ed. Diana Coole and Samantha Frost, 1–43. Durham, NC: Duke University Press.

Coordinadora Antirrepresiva LGBTTTIQP. 2016. "La Memoria no es un privilegio cis-heterosexual. A 40 años del golpe genocida, marchá con la Coordinadora Antirrepresiva LGTTTBIPQ [*sic*]." *Facebook*, March 23. www.facebook.com.

Copelon, Rhonda. 2008. "Gender Violence as Torture: The Contribution of CAT General Comment No. 2." *New York City Law Review* 11 (2): 229–63.

Corradi, Juan E., Patricia Weiss Fagen, and Manuel A. Garretón, eds. 1992a. *Fear at the Edge: State Terror and Resistance in Latin America*. Berkeley: University of California Press.

———. 1992b. "Introduction." In Corradi, Fagen, and Garretón, *Fear at the Edge*, 1–10.

Cosse, Isabella. 2014. "Infidelities: Morality, Revolution, and Sexuality in Left-Wing Guerrilla Organizations in 1960s and 1970s Argentina." *Journal of the History of Sexuality* 23 (3): 415–50.

Creed, Barbara. 1986. "Horror and the Monstrous-feminine: An Imaginary Abjection." *Screen* 27 (1): 44–71.

Crenshaw, Kimberlé. 1989. "Demarginalizing the Intersection of Race and Sex: A Black Feminist Critique of Antidiscrimination Doctrine, Feminist Theory and Antiracist Politics." *University of Chicago Legal Forum* 1989 (1): 139–67.

Crenzel, Emilio. 2011a. "Between the Voices of the State and the Human Rights Movement: *Never Again* and the Memories of the Disappeared in Argentina." *Journal of Social History* 44 (4): 1063–76.

———. 2011b. "*Present Pasts*: Memory(ies) of State Terrorism in the Southern Cone of Latin America." In Lessa and Druliolle, *Memory of State Terrorism in the Southern Cone*, 1–13.

Cubilié, Anne. 2005. *Women Witnessing Terror: Testimony and the Cultural Politics of Human Rights*. New York: Fordham University Press.

Cueto Rúa, Santiago. 2010. "HIJOS de víctimas del terrorismo de Estado; Justicia, identidad y memoria en el movimiento de derechos humanos en Argentina, 1995–2008." *Historia Crítica* 40 (January–April): 122–45.

Daleo, Graciela. 2010. "Las palabras de la Memoria." In *Acompañamiento a testigos y querellantes en el marco de los juicios contra el terrorismo de Estado: Estrategias de intervención*, 69–72. Buenos Aires: Secretaría de Derechos Humanos del Ministerio de Justicia, Seguridad y Derechos Humanos de la Nación.

Dandan, Alejandra. 2016. "Entre los 40 años y los cien días." *Página/12*, March 25. www.pagina12.com.ar.

Danner, Mark. 2004. *Torture and Truth: America, Abu Ghraib, and the War on Terror*. New York: New York Review Books.

D'Antonio, Débora. 2003. *Mujeres, complicidad y Estado terrorista*. Cuaderno de Trabajo no. 33. Buenos Aires: Centro Cultural de la Cooperación.

———. 2008. "Represión y resistencia en las cárceles de la última dictadura militar argentina." *La revista del CCC*, January/April, no. 2. www.centrocultural.coop.

———. 2009. "'Rejas, gritos, cadenas, ruidos, ollas': La agencia política en las cárceles del estado terrorista en Argentina, 1974–1983." In Andújar et al., *De minifaldas, militancias y revoluciones*, 89–108.

———, ed. 2015. *Deseo y represión: Sexualidad, género y Estado en la historia Argentina reciente*. Buenos Aires: Imago Mundi.

Daona, Victoria. 2013. "Mujeres, escritura y terrorismo de estado en Argentina: Una serie de relatos testimoniales." *Moderna Språk* 107 (2): 56–73.

Darghouth, Sarah, Duncan Pedersen, Gilles Bibeau, and Cecile Rousseau. 2006. "Painful Languages of the Body: Experiences of Headache among Women in Two Peruvian Communities." *Culture, Medicine and Psychiatry* 30 (3): 271–97.

Darré, Silvana. 2013. *Maternidades y tecnologías de género*. Argentina: Katz.

da Silva Catela, Ludmila. 2002. "El mundo de los archivos." In *Los archivos de la represión: Documentos, memoria y verdad*, ed. Ludmila da Silva Catela and Elizabeth Jelin, 195–219. Madrid: Siglo Veintinuno.

Davidovich, Karin. 2014. "Hablar desde el silencio: El silencio como verdad en las narrativas de mujeres sobrevivientes." *Catedral Tomada* 2 (3): 18–50.

de Certeau, Michel. 1984. *The Practice of Everyday Life*. Translated by Steven Rendall. Berkeley: University of California Press.

de Giorgi, Ana Laura. 2015. "Entre el pasado y el presente. Entre lo personal y lo político: Narrativas y apuestas de las ex presas políticas en Uruguay." *Tempo e Argumento* 7 (15): 202–28.

Deleuze, Gilles. 1988. *Spinoza: Practical Philosophy*. Translated by Robert Hurley. San Francisco: City Lights Books.

Del Rosso, Jared. 2011. "The Textual Mediation of Denial: Congress, Abu Ghraib, and the Construction of an Isolated Incident." *Social Problems* 58 (2): 165–88.

———. 2015. *Talking about Torture: How Political Discourse Shapes the Debate*. New York: Columbia University Press.

DeLuca, Kevin Michael. 1999. "Unruly Arguments: The Body Rhetoric of Earth First!, Act Up, and Queer Nation." *Argumentation and Advocacy* 36 (1): 9–21.

DeMello, Margo. 2014. *Body Studies: An Introduction*. New York: Routledge.

"Denuncia del CELS por requisas vejatorias a menores de edad en San Luis." 2014. *Todo Noticias*, June 18. http://tn.com.ar.

De Riz, Liliana, Luis Acosta, and Mariana Clucellas. 2002. *Aportes para el desarrollo humano de la Argentina 2002: Desigualdad y pobreza*. Buenos Aires: Programa de las Naciones Unidas Para el Desarrollo.

Deutscher, Penelope. 2008. "The Inversion of Exceptionality: Foucault, Agamben, and 'Reproductive Rights.'" *South Atlantic Quarterly* 107 (1): 55–70.

Diana, Marta. 1996. *Mujeres guerrilleras: La militancia de los setenta en el testimonio de sus protagonistas femeninas*. Buenos Aires: Planeta.

Dossa, Parin. 2003. "The Body Remembers: A Migratory Tale of Social Suffering and Witnessing." *International Journal of Mental Health* 32 (3): 50–73.

Downey, Anthony. 2009. "Zones of Indistinction: Giorgio Agamben's 'Bare Life' and the Politics of Aesthetics." *Third Text* 23 (2): 109–25.

Doyle, Kate. 2003. "The Tlatelolco Massacre." National Security Archive. http://nsarchive.gwu.edu.

Doyle, Laura. 2001. "Bodies Inside/Out: A Phenomenology of the Terrorized Body." In *Bodies of Resistance: New Phenomenologies of Politics, Agency, and Culture*, ed. Laura Doyle, 78–99. Evanston, IL: Northwestern University Press.

Druliolle, Vincent. 2011. "Remembering and Its Places in Postdictatorship Argentina." In Lessa and Druliolle, *Memory of State Terrorism in the Southern Cone*, 15–41.

DuBois, Lindsay. 1990. "Torture and the Construction of an Enemy: The Example of Argentina 1976–1983." *Dialectical Anthropology* 15 (4): 317–28.

Duffy, María Virginia. 2012. "El infierno de las Anónimas: Un compromiso pendiente para la justicia argentina." In Sonderéguer, *Género y poder*, 219–67.

Duhalde, Eduardo L. 1999. *El estado terrorista Argentino: Quince años después, una mirada crítica.* Buenos Aires: EUDEBA.

Edwards, Alice. 2006. "The 'Feminizing' of Torture under International Human Rights Law." *Leiden Journal of International Law* 19 (2): 349–91.

Einwohner, Rachel L. 2011. "Ethical Considerations on the Use of Archived Testimonies in Holocaust Research: Beyond the IRB Exemption." *Qualitative Sociology* 34 (3): 415–30.

"El horror que se transforma en una historia de esperanza." 2015. *Infojus Noticias*, April 18. www.infojusnoticias.gov.ar.

Enloe, Cynthia. 1989. *Bananas, Beaches and Bases: Making Feminist Sense of International Politics.* London: Pandora.

———. 1991. "'WomenandChildren': Propaganda Tools of Patriarchy." In *Mobilizing Democracy: Changing the US Role in the Middle East*, ed. Greg Bates, 89–96. Monroe, ME: Common Courage Press.

———. 2000. *Maneuvers: The International Politics of Militarizing Women's Lives.* Berkeley: University of California Press.

———. 2004. *The Curious Feminist: Searching for Women in the New Age of Empire.* Berkeley: University of California Press.

———. 2013. *Seriously! Investigating Crashes and Crises as If Women Mattered.* Berkeley: University of California Press.

———. 2016. *Globalization and Militarism: Feminists Make the Link.* Lanham, MD: Rowman & Littlefield.

Equipo Nacional de Pastoral Aborigen (ENDEPA). 2016. "A 40 años del golpe: ¿Qué pasó con los pueblos originarios durante la dictadura?" March 23. http://endepa.org.ar/?p=1513.

Eyerman, Ron. 2005. "How Social Movements Move: Emotions and Social Movements." In *Emotions and Social Movements*, ed. Helena Flam and Debra King, 41–56. New York: Routledge.

Falcón, Sylvanna. 2006. "'National Security' and the Violation of Women: Militarized Border Rape at the US-Mexico Border." In INCITE! Women of Color against Violence, *Color of Violence*, 119–29.

Faulk, Karen Ann. 2013. *In the Wake of Neoliberalism: Citizenship and Human Rights in Argentina*. Stanford, CA: Stanford University Press.

Feierstein, Daniel. 2011. "Sobre conceptos, memorias e identidades: Guerra, genocidio y/o terrorismo de Estado en Argentina." *Política y Sociedad* 48 (3): 571–86.

Feld, Claudia. 2002. *Del estrado a la pantalla: Las imágenes del juicio a los ex comandantes en Argentina*. Buenos Aires: Siglo Veintiuno de España.

Felder, Ruth, and Viviana Patroni. 2011. "Austerity and Its Aftermath: Neoliberalism and Labour in Argentina." *Socialist Studies/Études Socialistes* 7 (1/2): 259–81.

Felgueras, Santiago, and Leonardo Filippini. 2010. "La tortura en la jurisprudencia Argentina por crímenes del terrorismo de estado." CELS and ICTJ, November 29. www.cels.org.ar.

Felitti, Karina. 2000. "El placer de elegir. Anticoncepción y liberación sexual en la década del sesenta." In Lozano, Pita, and Ini, *Historia de las mujeres en la Argentina*, 155–71.

———. 2010. "Poner el cuerpo: Género y sexualidad en la política revolucionaria de Argentina en la década de 1970." In *Political and Social Movements during the Sixties and Seventies in the Americas and Europe*, ed. Avital H. Bloch, 69–93. Colima, Mexico: Universidad de Colima.

Felman, Shoshana, and Dori Laub. 1992. *Testimony: Crises of Witnessing in Literature, Psychoanalysis, and History*. New York: Routledge.

Filippini, Leonardo. 2011. "La persecución penal en la búsqueda de justicia." In Centro de Estudios Legales y Sociales and Centro Internacional para la Justicia Transicional, *Hacer justicia*, 19–47.

Fisher, Jo. 1993. *Out of the Shadows: Women, Resistance, and Politics in South America*. London: Latin American Bureau.

Flores, Leonor Eloina Pastrana. 2011. "La implicación del investigador en la pesquisa: Ejercicio de conocimiento intercultural." Paper presented at the XI Congreso Nacional de Investigación Educativa/12. Multiculturalismo y Educación, Mexico, November 7–11. www.comie.org.mx.

Fobear, Katherine. 2014. "Queering Truth Commissions." *Journal of Human Rights Practice* 6 (1): 51–68.

Forcinito, Ana. 2012. *Los umbrales del testimonio: Entre las narraciones de los sobrevivientes y las señas de la posdictadura*. Madrid: Iberoamericana.

Foucault, Michel. 1989. *Vigilar y castigar: Nacimiento de la prisión*. Translated by Aurelio Garzón del Camino. Argentina: Siglo XXI.

Franco, Jean. 1992. "Gender, Death, and Resistance: Facing the Ethical Vacuum." In Corradi, Fagen, and Garretón, *Fear at the Edge*, 104–18.

Franco, Marina. 2012. *Un enemigo para la Nación: Orden interno, violencia y "subversión," 1973–1976*. Buenos Aires: Fondo de Cultura Económica.

Fregoso, Rosa-Linda, and Cynthia Bejarano, eds. 2010. *Terrorizing Women: Feminicide in the Américas*. Durham, NC: Duke University Press.

Fried, Gabriela. 2006. "Piecing Memories Together after State Terror and Policies of Oblivion in Uruguay: The Female Political Prisoner's Testimonial Project (1997–2004)." *Social Identities* 12 (5): 543–62.

Fried Amilivia, Gabriela. 2016. *State Terrorism and the Politics of Memory in Latin America: Transmissions across the Generations of Post-dictatorship Uruguay, 1984–2004*. Amherst, NY: Cambria Press.

Frye, Marilyn. 1983. *The Politics of Reality: Essays in Feminist Theory*. Trumansburg, NY: Crossing.

Fuchs, Thomas. 2003. "The Phenomenology of Shame, Guilt and the Body in Body Dysmorphic Disorder and Depression." *Journal of Phenomenological Psychology* 33 (2): 223–43.

"Fuertes repercusiones por un editorial de *La Nación*." 2015. *La Nación*, November 23. www.lanacion.com.ar.

Funes, Patricia. 2007. "Los libros y la noche. Censura, cultura y represión en Argentina a través de los servicios de inteligencia del Estado." *Dimensões* 19: 133–55.

Fusco, Coco. 2008. *A Field Guide for Female Interrogators*. New York: Seven Stories Press.

Gaer, Felice. 2013. "Rape as a Form of Torture: The Experience of the Committee against Torture." *CUNY Law Review* 15 (2): 293–308.

Gago, Verónica. 2016. "Treinta años de espera, dos siglos de condena." *Página/12, Suplemento Las12*, March 4. www.pagina12.com.

Garaño, Santiago. 2010. "'Romper la vidriera, para que se vea la trastienda.' Sentidos, valores morales y prácticas de 'resistencia' entre las presas políticas de la cárcel de Villa Devoto durante la última dictadura militar argentina (1976–1983)." *Historia Crítica*, "Memoria, historia y testimonio en América Latina" 40 (January–April): 98–120.

Garland-Thomson, Rosemarie. 2002. "Integrating Disability, Transforming Feminist Theory." *National Women's Studies Association Journal* 14 (3): 1–32.

"Gender and Latin America's Pink Tide." 2012. *Politics & Gender* 8 (2).

Gioscia, Laura. 2015. "The Materiality of the Body and Women's Rights. Affects and the Political, a New Approach." Paper presented in "Precariedades, Exclusiones, Emergencias," Latin American Studies Association Conference, San Juan de Puerto Rico, May 27–30.

Glenn, Evelyn Nakano. 1985. "Racial Ethnic Women's Labor: The Intersection of Race, Gender and Class Oppression." *Review of Radical Political Economics* 17 (3): 86–108.

Glover, Jonathan. 2012. *Humanity: A Moral History of the Twentieth Century*. New Haven, CT: Yale University Press.

Goldstein, Donna M. 2003. *Laughter Out of Place: Race, Class, Violence, and Sexuality in a Rio Shantytown*. Berkeley: University of California Press.

Gómez-Barris, Macarena. 2009. *Where Memory Dwells: Culture and State Violence in Chile*. Berkeley: University of California Press.

———. 2010. "Witness Citizenship: The Place of Villa Grimaldi in Chilean Memory." *Sociological Forum* 25 (1): 27–46.

González, Carmen. 1992. "Violencia en las instituciones jurídicas." In *La mujer y la violencia invisible*, ed. Eva Giberti and Ana María Fernández, 171–87. Buenos Aires: Sudamericana.

Goodwin, Jeff, James M. Jasper, and Francesca Polletta, eds. 2001. *Passionate Politics: Emotions and Social Movements.* Chicago: University of Chicago Press.

Gordon, Avery F. 2008. *Ghostly Matters: Haunting and the Sociological Imagination.* Minneapolis: University of Minnesota Press.

Gottschalk, Simon. 2003. "Reli(e)ving the Past: Emotion Work in the Holocaust's Second Generation." *Symbolic Interaction* 26 (3): 355–80.

Grammático, Karin. 2011. *Mujeres Montoneras: Una historia de la Agrupación Evita 1973–1974.* Buenos Aires: Luxemburg.

Grandey, Alicia A. 2003. "When 'The Show Must Go On': Surface Acting and Deep Acting as Determinants of Emotional Exhaustion and Peer-Rated Service Delivery." *Academy of Management Journal* 46 (1): 86–96.

Green, Debbie, Andrew Rasmussen, and Barry Rosenfeld. 2010. "Defining Torture: A Review of 40 Years of Health Science Research." *Journal of Traumatic Stress* 23 (4): 528–31.

Grosz, Elizabeth. 1994. *Volatile Bodies: Toward a Corporeal Feminism.* Bloomington: Indiana University Press.

Guelar, Diana, Vera Jarach, and Beatriz Ruiz. 2002. *Los chicos del exilio: Argentina, 1975–1984.* Buenos Aires: El país de nomeolvides.

Guglielmucci, Ana. 2007. "Visibilidad e invisibilidad de la prisión política en Argentina: La 'cárcel vidriera' de Villa Devoto (1974–1983)." *A Contracorriente* 4 (3): 86–136.

Halbwachs, Maurice. 1980. *The Collective Memory.* Translated by Francis J. Ditter, Jr. and Vida Yazdi Ditter. New York: Harper & Row.

Halewood, Peter. 2012. "Sameness/Difference, International Human Rights Law, and the Political Meaning of Torture." *Berkeley La Raza Law Journal* 22 (1): 257–68.

Hannoun, Antoine B., Anwar H. Nassar, Ihab M. Usta, Tony G. Zreik, and Antoine A. Abu Musa. 2007. "Effect of War on the Menstrual Cycle." *Obstetrics and Gynecology* 109 (4): 929–32.

Haraway, Donna. 1988. "Situated Knowledges: The Science Question in Feminism and the Privilege of Partial Perspective." *Feminist Studies* 14 (3): 575–99.

Harding, Sandra. 1993. "Rethinking Standpoint Epistemology: What Is 'Strong Objectivity'?" In *Feminist Epistemologies*, ed. Linda Alcoff and Elizabeth Potter, 49–82. New York: Routledge.

Harris, Christopher. 2005. "Remembering 1968 in Mexico: Elena Poniatowska's La Noche de Tlatelolco as Documentary Narrative." *Bulletin of Latin American Research* 24 (4): 481–95.

Hartmann, Betsy. 1995. *Reproductive Rights and Wrongs: The Global Politics of Population Control.* Boston: South End Press.

Hassoun, Jacques. 1996. *Los contrabandistas de la memoria.* Translated by Silvia Fendrik. Buenos Aires: Ediciones de la Flor.

Hiller, Renata. 2013. "El activismo de la diversidad sexual en la Argentina." *Ciencia Hoy*, September 19. http://cienciahoy.org.ar.

Hiner, Hillary, and María José Azócar. 2015. "Irreconcilable Differences: Political Culture and Gender Violence during the Chilean Transition to Democracy." *Latin American Perspectives* 42 (3): 52–72.

Hirsch, Marianne. 2014. "Presidential Address 2014—Connective Histories in Vulnerable Times." *PMLA* 129 (3): 330–48.

———. 2015. "Small Acts: Mobilizing Memory across Borders." Keynote address at the "Translating Memory and Remembrance across the Disciplines" conference, SUNY New Paltz, October 8.

Hirsch, Marianne, and Leo Spitzer. 2009. "The Witness in the Archive: Holocaust Studies." *Memory Studies* 2 (2): 151–70.

Historias Debidas: Latinoamérica. 2014. "Pilar Calveiro." Video recording. Ana Cacopardo (host and interviewer), Andrés Irigoyen (director). Argentina: Estudios Pacífico, Canal Encuentro, Ministerio de Educación de la Nación.

Hochschild, Arlie Russell. 2003. *The Managed Heart: Commercialization of Human Feeling.* 20th anniversary ed. Berkeley: University of California Press.

Hollander, Jocelyn A. 2001. "Vulnerability and Dangerousness: The Construction of Gender through Conversation about Violence." *Gender & Society* 15 (1): 83–109.

Hollander, Jocelyn A., and Rachel L. Einwohner. 2004. "Conceptualizing Resistance." *Sociological Forum* 19 (4): 533–54.

Hollander, Nancy Caro. 1996. "The Gendering of Human Rights: Women and the Latin American Terrorist State." *Feminist Studies* 22 (1): 41–80.

Honwana, Alcinda. 2006. *Child Soldiers in Africa.* Philadelphia: University of Pennsylvania Press.

Hood, Roger, and Carolyn Hoyle. 2014. *The Death Penalty: A Worldwide Perspective.* Oxford: Oxford University Press.

hooks, bell. 2015. *Sisters of the Yam: Black Women and Self-Recovery.* New York: Routledge.

Howard, Judith A., Barbara Risman, Mary Romero, and Joey Sprague. 1997. "Series Editor's Introduction." In *Gendered Situations, Gendered Selves: A Gender Lens on Social Psychology,* ed. Judith A. Howard and Jocelyn A. Hollander, ix–xi. Thousand Oaks, CA: Sage.

Huyssen, Andreas. 2011. "International Human Rights and the Politics of Memory: Limits and Challenges." *Criticism* 53 (4): 607–24.

Hyams, Melissa. 2004. "Hearing Girls' Silences: Thoughts on the Politics and Practices of a Feminist Method of Group Discussion." *Gender, Place & Culture* 11 (1): 105–19.

Ibañez, Ximena Andión, Elisa Slattery, and Jaime Todd-Gher. 2010. *Reproductive Rights Violations as Torture and Cruel, Inhuman, or Degrading Treatment or Punishment: A Critical Human Rights Analysis.* New York: Center for Reproductive Rights.

INCITE! Women of Color against Violence, ed. 2006. *Color of Violence: The Incite! Anthology.* Cambridge, MA: South End Press.

Insausti, Santiago Joaquín. 2015. "Los cuatrocientos homosexuales desaparecidos: Memorias de la represión estatal a las sexualidades disidentes en Argentina." In D'Antonio, *Deseo y Represión,* 63–82.

International Criminal Court (ICC). 2011. *Rome Statute of the International Criminal Court.* The Hague: ICC. www.icc-cpi.int.

———. n.d. "The States Parties to the Rome Statute." http://asp.icc-cpi.int.

Jaggar, Alison M., and Susan Bordo, eds. 1989. *Gender/Body/Knowledge: Feminist Reconstructions of Being and Knowing*. New Brunswick, NJ: Rutgers University Press.

Jasper, James M. 2011. "Emotions and Social Movements: Twenty Years of Theory and Research." *Annual Review of Sociology* 37 (1): 285–303.

Jelin, Elizabeth. 2001. "El género en las memorias de la represión política." *Mora* 7 (October): 127–37.

———. 2003. *State Repression and the Labors of Memory*. Translated by Judy Rein and Marcial Godoy-Anativia. Minneapolis: University of Minnesota Press.

———. 2004. "Los derechos humanos y la memoria de la violencia política y la represión: La construcción de un campo nuevo en las ciencias sociales." *Estudios Sociales*, Año XIV, 27 (second semester): 91–113.

———. 2011. "Revisitando el campo de las memorias: Un nuevo prólogo." http://memoria.ides.org.ar.

———. 2013. "Militantes y combatientes en la historia de las memorias: Silencios, denuncias y reivindicaciones." *Meridional* 1 (October): 77–97.

———. 2014. "Las múltiples temporalidades del testimonio: El pasado vivido y sus legados presentes." *Clepsidra* 1 (1): 140–63.

Jurik, Nancy C., and Cynthia Siemsen. 2009. "'Doing Gender' as Canon or Agenda: A Symposium on West and Zimmerman." *Gender & Society* 23 (1): 72–75.

Juris, Jeffrey S. 2008. "Performing Politics: Image, Embodiment, and Affective Solidarity during Anti-corporate Globalization Protests." *Ethnography* 9 (1): 61–97.

Kaiser, Susana. 2015. "Argentina's Trials: New Ways of Writing Memory." *Latin American Perspectives* 42 (3): 193–206.

Kampwirth, Karen. 2004. *Feminism and the Legacy of Revolution: Nicaragua, El Salvador, Chiapas*. Athens: Ohio University Press.

Kaplan, Betina. 2007. *Género y violencia en la narrativa del cono sur, 1954–2003*. Woodbridge: Tamesis.

Kaplan, Temma. 2002. "Reversing the Shame and Gendering the Memory." *Signs* 28 (1): 179–99.

Kearney-Cooke, Ann, and Diann M. Ackard. 2000. "The Effects of Sexual Abuse on Body Image, Self-Image, and Sexual Activity of Women." *Journal of Gender-Specific Medicine* 3 (6): 54–60.

Kilbourne, Jean, and Sut Jhally. 2000. *Killing Us Softly 3: Advertising's Image of Women*. Northampton, MA: Media Education Foundation.

Kleinman, Arthur, Veena Das, and Margaret Lock. 1996. "Introduction." *Daedalus* 125 (1): xi–xx.

Kleinman, Arthur, and Joan Kleinman. 1994. "How Bodies Remember: Social Memory and Bodily Experience of Criticism, Resistance, and Delegitimation following China's Cultural Revolution." *New Literary History* 25 (3): 707–23.

La Casa Del Encuentro. n.d. "Feminicidios." www.lacasadelencuentro.org.

Lagarde, Marcela. 2001. "Democracia genérica: Por una educación humana de género para la igualdad, la integridad y la libertad." www.mujeresdelsur.org.

Lampasona, Julieta. 2015. "Re-construyendo la experiencia de la (propia) desaparición." *Nómadas* 46 (2). http://revistas.ucm.es.

Langbein, John H. 2006. *Torture and the Law of Proof: Europe and England in the Ancien Régime.* Chicago: University of Chicago Press.

Langton, Rae. 2005. "Feminism in Philosophy." In *The Oxford Handbook of Contemporary Analytic Philosophy,* ed. Frank Jackson and Michael Smith, 231–57. Oxford: Oxford University Press.

Latina Feminist Group. 2001. *Telling to Live: Latina Feminist Testimonios.* Durham, NC: Duke University Press.

Laub, Dori. 1992. "Bearing Witness or the Vicissitudes of Listening." In Felman and Laub, *Testimony,* 57–74.

Laudano, Claudia Nora. n.d. [1998]. *Las mujeres en los discursos militares.* Buenos Aires: La Página S.A.

Lazzara, Michael, María Rosa Olivera-Williams, and Mónica Szurmuk. 2013. "Violencia, memoria, justicia: Una entrevista a Pilar Calveiro." *A Contracorriente* 10 (2): 324–46.

Lenton, Diana. 2014. "Memorias y silencios en torno a la trayectoria de dirigentes indígenas en tiempos represivos." *Revista TEFROS* 12 (2): 190–211.

Lessa, Francesca. 2015. "Justice beyond Borders: The Operation Condor Trial and Accountability for Transnational Crimes in South America." *International Journal of Transitional Justice* 9 (3): 494–506.

Lessa, Francesca, and Vincent Druliolle, eds. 2011. *The Memory of State Terrorism in the Southern Cone: Argentina, Chile, and Uruguay.* New York: Palgrave Macmillan.

Levey, Cara. 2014. "Of HIJOS and Niños: Revisiting Postmemory in Post-Dictatorship Uruguay." *History and Memory* 26 (2): 5–39.

Levi, Primo. 1989. *The Drowned and the Saved.* Translated by Raymond Rosenthal. New York: Vintage International.

Lewin, Miriam, and Olga Wornat. 2014. *Putas y guerrilleras.* Buenos Aires: Planeta.

Llanos, Bernardita. 2016. "Caught Off Guard at the Crossroads of Ideology and Affect: Documentary Films by the Daughters of Revolutionaries." In *Latin American Documentary Film in the New Millennium,* ed. María Guadalupe Arenillas and Michael J. Lazzara, 243–58. New York: Palgrave Macmillan.

Llobet, Valeria. 2015. "'¿Y vos qué sabés si no lo viviste?' Infancia y dictadura en un pueblo de provincia." *A Contracorriente* 12 (3): 1–41.

Lock, Margaret. 2001. "Containing the Elusive Body." *Hedgehog Review* 3 (2): 65–78.

Longoni, Ana. 2007. *Traiciones: La figura del traidor en los relatos acerca de los sobrevivientes de la represión.* Buenos Aires: Norma.

———. 2016. "Una respuesta a Marcelo Birmajer y sus ataques al Parque de la Memoria." *Esfera Común,* March 9. http://esferacomun.com.ar.

Lorber, Judith. 1994. *Paradoxes of Gender.* New Haven, CT: Yale University Press.

Lorenz, Federico Guillermo. 2004. "Argentina's Coup: Social Myth, Memory and History." *History Today* 54 (1): 17–19.

Lorenz, Federico, María Celeste Adamoli, Matías Farías, Cecilia Flachsland, Pablo Luzuriaga, Violeta Rosemberg, and Edgardo Vannucchi. 2010. *Pensar la dictadura: Terrorismo de Estado en Argentina.* Buenos Aires: Ministerio de Educación de la Nación Argentina.

Lorenzetti, Ricardo L., and Alfredo J. Kraut. 2011. *Derechos humanos: Justicia y reparación.* Buenos Aires: Sudamericana.

"Los fundamentos de la condena a Etchecolatz." 2010. *Diario Judicial,* July 16. www.diariojudicial.com.

"Los juicios por crímenes de la dictadura seguirán adelante." 2015. *Clarín,* November 11. www.clarin.com.

Loveman, Brian. 2011. "Military Governments in Latin America, 1959–1990." Oxford University Press Bibliographies Online. www.oxfordbibliographies.com.

Lozano, Fernanda Gil, Valeria Silvina Pita, and María Gabriela Ini, eds. 2000. *Historia de las mujeres en la Argentina: Siglo XX.* Vol. 2. Buenos Aires: Taurus.

Lutz, Ellen, and Kathryn Sikkink. 2001. "The Justice Cascade: The Evolution and Impact of Foreign Human Rights Trials in Latin America." *Chicago Journal of International Law* 2 (1): 1–33.

MacKinnon, Catharine A. 2006. *Are Women Human? And Other International Dialogues.* Cambridge, MA: Harvard University Press.

MacManus, Viviana Beatriz. 2015. "'We Are Not Victims, We Are Protagonists of This History': Latin American Gender Violence and the Limits of Women's Rights as Human Rights." *International Feminist Journal of Politics* 17 (1): 40–57.

Macón, Cecilia. 2014. "Illuminating Affects: Sexual Violence as a Crime against Humanity. The Argentine Case." *Historein* 14 (1): 22–42.

———. 2015a. "On Not To Talk: Hope and Joy as Resilience. The Case of Female Victims of Sexual Violence in the Argentinian Crimes against Humanity Trials." Paper presented at "History of Twentieth-Century Historiography," Athens, June 18–20.

———. 2015b. "'Santa Evita Montonera': Envious, Therefore Empowered." *Journal of Romance Studies* 15 (1): 1–28.

Madhok, Sumi, Anne Phillips, and Kalpana Wilson, eds. 2013. *Gender, Agency and Coercion.* New York: Palgrave Macmillan.

Mahmood, Saba. 2001. "Feminist Theory, Embodiment, and the Docile Agent: Some Reflections on the Egyptian Islamic Revival." *Cultural Anthropology* 16 (2): 202–36.

Mainwaring, Scott, Daniel Brinks, and Aníbal Pérez-Liñán. 2001. "Classifying Political Regimes in Latin America, 1945–1999." *Studies in Comparative International Development* 36 (1): 37–65.

Mama, Amina, and Margo Okazawa-Rey. 2012. "Militarism, Conflict and Women's Activism in the Global Era: Challenges and Prospects for Women in Three West African Contexts." *Feminist Review* 101 (1): 97–123.

Mann, Bonnie. 2008. "Manhood, Sexuality, and Nation in Post-9/11 United States." In Sutton, Morgen, and Novkov, *Security Disarmed,* 179–97.

Margulis, Paola. 2006. "Formas y límites. Un estudio sobre la representación del cuerpo en Para Ti durante la década del 70." *Questión* 1 (10). http://perio.unlp.edu.ar.

Mario, Silvia, and Edith Alejandra Pantelides. 2009. "Estimación de la magnitud del aborto inducido en la Argentina." *Notas de Población* 87: 95–120.

Martínez, Paola. 2009. *Género, política y revolución en los años setenta: Las mujeres del PRT-ERP.* Buenos Aires: Imago Mundi.

Masotta, Carlos. 2006. "Imágenes recientes de la 'Conquista del Desierto.' Problemas de la memoria en la impugnación de un mito de origen." *Runa* 26 (1): 225–45.

Mateo, Joanna. 2011. "Street Gangs of Honduras." In *Maras: Gang Violence and Security in Central America*, ed. Thomas Bruneau, Lucía Dammert, and Elizabeth Skinner, 87–103. Austin: University of Texas Press.

Máximo, Matías. 2015. "La memoria no es un privilegio heterosexual." *Página/12, Suplemento Soy*, March 28. www.pagina12.com.ar.

May, Vivian M. 2014. "'Speaking into the Void?' Intersectionality Critiques and Epistemic Backlash." *Hypatia* 29 (1): 94–112.

McCall, Leslie. 2005. "The Complexity of Intersectionality." *Signs* 30 (3): 1771–800.

McSherry, J. Patrice. 2005. *Predatory States: Operation Condor and Covert War in Latin America.* Lanham, MD: Rowman & Littlefield.

Melzer, Patricia. 2015. *Death in the Shape of a Young Girl: Women's Political Violence in the Red Army Faction.* New York: New York University Press.

Memoria Abierta. n.d.-a. "Comunicado N°1 de La Junta de Comandantes Generales de las Fuerzas Armadas (24 de Marzo de 1976)." Audio recording. www.memoriaabierta.org.ar.

———. n.d.-b. "Who We Are." www.memoriaabierta.org.ar.

———. n.d. [2016]. "530 horas: El archivo audiovisual del juicio a las juntas (Argentina—1985)." www.memoriaabierta.org.ar.

———. 2002. "Testimonio de Francisco Amarilla." Written summary. Buenos Aires, July 19.

———. 2005. "La representación de experiencias traumáticas a través de archivos de testimonios y de la reconstrucción de espacios de represión." Paper presented at the Encuentro Internacional "El arte: Representación de la memoria del terror," November 4. www.memoriaabierta.org.ar.

Menchú, Rigoberta, with Elisabeth Burgos-Debray. 1984. *I, Rigoberta Menchú: An Indian Woman in Guatemala.* Translated by Ann Wright. London: Verso.

Menjívar, Cecilia. 2011. *Enduring Violence: Ladina Women's Lives in Guatemala.* Berkeley: University of California Press.

Menjívar, Cecilia, and Néstor Rodríguez. 2005. "State Terror in the U.S.-Latin American Interstate Regime." In *When States Kill: Latin America, the U.S., and Technologies of Terror*, ed. Cecilia Menjívar and Néstor Rodríguez, 3–27. Austin: University of Texas Press.

Milgram, Stanley. 1975. *Obedience to Authority: An Experimental View.* New York: Harper & Row.

Miller, Francesca. 2008. "Mothers of the Plaza de Mayo." In *The Oxford Encyclopedia of Women in World History*, vol. 3, ed. Bonnie Smith, 277–78. Oxford: Oxford University Press.

Mills, C. Wright. 1959. *The Sociological Imagination*. New York: Oxford University Press.

Ministerio de Educación. n.d. "SIG de la memoria." *SIG de la memoria*. www.mapaeducativo.edu.ar.

Mischel, Walter. 1968. *Personality and Assessment*. New York: Wiley.

Mochkofsky, Graciela. 2016. "Obama's Bittersweet Visit to Argentina." *New Yorker*, March 23. www.newyorker.com.

Mohanty, Chandra Talpade. 1988. "Under Western Eyes: Feminist Scholarship and Colonial Discourses." *Feminist Review* 30 (1): 61–88.

Moraga, Cherríe, and Gloria Anzaldúa, eds. 1983. *This Bridge Called My Back: Writings by Radical Women of Color*. New York: Kitchen Table/Women of Color Press.

Morgan, Lynn. 2015. "Reproductive Rights or Reproductive Justice? Lessons from Argentina." *Health and Human Rights* 17 (1): 136–47.

Mujeres en Igualdad (MEI). n.d. "Guía de recursos de asistencia a víctimas de violencia y/o trata." www.mujeresenigualdad.org.ar.

Mulvey, Laura. 1975. "Visual Pleasure and Narrative Cinema." *Screen* 16 (3): 6–18.

Municipalidad General Pueyrredón. 2015. "Se presentó en sociedad el libro 'Marimosa y las hormigas.'" Video recording, April 16. www.youtube.com/watch?v=hR7l3xpBU24.

Nesiah, Vasuki, et al. 2006. *Truth Commissions and Gender: Principle, Policies and Procedures*. New York: International Center for Transitional Justice.

"No más venganza." 2015. *La Nación*, November 23. www.lanacion.com.ar.

Oberti, Alejandra. 2005. "Violencia política, identidad y géneros en la militancia de los '70." In Andújar et al., *Historia, género y política en los '70*, 260–76.

———. 2015. *Las revolucionarias: Militancia, vida cotidiana y afectividad en los setenta*. Buenos Aires: Edhasa.

Office of the United Nations High Commissioner for Human Rights. n.d. "Convention against Torture and Other Cruel, Inhuman or Degrading Treatment or Punishment." www.ohchr.org.

O'Keefe, Theresa. 2014. "My Body Is My Manifesto! SlutWalk, FEMEN and Femmenist Protest." *Feminist Review* 107 (1): 1–19.

Olick, Jeffrey K., Vered Vinitzky-Seroussi, and Daniel Levy. 2011. "Introduction." In *The Collective Memory Reader*, ed. Jeffrey K. Olick, Vered Vinitzky-Seroussi, and Daniel Levy, 3–62. New York: Oxford University Press.

Olivera, Héctor, dir. 1986. *La Noche de los Lápices*. Film.

Oosterhoff, Pauline, Prisca Zwanikken, and Evert Ketting. 2004. "Sexual Torture of Men in Croatia and Other Conflict Situations: An Open Secret." *Reproductive Health Matters* 12 (23): 68–77.

Osorio, Carlos, and Peter Kornbluh. 2016. "Obama Agrees to Declassify US Records on Argentine Dirty War." National Security Archive Briefing Book No. 545, March 18. http://nsarchive.gwu.edu.

Otero, Rocío. 2010. "La repolitización de la historia de los sesenta y setenta: Una nueva etapa en la representación del pasado reciente." In *La sociedad argentina hoy frente a los años '70*, by Claudia Medvescig, Rocío Otero, Valentina Salvi, and Alejandro Villa, 66–111. Buenos Aires: EUDEBA.

Outman-Kramer, Miranda, and Susana Galán, eds. 2014. "*Comparative Perspectives Symposium*: Gendered Bodies in the Protest Sphere." *Signs* 40 (1).

Outreach Programme on the Rwanda Genocide and the United Nations. n.d. "Background Information on Sexual Violence Used as a Tool of War." www.un.org.

Park, Rebekah. 2013. "Remembering Resistance, Forgetting Torture: Compromiso and Gender in Former Political Prisoners' Oral History Narratives in Post-dictatorial Argentina." *History of Communism in Europe* 4: 87–111.

———. 2014. *The Reappeared: Argentine Former Political Prisoners*. New Brunswick, NJ: Rutgers University Press.

Parkins, Wendy. 2000. "Protesting Like a Girl: Embodiment, Dissent and Feminist Agency." *Feminist Theory* 1 (1): 59–78.

Parson, Nia. 2013. *Traumatic States: Gendered Violence, Suffering, and Care in Chile*. Nashville: Vanderbilt University Press.

Partnoy, Alicia. 1986. *The Little School: Tales of Disappearance & Survival in Argentina*. Pittsburgh: Cleis Press.

———. 2006. "Cuando Vienen Matando: On Prepositional Shifts and the Struggle of Testimonial Subjects for Agency." *PMLA* 121 (5): 1665–69.

———. 2009. "Disclaimer Intraducible: My Life/Is Based/on a Real Story." *Biography* 32 (1): 16–25.

Pasternak, Alfred, and Philip G. Brooks. 2007. "The Long-Term Effects of the Holocaust on the Reproductive Function of Female Survivors." *Journal of Minimally Invasive Gynecology* 14 (2): 211–17.

Patai, Daphne. 1993. *Brazilian Women Speak: Contemporary Life Stories*. New Brunswick, NJ: Rutgers University Press.

Pateman, Carol. 1989. *The Disorder of Women: Democracy, Feminism and Political Theory*. Stanford, CA: Stanford University Press.

Payne, Leigh A. 2008. *Unsettling Accounts: Neither Truth nor Reconciliation in Confessions of State Violence*. Durham, NC: Duke University Press.

Peller, Mariela. 2013. "Vida cotidiana y militancia armada en los años '70 en la Argentina: Problemas conceptuales e hipótesis de lectura." *INTERthesis* 10 (1): 37–64.

Perera, Verónica. 2016. "Los límites de un homenaje: Imagen y memorias en Teatro Abierto 2013." *Clepsidra* 3 (5): 84–105.

Peterson, Abby. 2001. "The Militant Body and Political Communication: The Medialisation of Violence." In *Contemporary Political Protest: Essays on Political Militancy*, 69–101. Aldershot: Ashgate.

Philipose, Liz. 2007. "The Politics of Pain and the Uses of Torture." *Signs* 32 (4): 1047–71.

Pigna, Felipe. 2013. "Lo Pasado Pensado-Felipe Pigna-La Conferencia de Videla (1979)." Video recording, April 25. www.youtube.com/watch?v=1CHnHsPfDMo.

Plotkin, Mariano Ben. 2001. *Freud in the Pampas: The Emergence and Development of a Psychoanalytic Culture in Argentina*. Stanford, CA: Stanford University Press.

Potes, Marisa. 2014. *Marimosa y las hormigas*. Illustrated by Adrián Icasati. Mar del Plata: Municipalidad de General Pueyrredón.

Puar, Jasbir K. 2004. "Abu Ghraib: Arguing against Exceptionalism." *Feminist Studies* 30 (2): 522–34.

———. 2005. "On Torture: Abu Ghraib." *Radical History Review* 93 (Fall): 13–38.

Puig, Manuel. 1969. *Boquitas pintadas*. Buenos Aires: Sudamericana.

Punamäki, Raija-Leena, Katri Kanninen, Samir Qouta, and Eyad El-Sarraj. 2002. "The Role of Psychological Defences in Moderating between Trauma and Post-traumatic Symptoms among Palestinian Men." *International Journal of Psychology* 37 (5): 286–96.

Putnam, Frank W. 2013. "The Role of Abusive States of Being in Interrogation." *Journal of Trauma & Dissociation* 14 (2): 147–58.

Quijada, Mónica, Carmen Bernand, and Arnd Schneider. 2000. *Homogeneidad y nación, con un estudio de caso: Argentina, siglos XIX y XX*. Madrid: Consejo Superior de Investigaciones Científicas.

Rabotnikof, Nora. 2007. "Memoria y política a treinta años del golpe." In *Argentina, 1976. Estudios en torno al golpe de estado*, ed. Clara E. Lida, Horacio Crespo, and Pablo Yankelevich, 259–84. Mexico: El Colegio de México.

Ramus, Susana Jorgelina. 2000. *Sueños sobrevivientes de una montonera: A pesar de la ESMA*. Buenos Aires: Colihue.

Randall, Margaret. 2003. *When I Look into the Mirror and See You: Women, Terror and Resistance*. New Brunswick, NJ: Rutgers University Press.

REDLACTRANS. 2012. "The Night Is Another Country: Impunity and Violence against Transgender Women Human Rights Defenders in Latin America." http://redlactrans.org.ar.

Regueiro, Sabina. 2008. "Maternidades clandestinas de Campo de Mayo. Tramas burocráticas en la administración de nacimientos." In Tarducci, *Maternidades en el siglo XXI*, 87–135.

Rejali, Darius M. 2007. *Torture and Democracy*. Princeton, NJ: Princeton University Press.

Riaño-Alcalá, Pilar, and Erin Baines. 2011. "The Archive in the Witness: Documentation in Settings of Chronic Insecurity." *International Journal of Transitional Justice* 5 (3): 412–33.

Riley, Robin L., Chandra Talpade Mohanty, and Minnie Bruce Pratt, eds. 2008. *Feminism and War: Confronting U.S. Imperialism*. London: Zed Books.

Roberts, Dorothy E. 1997. *Killing the Black Body: Race, Reproduction, and the Meaning of Liberty*. New York: Pantheon Books.

Romanin, Enrique Andriotti. 2013. "Decir la verdad, hacer justicia: Los Juicios por la Verdad en Argentina." *ERLACS* 94: 5–23.

Romero, Luis Alberto. 2013. *A History of Argentina in the Twentieth Century*. University Park: Pennsylvania State University Press.

Ross, Loretta. 2006. "The Color of Choice: White Supremacy and Reproductive Justice." In INCITE! Women of Color against Violence, *Color of Violence*, 53–65.

Rothberg, Michael. 2013a. "Beyond Tancred and Clorinda: Trauma Studies for Implicated Subjects." In *The Future of Trauma Theory*, ed. Gert Buelens, Samuel Durrant, and Robert Eaglestone, xi–xviii. New York: Routledge.

———. 2013b. "Multidirectional Memory and the Implicated Subject: On Sebald and Kentridge." In *Performing Memory in the Arts and Popular Culture*, ed. Liedeke Plate and Anneke Smelik, 39–58. New York: Routledge.

Safa, Helen Icken. 1990. "Women's Social Movements in Latin America." *Gender & Society* 4 (3): 354–69.

Salerno, Melisa A. 2009. "'They Must Have Done Something Wrong . . .': The Construction of 'Subversive' Social Categories and the Reshaping of Subjectivities through Body and Dress (Argentina, 1976–1983)." In *Memories from Darkness: Archaeology of Repression and Resistance in Latin America (1960–1980)*, ed. Pedro P. Funari, Andrés Zarankin, and Melisa A. Salerno, 81–103. New York: Springer.

Salvi, Valentina. 2010. "La familia como nación: Memoria y política en el discurso de las agrupaciones de 'Memoria Completa.'" Paper presented at the III Seminario Internacional Políticas de la Memoria, Buenos Aires, October 28–30. www.derhuman.jus.gov.ar.

Sanford, Victoria. 2008. "From Genocide to Feminicide: Impunity and Human Rights in Twenty-First Century Guatemala." *Journal of Human Rights* 7 (2): 104–22.

Sasson-Levy, Orna, and Tamar Rapoport. 2003. "Body, Gender, and Knowledge in Protest Movements: The Israeli Case." *Gender & Society* 17 (3): 379–403.

Scarry, Elaine. 1985. *The Body in Pain: The Making and Unmaking of the World*. New York: Oxford University Press.

Scheff, Thomas J. 2003. "Shame in Self and Society." *Symbolic Interaction* 26 (2): 239–62.

Scheper-Hughes, Nancy, and Philippe Bourgois. 2004. "Introduction: Making Sense of Violence." In *Violence in War and Peace: An Anthology*, ed. Nancy Scheper-Hughes and Philippe Bourgois, 1–31. Malden, MA: Blackwell.

Scott, James C. 1985. *Weapons of the Weak: Everyday Forms of Peasant Resistance*. New Haven, CT: Yale University Press.

Scott, Joan W. 1986. "Gender: A Useful Category of Historical Analysis." *American Historical Review* 91 (5): 1053–75.

———. 2001. "Fantasy Echo: History and the Construction of Identity." *Critical Inquiry* 27 (2): 284–304.

"Se entregaron ejemplares de 'Marimosa y las hormigas.'" 2016. *Radio Claridad*, March 25. www.am1080.com.ar.

Segato, Rita Laura. 2014. *Las nuevas formas de la guerra y el cuerpo de las mujeres*. Puebla: Pez en el árbol.

Serano, Julia. 2013. *Excluded: Making Feminist and Queer Movements More Inclusive*. Berkeley: Seal Press.

Seri, Guillermina. 2008. "Terror, Reconciliation, Redemption: The Politics of Memory in Argentina." *Radical Philosophy* 147 (January–February): 8–13.

Shanks, Torrey. 2015. "Toleration and Democratic Membership: John Locke and Michel de Montaigne on Monsters." *Political Theory* 43 (4): 451–72.

Shepherd, Laura J., and Laura Sjoberg. 2012. "Trans-Bodies in/of War(s): Cisprivilege and Contemporary Security Strategy." *Feminist Review* 101 (1): 5–23.

Shildrick, Margrit. 2002. *Embodying the Monster: Encounters with the Vulnerable Self.* London: Sage.

Sifris, Ronli. 2013. *Reproductive Freedom, Torture and International Human Rights: Challenging the Masculinisation of Torture.* New York: Routledge.

Sikkink, Kathryn. 2011. *The Justice Cascade: How Human Rights Prosecutions Are Changing World Politics.* New York: Norton.

Sikkink, Kathryn, and Hun Joon Kim. 2013. "The Justice Cascade: The Origins and Effectiveness of Prosecutions of Human Rights Violations." *Annual Review of Law and Social Science* 9 (1): 269–85.

Sjoberg, Laura, and Sandra Via. 2010, eds. *Gender, War, and Militarism: Feminist Perspectives.* Santa Barbara, CA: Praeger.

Skaar, Elin, Jemima García-Godos, and Cath Collins, eds. 2016. *Transitional Justice in Latin America: The Uneven Road from Impunity towards Accountability.* New York: Routledge.

Smith-Ayala, Emilie. 1991. *The Granddaughters of Ixmucané: Guatemalan Women Speak.* Toronto: Women's Press.

Söderbäck, Fanny. 2012. "Revolutionary Time: Revolt as Temporal Return." *Signs* 37 (2): 301–24.

Sonderéguer, María, ed. 2012. *Género y poder: Violencias de género en contextos de represión política y conflictos armados.* Bernal: Universidad Nacional de Quilmes Editorial.

Spade, Dean. 2013. "Intersectional Resistance and Law Reform." *Signs* 38 (4): 1031–55.

Spelman, Elizabeth V. 1982. "Woman as Body: Ancient and Contemporary Views." *Feminist Studies* 8 (1): 109–31.

Spillman, Lyn, and Brian Conway. 2007. "Texts, Bodies, and the Memory of Bloody Sunday." *Symbolic Interaction* 30 (1): 79–103.

Spinola, Eduardo. 2014. "Casos de afroamericanos víctimas del terrorismo de estado | Argentina investiga." *Dirección General de Comunicación y Medios, Universidad Nacional de La Plata*, February 10. http://argentinainvestiga.edu.ar.

Stephen, Lynn. 1997. *Women and Social Movements in Latin America: Power from Below.* Austin: University of Texas Press.

Stern, Steve J. 2016. "Memory: The Curious History of a Cultural Code Word." *Radical History Review* 2016 (124): 117–28.

Stockwell, Jill. 2014. "'The Country That Doesn't Want to Heal Itself:' The Burden of History, Affect and Women's Memories." *International Journal of Conflict and Violence* 8 (1): 30–44.

Strejilevich, Nora. 1997. *Una sola muerte numerosa.* Miami: North-South Center Press.

———. 2016. "Genres of the Real: *Testimonio,* Autobiography, and the Subjective Turn." Translated by Judith Filc. In *The Cambridge History of Latin American Women's Lit-*

erature, ed. Ileana Rodríguez and Mónica Szurmuk, 433–47. New York: Cambridge University Press.

Sutton, Barbara. 2007a. "Naked Protest: Memories of Bodies and Resistance at the World Social Forum." *Journal of International Women's Studies* 8 (3): 139–48.

———. 2007b. "*Poner el Cuerpo*: Women's Embodiment and Political Resistance in Argentina." *Latin American Politics and Society* 49 (3): 129–62.

———. 2008. "Contesting Racism: Democratic Citizenship, Human Rights, and Anti-racist Politics in Argentina." *Latin American Perspectives* 35 (6): 106–21.

———. 2010. *Bodies in Crisis: Culture, Violence, and Women's Resistance in Neoliberal Argentina.* New Brunswick, NJ: Rutgers University Press.

———. 2015. "Collective Memory and the Language of Human Rights: Attitudes toward Torture in Contemporary Argentina." *Latin American Perspectives* 42 (3): 73–91.

———. 2017. "Zonas de clandestinidad y 'nuda vida': Mujeres, cuerpo y aborto." *Estudos Feministas* 25 (2): 889–902.

Sutton, Barbara, and Elizabeth Borland. 2013. "Framing Abortion Rights in Argentina's *Encuentros Nacionales de Mujeres.*" *Feminist Studies* 39 (1): 194–234.

———. 2015. "Abortion and Women's Human Rights in Argentina." Paper presented at "Sexualities," American Sociological Association annual conference, Chicago, August 23.

Sutton, Barbara, Sandra Morgen, and Julie Novkov, eds. 2008. *Security Disarmed: Critical Perspectives on Gender, Race, and Militarization.* New Brunswick, NJ: Rutgers University Press.

Sutton, Barbara, and Kari Marie Norgaard. 2013. "Cultures of Denial: Avoiding Knowledge of State Violations of Human Rights in Argentina and the United States." *Sociological Forum* 28 (3): 495–524.

Svampa, Maristella. 2005. *La sociedad excluyente: La Argentina bajo el signo del neoliberalismo.* Buenos Aires: Taurus.

Tarducci, Mónica, ed. 2008a. *Maternidades en el siglo XXI.* Buenos Aires: Espacio.

———. 2008b. "Presentación." In Tarducci, *Maternidades en el siglo XXI*, 9–13.

Taussig, Michael T. 1999. *Defacement: Public Secrecy and the Labor of the Negative.* Stanford, CA: Stanford University Press.

Taylor, Diana. 1997. *Disappearing Acts: Spectacles of Gender and Nationalism in Argentina's "Dirty War."* Durham, NC: Duke University Press.

———. 2003. *The Archive and the Repertoire: Performing Cultural Memory in the Americas.* Durham, NC: Duke University Press.

Taylor, Verta, Leila J. Rupp, and Joshua Gamson. 2004. "Performing Protest: Drag Shows as Tactical Repertoire of the Gay and Lesbian Movement." In *Authority in Contention*, ed. Daniel J. Myers and Daniel M. Cress, 105–37. Bingley: Emerald.

Taylor, Verta, and Nella Van Dyke. 2004. "'Get Up, Stand Up': Tactical Repertoires of Social Movements." In *The Blackwell Companion to Social Movements*, ed. David A. Snow, Sarah A. Soule, and Hanspeter Kriesi, 262–93. Malden, MA: Blackwell.

Theidon, Kimberly. 2011. "Género en transición: Sentido común, mujeres y guerra." *Cuadernos Pagu* 37: 43–78.

———. 2014. "How Was Your Trip? Self-Care for Researchers Working and Writing on Violence." DSD Working Papers on Research Security, No. 2. Brooklyn, NY: Social Science Research Council, Drugs, Security and Democracy Program.

Tilly, Charles. 1978. *From Mobilization to Revolution*. Reading, MA: Addison-Wesley.

———. 1995. *Popular Contention in Great Britain, 1758–1834*. Cambridge, MA: Harvard University Press.

Tortti, María Cristina. 2006. "La nueva izquierda en la historia reciente de la Argentina." *Cuestiones de Sociología* 3: 19–32.

Traverso, Enzo. 2007. "Historia y memoria: Notas sobre un debate." In *Historia reciente: Perspectivas y desafíos para un campo en construcción*, ed. Marina Franco and Florencia Levín, 67–96. Buenos Aires: Paidós.

Treacy, Mary Jane. 1996. "Double Binds: Latin American Women's Prison Memories." *Hypatia* 11 (4): 130–45.

Tuana, Nancy. 2001. "Introduction." In *Engendering Rationalities*, ed. Nancy Tuana and Sandra Morgen, 1–20. Albany: State University of New York Press.

Turner, Bryan S. 1984. *The Body and Society: Explorations in Social Theory*. New York: Blackwell.

———. 2006. *Vulnerability and Human Rights*. University Park: Pennsylvania State University Press.

United Nations Development Programme (UNDP). 2010. "Argentina: Campaign to Reduce Violence against Women." *UNDP Success Story Leads*. http://undp.org.

United Nations, Division for the Advancement of Women, Department of Economic and Social Affairs. 1998. "Sexual Violence and Armed Conflict: United Nations Response." www.un.org.

Ussher, Jane M. 2006. *Managing the Monstrous Feminine: Regulating the Reproductive Body*. New York: Routledge.

"US Woman Soldier Unrepentant over Abu Ghraib." 2009. *BBC News*, August 13. http://news.bbc.co.uk.

Vacarezza, Nayla. 2015. "Aborto, experiencias, afectos." In *Código rosa: Relatos sobre abortos*, by Dahiana Belfiori, 137–41. Buenos Aires: La Parte Maldita.

Vaisman, Noa. 2017. "Variations on Justice: Argentina's Pre- and Post-transitional Justice and the Justice to Come." *Ethnos* 82 (2): 366–88.

Vásquez, Juana. 1991. "We Value Life Very Deeply: Five Centuries of Struggle." In *The Granddaughters of Ixmucané: Guatemalan Women Speak*, by Emilie Smith-Ayala, 45–58. Toronto: Women's Press.

Vassallo, Marta. 2011. "Introducción." In Aucía et al., *Grietas en el silencio*, 11–25.

Vecchioli, Virginia. 2001. "Políticas de la memoria y formas de clasificación social: ¿Quiénes son las 'víctimas del terrorismo de estado' en la Argentina?" In *La imposibilidad del olvido: Recorridos de la memoria en Argentina, Chile y Uruguay*, ed. Bruno Groppo and Patricia Flier, 83–102. La Plata: Editorial Al Margen.

———. 2005. "'La nación como familia.' Metáforas políticas en el movimiento argentino por los derechos humanos." In *Cultura y política en etnografías sobre la Argentina*, ed. Sabina Frederic and Germán Soprano, 241–70. Buenos Aires: Ed. UNQ/ Prometeo.

Veiras, Nora. 2011. "¿Cómo habría actuado yo?" *Página/12*, November 28. www.pagina12.com.ar.

Verbitsky, Horacio, and Juan Pablo Bohoslavsky, eds. 2013. *Cuentas pendientes: Los cómplices económicos de la dictadura*. Buenos Aires: Siglo Veintiuno.

Vezzetti, Hugo. 2013. *Sobre la violencia revolucionaria: Memorias y olvidos*. Buenos Aires: Siglo Veintiuno.

Vilar, Natalia Pérez. 2009. "La tortura como inscripción del dolor en el cuerpo." *Tramas* 32: 99–120.

Villalón, Roberta. 2010. "Passage to Citizenship and the Nuances of Agency: Latina Battered Immigrants." *Women's Studies International Forum* 33 (6): 552–60.

Villani, Mario, and Fernando Reati. 2011. *Desaparecido: Memorias de un cautiverio: Club Atlético, el Banco, el Olimpo, Pozo de Quilmes y ESMA*. Buenos Aires: Biblos.

Viñas, David. 2002. "The Foundation of the National State." Translated by Mark Alan Healey. In *The Argentina Reader: History, Culture, Politics*, ed. Gabriela Nouzeilles and Graciela Montaldo, 161–69. Durham, NC: Duke University Press.

Viterna, Jocelyn. 2013. *Women in War: The Micro-processes of Mobilization in El Salvador*. New York: Oxford University Press.

Volo, Lorraine Bayard de. 2012. "A Revolution in the Binary? Gender and the Oxymoron of Revolutionary War in Cuba and Nicaragua." *Signs* 37 (2): 413–39.

Washington Office on Latin America (WOLA). 2016. "Brave Women Break Silence and Impunity in Guatemala: The Sepur Zarco Case." March 3. www.wola.org.

Weitz, Rose. 2001. "Women and Their Hair: Seeking Power through Resistance and Accommodation." *Gender & Society* 15 (5): 667–86.

Welch, Michael. 2003. "Trampling Human Rights in the War on Terror: Implications to the Sociology of Denial." *Critical Criminology* 12: 1–20.

Weld, Kirsten. 2014. *Paper Cadavers: The Archives of Dictatorship in Guatemala*. Durham, NC: Duke University Press.

West, Candace, and Don H. Zimmerman. 1987. "Doing Gender." *Gender & Society* 1 (2): 125–51.

White House, Office of the Press Secretary. 2016. "Remarks by President Obama and President Macri of Argentina at Parque de La Memoria." March 24. www.whitehouse.gov.

Whitmer, Ali, Laura Ogden, John Lawton, Pam Sturner, Peter M. Groffman, Laura Schneider, David Hart, et al. 2010. "The Engaged University: Providing a Platform for Research that Transforms Society." *Frontiers in Ecology and the Environment* 8 (6): 314–21.

Wolff, Cristina Scheibe. 2015. "Pedaços de alma: Emoções e gênero nos discursos da resistência." *Estudos Feministas* 23 (3): 975–89.

World Bank. 2015. *Indigenous Latin America in the Twenty-First Century*. Washington, DC: World Bank.

World Health Organization. 2013. "Global and Regional Estimates of Violence against Women: Prevalence and Health Effects of Intimate Partner Violence and Non-partner Sexual Violence." http://apps.who.int.

Yanzon, Rodolfo. 2011. "Los juicios desde el fin de la dictadura hasta hoy." In Andreozzi, *Juicios por Crímenes*, 137–53.

Zerubavel, Eviatar. 1996. "Social Memories: Steps to a Sociology of the Past." *Qualitative Sociology* 19 (3): 283–99.

Ziarek, Ewa Płonowska. 2008. "Bare Life on Strike: Notes on the Biopolitics of Race and Gender." *South Atlantic Quarterly* 107 (1): 89–105.

Zurutuza, Cristina. 2011. "Crímenes sexuales en contextos concentracionarios: Violencia, género, subjetividad." In Aucía et al., *Grietas en el silencio*, 69–114.

INDEX

abortion, 11, 19, 116; body-for-others construction and, 116; clandestinity and, 273n7; state power and, 243–45

Abu Ghraib prison (Iraq), 107, 242; sexualization and, 105

accommodation, 133–34

Achugar, Mariana, 215

Acosta, "Tigre," 78

Actis, Munú, 47; bodily marks and, 175; embodied care and, 160; embodied emotions and, 155–56; *Ese infierno*, 58; mind/body split and, 146; passion and, 205–6; *poner el cuerpo* and, 62; recuperation processes and, 266n5; sexualization and, 110–11; voice and, 176

active listening, 34–35

activism, 193–97, 200–203; dehumanization and, 75; democratic culture and, 222–27; discourse on the future and, 180, 182–84; embodiment of, 203–5, 209–12; identity and, 169; joy and, 49, 207–8; Kirchners and, 270n2; *machismo* and, 192; micro-actions and, 198–99; Mothers of the Plaza de Mayo and, 16; passion and, 205–6; perseverance, 209–11; political voices and, 184–87, 191–93; pregnancy and, 118; radicalization and, 43; revolutionary movements and, 187–91; state terror and, 46–48; victimization and, 250. *See also* futurity

Afghanistan, 38

Afro-Argentines, 11, 237

afterlife of violence, 71, 266n19

Agamben, Giorgio, 5, 56; bare life concept and, 68; forms of agency and, 134; psychological torture and, 72

agency, 6–7; bodily marks and, 175; care and, 250–51; embodied memory and, 139; embodied narratives and, 246–53; everyday acts of, 250; forms of, 132–35; mind/body split and, 140; political voices and, 184–87, 191–93; reclamation and, 169–70; revolutionary movements and, 187–91; sexual choice and, 265n10; silence and, 63; tactical performance and, 148, 268n1; temporality and, 251–52; transitional justice and, 229; truths and, 249–50; victimization binary with, 52–53, 64, 176; vulnerability and, 127, 177, 246–49

age performance, 153–54

Agger, Inger, 107

Agrupación Evita, 188–89. *See also* Montoneros

Ahmed, Sara, 207

Alfaro, Elena, 117

Alfonsín, Raúl R., 7, 218

Álvarez, Marta, 19, 49, 54, 57; activist embodiment and, 204; crazy label and, 78; feminine performance and, 150, 153; *machismo* and, 192; passion and, 206; pregnancy and, 114

Amarilla, Luisa Blanco de, 196–98, 271n10

amenorrhea, 97–98. *See also* menstruation

Andrews, George Reid, 237

animal cruelty, 86

Antaki, Mark, 173, 266n3

temporality and, 82. *See also* dehumanization
human rights, 6–7; Afro-Argentines
and, 237; body narratives and, 84–85,
97; democratic culture and, 222–27;
dictatorship and, 12–14; discourse of, 4,
250; feminism and, 21–22; futurity and,
181; gender noncomformity and, 235;
indigenous people and, 236; Kirchners
and, 7–9; logic of the perpetrators and,
267n8; Macri and, 230–31, 233; making
collective memory and, 9–11; military
governments and, 12–14; monumental
memory and, 176–77; official denial
and, 96; Operation Condor and, 232;
perseverance and, 209–11; Rights of
Man language and, 86; silence and,
234–35; transitional justice and, 229–38;
United States and, 230–31; universalism
of, 11; women's rights and, 261n26
humiliation, 126; self and, 137; sexualization and, 104–5. *See also* degradation;
dehumanization; shame
Huyssen, Andreas, 11
hyperawareness, 123–25, 130

identity, 23; essentialism and, 25; feminine
performance and, 152; gendered names
and, 262n35; monstrosity and, 128;
travestis and, 169; "women" as category
of, 23–24. *See also* gender
Illia, Arturo, 44
implicated research, 32, 36–39; active
listening and, 34–35; childhood memories and, 32–34
impunity, 7–10, 14, 18, 20; abortion and,
244; annulment of, 30, 264n1; appropriation of children and, 271n16; body
narratives and, 97; embodied care
and, 165; embodied emotions and, 156;
justice and, 216–17; justice aspirations
and, 220; male gaze and, 110; normalization and, 241; perseverance and,

209; psychological torture and, 71–72;
sexualization and, 106; sexual violence
and, 238–39, 241; silence and, 51; trial
of the Juntas and, 221; vulnerability
and, 126
Insausti, Santiago Joaquín, 269n13
indigenous peoples, 11; body narratives
and, 94; collective memory and, 236;
colonialism and, 85
indistinction, zones of, 72–73, 266n22
individualism, 159, 190
inequality, 187–91; feminine performance
and, 149; femininity scripts and, 120–
21; gender logics and, 192; intersectionality and, 262n34; sexual violence and,
242; social justice and, 217–19
innocence, 182
INSGENAR (Instituto de Género,
Derecho y Desarrollo), 261n28
"Integral Protection to Prevent, Punish, and Eradicate Violence against
Women in the Realms in Which They
Develop Their Interpersonal Relations" law, 261n27
Inter-American Commission on Human
Rights, 209, 267n9
intergenerational relations, 213, 215; activism and, 271n10; embodied emotions
and, 158. *See also* children; futurity;
memory: transmission of
internal enemies, 13, 77; construction of,
270n1
internal exile, 47
International Criminal Court, 22
international treaties, 260n15
intersectionality, 23, 262n34
interviews, 27, 29–30; prioritizing of,
263n38. *See also* Memoria Abierta
Iraq, 38, 242; Abu Ghraib and, 105, 107

Jasper, James M., 208
Jelin, Elizabeth, 17; activism and, 270n2;
discourse on the future and, 180

recuperation (*recuperación*), 19; feminine performance and, 150–51; gender ideology and, 87; systematized processes of, 266nn4, 5. *See also* femininity

REDLACTRANS report (2012), 239

Regueiro, Sabina, 115, 268n22

regulation, modes of, 238; clandestinity and, 246; normalization of gender and, 241; reproduction and, 243

relational world, 48–50, 136–38; corporeality and, 139; embodied care and, 162–66; resistance and, 136–38; vulnerability and, 251

reproduction, 88–89; state power and, 238, 243–46. *See also* abortion; children

resignation, 135

resilience, 39; body narratives and, 94; clinging to life and, 135–36; ethical positioning and, 252; femininity and, 103–4; femininity scripts and, 121; forms of agency and, 132; vulnerability and, 127. *See also* perseverance; resistance

resistance, 6; agency and, 249; body narratives and, 84; care and, 159–62; clothing and, 166–68; collective memory and, 234; *compromiso* and, 179; creativity and, 142–43; embodied emotions and, 158; embodied gestures and, 251, 253; embodied memory and, 139; everyday acts of, 177–78, 250; everyday life and, 177; femininity scripts and, 121; forms of agency and, 132–35; materiality and, 165–66; mind/body split and, 139–42, 144–48; non-clandestine prisons and, 269n11; performance and, 138; pregnancy and, 118; "psy culture" and, 268–69n7; relational world and, 136–38; social memory and, 228; solidarity and, 162–65, 168–70; vulnerability and, 127. *See also* activism; perseverance; resilience

revolutionary movements, 187–91; class and, 193; commitment and, 200, 203; discourse on the future and, 184; gender logics and, 192; logic of the perpetrators and, 202; revolutionary time and, 183. *See also* activism

Reyes, Susana, 67, 125; crazy label and, 78; embodied care and, 160; justice aspirations and, 219; pregnancy and, 116–17, 119; privacy and, 125; sexualization and, 108

Riaño-Alcalá, Pilar, 60

Rights of Man language, 86

Romero, Luis Alberto, 45

Rome Statute (International Criminal Court), 22

Rothberg, Michael, 37

Ruiz, Julia, 74, 195, 218–19

Rwanda, 22, 106

Sacolsky, Rebeca "Tita," 73, 91, 222

Salerno, Melisa A., 166, 170

Salvi, Valentina, 11

Sanford, Victoria, 20

Sartre, Jean-Paul, 201

Scala, Susana Martínez de, 214

Scarry, Elaine, 267n12; fiction of power and, 172; inexpressibility of pain and, 102, 266n1

scars. *See* markings

Schachter, Laura, 49–51, 56, 58–59; body narratives and, 100; double morality and, 111; feminine performance and, 153; passion and, 206

Scheper-Hughes, Nancy, 20

Scott, Joan, 3, 23–24

scripts, 6; body hyperawareness and, 123–25; dehumanization and, 120–23; monstrosity and, 127–30; Mothers of the Plaza de Mayo and, 16; sexualization and, 104–5; vulnerability and, 125–27. *See also* gender

violence and, 242; September 11 and, 38; slavery and, 158; torture debates in, 265n17; "war on terror" and, 38, 105, 231, 242
unreality, 73–74, 76
Uruguay, 118; abductions from, 268n3; co-operation with Argentine CDCs and, 263n37; justice aspirations and, 221
utopia, 49, 180, 193–94. *See also* futurity; revolutionary movements

Vaisman, Noa, 216–17, 219
"Variations on Justice" (Vaisman), 216
Vassallo, Marta, 163; commitment and, 199; memory transmission and, 215
victimization, 6; activism and, 250; agency binary with, 52–53, 64, 176; discourse on the future and, 182; masculinity and, 87; political voices and, 184
Videla, Jorge Rafael, 72
Villalón, Roberta, 132–33
Villani, Mario, 110; *Desaparecido*, 32
voice, 5–6; agency and, 184–87, 191–93; bodily markings and, 170, 172–75; body and, 60–62; discourse on the future and, 181–84; embodied care and, 165; embodied memory and, 170–76; feminine performance and, 151–53; gender and, 82; metatestimony and, 176; Mothers of the Plaza de Mayo and, 15, 18; pain and, 173; political nature of, 5; *poner el cuerpo* and, 62–63; revolutionary movements and, 187–91; sensory memory and, 170–72; *testimonios* and, 63–67
Volo, Lorraine Bayard de, 191
vulnerability, 7, 130; agency and, 177, 246–49; care and, 250–51; double

meaning of, 137; embodied care and, 165; femininity scripts and, 125–27; forms of agency and, 134; paradoxical carnal logic and, 135; relational world and, 136–38; tactical performance and, 148; temporality and, 251–52; transitional justice and, 229; truths and, 249–50

weapons of the weak, 149, 160
Weld, Kirsten, 27
Western civilization, 129, 139
"whore" stigma, 54; gender ideology and, 90–91; Madonna binary with, 111; pregnancy and, 114; prostitution and, 267n6; revolutionary movements and, 190. *See also* prostitution
women's movements, 18, 54; globalization of, 86. *See also* activism; feminism; Mothers of the Plaza de Mayo
Workers' Revolutionary Party–People's Revolutionary Army (Partido Revolucionario de los Trabajadores–Ejército Revolucionario del Pueblo, PRT-ERP), 46, 188–90, 201
World Health Organization, 246
World Medical Association, 69
Wornat, Olga, 267n13

Yanzon, Rodolfo, 271n16
Y nadie quería saber: Relatos sobre violencia contra las mujeres en el terrorismo de estado en Argentina (Bacci, Capurro Robles, Oberti, & Skura), 52, 262n28
Yugoslavia, 22, 106

Ziarek, Ewa Plonowska, 134
Zurutuza, Cristina, 109

ABOUT THE AUTHOR

Barbara Sutton is Associate Professor in the Department of Women's, Gender, and Sexuality Studies at the University at Albany, SUNY. She is also affiliated with the Departments of Sociology and of Latin American, Caribbean, and U.S. Latino Studies. She is the author of *Bodies in Crisis: Culture, Violence, and Women's Resistance in Neoliberal Argentina* (2010).